YASMIN KHAN

Yasmin Khan is a British writer and historian. She is an Associate Professor of History at the University of Oxford and a Fellow of Kellogg College. Her first book, *The Great Partition: the Making of India and Pakistan*, won the Gladstone Prize from the Royal Historical Society in 2007 and was longlisted for the Orwell Prize in 2008.

16 FEB 2024

EAST S

D1421898

04397639

ALSO BY YASMIN KHAN

The Great Partition: the Making of India and Pakistan

YASMIN KHAN

The Raj at War

A People's History of India's
Second World War

VINTAGE

1 3 5 7 9 10 8 6 4 2

Vintage
20 Vauxhall Bridge Road,
London SW1V 2SA

Vintage is part of the Penguin Random House group of companies
whose addresses can be found at global.penguinrandomhouse.com.

Copyright © Yasmin Khan 2015

Yasmin Khan has asserted her right to be identified as the author
of this Work in accordance with the Copyright, Designs and
Patents Act 1988

First published by Vintage in 2016

First published in Great Britain in 2015 by The Bodley Head

A CIP catalogue record for this book is available
from the British Library

ISBN 9780099542278

Typeset in Dante MT Std by Palimpsest Book Production Limited
Falkirk, Stirlingshire

Printed and bound by Clays Ltd, St Ives plc

Penguin Random House is committed to a sustainable future for
our business, our readers and our planet. This book is made from
Forest Stewardship Council® certified paper.

MIX
Paper from
responsible sources
FSC
www.fsc.org FSC™ C018179

'You want to know the names of the men who have joined the army from our village. They are too many to be mentioned.'

An Urdu letter from an unknown man in the North-West Frontier Province to his son, 1943.

'And war is many things.'

Richard Flanagan, *The Narrow Road to the Deep North*

Contents

Prologue

On 3 January 1946, three men, Prem Kumar Sahgal, Gurbaksh Singh Dhillon and Shah Nawaz Khan, quietly emerged from imprisonment in Old Delhi's Red Fort. The Government of India had held them there for three months. Just four days earlier the trio had been convicted of waging war against the King-Emperor and sentenced to transportation for life. They were leading officers of the Indian National Army (INA) and had been in the vanguard of Subhas Chandra Bose's renegade force. They had fought for the Axis in Burma and South-East Asia. Now they were free men and, within days, found themselves national heroes. The Commander-in-Chief of the Indian Army had remitted their sentences; although technically found guilty, their punishment had been quashed. People interpreted their release as a decisive victory against the British Raj.

The trials had been a disaster for the British rulers. The bungled attempt at a public prosecution had resulted in the 'hero worship of traitors' in the words of Archibald Wavell, the Viceroy of India in 1946. He admitted frankly that the affair was 'embarrassing'.[1] Since November, the trial had gripped the imagination of the Indian public. People had bought reports of the court case, autobiographies of the officers, panegyrics of Bose and pamphlets about all aspects of the Indian National Army, on sale at every pavement stall and bookshop. The way in which Bose and his followers had established a breakaway army to side with the Japanese had been told in full for the first time, without the full force of wartime censorship in place.

As the word spread of the men's release they were swept along the cramped streets of Old Delhi in a growing tide of supporters, cheered and hoisted on shoulders. Soon they were forced to stand on the roof of a car because of the crush of the crowds. Everybody clamoured to shake their hands and to fill their mouths with sweets. Indian National Congress politicians rushed to the scene to be among the first to congratulate them. Over the coming days, the men paraded around Delhi, Lahore and across the country. They were hosted at massive rallies. Everywhere they went admirers mobbed them, thrust forward autograph books and strung heavy garlands of flowers around their necks. The crowds were hundreds of thousands strong. 'People wanted to see us, touch us, hear us speak and garland us. They had gone mad with the joy of our release. Young girls cut their fingers with razor blades and applied blood to our foreheads instead of vermillion', recalled Gurbaksh Singh Dhillon, one of the released prisoners.[2] Policemen, magistrates and officials looked on, powerless to intervene or to stem the tide.

The Red Fort, the sandstone fortress built by the Mughal emperors in the heart of New Delhi, was spectacularly ill-chosen as the location for the trial. The fort, which had been used as a barracks by the Indian Army ever since the uprising of 1857, was the symbolic seat of South Asian power. So, too, the British decision to try the three officers together, a Sikh, a Hindu and a Muslim. This just added piquancy to the symbolism of the event. The Congress Party used the trials as a way to try to build pan-religious solidarity and some of the finest legal minds in the country, including Jawaharlal Nehru, the foremost Congressman of the era, had represented the men as their defence barristers. Any earlier ambivalence the Congressmen had felt about the militarism and unabashed pro-Axis stance of the INA was swept aside in the fervour of the moment.

The vehement outpourings of anger that greeted the INA trials, and widespread rejoicing at the release of the prosecuted men, were the result of a hardened form of nationalism. Everywhere there was a new belief in the power of violence to release India from colonial control, and an upsurge of post-war euphoria which gripped civilians and soldiers alike. Policemen, magistrates and military generals became reluctant to intervene in a cause célèbre which had captured the imagination of people of all regional and religious backgrounds. Military commanders of the Indian Army had feared mutiny if the INA men received the death sentence. As it was, over 20,000 members of the Royal Indian Navy would mutiny during the coming weeks in any case.

The upsurge of political zeal was inextricably linked with ongoing demobilisation. As over 2 million Indian soldiers were demobilised from the Indian Army in the aftermath of the war, and began to return to their villages, they started to ask how they would be rewarded for their sacrifices during the war. As one Pathan soldier told the Indian civil servant Malcolm Darling, 'We suffered in the war but you didn't . . . we bore with this so that we might be free.'³ This was the moment that British rule in India became untenable. It marked a decisive break with everything that had gone before. Imperial rule had lost its final shreds of legitimacy. The Raj had unravelled under the pressure of war.

The elation greeting the released prisoners would have been unthinkable in 1939. At the start of the war, nobody would have anticipated in Mahatma Gandhi's India that it would be military men who would soon be in the vanguard of nationalism. But six years of war had changed the political language. By 1946 Gandhi was barely heeded by a new generation of protesters who were angry, strident and determined to achieve Independence. Their hero was Subhas Chandra Bose and their battle cry was 'Blood is calling to blood'.

By contrast, in August 1939 as the world waited for the news of the outbreak of war, a government spokesman in Simla, the summer capital of imperial India, declared, 'We only have to press a button and the whole organisation prepared to meet a war emergency will slide smoothly into action.'⁴ This was propaganda, of course, but it also suggests the easy complacency with which India was plunged into war in 1939.

At the start of the war, Europe's troubles had seemed far-distant and removed from India. Living in the cantonments and bungalows of the imperial state, the older guard of army officers and officials believed that India could be insulated and protected from the swirl of ideologies taking place in Europe. The war would be framed in terms of loyalty and disloyalty to the Crown and would be a repeat perfor-mance of India's role in the First World War: the landed and the wealthy would take the lead and Indian subjects would fall in step behind them. India would come to the aid of the motherland, and the state would draw on manpower and resources as it saw fit. The prospect of total war, of a threat of invasion reaching India's borders, of deeply transformative social change, of the erosion and eventual collapse of the power of the imperial state, would have seemed outlandish to many of these officers in the late 1930s.

* * *

Some years ago, I wrote a book about the Partition of India, about the tragic violence, refugee movements and the breakdown of trust, which resulted in the making of the two new nations of India and Pakistan. That book focused on the pivotal year of 1947. But in the course of writing it I was often struck by how profoundly transformed India had been in the 1940s, and, in particular, how the Second World War had determined so many aspects of decolonisation and Partition. Muhamad Ali Jinnah, the leader of the Muslim League, had made his very first public demand for Pakistan within months of the war starting. I realised that it is necessary to dig back into the preceding years, and to understand the whole wartime transformation of India in order to really comprehend the exit velocity of the British, the crisis that accompanied Independence in 1947 and the Partition of the subcontinent. Once I began to trawl back into the 1940s, I realised just how critical these years had been to the collapse of the empire and to the making of modern South Asia.

In Britain, in recent years the sheer scale of the contribution of the British Empire to the war effort, in both the First and Second World Wars, has become apparent. No longer is it simply an island story of heroic, plucky Britain fighting against Nazi-occupied continental Europe; it has now become increasingly customary for historians to refer to the contribution played by Asian, African and Caribbean servicemen in the 1940s. This is only fitting. Some 5 million joined the military services of the British Empire during the Second World War, almost half of them from South Asia. It was only in 2002 that the Commonwealth Gates Trust installed a memorial on Constitution Hill in London to honour the role of these men. Museum exhibitions, oral history projects and television documentaries have continually probed and elucidated the role of imperial and Commonwealth servicemen and their lesser-known participation in the war, to reveal how crucial they often were to the action, the sacrifices that they made in the face of terrible odds, and also to divulge individual stories of great bravery and intrepid action.

It is no longer true to suggest that this is an entirely forgotten story. From the life histories of Sikh pilots in the Royal Air Force to the memoirs of Caribbean seamen on board merchant vessels in the Atlantic, we now know more than ever before about the global mobilisation and deployment of men from across the empire. At El Alamein, Monte Cassino and Kohima, 'British' victories belonged to an extraordinarily diverse and international cast of men from the continents of Australasia, Africa, North America and Asia. These kinds of memorialisation have had an echo in India, with regimental museums and military historians speaking more vocally about Indians who won the Victoria Cross and South Asian participation in battles. Britain did not fight the Second World War, the British Empire did.

However, this book aims to go one step beyond this. Rather than just looking at the contributions of South Asians to the war in Europe and Asia, it seeks to understand how the Indian subcontinent itself was reshaped by the war. How did the war impact on India's 'home front'? How did gearing up for total war, and the rapid re-purposing of the Indian state into a garrison, barrack and training camp for a vast army, affect and shape South Asian society? Beyond the well-trained and relatively well-paid infantryman or officer, which men and women propped up the Indian Army over thousands of miles of supply lines? How was the war experienced in small villages abutting aerodromes, or by young nurses in Indian General Hospitals?

As well as acknowledging the role of South Asian men and women, then, this means asking some hard questions about the social costs of war and the coercion that accompanies such a massive military commitment. It also demands that we pay proper attention to the people who have tended not to feature so prominently in military histories: the non-combatants and camp followers, the Lascars, prostitutes, nurses, refugees and peasants whose lives changed because of the demands of military commitments.

This book ranges across the subcontinent, from the commanding heights of New Delhi to the scrublands and jungles inhabited by *adivasis* and the villages of low castes and *dalits*. It is a story told in many voices, by individuals – Indian, British and many other nationalities too – who experienced the war in various and often contrasting ways. It reflects the diversity of wartime experiences in India. Merchants, industrialists, soldiers, merchant seamen, agriculturalists or black marketeers, in small towns or mega-cities, on coastal water-ways or in the mountains, all had their own ways of negotiating the challenges and opportunities of war. Some profited and many were impoverished. This book aims to give the flavour of these plural, and often hidden, voices.

Some of the experiences recounted here are universal staples of wartime: families separated over wrenchingly long years and vast distances, bravery in the midst of battle, the astonishing mushrooming of the state as it expanded and juggled the many tasks necessitated by the war, from postal services to ports. A defining feature of the war across the world was the upheaval of refugees and the movement of people on an unprecedented scale. The attrition of resources, the disruptions to labour and the effects of inflation caused by war are only just being recognised and fully researched as civilian dramas with similar contours, from North Africa to the Middle East and South-East Asia.

This book focuses on this nexus between warfare and society. Understanding the Indian home front is a way of understanding the pernicious, unforeseen and often deadly consequences of war on the lives of ordinary people. It is also crucial to understanding the revolutionary turn of events leading up to India's Independence and the end of the Raj.

Looking at the events of the 1940s from the bottom-up or human perspective, rather than from the sweeping global panorama of war, also involves a moral dimension. The war was a just war against fascism in Europe and Asia, a necessary but painful corrective to the rising tide of fascist and expansionist politics, which threatened the rights of millions of people. But it also had other implications and costs, many of which could hardly be foreseen or anticipated by its protag-onists. The priorities of war forced people into difficult moral and personal choices. Imperial subjects could not necessarily evaluate the war as a 'good' or 'just' war whilst they witnessed the effect on their own lives, as they faced astronomical price rises, lethal food shortages and famine, the loss of young men on unknown foreign battlefields, requisitioning and other disruptions to their everyday existence. The war sharpened dichotomies between the wealthy elites and the vast number of the very poor, heightened social tensions and exacerbated differences of class, caste and religion.

Many societies have used histories of war or stories of national liberation to bolster their own cohesion and sense of national belonging. The 1940s have often been remembered in ways that have served national stories and myths. There is nothing unusual about this anywhere in the world. In India and Britain, after the decolonisation of the Raj in 1947, and in the latter part of the twentieth century, school curricula, textbooks, national myths and heroes developed along divergent tracks. For Britons, there was little reflection about the twilight of imperial rule and there was often amnesia about horrors such as the Bengal famine of 1943 that occurred on the imperial watch.

In India, similarly, the war was also overlooked or remembered in partisan ways. The Second World War seemed sometimes, from an Indian perspective, an obscure or even irrelevant subject for research or the preserve of nostalgic militarists. Although wartime had a defining impact on nationalist politics, the historical emphasis was on the Gandhian campaigns of national liberation and on the creation of the new states of India and Pakistan in 1947. Crucially, the leading nationalists had been absent from many of the major wartime events as they were incarcerated. Nehru, the pre-eminent leader of his generation and the first Prime Minister of independent India, personally remembered the 1940s as 'the quiet uneventful past'. He spent nearly three years in prison, his ninth period of detention: 'We could only hear very distantly the far-off drums of the Great World War that was going on then.'[5]

The social history of the war itself – the arrival in India of soldiers and nurses from around the world, the employment of millions of labourers, the recruitment and overseas service of thousands of Indian soldiers, the panic and rumours about possible invasion by the Japanese and the profound economic hardship (and, for a lucky few, profits) – has remained outside the scope of South Asian history-writing, apart from in the work of a few exceptional historians.[6] Yet a better awareness of the war's effects also helps us to understand the foundations of modern South Asia. As in Britain, it made the subcontinent a more recognisably modern place. Cities such as Karachi and Bangalore boomed, the infrastructure of airlines, companies and road networks was laid by wartime projects, and consumer imports from tinned food to fridges came onto the market. The Americans became more economically and socially influential than ever before. Middle-class women found new freedoms in work and activism, jazz and cinema thrived and, as in Britain, social expectations soared regarding what life would be like after the war. Nehru's planned economy and the welfare-oriented, developmental state that he tried to craft after 1947 had roots in the Raj's transformation of the 1940s. The explicit trust placed in the ability of the government to provide better healthcare or education was an offshoot of the wartime changes, just as it was in Europe.

The war flattened out the pretensions of empire, making ceremonial and ritual excesses look archaic, challenging old compacts between the King-Emperor and the landed elites. It mobilised women, workers and the urban middle classes in radical new ways. It heightened nationalism, both in India and in Britain, so that older forms of transnational solidarity became dated and obsolete. The Raj was left in debt, morally redundant and staffed by exhausted administrators whose sense of purpose could not be sustained. Development and democracy were the new political aspirations for politicians in Delhi and in London. Ultimately, the war delivered decolonisation and the Partition of 1947 – neither of which were inevitable or foreseen in 1939. All this is not to undermine the considerable achievement of the nationalists over the long duration, their sustained resistance to the Raj was also essential in knocking down its foundations and creating the possibility of a new order. Both elements interlocked. But ultimately, the timing of decolonisation relied heavily on the damage done to the structures of the state by the war, and by the empire's complete lack of legitimacy when the conflict finally ended.

I

An Empire Committed

'Everyone is buying or if they can hiring radio sets', Sydney Ralli recorded in her diary in Karachi in September 1939. A broadcaster and journalist, Ralli was married to an imperial tycoon, Charles, heir to a cotton textile and shipping fortune. News from Europe arrived by radio, newspaper and through family letters. Elites in India had a sharper appreciation of the threat of war in 1939 than many others because they were more likely to have access to a radio. 'Every single person walks around with a gas mask . . . all the shops are practically empty, most of them closed at 5 o'clock. Everyone is doing some sort of national service. Sandbags everywhere. Everything is pitch-black at night and one is advised not to be out after dark as it is dangerous',[1] Ralli wrote home, determined to share in the grittiness of war's outbreak and to play her own part in the international drama unfolding.

The Government of India was busily announcing preparations for the defence of the Raj, air raid wardens had begun drilling and officials ordered the mobilisation of machinery and weaponry and began seeking contributions to the War Fund. The war also resonated through a network of family and friends back in Britain who sent detailed letters, riddled with mounting tension and apprehensions. Ralli even heard the details of other people's letters, leaked by a friend stationed in the censor's office in Karachi. But this initial sense of drama was short-lived and soon melted away. Ralli herself could not keep up the sense of suspense, when everyday life soon slipped back to normality. Within weeks, the atmosphere had returned very much to business as usual, with the war soon taking on a dream-like, fantastical quality.

India soon became a site of escape and release from war-torn Britain, a place where there was less scarcity and more security for Britons. This was still the time of the funny or phoney war. Despite premonitions of future destruction, such as the wide distribution of gas masks among the well-off, the war felt surreal and distant in India. Parents called back their children from European boarding schools believing they would be safer in India. When the newspaper editor Desmond Young's wife and teenage daughters came to India, 'they left shamefaced, for all three felt that they ought to stay whatever might be in store for England'.[2] As children were evacuated from the cities of England to the countryside, many of the children of the Raj came to India, especially after the fall of France, and found places in boarding schools in the hill stations of Mussoorie and Dehra Dun instead. 'With the more modern living conditions, fridges, and better though scarce medicines the old theory that children could not stand the climate for long was partly confounded, neither was it found to affect their schooling to any great extent', remembered Margaret Stavridi, the wife of an East Indian Railway engineer.[3]

Men in the Indian Civil Service (ICS) were exempted from military service and army officers looked less likely to be called straight to a fighting front. There were long delays creating a National Service system, and even once some 15,000 Britons had been registered, allocation to military roles was sluggish. In September, Sydney Ralli persuaded her husband not to sign up, encouraging him to continue working in the Naval Control Service in Karachi. She won her husband round. 'After all it is far better for him to do a job here, where he knows conditions than running up mountains with Gurkhas as a second lieutenant, tramping with his troops over the plains of central India. He seemed to think at first that he was shirking things but eventually became convinced.'[4] Ian Hay Macdonald, an Indian Civil Service officer based on the other side of the country in Orissa, looked on with some disbelief as the war unfolded in Europe and as he learned of his brother's enlistment in the Royal Navy at Portsmouth and of bombers sighted over his family home in Scotland. Within a year several of his university class-mates would be dead. Later he would describe watching the war as if it was a show, 'it is like being in a grandstand watching some game or other, we are so cut off from it here'.[5] As in Singapore, Hong Kong and the other great Eastern imperial cities, the war was impinging on life in random, occasional ways rather than apparently causing any real restructuring of the Raj. This brought guilt but also a sense of relief. The empire provided an extended British sphere, beyond the British Isles, in which some subjects could find sanctuary.

★　★　★

The colonial class in India felt indulged and fortunate compared to their relatives in Britain. Here they were protected by large whitewashed villas, long lawns, servants and drivers, and could acquire all manner of goods on the black market. 'You would certainly not think there was a war on if you saw us here', Macdonald reported from a relatively remote town in Orissa. 'We get as much butter and bacon as we want etc. and there is no shortage of British goods, all sent out presumably to keep up the export trade . . . I must say I have had bad attacks of conscience at the easy life we lead.'[6]

The Raj protected the prestige of the European community and explicit segregation along the lines of race was common. Hazratganj, the main thoroughfare of Lucknow, where glass-fronted shops lined the streets, and diners enjoyed the city's famous biryanis, was out of bounds to Indians during certain hours of the day and they were banned from walking on certain sections of the pavements. Although never pursued as ruthlessly as in South Africa, the racial division was a recurrent affront to people. Signs saying Whites Only on railway platforms and in waiting rooms were still on display. A number of elite clubs, such as the Bombay Gymkhana, refused Indians membership. At Breach Candy, a racially segregated beach, 'Europeans only' could swim. Planters and factory managers unthinkingly prodded workers with rattan canes; police used *lathis* to strike at unruly crowds.

Nonetheless, Indian landowners, princes, industrialists and a small but powerful middle class of lawyers, journalists and academics lived comfortably too, and sometimes exceptionally well. Santha Rama Rau, a sixteen-year-old from an affluent family, returned to India in 1939 after ten years in Britain, to the relative comforts and safety of Bombay. She was learning again how to be an 'Indian' in an unfamiliar environment, and her memoir charts her growing racial consciousness in 1940s India, on seeing benches on a railway station marked 'Europeans only', her increasing sense of 'us' and 'them', coming from 1930s London where, as the daughter of a diplomat, she had had an elite, cosmopolitan and charmed childhood. As Santha Rama Rau admitted honestly on her return to life in a prosperous suburb of New Delhi, it was possible to insulate oneself from the sounds of economic desperation in the countryside. She could spend a whole day 'not thinking about the majority of Indians who are as foreign as the Germans or the French'.[7] For India's most wealthy minority, as for the British, the start of the war was of little consequence to their everyday lives, creating the inconvenience of steeper prices and the need to acquire things on the black market, but barely denting the routine business of life.

Since the 1920s and the first wave of reforms which encouraged the participation of Indians in the running of the state, there had been a slow recognition of the rights of people to participate in the running of their own country. The devolution of power to provincial assemblies and the promotion of Indians to civil and military positions of leadership had been accepted as policy. Indianisation had been fully accepted in principle.[8] However, this 'Indianisation policy' did not automatically translate into an inevitable trajectory towards Independence. On the contrary, Indianisation was in some ways used to forestall change. Any devolution of power still had a number of vocal opponents, both within and beyond India, and the actual deadline for the British leaving India had never been enunciated. The 'readiness of the Indian to govern himself' was forever moving further away on the horizon, always subject to another set of qualifications or objections, always open to the charge that progress and liberalism had not yet been fully embedded. A new generation of administrators within the ICS – both British and Indian – had very different ideas: they sympathised deeply with nationalism, believed in ideals of material and political betterment and worked hard towards the ideal of a developed and more prosperous land. Indeed, these men would be in the ascendancy in the 1940s.[9] But even Nehru admitted in the late 1930s that his best hope was for Independence within a decade. A futuristic novel set in 1957, in which maniac Indians turned on their British masters 100 years after the mutiny, only to be crushed by the power of aerial bombardment, could still be published without any irony in Britain in the 1930s. There was no inevitability about Independence.

★   ★   ★

Lord Linlithgow, viceroy at the outbreak of war, had been in India since 1936. He had cut his teeth on Indian politics, not in the villages and towns of India but in Whitehall, by chairing important committees on Indian affairs in the 1920s and 1930s. A viceroy with no passion for India and only a little prior exposure to the country, he did not know the local languages and was similarly deaf to the nuances of Indian politics. Linlithgow's stiff, towering body looked almost designed for the viceregal robes and he made an imposing impression standing next to his wife, who was six feet tall. He had a touching fondness for his own children and grandchildren but everyone else found there was a touch of granite about him. He was described in *Time* magazine as having a 'half-dreamy, half-cranky' face, but Nehru less charitably assessed him as 'Heavy of body and slow of mind, solid as a rock and with almost a rock's lack of awareness'.[10] His limitations provided a rare point of agreement between Indian nationalists and many British civil servants. The Viceroy's own enthusiasm for the role had also rapidly diminished. When the Bombay provincial ministry brought in the prohibition of alcohol he found it 'something of a trial at public functions where a little

anaesthetic is at times so very welcome'. He would ask for retirement on several occasions throughout the war, only to be
compelled by Churchill to extend his term.[11] He would have been
a passable viceroy during a quiet spell of the nineteenth century
but was no match for Gandhi or for the formidable changes that
the war would bring to India.

Linlithgow's weakness was that he imagined that his Indian subjects
would feel the same way about war as him, that they would share
the same fears about German expansionism, the same need to defeat
fascism, and would unquestioningly support the prioritisation of war.
Linlithgow, whose own twin sons were now fighting in Europe, took
the British case for war as self-evident: 'our moral case is so strong it
ought, I feel, to make an appeal to anyone who is prepared to approach
it with an open mind'. This was a risky and foolhardy position to
adopt for a viceroy charged with convincing a sceptical Indian public
about British war intentions.[12] His failure to consult and to make a
concerted effort to join forces with Indian leaders at the very start of
the war would have catastrophic consequences for years to come;
within eight weeks, the new political settlement of 1937, which delivered Indian rule at the regional level, had imploded. The Congress
ministries in United Provinces and Bombay resigned, followed by
ministries in Orissa, Central Provinces and the North-West Frontier
Province.

To many in Britain the Second World War was a 'just war', an epic
ideological struggle. In 1939 for many imperial subjects, without any
clear promise of emancipation from British rule even at the end of
the war, matters were far less clear-cut. Linlithgow had a blind spot:
he was completely unable to see the need to persuade or convince
his Indian subjects of the moral necessity to fight, assuming that right-
thinking individuals would see it with simple clarity. Several weeks
into the commencement of the war he wrote, 'I see no reason why
we should let ourselves become entangled in an academic argument
about the merits or demerits of democracy.'[13] His calculation was that
the majority of Indians would come to their senses and support the
war effort. He was warned by numerous advisers not to miss
the psychological moment and to win over public opinion to the cause.

But the Viceroy stalled, returning to old stalwarts of the colonial regime, spending his time meeting princes and other old friends of the British in India. He admitted to being 'baffled' about how to recruit men and to get a war plan in order without any clear plan of action coming from London.[14]

There was a bastion in the Viceroy's calculations: 600 princely states, some with land masses as large as France or with populations to rival those of European countries. The Nizam of Hyderabad had been featured on the front cover of *Time* magazine in 1938, celebrated as the richest man in the world. These princes, who ruled one third of the subcontinent's population directly but owed their strength to the Raj, liberally opened their purses and palaces, offering their services. One by one, maharajas offered their help to the Crown. The day after war was declared the Maharaja of Kashmir offered to leave for any theatre of war immediately in a letter of fealty to the British state: 'I have available in Jammu a reserve of man-power which has been judged . . . excellent fighting material and of this I have decided to give the benefit to His Majesty's Government.' He also offered for immediate active service two infantry battalions and one mountain battery for use anywhere in the world. The princely state would pay for these men and support their families while they were away from home; the government need only feed them in the field and meet their other daily requirements. The maharaja also invited the government to send recruiting parties into Kashmir as long as they co-operated with the local authorities.[15] The Rajput princes of Jodhpur and Bikaner made similar offers and within days several more states were making lavish donations: Indore gave five *lakhs*, Travancore six *lakhs*, Bikaner one and a half *lakhs*, the Nizam of Hyderabad set aside over £100,000 for the air ministry, and Maharaja Jam Sahib of Nawanagar promised to contribute a tenth of the gross revenue of his state to the war effort. The Nawab of Bhopal was so keen to get to the front or to serve in some other capacity that he had to be persuaded to stay in his city. The Maharaja of Jaipur was soon in North Africa inspecting troops.

The princes knew from their experiences of the First World War that this was an opportunity to cement their loyalty to the British and to prop up the existing political order. Many of them also had close ties to the military, had been educated at Sandhurst or in British schools and felt a strong affinity with the cause. The Nepali regent, desperate to defend his country's own sovereignty, surprised the Commanding Officers by his obsequiousness. 'If money was needed, the Maharajah sent it', wrote the Indian Army officer Lieutenant General Francis Tuker.[16] In return, Linlithgow and the Marquess of Zetland, the Secretary of State for India, positively gushed at the loyalty and largesse of the princes.

This was not an uncomplicated story of Raj loyalism, devoid of more ambivalent undertones. The princes of India, albeit a diverse and vastly varied bunch of sultans, maharajas and nawabs, had long been anxious about safeguarding their constitutional future and preserving their power in the face of the waning of the British power that supported them. Agitations and rebellions in their states had been erupting with uncomfortable regularity in the late 1930s. They had long sought guarantees of their sovereignty, inviolability and continued leadership in any kind of post-British state. Both the British and the Congress during the 1930s had urged autocratic maharajas to reform their constitutional positions and to devolve more power to the people in their states. The princes now saw a sliver of opportunity to entrench their position and to curry British favour on an unprecedented scale by volunteering men, materials and money. The princes would continue to play the role of loyalists to the Crown throughout the war, and their own states would often witness rapid economic growth as a result. These apparently unconditional promises of loyalty were firmly predicated on an expectation of mutual support from the British Crown, an expectation which, ultimately, would be sorely misplaced.

For the majority of Indians, the start of the war was more disquieting and confusing. Abul Kalam Azad, who would soon become President of the Congress Party and was a close confidante of many key leaders, remembered the uneasy feeling after war was declared:

'Everybody seemed to be waiting for something to happen but their formless fears were vague and undefined. In India also there was a sense of expectancy and fear.'[17]

For South Asian politicians, international politics *did* matter. Nehru had been absorbed by the Spanish Civil War during his stay in Europe in 1936, speaking out in favour of the Republicans in Trafalgar Square in London. The settlement of Jewish refugees, hounded out of central Europe, was already a subject of concern for sympathetic politicians in India. By December 1938 Nehru was urging his old friend, the provincial chief minister in United Provinces, to offer government positions to skilled Jewish refugees and stressing the urgency of offering them help: 'I have received information that things are moving so fast', he wrote to Pandit Pant, 'that perhaps many of these unfortunate persons may simply be crushed out of existence unless some way out is found for them.'[18] The politics of the Middle East was always avidly followed in India and Muslims in particular watched the Palestinian question with concerned curiosity, following the Arab revolt and the British machinations regarding the creation of a Jewish homeland in the newspapers.

Fascism and communism had left deep impressions on Indian minds and on South Asian political organisation in the 1930s. Hitler, Stalin and Mussolini had millions of admirers and books about them sold in great numbers, and their photographs regularly dominated the front pages of newspapers. India had its own forms of local militarism. Militant youth movements, including the Khaksars, Muslim League National Guards and Congress youth wings, had attracted surging numbers of young people who drilled, exercised, sang songs and marched through the alleyways and marketplaces of Indian towns. Some, such as the religious militants in the Rashtriya Swayamsevak Sangh (RSS), celebrated a future vision of an exclusively Hindu India, and their leaders openly celebrated Hitler's ideas and methods. The cross-currents of international fervour had distinct echoes in India.

As the Spanish Civil War ended, the Munich crisis unfolded and Hitler and Stalin began to align, Europe's troubles and the growth of fascism provoked a highly charged intellectual and divisive debate in metropolitan coffee houses and university common rooms. The assault on China by Japan was closer to home and watched with deep interest and concern. But even the internationally astute Jawaharlal Nehru could confidently state, 'I do not think there is the slightest chance of a German or Japanese invasion of India.'[19] Even as global events became daily more critical, and dominated the headlines, the threat of actual warfare on Indian soil was still far-distant; there were too many pressing concerns within India's own borders.

Many Indian leaders had some sympathy for the war. They wanted to know what India would get in return for fighting a war in the name of freedom. As Nehru saw it, the old world order was dead and the war would inevitably bring seismic change and a new world in its wake. The leaders of the major parties were under pressure from the public not to come away empty-handed and often the party followers wanted to go further than their leaders in using the war as an opportunity for pushing nationalist goals. But there was also a sense of uncertainty about taking advantage of Britain's great vulnerability. Gandhi told how as he was boarding a train in Delhi, people in the crowd were smiling at him 'whilst they were admonishing me not to have any understanding with the Viceroy'.[20] Jinnah's words to the Viceroy the same week held some revealing echoes of Gandhi's. 'He, Mr Jinnah, personally shared those sentiments of loyalty and that same readiness to give his full support [to the war effort]. But he was a public man and had to think about his followers.'[21] Subhas Chandra Bose made clear, a week before the war started, 'if war broke out between Germany and Poland the sympathy of the Indian people would be with the Poles'. But he then followed this with the pivotal question, 'Whatever our subjective reactions in this international conflict may be, what are we to do as a nation?'[22]

Different priorities, between the British and the Indians, started to show and drive rifts even where cordial relations and common purpose had previously prevailed. 'Feeling hardened on both sides', the newspaper editor Desmond Young recalled.[23] The pre-eminent industrialist Ghanshyam Das Birla, whose factories were soon booming with wartime contracts, talked of British 'wooden-headedness' in private, while an ICS officer wrote to his parents that 'The Indian race must I think be quite the most contemptible on earth at least the bits I have seen of it', declared the Congress 'incapable of running a Sunday school picnic' and admitted that he had recently become 'a confirmed diehard' on the political question.[24] This estrangement was a tragedy for those on the left of the Congress. They had long championed the anti-fascist cause from Spain to Abyssinia, and detested Hitler but felt embittered by the British stance. Nehru felt deeply let down by old British friends whose sights were now fixed single-mindedly on Europe: 'It shows the enormous gap between India and England. I had not realised, when I was in England last, that this gap, which was obviously present, was quite so wide and unbridgeable as I now feel it is. Of course the war makes a difference and confuses people's minds. But what a difference!' Later he wrote to Rajendra Prasad, 'What has surprised me more than the invasion of Holland etc., has been the quite singular obtuseness of the British.'[25]

As the war proceeded, many British people, from journalists to Tommies, would come to sympathise with the Indian cause for polit-ical freedom, as we shall see, and the division was never simplistically along racial lines. However, this sense of two worlds drifting apart, of two peoples less entwined than they had been in the past, runs through many accounts of the time. The sheer geographical distance and the diverse priorities of imperial subjects and metropole pulled people in different directions. Across the world, empires were giving way to nation-states.

*   *   *

The Raj had a renewed sense of uncompromising confidence, as the democratic gains of the late 1930s were rolled back. As a wartime state, under the Defence of India Act passed in 1939, policemen

and civil servants acquired unprecedented power and the state
began to use its security apparatus for internal defence. Provincial
governors could detain indefinitely anyone whom they believed
jeopardised the war effort. These powers went far beyond any that
had been in place in India since the First World War. 'This is the
largest district in India – 12,000 square miles I think – of which I
am now lord of 4,000', Ian Macdonald, who was rapidly promoted
to new responsibilities, joked in a letter home to his parents, only
partly in jest.[26] The Act gave civil servants extraordinary powers:
to control food distribution, to suspend newspapers, to seize property. In fact, the Act enabled the government to do *anything* considered 'necessary or expedient for securing the Defence of British
India, the public safety, the maintenance of public order or the
efficient prosecution of the war'.[27] Defence Acts were not unusual
in wartime, and were also passed in Britain, but the difference in
India was the great discretion suddenly centralised in the hands of
a local magistrate. The Chief Press Adviser at the time, Desmond
Young, well understood that there could be a blurring between the
powers required to effectively fight a war and to run a disgruntled
empire, particularly when nationalist protest had preceded the war
by two decades. 'Press criticism which in peacetime was just tolerable, provided always that it was "constructive" (or favourable),
was now "disloyalty".'[28] These binaries of loyalty and disloyalty
were the prism through which all political action was increasingly
viewed.

This logic was also applied to foreign nationals. Rules of internment varied considerably across South Asia, so that scattered
German and Italian nationals had diverse experiences. India had
small but significant communities of Germans and Italians in
1940, around 1,500 Germans and over 700 Italians. Many worked
for the consulates; some of them were employed by firms such
as Siemens Schukert and Agfa. They worked in businesses and
companies, as doctors, missionaries and teachers. As elsewhere
in the British Empire, as war loomed closer these individuals
came under surveillance. The process was patchy and riddled
with inconsistencies. In India, police faced particular difficulties

in deciding who was potentially troublesome. The British Empire had by its very nature attracted global explorers and nurtured hybrid romances and it was not always easy to pigeonhole people by nationality. Border and passport control was rudimentary and less carefully controlled than in Britain, and the number of continental Europeans arriving in India was growing all the time as Europe's ethnic patchwork came under ferocious attack from many sides.[29]

Police detained some of these Europeans, including women and children, as soon as the war started. An Austrian mountaineer, Heinrich Harrer (who became famous for his escape from detention and time in Tibet), recalled that once the war started the arrests went 'like clockwork'.[30] A large troop of police entered the restaurant garden in Karachi where he was eating and detained him immediately. At the Bombay Talkies, the German technicians and cameramen were arrested, including the director Franz Osten, who was later expelled and sent back to Germany. Whilst some Italians and Germans were allowed to roam freely, some were confined to the limits of a controlled environment within a two-mile radius of a particular police station.

Nevertheless, despite the hostilities in Europe local relations between Europeans in India and the British rulers were often cordial, less coloured by the conflict taking place in Europe than by the prior dynamics of the Raj. German Lutheran missionaries in Orissa entertained members of the Indian Civil Service at a Christmas party in 1940 and later baptised the baby of the District Magistrate by reading out the Church of England Service when no other clergymen were available.

Magistrates and policemen often based decisions on political risk as much as nationality. Jewish central Europeans could easily fall into the net if they also seemed politically suspect. The taint of communism or radicalism was a way to put troublesome characters behind bars. Leopold Weiss, better known as Muhammad Asad, was one of the first to be seized. A Viennese Jewish convert to Islam, he had been on the police radar for a number of years, labelled as a Bolshevik. He was interned in

Lahore, and remained in the hill station of Dalhousie for the next six years. Surrounded by barbed wire, Nazis and anti-fascists lived inches from each other. Weiss was deeply worried about his relatives back in Vienna, aware of the pogroms and deportations taking place. His concern was justified; the entire family had been rounded up and sent to their deaths. His father, stepmother and sister did not survive the war. When asked many years later about his Indian internment he still recalled it with resentment. What did he do in the camp, for six long years? 'Nothing. We were housed in seventy-man barracks. What could we do there?' he remembered with some bitterness. 'Once, at Christmas, we fought with the Fascists. We won, because we were sober and they were drunk.'[31] Asad later became a prolific author on Islamic reform, but spoke only rarely of his years in the internment camp.

A number of other Jewish refugees found themselves interned in India. One Mr Joschkowitz, who had been born in Germany to Jewish parents and described himself as 'a victim of Nazi and anti-Semitic prosecution', had fled Germany and stayed temporarily in France, England, Egypt and Iraq before finding himself in India, where he was interned at Dehra Dun. He appealed with desperation for release. 'Several times I have tried to explain to the Authorities the paradox of my position but . . . without result.'[32] Others worried about their association with or marriage to Germans. A Mrs Pohlmann, in Calcutta, who had married a German at the turn of the century, pleaded that she should not be interned or sent out of India.[33]

As the provincial governments and local magistrates extended their powers under the Defence of India Act, surveillance was devolved to local and provincial police and from early 1940 it was they who made ad hoc decisions about internments. Christoph von Fürer-Haimendorf, an Austrian who had trained as an anthropologist at the University of Vienna, had a German passport. He was friendly with senior government officials, so instead of camp internment he was 'confined' to Hyderabad State, in reality living as a guest of the wealthy nizam, for the first part of the war. 'I was in the position of an enemy alien, but fortunately I had good connections', he later recalled.[34] In the 1940s he was carrying out anthropological fieldwork amongst local tribes, which laid the basis for his future career at the School of Oriental and African Studies.

Special branches often had only names and addresses to work with and the police often lacked the necessary linguistic skills to investigate properly. Detection was an imprecise science. 'Our own records . . . were practically non existent as previously they had given no cause for investigation. We did not even know whether there was a Nazi Party among the big German community, or what the relation was between the Germans, Italians and Japanese following the formation of the Axis', one police chief from Bengal, Philip Finney, recalled.[35] His own attempts to establish investigations into Axis fifth columnists involved finding a British policeman who had German parentage and could speak German, whom he ran as an undercover agent.

Finney ran a network of Indian agents including house servants, chauffeurs and the head waiter at the German Club, who spoke both English and German. Interception of the mail of foreign nationals, which should have been authorised instead by the Indian Home Office, was taken up energetically by the police force ('I felt this was a case where one should act illegally') and accordingly when German and Japanese mail arrived at the post office it was temporarily smuggled out before being returned to the sorting office. 'We didn't really find out much about German spying, although two people I can recall caused us considerable thought and some anxiety.'[36]

Across the cities of South Asia, routine policing and administrative duties now became saturated with the concerns of the war. It was difficult to separate out civil and military imperatives and this would become ever more apparent as the internal and external defence functions of the state blurred, and the policing apparatus was turned ever more inward, towards the Indian populace.

Underneath this controlled surface, there was a strong streak of active resistance. The great ferment of political ideas of 1940s India was already in full swing and tussles over political ideologies were deeply and bitterly felt. Politicians struggled to articulate a response to an international war which was meaningful for their followers. Some *dalit* leaders thought of their own community's share of military jobs. Some Sikhs wanted to protect their historic advantages in the army. Jinnah began articulating a powerful new brand of religious nationalism. Jailed communists protested by hunger-striking. For peasants, with less contact with the state, the war was even more obscure – a quarrel between Europeans not rooted in Indian conditions – but they were also on the march, campaigning for their own freedoms. *Kisans* protested everywhere for more land and more rights against the predations of landlords.

By mid-1940 small pockets of resistance had begun erupting all over the country. Allah Ditta and Ghulam, both butchers in a village of Montgomery district, were prosecuted for exhorting people not to give money to war collections. Ghulum Nabi Janbaz of Amritsar was imprisoned for 'Delivering [an] objectionable speech, speaking highly of Herr Hitler and condemning the British', and one Sohanu of Bhanala for making anti-government and anti-recruitment utterances.[37] Mulk Raj of Rahbur was sentenced to one year's imprisonment for printing anti-war statements. In Punjab 'a small Muslim boy' was arrested in Lahore for singing an anti-recruitment song. Women sang songs cursing the railways that swept off their menfolk to war. A memo was issued to policemen across India to watch out for agents provocateurs who dissuaded young men from signing up as soldiers. 'The volume of specific reports reaching army headquarters of attempts to dissuade would-be recruits from joining is considerable and comes from a wide area though chiefly in the United Provinces and Punjab.' The memo warned of 'anti-recruitment propagandists travelling in trains and talking to serving soldiers and recruits', also of anti-recruitment activists turning up in villages at the same time as paid or volunteer recruiting parties arrived, talking men out of joining up on the spot.[38] Intelligence officers had a tendency to see organised agents lurking behind random events. Not all defiance was organised on the grounds of nationalism but it did have an inner logic. People feared being sent away to fight in far-distant lands to battle against what ever more appeared to be a superior enemy. Villagers engaged in their own debates about the wisdom of joining up, and arguments started up between ordinary passengers on trains about the value of the war.

2

Peasants into Soldiers

Fifty-three thousand men were enlisted in the Indian Army in the first eight months of the war. By late 1940, 20,000 a month were joining up. By the end of the war the army was over 2 million men strong, a vast intricate machine which needed to be fed, clothed, equipped with arms, moved and housed. The Indian Army was never a singular entity. Some of the toughest infantrymen and artillery would trek across the deserts of North Africa and the Middle East before moving on to the completely different demands of jungle warfare in Burma and north-east India. Many would be away from home for three years or more. Some would revolt and leave the Indian Army altogether, defecting to the Japanese. Some were officers from privileged families, trained at Sandhurst or Dehra Dun, more at ease with their fellow British officers than with the men under their command. Others were doctors in Indian Military Hospitals. Some would have a more comfortable war, manning depots, teaching languages, plotting air-routes, fixing vehicles, working on scientific schemes. And behind them all stood the non-combatants who made the Indian Army function: the washermen, tailors and boot-makers who maintained, repaired and replaced uniforms, the barbers and cooks who looked after the needs of the men, the nursing orderlies and the sweepers, who mopped up the camp and latrines. Religious teachers, *pandits* and *munshis*, mule-handlers and vets, all accompanied the troops. Behind the caricatures of 'martial races' were millions of people with miscellaneous backgrounds, ambitions, fears and needs.

Indian soldiers had long been used for a dual purpose: sent overseas to fight for the empire and used closer to home to conquer territory and to secure the frontiers of the Raj, as it expanded ever outwards and absorbed Indian-ruled territories into the empire, piece by piece. Indian soldiers were the motor of expansion and in the vanguard of imperial defence from the nineteenth century in Java, Malacca, Penang, Singapore and China. Indian troops fought against the Mahdi uprisings in Sudan, in the Boxer Rebellion in China, in the Afghan wars and in Tibet. They both triggered and helped suppress the Indian uprising of 1857. In the First World War, 1,302,394 Indian soldiers had left the subcontinent to fight in France and Belgium, in Gallipoli, Salonika and Palestine, in Egypt and Sudan, in Mesopotamia, at Aden and in the Red Sea, East Africa and Persia.

In 1939 the novelist Mulk Raj Anand, who was born in Peshawar and had grown up in the military cantonments of North India, published a novel dedicated to his father, Lal Chand, a metalworker turned soldier who had fought in the First World War as a sepoy. His book, timing uncannily with the start of the next global war, told the story of a company of sepoys from a village, thrown into the disloca-tion and horrors of Ypres. It emphasised the faraway nature of the First World War, its eerie other-worldliness for men coming from north-west India, their difficulty in making sense of the trenches. The first scene depicts the ships carrying the men towards the ports of France:

> 'Is the war taking place there then?' a sepoy asked. No one answered him as most of the sepoys did not know where the war was . . . 'So we have come across the black waters safely then,' he said to himself apprehensively, as if he really expected some calamity, the legendary fate of all those who went beyond the black seas to befall him at any moment.[1]

In 1939, many of the First World War veterans could still be seen, sitting chatting by tea shops or sitting on *charpoys* in the villages of Punjab. Some still wore items of uniform, a faded jacket or hat. If you asked them they would fetch their medals from old tin boxes or wrapped up in cotton bundles. They told tales not only of horror, but also of heroism, adventure, travel and exotic women. Elderly veterans helped to round up new recruits. In Rajinder Singh Dhatt's estimation, there were twenty to thirty men in his village in East Punjab who had also been in the First World War. The First World War had brought price rises, revenue hikes of over 15 per cent and political dislocation to India, alongside some 74,000 deaths. Yet the war itself had always been remote, something heard about by civilians but less often seen. The idea of a total war, which brought calamity right into Indian households, was not really contemplated. At the start of the Second World War many people drew a parallel with the First and believed this new war would follow the same script. They did not expect it to come to their own shores.

As yet, few knew where it would be fought or for how long. When people contemplated war, they cast their eyes northward to the frontier with Afghanistan. Over a third of the army was stationed on this frontier in 1939 and the army had grown accustomed to thinking of the enemy as rebellious Pathans and murderous mullahs, 'not only fanatical but armed to the teeth' in the words of the Viceroy, who was absorbed by the frontier through the first months of the war.[2] The army had been beating back the followers of a charismatic and evasive Pathan chieftain, the Faqir of Ipi, since the late 1930s. He had been trying to push the British out of the frontier country, especially around the region of Bannu, and had started to be accredited with miraculous powers, as he repeatedly escaped capture and death. The fighting was tough and sustained. The faqir's followers mined roads and set booby traps at junctions and on bridges; his band of roaming guerrillas launched surprise attacks on soldiers with rifles, grenades and swords. Weekly news arrived of kidnappings of civilians and soldiers, daylight raids and ambushes on main roads and frontier towns. The frontier tribes looted mail trucks and fired directly on the military.

In response the government spent over 15 million rupees in a year trying to pacify the rebels; the RAF and the Royal Indian Air Force (RIAF) dropped red warning notes from the air before bombing villagers in Waziristan into submission, strafing them from the air and machine-gunning them from armoured cars. 'The embarrassment in the present position', confided the province's governor about the unclear aims of the campaign, 'is that we maintain a large military force in a potentially hostile country, while at the same time, seldom if ever is any real military objective offered.'[3] By 1939 the rebels were losing ground. But the worst fears of the Government of India still turned on the 'Russian menace' and the idea of the Great Game, the fear of Russia taking advantage of the volatile frontier to break into the British Empire.

The state issued plans for action in the event of a Russian invasion, with a northern line to support the Afghan government in Kabul and a southern line to forestall Soviet troops around Kandahar. A Nazi or Italian enemy seemed far-distant and less pressing.

The Indian Army was slowly trading horses for tanks. Indian Army chiefs saw this as a way to fortify South Asian defence but London soon started pressing for increasing numbers of troops to be sent to the Middle East, where the Italians had declared war on 10 June 1940, which expanded the theatres where Britain needed to send men. Force Trout was sent to Iraq in August 1940 in order 'to stiffen the morale of the Iraqi government', to protect the refinery at Abadan against sabotage and to protect the line of communication to Palestine.[4] There was a tension between these domestic and international needs; manpower was stretched like a very thin skein around the Middle East and Asia in 1940 with too little equipment, training or shipping available. The Indian Army was already widely spread all over the world, even in the very first year of the war. The soldiers of the 6th Rajputana Rifles, for instance, could be found from the Mediterranean to East Asia as early as September 1940. The 1st and 4th battalions were readying to fight the Italians in North Africa, the 2nd and 3rd were battling tribes in the North-West Frontier Province, the 5th battalion was doing garrison duty in Hong Kong and the 6th was still being formed in northern India, and was soon destined for Bengal. The Indian Army existed to protect and fortify British regions of interest.

This was, though, an army being scrambled for action in the face of unprecedented challenges. The army still lacked motorised transport and was heavily reliant on mules and horses. It was also severely short of everything from guns to boots. Delays in raising regiments and in sending them out to operations occurred while equipment was shuttled from place to place. Some in Delhi believed that the internal defence of India should still be prioritised and remained reluctant to leave holes in India's own defence, wary of the situation at the frontier and the strength of the rebellion there, while others in London wanted troops extracted for the European and African fronts as quickly as possible. Numerous internal tussles over money, equipment and men ensued. Some regiments were left with second-hand equipment and substandard training. The sepoys at war on the Afghan border did not know that very soon long days in rugged hill country would be replaced with the deserts of North Africa.

The vast, almost unfathomable expansion of the Indian Army was beginning. Joining up as a volunteer after the start of a war in Europe still involved a leap of faith, a step into the unknown. As propaganda regularly reminded the world, this was a 'volunteer army' not raised by conscription. It was far easier for men from the traditional recruiting lands of North India to learn the ropes. Many Jats, Rajputs, Pathans and Sikhs from North and north-west India had come from generations of military service, had always expected to join up, in war or peace, and regarded themselves as tied to the *sarkar* by bonds of fealty. In parts of Punjab, Rajasthan and west United Provinces family expectations and traditions, the more prominent presence of the military in the daily lives of the village, and the welfare and resources provided by military investment to their areas, had all cemented bonds with the Indian Army. Punjabis still made up 60 per cent of the army in 1939. In these districts, villages had been carefully cultivated, government had given strategic assistance over the years to the local farmers and the expectations and experiences of war were part of local folklore. The systems of promotion, leave and pay were all understood.

In Punjab, medals and scars of war were worn proudly as heroic symbols. In the irrigated tracts of the southern Punjab, landholders with sprawling estates could be relied upon to drum up men and to provide them for the *sarkar* as soldiers. In return, these local landlords had untrammelled power on their own estates, received the benefits of government investment in irrigation, the ability to continue to cultivate and sell, to hunt and to live their lives undisturbed by the rulers, while retaining the ear of the governor if any small difficulties needed easing. By 1940 some of these older solidarities had started to break down and the *zamindari* families that the British looked to, to prop up their rule in the region, had often begun an interminable decline into genteel poverty. Henry Craik, the aristocratic Governor of Punjab, had been in India since 1899, and now feared that the 'old families who have for generations used their influence in support of the administration' faced sinking into 'comparative insignificance or poverty'.[5] But the days of the great loyalist *zamindars* were not numbered just yet, and when war broke out some of these old links between crown and country were revitalised.

Here, the military was a well-known and domesticated beast. 'I
went with happiness. My whole family for generations has been in
the army and it was my dream to do army service', remembered Ali
Akbar. But even for these men, real information about the war was
sometimes scarce. 'When I enlisted that's when I found out that the
war had started', Ali added.[6] Among the Sikhs, recruitment was a
traditional avenue for employment and income, leaving a number of
nationalist Sikh leaders in an awkward position in 1940, caught between
the desire to furnish their followers with jobs and their own ambivalence about serving the British. Master Tara Singh wrote to Gandhi
asking him not to do anything that would limit Sikh army recruitment,
to which Nehru tartly remarked it was not possible 'to have it both
ways'.[7] Some leaders had long been straddling the uncomfortable
position between their own anti-imperial sentiments and their
followers' reliance on the state for jobs and resources.

But in other areas, recruitment was less straightforward. In 1940
the political agent in the remote region of Sabar Kantha – a princely
state in what is today the Gujarati-Rajasthani border, a scrubland, far-
removed from big cities and in the shadow of the Aravali hills – sent
out a circular. He wrote to chiefs and landlords seeking Rajputs to
join the army. He was looking for men aged sixteen to twenty-five,
with a minimum height of 5 feet 5 inches, a chest of 33 inches, and
weight of at least 112 pounds. The local landed magnates or *thakurs*
wrote back dutifully one by one, politely informing him that no one
was suitable or interested or available. 'Now there is not a single
Rajput available for recruitment in the Indian Army', replied one.
'There is no possibility', wrote another. 'I have the honour of informing
you that the Rajputs and Mohammedans residing in this state were
called by me for recruitment and exhorted to join the military service,
explaining the terms stated in your letter but I regret that none shows
his willingness to join the army and so no suitable candidate at present
is available from here.' Another told the agent: 'Regret to inform you
no response whatsoever'. Some blamed 'a lack of warlike and martial
spirit', others the 'backwardness' of the area. The agent reminded the
thakurs in further letters of the advantages of joining the army,
the free rations, clothes, and games that soldiers would be able to
access. Development and the promise of a more modern future were
used as enticements to induce the men to sign. The *thakurs* were asked

to tell the men that they would have electric lighting and the chance to learn to read. But still nobody was forthcoming. In Malpur State, the young males asked for more time 'to think over the matter'.[8]

Men entered the army in numerous different ways and for diverse reasons. 'Voluntary' recruitment spanned the whole spectrum from loyalist, pro-British families to those who had their arms heavily twisted and felt direct pressure from their landowners or overseers. Service in the army had long been recognised as a way of securing a guaranteed supply of rice or bread. As the war progressed, Recruitment Officers spread their net ever wider and trawled the countryside for men, changing the character of the pre-war Indian Army beyond recognition. Landlords and policemen placed casual pressure on young men to try to comply with the *sarkar's* desires. Some new recruits had bodies visibly atrophied by malnutrition; they had been subsisting at the barest level, even before the war raised food prices. Even in Punjab, where incomes had been rising steadily for several decades, the early months of the war were also marked by a devastating famine which ravished tenant-cultivators in the south-eastern districts of Hissar, Rohtak and Gurgaon, the worst experienced for forty years. A place in the Indian Army meant a job and a full belly. People, in the countryside and the cities, remembered all too vividly the depression decade, when men had camped outside the factories in vain waiting for work, when those inside might be dismissed, put on short work or find their wages slashed without notice. Above all, the army promised a way to extend support to other family members; new recruits became not only breadwinners for their own immediate kin but sometimes for numerous dependants.

Young men could also be pressurised into leaving their homes to join a remote war although many resisted such pressure. In Valasna, the following year, the political agent was still persisting in trying to root out suitable men. Three men had been identified by the *thakur* as potentially promising offerings to the colonial state. One of them, a Muslim tailor, had slipped away to live in a village ten miles away. Now that the day had come and they were being called to join up, the *thakur* reported, 'I called him too to come and see me personally. I deputed his own cousin from here to call him but the man avoided him sending me a reply that he was sick.' The other two men had come to see him but had agreed to go and see the

Recruiting Officer 'very reluctantly'. He had practically had to bribe them, offering the money for their travel expenses. But two days later they had not returned to collect the cash. The *thakur* wrote in anguished tones, 'I myself do cherish very great zeal and interest on the subject, as a matter of personal belief and conviction and had hoped to do my possible bit,' but he now recommended that the Assistant Recruitment Officer cancel his forthcoming trip: 'his most precious time and labours, I fear, would not be turned to good account'.[9]

A handful of potential recruits did come forward: in Vadgam two men had put their names forward and showed 'ardent desire' to join the army. One, a former police constable who had previously worked as a peon for three years, appeared 'a promising young man full of budding hopes and enthusiasm'. The twenty-four-year-old Rajput had been forced to resign his new position in the police as a constable eight months earlier because of his mother's illness. The other keen candidate was described in four simple sentences:

Candidate Kishorsinhji is a Rathod Rajput of about 25 years of age. He has no parents. He is all alone and he maintains himself by working as a day labourer. He seems to be an energetic Rajput.[10]

Both these men wished to join the army because of their personal circumstances and poverty. Both were sent to Sadra, the market town, in order to meet the Assistant Recruiting Officer at the police station at ten o'clock in the morning on the allotted day. The file runs out at this point and we are left to wonder whether they managed to achieve their ambition and what fate held for them.

Recruitment had long relied on an idea of collective types; on the idea that certain 'martial races' should be the mainstay of the Indian Army and that it was possible to discern the quality of a potential soldier from the ethnic or linguistic group to which he belonged. Men had, for generations, not been assessed as individuals but as representatives of their race, a complex business in a land of such variation. They were first and foremost physical specimens, expected to match the ideal type of their caste or tribe. Breadth of chest, decent eyesight and the ability to follow basic orders were essential. If they had additional skills, or could read and write, they might have a chance of promotion. The physical inspection was rudimentary. Stripped down to their underwear, the men stood for measurement and medical inspection in a line before arriving in front of the Recruiting Officer. If he was pleased with what he saw he often inscribed their chests with a large chalk 'tick'.

In Rajasthan, Recruitment Officers carried with them a slim printed volume with a pale green cover, *The Recruiting Handbook for the Rajputana Classes*. This had been compiled by one Major Brian Cole, a Recruiting Officer for Rajputana and central India, who wrote the handbook in 1921 based on his own experiences of drumming up men during the First World War. The handbooks were supposed to be the bible for all recruiters. Although reliance on them can be exaggerated, they were still being used as reference manuals into the 1940s. The Government of India published numerous similar handbooks from the 1890s onwards which described the different martial types from Madrassis to Kumaonis to Pathans and Rajputs. These handbooks catalogued 'types' of men and were supposed to give the Recruiting Officer an idea of what to expect in the area he was visiting, and, most importantly, *who* to recruit from the various castes and tribes of India, pointing out the sub-groups seen as suitable material for military recruitment. For instance, the handbook recommended: 'Rajputana Jats are on the whole a fine lot physically, especially those of Bikaner. They do not run to anything unusual in the way of height but have splendid chests and thighs.'[11]

Running through these handbooks was the assumption that different ethnic groups in India had entirely different levels of physical fitness, intelligence and martial qualities, alongside a host of other attributes. The handbooks also gave stern warnings about the types to avoid recruiting: in the Kumaoni hills, for example,

the short stocky lad with a fair complexion of about 5 ft. 4 in. (or 5 ft. 2 in. if young) with a chest measurement of at least 33 inches at the age of 17 years or 18 years is likely to provide the best material. The types found in the bazaars of Almora and Ranikhet and in the vicinity of the larger temples should be definitely rejected. The long lanky lad who will have outgrown his strength should not be taken.[12]

Underpinning these assumptions about race (which had pan-imperial appeal in the 1920s and 1930s) was also the idea that certain types of personality and psychological disposition could be detected by the physical appearance of the potential recruit. On the Rajputs again, the recruiting handbook opined,

> As soldiers they are brave, obedient and undemonstrative and have great pride of race. They are singularly free from caste prejudices and would never subordinate military efficiency to religious prejudice. They give no trouble in barracks and are singularly free from intrigue. When led by officers that they know and trust they will go anywhere and do anything.[13]

The handbooks also featured appendices, maps and population statistics, all intended to make the job of the Recruiting Officer easier. The numbers of men, district by district, taken from the government's decennial census, were published in tables at the back of the handbooks. The officers were also urged to consider rainfall and the best seasons for recruiting. Sometimes districts would be malarial or men would be preoccupied with harvesting. These efforts to catalogue, map and identify India for the benefit of its own administration had a long history and had often been completed with the willing assistance and participation of Indians themselves, who by 1940 were making up an increasing proportion of the Recruiting Officers. Yet the notions expressed in these handbooks belonged to an earlier age and would soon be of little use. The extended scope of recruitment in the 1940s and the sheer need for manpower changed the basis of the army, even if, in the most highly prized infantry regiments, regimental traditions appeared on the surface to look continuous with the past. During the 1940s, imperial systems dating from the nineteenth century and present wartime realities would become ever more dissonant.

As the Indian Army grew and the demand for recruits surged, so the recruiting methods changed and became less selective. 'I found that the most productive source of recruits were the *melas* or country fairs which would be held almost every week in different parts of Bihar – thousands buying, selling, beggars, holy men, stalls', John Ffrench, a British Recruiting Officer, recalled. 'We had only to drive our truck onto the ground, raise a flag and bang a drum. The problem then was to sort the men from the boys and weed out the few with medical problems, leaving us with forty or fifty strong young men.'[14]

The reasons why men entered the army also became more diverse and spurred by individual circumstances. Many of those raw recruits themselves were struck with wonder, as older men, looking back at their own youthful lack of inhibition, the bold naivety and the cavalier way that some of them approached war. 'Actually there was a teacher of mine who said that when you join the army and you swear an oath you should fully carry out what you have sworn to do so even if that meant your fellow soldiers dying next to you. You should strive to fulfil your duties', recalled Sardar Ali. Some were driven by a sense of adventure and exploration. 'I had no idea about what I was headed for. I was just so excited because I was young and safety was not a priority', Sardar Ali added.[15] In Punjab, a seventeen-year-old named Mohammed Khan was keen to join up, freely going to his local recruiting station and soon signed to the 9th Baluch Regiment. He later recalled that it was because he wanted to defend Britain. But what was Britain to him? He came from a village of agriculturalists and had seen two British families in his life before joining up, living about thirty miles away from his village. He did not know any English, although he would come to learn it to a point of fluency in the army.[16]

The traditional recruiting area would quickly be drained of men. New kinds of recruits, untouchable leather-workers or Bengali urbanites, became temporary soldiers. These men came into the army because of hunger, the chance for a steady wage and the opportunity to become a breadwinner for their family. Enthusiasm for recruitment depended not only on family traditions but also on familiarity with the military and an understanding of what joining the army meant. In places like Punjab and United Provinces, where proud and relatively comfortable veterans resided in *pukka* houses with decent furniture, wearing wristwatches and good-quality clothes, it is hardly surprising that young men might be interested in becoming sepoys. In other places, doubts about leaving farms untended or the pull factor of high wartime prices for crops like cotton meant that some farmers had less incentive to leave than others. Elsewhere, especially if people had heard stories of terrible wartime experiences, injuries and losses, or where there was deep suspicion of the army and of the colonial state, recruiters did not have such an easy task.

There was also the influence of role models and respected elders, teachers or British officers, friends or relations who may have been met in a chance encounter but made a strong impression on a youthful mind. Nineteen-year-old Nila Kantan met a British officer and within two days had signed a commitment to going anywhere in the world on service: 'They gave me a uniform and the rank of Indian Warrant Officer. Then, my God! I got in this troopship, without any training whatsoever – it was very peculiar.'[17]

Young people made decisions without the agreement of their parents, ran away from home or found themselves overseas for far longer than they had ever expected. This could also be a way of escaping family feuds, domestic violence, unwanted marriage arrangements or strained relations with parents. The official recruitment age was far from set in stone. Indian teenagers and even boys presented themselves, and pressurised Recruiting Officers did not strictly adhere to the age limit. There were few birth certificates in a peasant society with high rates of illiteracy. It was very easy for keen aspirant soldiers to pass themselves off as older than they were and for collusion to occur between Recruiting Officer and recruit. Mangal Singh went to see the Recruitment Officer when his parents were away from his village in Punjab. That same day he passed the cursory medical inspection, signed enrolment certificates, was issued with railway passes and kit, given advance money on his wages and a small bonus for joining up and instructed to proceed to the Signal Training Centre at Jabalpur, several hundred miles away from his village. He did not see his parents again for two years. He sent a letter to his family to tell them that he had joined the Indian Army.

* * *

In Nepal, at the same time, the recruiting parties set out in trucks, travelling rocky, treacherous roads, reaching up into remote villages, and stripping the hills of all the young and able-bodied men: Gurungs, Rais, Limbus. These men from widely different ethnic groups and long-distant parts of Nepal would become famous under one label, known collectively as the Gurkhas. The Gurkhas have long played a distinctive role in the military history of Asia. Very old traditions of

migration to find military labour or other work on the warmer plains
to the south pre-dated British rule in South Asia. The local word for
Gurkha, 'Lahure', suggests a man who travels to the city of Lahore
to join the military and probably dates back to at least the eighteenth
century. The British perception of the Gurkhas as tough, unified, loyal
and willing fighters was well crafted by wartime propaganda which
never failed to celebrate their role.

The rulers of Nepal, who resisted British conquest, and constantly
and cleverly defended the sovereignty of their mountain kingdom,
had since 1815 sent men to the British as a trade-off for Independence.
It was a way to secure their kingdom's relative isolation from the
West and their own power; only 153 Europeans even set foot in
Nepal between 1885 and 1925. The British warmed to the sturdy
hill-men, celebrating their loyalty and toughness, and turning their
bravery almost into a mythic cult. Gurkhas seemed distinctive and
stayed aloof from the Indians and therefore appeared perfect for
suppressing revolts and doing garrison duty inside India. Their
origins in the hills, their valleys surrounded by the exquisite crystal-
line peaks of the Himalayan range, captured something in the
imagination. Disparate men from the hills were recast into an ideal
type, the valiant but boyish Gurkha who gave unquestioning loyalty
to the empire.

High up in the Himalayas, recruitment was being intensified among
the Gurkhas of Nepal. The Maharaja Jhuddha of Nepal gave his
blessing and encouragement to the recruiters, but he was more
cautious about some of the more extreme British demands. Recruitment
in Nepal was not straightforward. Rainy summer months made it
difficult to communicate across the mountainous terrain and for the
young men to come down from their villages into the valleys. Labour
parties competed to acquire healthy young men. The British recruiters
also had to tread carefully to make sure that they did not interfere
with harvest season. Recruitment was staggered between eastern and
western districts. The British agent at the court in Kathmandu used
sycophancy, gifts and gentle persuasion to extract more men from the
mountain kingdom:

There is just now a slight tendency to show a natural drying up of the
well, but with his Highness' magic wand he [the British Recruiting

Officer] feels sure that sufficient water can be obtained from the well so that complete demands may be met by 28th February after which the weather really gets too hot for recruits to come in. Knowing what wonders your Highness' magic wand can work and knowing also how wonderfully good your Highness has been in assisting our demands for the expansion of the Gurkha Regiments, I wonder if your Highness would be so good as to wave it so that Col. Strahan may be able to complete the demands by 28th February. It would indeed be a marvellous achievement.[18]

The maharaja soon applied his 'magic wand' and the initial British appeal for an extra six battalions had soon swollen to ten. Extraordinary measures were used – all reservists were called up and then men on leave from the army were encouraged to return with willing recruits from their villages.

The Gurkhas, like the Indian soldiers, would play crucial roles in the combat to come. However, again, the freedom to join the army voluntarily can be exaggerated. For many, there was no choice at all. After all, Nepal had abolished slavery only fifteen years earlier. Headmen and landlords, responding to demands from higher up the hierarchy, needed to supply men as proof of loyalty to the regime. The poorest or the indebted would be sent off to the army. Tempting gifts of land or money lured other men into service, and those changing their mind or deserting had land confiscated. 'What do the young men know? Nothing!' recalled a Lahure who would become a prisoner of war in Singapore:

We saw lots of rupees in these recruiters' pockets and their nice warm 'sweaters'. They told us we would eat rice every day, see new places. What did we know about war? Nothing! . . . The recruiters didn't talk to us about war, only about pensions and food and clothing. They were very clever. When you are young and have always been with your mother and father what do you know of the suffering of going to a foreign country? Nothing![19]

The greatest resistance came from women. Mothers hid their sons, trying to keep them away from the recruiting parties, sending them up into the more isolated hills or out of the village to stay with relatives. The richer the family, the more likely its young men were to escape the recruiting parties. Other mothers resorted to pleading and emotional blackmail to try to stop their sons from going. One Nepali captain who served in Burma believed almost half of Gurkhas in the Second World War left without parental permission.[20] Mary Des Chene, an anthropologist who worked closely with the families of Gurkhas in one Nepali village, recorded the distinct feelings of misery and hardship associated with wartime many decades later. As one old woman, a widow from the war, told her, 'Before they took our food but during that war they grabbed our people too.'[21] Some of these women never had a chance to get to know their husbands: typical is Santamaya Limbu, who was married at the age of fifteen to a man she barely knew, who left for his post within a month of marriage. After ten months he came back for a number of days and then she never saw him again. He was presumed dead but she never had confirmation. She keeps his photograph and medals to this day.[22]

The word *dukha*, sadness, resurfaces in many memories of the time. Brothers, husbands and fathers vanished and there was little support extended to the women left behind. Women were left with hungry mouths to feed and farmland and paddy to plough and harvest. Their days might start now at five in the morning, ending at ten or eleven at night, husking rice, cooking and cleaning, collecting firewood, water and fodder. Children and old men adjusted to the new conditions, worked longer and harder in the fields. As a Nepali woman recalled, 'I hear the whole world was fighting but why they needed my son's father to settle it, I can't understand.'[23] Sometimes men crept away in secrecy, fearing their mother's displeasure. There was little ceremony or fanfare.

'Mother May Ask Where My Son Has Gone' is the title of one of the most popular folk songs of Nepal, still well known today. The song was popularised by the legendary folk singer Jhalakman Gandharva, who served as a Gurkha later in the century. The lament recalls the sadness of families left without their young men and the loss of kin, and captures the ways in which the recruitment of a family member echoed throughout a family. Its continued popularity perhaps suggests the profundity of wartime experience in Nepal.

House to House, door to door
They came to recruit
Asking if we would like to be a Lahure
Our hearts concurred
The major *saheb* in the corner, he checked
The squint eyed and the deaf, they went out
The healthy went to the hospital
And were taken in
Six months to that day
We paraded barefoot
Many are wounded in the chest, and many more in the head.
When I remember the wound in the head, my heart shakes.

Poor Souls![24]

3

Into the Middle East and North Africa

In Bombay, by 1940, the loading of troop ships was becoming a familiar sight: the departure of long columns of men, kitbags slung over their shoulders. The troop ships were tugged out from the harbour when the tide came in before being released onto the open sea. As everywhere, the destination was a closely guarded secret, causing much speculation, although the painting of the desert camouflage on regimental vehicles was one sign that the destination would be in the Middle East or North Africa. Harnarain Singh stood on deck as his ship pulled away from the Indian coastline and later remembered the many destroyers, troop ships and battleships as a beautiful sight. Others felt more nervous. Shells and bombs became a constant threat for soldiers as well as for Lascars; Nila Kantan was in a convoy, escorted by three cruisers and six destroyers as he sailed through the Red Sea:

> There was a naval action – the Italians started attacking in the middle
> of the night. I tried to go to my action station, but the naval people
> were so quick that they completely blocked all the watertight compart-
> ments. I got stuck in one. When the ships started firing I began weeping
> like children – because I had never seen all these things. Then a naval
> officer came and said, 'don't cry lad.'[1]

Many men longed for action and felt the excitement and tension mounting, especially as they reached their destination and came within sight of enemy aircraft. Harnarain Singh remembered how tense the men were; as his troop ship drew close to the North African coastline the men spotted enemy planes, and immediately picked up their rifles, yelling, firing into the sky with no hope of hitting their target.

Boredom was the chief danger though. And conditions on board ship could be tough. Officers and Other Ranks experienced the same voyage very differently. An Indian officer, Krishna Kumar Tewari, recalled his journey from South India to Burma: 'The ship was absolutely packed. Indian Other Ranks were accommodated on the lowermost deck . . . a number of men fell sick. This was due more to the overcrowding in the lower decks than to the roughness of the sea.'² Indian troops were frequently accommodated on the open decks. For villagers from inland districts, perhaps never having seen the sea before, it was a disconcerting and alien journey.

British Tommies setting out for India, sailing in exactly the other direction, also suffered.

They [Other Ranks] ate at long tables nearly the width of the ship, men on both sides and very cramped, and they slept on a hammock above the table, or on the table, or on the floor beneath the table. Food was delivered in buckets and very large tureens to the top end of each table and then ladled out to be passed along to the far end until all were served. The atmosphere was fetid at all times but much worse during the period of seasickness as through the Bay of Biscay.³

John Ffrench remembered the toilets as 'just frightful. They were quite inadequate for our needs and usually became blocked and ankle deep in water by mid day.' On the SS *Andes* sailing from Bombay, there were no facilities for Indian cooking and the cooks could only use petrol burners on the open deck: 'You can imagine the difficulties in preparing chapattis in the howling gale we ran into off Aden. None of the recruits had ever been far from their villages, much less overseas, so that they did not turn out to be good sailors either.'⁴ Men whiled away their time, playing carrom and chess, cards, reading, sleeping, talking, pacing the decks in order to try and keep fit, while the rot set in and muscles weakened and training faded from memory.

Thirty-one thousand Indian troops had already started arriving in the Middle East to fight the Italians in North Africa. Commanded by General Wavell, who would later become the penultimate Viceroy of India, they destroyed ten Italian divisions. They captured 130,000 prisoners and swept over 500 miles. This was the first good news of the war for the British. The men of the 4th and 5th Indian Infantry divisions would be celebrated across the empire, their victories announced with great pride in India.

Back in India, what did people know of the battles taking place elsewhere? And what kinds of information did soldiers and their distant families share? Like everywhere in the world, people wanted mundane news: of births, deaths and marriages, of men who had joined the army or had returned on leave. As ever in war, it was difficult for men to share their experiences of battle with their loved ones. Premindra Singh Bhagat, a cheerful twenty-two-year-old officer from the Royal Bombay Sappers and Miners, was in East Africa in 1941 and was particularly eloquent when trying to capture the details of battle. He wrote a long evocative letter for his seventeen-year-old sweetheart, Mohini, who was waiting for him back in Poona, trying to share with her what he had experienced:

> Sorry to sound so melodramatic, but the truth is the last few days have altered my outlook, not that I am pessimistic. In actual battle one is heavily bombed from the air, there are mines on the ground and machine gun bullets in the air. I have been in an area, mentioned twice on the wireless, where in forty minutes some fourteen aeroplanes just littered the place with bombs. I lay flat on the ground, and after the bombing was over I was covered with earth, two bombs having dropped just five yards away. That was my first escape; the second from bombs was two days ago. They say I have been very brave for some small thing I did, but believe me I was the most scared person in the world.[5]

Many could not find the words to express themselves and the illiterate relied on letter-writers and fellow soldiers in any case. The presence of the censor was well understood and letters made subtle gestures towards more explicit meanings. Like soldiers everywhere, the men also wanted to reassure and console their loved ones. Premindra later regretted his 'sloppy letter', wishing that the censor had stopped it. Letters were usually far more concerned with the basic stuff of life: family marriages, petty local disputes, the health and protection of elderly parents and children, how to handle savings accounts and matters of buying and selling, land disputes, relationships with kin and neighbours, spats and feuds. As the head of the family or at least as the main breadwinner, soldiers often carried the heavy responsibility for family well-being on their shoulders. They took great care to respond to household matters and to suggest ways of protecting their relatives, even from hundreds of miles away.

The Indian Army encouraged contact between men and their families. The officers knew that this was essential for morale and that worries about domestic life would weigh upon the soldiers, especially when so far from home. But the cost of postage was a burden for families with sons overseas; in 1940 and 1941 so many letters were being posted without stamps that it became a government matter. In May 1941, the Defence Department agreed to pay the difference on letters and parcels that were not sufficiently stamped, finding that returning them to the sender 'could give the wrong impression'. Soldiers were issued with free 'safe arrival' postcards to send to their loved ones.[6]

But for many families, there were very long absences and poor communications, given the remoteness of some of the theatres in the desert, and later the jungle. Mohini, Premindra Singh Bhagat's beloved, remembered 'days when she didn't get letters for a while and would panic'.[7] Sepoys' families looked for help from local District Welfare Boards, set up to provide support. Originating in Punjab for soldiers demobilised from the First World War, the system had spread and boards sprung up in North-West Frontier Province, United Provinces, Poona, Madras and Rajasthan by 1940. Manned by retired officers (often with the help of their wives), these boards operated in diverse ways. In Punjab they tended to be more elaborate and reputable, with local *tehsil* subcommittees manned by retired soldiers who knew the villages and the regiments well. Elsewhere, they were underfunded or less well established. The ideal was a one-stop shop for all the grievances that affected soldiers' families – news of the progress of the war, employment for ex-soldiers, gratis payments and grants for widows and the elderly who had run into trouble, helping the wounded to receive treatment in government hospitals and sending retired or wounded men to homes or training institutes where they might learn a trade. They were there to help if disease or famine struck a family, to give out free airmail letters to relatives and to forward news from regiments.

The boards were also the chief channels for remittances, an important function as men often handed over more than three-quarters of their wage to their families. The thousands of appeals and petitions to the boards by families suggests that there was a considerable amount of faith placed in this institution. The idea was to smooth the path of the soldier and his family, and to help dodge red tape or even the law courts if necessary. If a soldier was serving overseas or in a war area then any court proceedings naming that soldier would be suspended. In Punjab, the tuition fees for children whose fathers were on active service overseas were waived up until eighth class. District boards also had a good grasp of detail. They advised families about how best to support their men, recommending the ideal contents of parcels: chocolate, cigarettes, chewing gum, cottons, silks, knitwear, pens, pencils, pipes/tobacco pouches, safety razors and blades, small musical instruments, soap, face cloths and sponges.[8] But they also had a more political role; in 1940–1941 the Punjab Board was mainly preoccupied with helping to enlist men and 'counteracting anti-recruitment propaganda'. In Assam, the war board was being used to 'deny false rumours spread by enemy agents'.

In Punjab, the leading politicians stayed closely entwined with the military. Sikander Hyat Khan, the chief minister of the province, had his sons enlisted in the armed forces and early in the war went on a tour of the Middle East and North Africa. The army's careful nurturing of links to the homeland was another way of enforcing discipline; the disapproval of a father or uncle might be feared more than the stern words of an officer. Reporting back to the head of the family on the conduct of a soldier was another way of keeping him in check. The army's reach stretched, then, right back into the soldier's home. And many of the families from the older, established recruiting grounds had been inculcated with loyalist values which they passed on to their children, even as they watched them depart for war, urging them to keep the oath they had pledged to the military, telling them often to face bullets squarely, not to take one in the back. Exhortations to behave and to avoid getting into trouble frequently peppered letters to soldiers.

News from the war reaching India could be patchy. Taking possession of the letter in the first place was not always straightforward. At least one postman was accused of charging for handing over a letter and routine complaints about the post office flooded in. Postmen were the bearers of news – good and bad. 'The postman's statement that I am dead is baseless', wrote an infantryman to Kanpur. 'You should forget that. It is quite wrong. I am quite well here by the grace of God. I am not feeling bad here. Ask the postman how he came to know that? Forward me too a clear statement from him.'⁹ Soldiers reprimanded their families for overpaying postage costs, telling them not to waste money, while families complained about the cost of postage, some even using it as a reason for not writing. From Dera Ismail Khan, 'You must have thought that Khuda Bux is angry with you, but that is not the case. The cause of my silence is that the time is very critical now . . . An average family man can't post you a letter with eight *annas* stamp at such a hard time.'¹⁰

Tempers could fray when letters were delayed or lost, each sender defending his record of writing or making convincing excuses. A Sikh Recruiting Officer wrote to another Sikh officer in his regiment testily, 'I have written you two letters before I went on tour, I can't say why you don't get them. Well I can't answer it myself but I have been writing to you. Now it is up to you to believe it or not.'¹¹ For those engaged directly in battle finding the opportunity to write was more difficult. While Harnarain Singh served as an officer in the Middle East for three years, including at Keren and Tobruk, his new bride remained in Punjab and like so many other wives wondered whether her husband was alive or dead. For one year of the three she heard nothing from him at all – none of the letters that they wrote to each other reached their destination. For the bride who, in keeping with tradition, had moved in to live with her in-laws and had a new baby daughter to look after, this was a testing time.¹²

As time passed, the wives embroidered shoulder flashes for military uniforms, wrote and waited for letters and carried out harder and longer menial tasks. From Nepal, an observer recorded shortly after the war the ways in which villagers thought about the Lahure who had gone away to fight in foreign places.

He is always in the thoughts of those who are in the village. During the evenings they talk a lot about him, commenting on letters they have got, and information given by men on leave. They anticipate what they will do during his leave: a marriage, a ceremony for the end of

mourning. A mother makes a wish that one of her children who is
sick will be better before her husband comes back, so that he finds all
the family in good health.[13]

As elsewhere in the world, the Second World War for many women
in Asia was a time of waiting and worrying.

At the same time, the Government of India struggled to convey a
consistent propaganda message. How to convey to the public what
was happening overseas and how to make the war 'real' to those who
felt very far away from its heartland? 'The war, its causes and effects
and implications will never, to my mind, be understood by the simple
country folk of villages', wrote Henry Twynam, the Governor of the
Central Provinces, to the Viceroy.[14] There was a great deal of unease
in colonial circles about how much villagers did – and should – know
about the war. Of course, knowledge and understanding of the war
varied from region to region, person to person. For the literate, detailed
coverage of events was available in English and vernacular newspapers.
The number of foreign correspondents based in India grew as the
fighting escalated in Asia. Politics was hotly and strenuously debated
and many people followed the news closely and were intensely
concerned to know about British fortunes, in particular as France fell
and Russia was invaded.

The radio was becoming a crucial source of information and –
although still mostly available only to rich households – radio sets
with loudspeakers would be placed in public parks and outside shop-
fronts, particularly when a vital piece of news was about to be
broadcast. One challenge keenly felt by the British was the popularity of German radio, strictly forbidden although extensively
listened to. German services in Hindustani reached wide audiences;
when 13,507 listeners were surveyed in 1940 by All India Radio the
preference for German radio was striking.[15] The government prohibited the public dissemination of Axis broadcasts in June. Sayeed
Hasan Khan, at the time a child in Bareilly, United Provinces, remembers the family gathering around the wireless to hear German radio
broadcasts, while the shutters were kept closed and a servant
stationed at the door as a guard.[16] Even the ICS was not immune to
the appeal of the German programmes. Almost everyone who could
listened to them. Ian Hay Macdonald told his family that the BBC

compared 'very unfavourably with the German wireless', both in terms of reception and quality, and that the German broadcasts were 'more musical, bright and chatty'.[17]

Another source of information was the Indian Civil Service officer, who exchanged bits of news in the villages while making his paternalistic tours. Manzoor Alam Quraishi held camp-fire meetings, distributing free cigarettes and snacks to villagers who gathered around to listen to his talks about the progress of the war. 'They were interested to know the welfare of our national leaders', recalled the District Magistrate, 'I used to utilize this occasion to make appeals for voluntary donations and recruits, which usually met [a] good response.'[18] Over time the British propaganda machine became more systematic and slick, but in the main the Indian villager pieced together an understanding of the war based on bricolage, stories gleaned from the families of soldiers, newspaper articles read aloud at village gatherings, radio broadcasts from a shop in a district town, the official visit of a civil servant or landlord, and counter-propaganda circulated by the Congress and the Axis. Posters were hammered onto telegraph poles and newspapers ran through hundreds of hands, often weeks after printing. Factual truths became hard currency. In one district in Punjab a rumour spread that 'the corpses of Indian troops litter both sides of the Suez canal'.[19]

Competing narratives of the war were in circulation already and while the government feared misinformation, propaganda and false rumours, ordinary people were equally wary of the accuracy of information that was being fed to them. 'Even the news that comes is terribly lop-sided', Nehru lamented. 'The censor is always there.'[20] The government fervently clamped down on papers that published false rumours, of air raids on Indian soil or sightings of submarines off the coastline. Officers constantly struggled to place suitably rousing articles in the local press. The Punjab government allotted 75,000 rupees for propaganda efforts and was 'getting excellent stuff into the local dailies, including reproductions of some of the most striking cartoons of Hitler etc. published in English papers' within the first few weeks of the war.[21] Once again, there was murky confusion between sedition, poor taste and outright national threat. The state took the censorship opportunity to ban unpalatable literature on subjects ranging from communism to sex, raiding bookshops and printers. In early 1940, police carted off thousands of books from a bookshop in Allahabad called Kitabistan, including books on Russia, the Spanish Civil War and socialism. Nonetheless, Clive Branson found Hitler's *Mein Kampf* 'on sale prominently at *every* bookstall' alongside novels, romantic pulp fiction and religious literature.²² But the pre-occupation with rumour and false information would continue to plague the Raj and only increase as the profundity of disenchantment with the war effort became more apparent over time.

*   *   *

Premindra Singh Bhagat continued to write from North and East Africa to his sweetheart Mohini. She was very much on his mind. The couple had wanted to marry before he departed for the war but had been prevented by her father, a colonel in the Indian Army, who found the officer too irresponsible as a suitor. Premindra was typical of some of the professional high-ranking officers coming into the army in the 1930s; the son of an erudite and successful government engineer, he had been educated at the Indian Military Academy at Dehra Dun. He was a tennis player and golfer who, back home, drove a Model T Ford. His background was very different to the sepoys from the villages. Middle-class, educated men were often attracted to the army because of the technical skills they could develop and the chances for training and travel. Now near Metemma, in present-day Ethiopia, the young sapper had been clearing mines. The retreating Italians on their way between Gallabat and Gondar had left the roads embedded with explosives. The plan was to follow the Italians, to clear and set a path through these extensive minefields. Premindra Singh Bhagat faced potential explosions on every side as he worked to defuse the bombs. 'The last ten days have been quite a revelation to me of war. Dead bodies lying on the road, some mangled and no one taking any notice of them. To think the very same body had life and enjoyed himself a few hours before is preposterous', he wrote back to India.

His letters were artfully modest and understated. 'The last ten days have been a bit trying', he told the seventeen-year-old woman he hoped to marry. His right eardrum punctured, he had been inva-lided to hospital after detecting and supervising the defusing of mines constantly over four days, working in intense conditions from dawn to dusk. His carrier had been blown up twice, leaving his fellow soldiers bleeding and dismembered around him, and on a third occasion he had been ambushed and had carried on with his task under close enemy fire. 'I have been congratulated for getting blown up twice by the red hats. Though personally it does not make sense to me. After all, there were some people killed, and I was the lucky one to escape.'[23] His ambivalence about the Victoria Cross that he was going to be awarded while so many of his colleagues had died, and the shock with which he reeled in the aftermath of battle, are still palpable. He would be the first Indian to receive the Victoria Cross in the Second World War.

4

Free and Willing Human Beings

On the evening of 13 March 1940 Udham Singh, an itinerant radical and peddler living in London, shot dead a seventy-four-year-old man at Caxton Hall, in the heart of Westminster, a stone's throw from Westminster Abbey and within minutes of the Houses of Parliament. The victim was Sir Michael O'Dwyer, who had been the Governor of Punjab at the time of the Amritsar massacre in 1919. He had been taking part in a discussion on the future of Afghanistan. The BBC broke the news on the nine o'clock bulletin.

The assassin was a rootless London resident, who had worked as a travelling salesman and a film extra and was a passionately committed nationalist. He shot the retired governor twice in the chest with a revolver and the former Raj official died shortly afterwards. In the trial that followed, Singh declared loudly that he had sought retribution for O'Dwyer's role in imposing martial law and defending the perpetrators of the Amritsar killings at the end of the First World War, almost exactly twenty-one years earlier. When Scotland Yard released the files on his trial they revealed his reaction when the judge gave the verdict: he spat and swore 'against the King and Emperor' and declared that he wasn't afraid of death and that when he had gone 'thousands of [my] countrymen would drive you dirty dogs out of my country'.[1]

The Caxton Hall assassination was carried out at a time when Britain was intensely vulnerable. The assassination shrank the distance between Amritsar and London, collapsing time between 1919 and 1940. It brought back to the newspapers, and to the memories of many, the bloody scenes at Jallianwala Bagh, where hundreds of innocent men, women and children had died. The Caxton Hall murder reawakened those events thousands of miles away and many years ago in Punjab.

Udham Singh's case was a gift for the Nazi propaganda machine and within hours of the news the British Nazi 'Lord Haw-Haw' was broadcasting on the subject from Berlin. The case was conducted *in camera* with a small number of spectators and the transcripts of the trial were kept closed until the mid-1990s. The jury found Udham Singh guilty of murder and he was sentenced to hang.

The Indian press and Indian politicians universally condemned the murder of O'Dwyer, and remained ambivalent about the death sentence passed in response. Nehru distanced the Congress from the killing, while Gandhi made his outright condemnation clear, calling it 'an act of insanity' and sending condolences to O'Dwyer's family. The Bengal and Punjab Legislative Assemblies passed resolutions condemning the murder, as did the Congress Working Committee. But some members of the British public wrote letters pleading against the death penalty for Singh. Joyce Tarring wrote to the Secretary of State for India from a hotel in Cumberland to say that 'it would be a great act of clemency which would touch the heart of India'. Another woman from Hampstead was concerned that 'there is a real danger of this affair being misinterpreted in India'. The scholar and champion of Indian rights Edward Thompson also urged the Secretary of State for India to show leniency.[2]

Regardless, Udham Singh was hanged in Pentonville Prison at dawn on 31 July 1940, just as the Battle of Britain was underway over southern England and along the coastline, and clashes began above the English Channel which would intensify in ferocity over the coming weeks. He was buried in an unmarked grave in the grounds of Pentonville Prison, and his execution received scant mention in the newspapers and went mostly unnoticed around the empire. The story had been successfully relegated to the small-print columns inside the newspapers and Udham Singh was cast as a lunatic rather than as a committed, if unhinged, terrorist. The story soon fizzled out and was not given much more attention during wartime, although Sikhs, who particularly claimed Udham Singh as their own, circulated stories about his heroism and his bravado. The murder had been a warning shot across the bows of the British Empire, indicating the zealous strength of nationalist feeling, and the readiness of some to turn to violence instead of non-violence. It heralded the start of a tempestuous time ahead, but news about India was drowned out by the crushing drama of the war in

Britain: the anxieties about France and the growing fear of a German bombing campaign. Indian problems were a very distant and secondary question.

In Britain dogfights and clashes above the channel would intensify in ferocity over the coming weeks. Fears of German invasion, palpable if only fleeting, galvanised the British public in a new determination and national unity towards the war effort.[3] But, with the fall of France, Britain was increasingly an island that regarded itself as standing alone. Britain struggled to integrate imperial subjects living thousands of miles away, subjects who wanted the freedom to choose whether to support the war or not, or who thought, in the words of one Indian peasant, that it was simply 'not our quarrel'.

*   *   *

There were also many Indians living in Britain who did experience the real dangers and hardships of wartime cities at first hand. When the first phase of the Blitz was unleashed in September 1940, the Indian YMCA hostel in Bloomsbury was bombed and had to be evacuated. Savitri Choudhary, who was married to a doctor in Kent, slept in an Anderson shelter in her back garden with her husband, maid and children, and comforted local women whose sons had gone to war and were missing or killed. 'Many a fierce battle was fought over us while we hid in our shelters like primitive cavemen and women, hoping and praying that they wouldn't drop their load on us.'[4] Mira Lam and his family were bombed out of the Toxteth area of Liverpool. Dr Baldev Kaushal, a Punjabi with a large surgery in Bethnal Green, was awarded an MBE for his 'gallant conduct' during the Blitz. By the end of the year, Indian Lascars recruited from ports and docks into the Military Pioneer Corps were clearing debris from the bombed tube station at Sloane Square.[5]

Ideological demands for Indian freedom were entirely compatible with participation in the war effort. 'We want to serve as free and willing human beings', declared Aftab Ali, the president in 1940 of the Indian Seamen's Federation in Calcutta, which supported Indian merchant seamen.[6] Many of these seamen or Lascars originated from eastern India. They could be seen meeting each other in cheap cafés frequented by Indians, smoking, going for prayers, sitting around together in their overalls and distinctive *topis*. Many were illiterate but would find someone to write a letter back to a home village. Badly dressed, particularly for the British winter, and with meagre wages in their pocket, some found shelter and comforts at establishments like the Mersey Mission to Seafarers, where they might play board games or listen to the radio. Many of these men had been on the crews of ships that were now being refitted for war and as they waited for the ships to be turned around, some ventured inland. They made calculations about the risks that might be involved in sailing across the Atlantic or through the Mediterranean. Around the ports of empire, from Liverpool to Calcutta to Hong Kong, seamen had started to raise their voices, demanding war bonuses, compensation in case of death and increased wages in the face of the rising prices of commodities.

The Lascars had been hired on ships for three centuries as cheap labour. They had hard and peripatetic lives. Their monthly pay was £1 17 shillings compared to the £9 12 shillings earned by European seamen for the same work at the start of the war. By 1938, 50,700 of the sailors employed on British merchant vessels were Indian or just over a quarter of the total number.[7] The Lascars had a poorer clothing allowance, worked longer and less regulated hours and slept in more cramped quarters. They ate a cheaper diet and suffered more ill-health. The system had barely evolved since Victorian times and was a particularly suitable target for labour leaders both in Britain and in India. Anachronistic even by the standards of the time, it was criticised by the Labour politician Aneurin Bevan as providing 'cheap human fodder' and a potential source of embarrassment for the British government. The war proved the catalyst that would lead to at least some changes in the Lascars' conditions, although real change would only come after the war.

A wave of strikes and protests broke out in ports around the empire in late 1939 and early 1940. Mass arrests took place. Some Lascars had prison sentences with hard labour for up to twelve weeks. At the end of October 1939, forty Indian seafarers from the SS *Clan Alpine* got two-month sentences for 'willful disobedience of lawful commands' and men from other ships berthed in London, SS *Britannia*, SS *Somali* and SS *City of Manchester*, received prison sentences for striking. Four hundred Lascars were imprisoned in the UK at the end of December 1940. Strikes erupted in other ports as far afield as Cape Town, Burma and Australia as the word spread around the seafarers' global networks. Eighty-three men from the SS *Prome*, who had been stuck at port in Liverpool for several months, too poor to afford telegrams back home to their families or to buy tobacco on shore or from the ship store, garnered considerable local sympathy in Liverpool when they started to strike, and the local superintendent refused to arrest them.[8] The Liverpool Lascar Welfare Officer, Mr Bukht, advocated their cause, citing their poverty and subsistence wages. The case was mediated successfully and the ship-owner handed out extra supplies. The ship finally set sail for Ceylon in February 1941. Nehru's friend and ally based in London, Krishna Menon, was in communication with Aftab Ali, the union leader for many of the men from Calcutta. Menon joined his voice to the pleas for Lascar welfare, lobbying MPs on their behalf. He was just one of several advocates and representatives of Asians in London, men who were speaking up more loudly than before but were also falling into factions and disagreements with each other. The war jolted the government into making improvements to the Lascars' conditions: for instance, the Indian Comforts Fund, initiated by British women, provided humanitarian relief and was dedicated to the needs of Indian troops and Indian seamen in Europe, knitting scarves and balaclavas for the men and packing up parcels of tinned food for Indian prisoners of war.

Some of the Lascars came from families with generations of ex-perience on sailing craft that plied the Indian Ocean or the Konkan coast. Goan Catholics worked as stewards, Muslim smallholders from Chittagong and Sylhet manned the decks, Punjabi and Pashtun 'ag-wallahs' (literally fire-men) stoked the engines in the boiler rooms. Others took to seafaring from rural inland districts and had never seen the ocean before. They were rounded up by *serangs*, the middlemen who acted as boss, big brother and overseer to the seamen. Even when away from home for years at a time, the Lascar still thought of home. By leaving home, the Lascar removed an extra mouth to feed, and while siblings tilled the land, or wives wove and stitched handicrafts, they sent back remittances, enabling the family to buy more animals or a small patch of land. Far inland, children of the Lascars looked at pictures of steamships sometimes proudly kept in the family home, imagining their absent fathers.

Lascars showed tremendous concern for their families back in India, over long periods of separation. One of the first thoughts on the outbreak of war was how to secure the future of their wives and children should their ships be torpedoed or bombed. The demands put forward by Atur Mian of the SS *Clan Rose* and Abdul Majid of the SS *Clan Macbrayne* in September 1939 are revealing of the hardships and the concerns of the Lascars: they asked for back-dated double wages, overtime and more leave, but also for two suits of warm clothing for each sailor, half a pound of tobacco and one piece of soap to be given to each man every week, and also, notice-ably, that half their wages would be taken to be wired as remittance to their family by the state. They demanded that an officer visit their ships and 'take the names and addresses of each member of the Indian crew and their heirs in India who are to receive this money'.[9] The final demand of the strikers was again intended to secure the welfare of their communities back home: 'Compensation for death or disablement due to war injuries will be paid to the Lascar or his heirs in accordance with the rules which the government are now framing.'[10] Wartime journeys would be perilous and different to the work of peacetime. The men worried about wives and children back in India, and wanted to provide for them, whether dead or alive. Throughout the years to come, a number of wartime workers, from road builders to soldiers, would face dilemmas similar to the Lascars' and seek to champion their own rights in the face of wartime trans-formation. The war would bring the possibility of novel forms of work, with higher wage packets, and many would try to negotiate or manoeuvre to maximise their own advantage. But ultimately this had to be reckoned alongside the risk of death, long and arduous absences from home and the uncertainty of a long war beyond Indian political control or influence.

* * *

On 18 September 1940 a German U-boat torpedoed the SS *City of Benares* in the Atlantic. Seventy-seven British children, many as young as five or six, who had been sent as evacuees from Britain to Canada perished. This tragedy stunned the empire. But less well known was the fate of the Indian crew manning the ship. Of the 160 Lascars

aboard, 101 were drowned or died in the shipwreck.[11] Many of them
have only ever been remembered by their forename, without a
recorded date of birth and with the simple epithet 'boy' or by the
basic description of their duty on board the ship. Soria the apprentice,
Sheikh Labu, a pantry boy, and Mubarak Ali, a baker, were among
those who perished: they remain little more than ghostly traces in the
archive. Abbas Bhickoo, who was twenty-two years old, and from
Sangameshwar, Ratnagiri, in present-day Maharashtra, was one of the
Lascars who managed to scramble onto a lifeboat. With other survivors, he lay adrift on the lifeboat for eight days until they were eventually picked up and taken to the west coast of Scotland. But Bhickoo
died shortly afterwards, presumably from exposure. His grave still
stands in Greenock in western Scotland. Yousuf Choudhary, who was
a child in Sylhet at the time, in present-day Bangladesh, remembered
how the news of a seaman's death would ripple through the community. 'As the news came, the dead seamen's relatives and friends would
gather and begin crying and shouting . . . soon the bad news spread
from house to house, village to village. The people became nervous,
worrying that they would be next in line for this shock. The British
public never heard the cry of the seamen's widows.'[12] Shivers rippled
through seafaring communities whenever a torpedoed ship was
reported: over the course of the war 6,600 Indian merchant seafarers
would lose their lives, over a thousand would be badly wounded and
over 1,200 would be taken as prisoners of war. Although the war was
still far from Indian towns and cities, the experiences of networks of
seamen and soldiers, already engaged in wartime service, were starting
to colour perceptions of the war back in India.

5

Not a Paisa, Not a Man

The war needed funding. In anticipation of the looming costs of conflict, the Indian and British governments had hammered out agreements in 1939 and 1940, dividing the cost of the war between the two exchequers. Put simply, this resulted in India continuing to pay for her own defence, in the form of the fixed costs of a peacetime army, while Britain footed the bill for any additional wartime expenditure. Britain would pay for the vast increase in recruitment, the assignments of soldiers overseas and the capital costs of developing industry and infrastructure. This looked, at first sight, like a fair deal for India, and was undergirded by political considerations. The headline story was that Britain was paying the cost of the war. Churchill was painfully sensitive to this fact, bursting into a 'Wilsonian Volcano' at the mention of the debts that were accruing to India in the form of sterling balances.[1] But in reality, this was a payment deferred. Sterling credits were lodged with the Reserve Bank of India for use after the war – a tempting prospect for those dreaming of post-war reconstruction and nationalist projects. During the war years themselves, however, the money had to be raised within India. The government turned to tax, borrowing and ultimately, to devastating effect, to increasing the amount of money in circulation.[2]

The Indian public was asked to pay its share not only through taxation but also through voluntary collections and subscriptions to special funds. The War Fund, a voluntary fund established in 1939, and collected by District Magistrates on behalf of the government, soon placed a new burden on reluctant 'donors'. This afflicted peasant cultivators and affluent middle-class elites alike and contributed towards the public disenchantment with the war. The War Fund, in the hands of local administrators, came to serve as an acid test of loyalty to the imperial state. Payments to the fund could also be used to secure small favours from officials and to untie red tape.

The War Fund was widely resented. In the eyes of many villagers this was a semi-voluntary tax. If a man needed a favour from local officials or was submitting a job application for state service, a subscription to the War Fund became all but obligatory. Princes and feudal landlords made extravagant donations but traders and smaller farmers were also expected to contribute. 'Petty government servants and minor officials dare not say "no" when they are asked to contribute. I just had a case like this from Allahabad district', Nehru wrote, referring to his home town in United Provinces. 'A poor village shopkeeper was asked to give Rs 15 or Rs 20. He said the most he could possibly give was Rs 5. He was cursed and sworn at and immediately a notice was given to him . . . Defence of India Rules . . . His case is up today in a court here.'[3] Nehru's antipathy to the War Fund is corroborated by other sources from the same province. There was pressure on local civil servants to generate funds and the amounts that they amassed were reported back to their superiors (along with the number of men recruited) in a pyramid of extraction. For Manzoor Alam Quraishi, a junior civil servant in United Provinces at the start of the war, the collection of war funds became part of his daily routine: 'The entire district staff from the Collector to the *patwari* had to give topmost priority to "War Work" which meant mostly at our level, "collection of donations for War Funds" and help in the recruitment of soldiers.' All routine deskwork was suspended. 'Intensive touring had to be done by all the officers for war work.' Quraishi remembered how the District Magistrate used elaborate rituals in the villages to celebrate large donations, wearing full ceremonial dress, as villagers looked on.[4]

In response, resistance mounted. Protesters chanted, 'Na ek pie, na ek bhai' (Not a penny, not a man). It is telling that in a classic Hindi novel of the time, *Aadha Gaon* (Half a Village), when the character Phunnan Miyan, the father of a soldier serving abroad in the military, is asked to donate to the War Fund, he retorts, 'I'm not giving an *anna* to the war fund. Do whatever you like.' By the end of 1941, 55 million rupees had been collected for the War Fund, more than had been donated to the fund in the whole duration of the previous war.[5] Large gifts to the War Fund signalled to administrators that the donor was a reliable fellow. 'Good' families had a reputation for loyalism and a long history of service. When a District Magistrate penned a note on the promotion file of one Maharaj Singh from Muzaffarnagar district, he noted that his family had been conspicuously loyal, 'supplying' 1,502 recruits to the Indian Army, purchasing war bonds of 352,000 rupees, donating 6,500 rupees towards the War Fund and the Red Cross and making payments towards funding propaganda and other war activities.[6] In essence, the landed often paid into the War Fund to secure access to government services and to certain rights. When the Katjus, members of a prominent Congressman's family, tried to purchase a house in the coastal resort town of Puri in 1940, to their surprise, despite all their papers and finances being in order, the government refused the sale on the basis that no contribution had been received to the War Fund.[7]

The extraction of cash for war funds could involve arm-twisting or promises of favours in exchange. The Viceroy's War Purposes Fund raised £3,500,000 of which half was sent directly to Britain – £150,000 to go to the victims of the Blitz, with other money forwarded to victims of Nazi aggression in Europe. But this money was not just extracted from the landed, but also raised by burdening poor peasants who were already struggling under inflation and the dazzling rises in the cost of wheat and cloth. The collection of the War Fund was part of the Raj's struggling attempt to cement people together in fellow feeling about the war effort, to psychologically bond peasants and soldiers. In reality, it brought an extra pressure to bear on the Indian peasant and added to his growing suspicion of the *sarkar*. The War Fund and recruiting were often spoken about in the same breath. The government expected people to supply money or manpower and families complained to their soldier-sons serving abroad about the extortion: a long complaint from Gorakhpur in United Provinces was sent to the Middle East about how the village had been 'disgraced' when local landlords and a police superintendent turned up at the village with a gang of policemen to collect the War Fund. 'They treated the Headmen and other respectable men of the village in a very disgraceful manner' and forcibly collected subscriptions of 'half the land revenue from everybody' by entering houses, searching, and asking for details of accounts. 'We have always been a loyal village', the letter-writer protested, 'with 100–125 recruits serving at present in the army.'[8]

Within months of the start of war, the Viceroy was worrying about the manner of collection for the war funds. Congress seized on examples of intimidation. Tales of arm-twisting floated upwards. In a wonderful piece of viceregal euphemism, Linlithgow noted 'a considerable amount of testimony which might be interpreted as throwing doubt on the spontaneity of the contributions now being made'.[9] Across India all kinds of innovative methods were being perfected in order to encourage 'spontaneous' giving. In Assam, the Governor admitted some problems with 'over zealous officers'.[10] In Sind the government had considered using 'assessed demand' – in other words an involuntary tax for landowners. One notable, Nabi Baksh Bhutto, doubled his original subscription of 1,000 rupees after a dressing-down by the Governor, who wrote him a letter expressing his disappointment with the paltry size of his donation. There was also evidence of prized gun licences being granted in exchange for War Fund donations. In Punjab, the Governor admitted that there was a certain amount of 'grumbling' among the rural folk, and in United Provinces they decided to tighten the rules so that appeals should only be made to 'well to do gentlemen' with 'no further collections from tenants or small landholders'. Pressure was also being applied to clerks in the civil service hierarchy with some government servants being encouraged to give one day's pay a month.

When Linlithgow considered completely changing the system he met a wall of resistance from civil servants. They reassured him that although there had been certain attempts to 'curry favour' the War Fund was a success story that could not be scaled back, for fear of defeatism. In fact, any change would have a deplorable effect and be seen as backtracking on the war effort. The truth was that collecting the war funds gave British officials in India something concrete to deliver in support of the war. It connected them directly to the effort and generated a sense of purpose. Stationed far from the centre of war, while their brothers and cousins back in Glasgow or London were enlisted, many officials felt deeply frustrated and enervated, cut off from the real action in Europe. Much later, in the 1940s and afterwards, this feeling of having been denied a real wartime role afflicted numerous colonial officials stationed in the more remote districts. Collecting for the war funds was a small but decisive way to do one's bit.

A new generation of British officers had been arriving in India. Of course, the Raj was not as timeless as some of its advocates liked to pretend. By the 1930s, debates among British leaders about the right course for India had become more polarised. Within the administration there had been a sea change over the course of the interwar years in the kind of men who ruled India. No longer exclusively drawn from a narrow circle, or the same small stock of the most elite private schools, the men who arrived in India by the 1930s were usually middle class rather than elite, curious and adventurous rather than classical orientalists. In comparison to their predecessors they often had less prior familiarity with each other or with India.

Many British men had started to turn away from a life in the Indian Civil Service, either troubled by moral compunction or realistic about the fact that the empire might well draw to a close over the coming decades. There was more scepticism about the long-term prospects in the service. British men in the ICS reportedly suffered higher rates of depression, premature retirement and disillusionment than in the past. Governors made assiduous attempts in order to keep some white representatives visible in the administration; 'It would be a disaster if the small British element in this vitally important branch of the administration should disappear altogether', wrote Henry Craik, the Governor of Punjab, regarding a vacancy in the Public Works Department in 1937, although failing to specify what this disaster might entail. On the other hand, when British men did present themselves for service, they still needed, in the view of the old guard, to be of the 'right' sort.[11] The Indian Civil Service was changing, racial lines were blurring and it was not as impenetrable for Indians or for middle-class British as it had been in earlier decades. Yet, in the highest echelons of power, and where it most mattered, the British still kept a firm grip on the functions of the state: most provinces did not see an Indian Inspector General of Police until after Independence.

Men now arrived in India to take up positions in the Indian Civil Service having read E. M. Forster's *Passage to India* and George Orwell's *Burmese Days*. They were not immune to debates in the British press and had often a deeply complex relationship with the idea of empire, and their views had been influenced by socialist and communist ideas in Britain. They were reflexive about their own purpose and the moral propriety of empire. They were rarely uncompromising diehards on the question of the British imperial mission, although they often maintained an idealised notion of taking moral and material better-ment to the East.[12] Many men who would serve in India during the war and beyond, such as Malcolm Darling and Penderel Moon, had an enlightened and optimistic attitude towards eventual self-governance. They particularly believed in the power of modern science, and the application of development in all of its guises, from tube wells to aero-planes, to deliver a better quality of life to the average Indian peasant.

Compounding the sense of frustration and uncertainty among British administrators was the plain fact that British rule had self-evidently not delivered on its promises: 90 per cent of the population of the country still faced dire and inescapable poverty. The vast majority of people lived in villages, and relied on crops for sustenance. More than half the population did not own or rent any land at all, and relied on day wages or seasonal labour to make ends meet. India's poverty was endemic. A small number of rich lived in a country that was overwhelmingly poor. Three hundred and eighty million people lived in India and most of them lived as subsistence farmers relying on their crops, subject to indenture and debt, victims of landlords and their henchmen, living precarious lives vulnerable to small changes in wage patterns, natural catastrophes or calamities. Caste discrimination, which put *dalits* at the bottom of the social pyramid, had been chal-lenged by Gandhi and by the *dalits'* own leader, Dr Bhimrao Ambedkar, but had not been radically transformed.

Malnourishment and undernourishment were commonplace. At the time of the outbreak of the Second World War, south-eastern districts of Punjab were suffering some of their worst famine condi-tions for a generation. Poverty was becoming more of a public concern across the world, nourished by the apparent successes of Soviet pol-icies in feeding and developing the Russian populace and fuelled by a new belief in man's ability to redress the balance of rich and poor. But this concern cut across the political spectrum and included conser-vatives and Gandhians. Gandhi was occupied with practical remedies to alleviate hunger and malnourishment in the late 1930s, and recom-mended certain types of leaves and grains as a way for the hungry to forage and sustain themselves. He spelt out the predicament of life for the majority: 'No one has, to my knowledge, said that the Indian villager has enough to keep body and soul together.'[13]

The state was expected to take the lead in addressing poverty. This was a consensus shared in surprising quarters and by Indian and British leaders of all different political backgrounds. 'We are conscious that, for the man in the street and the man in the fields, life often lacks not only all that may provide comfort and dignity, but even the greater part of that which is necessary to sustain life itself', said Sir Muhammad Zafarullah Khan, a loyalist follower of the Raj, who represented the Viceroy's Council in a speech at the start of the war.[14] The belief that the very poor could be helped by the right kinds of state intervention, by sanitary housing, improved healthcare or population control, was emerging everywhere as a hallmark of the age. Shortly after the commencement of war, Sir Joseph Bhore, a self-styled Indian version of William Beveridge, chaired a report investigating the state of public health which underlined how precarious lives were in India, reflecting on the 'large amount of preventable suffering and mortality'.[15] With measured but damning effect, the report pointed to social causes ranging from state neglect, poverty and unemployment to illiteracy and social customs. The literacy rate in India on the eve of the Second World War was 12.5 per cent and life expectancy was twenty-six years of age. Blatant poverty, in the aftermath of the Great Depression, fuelled the nationalist cries for Independence. The Indian National Congress, and to some extent the Muslim League, as well as smaller but influential parties which represented Sikhs, socialists, *dalits*, Anglo-Indians and Hindu nationalists, based their demands for immediate Independence not simply on nationalism alone but on the widely held belief that British rule had reversed earlier Indian chances of prosperity by encouraging reliance on extractive cash-crop markets and free trade, and that not only the political rights of people but the economic welfare of the country were at stake. The Raj had delivered on few promises of development.

*　*　*

Gandhi announced his own formal programme of resistance to the Raj in October 1940. It began haltingly, only really taking on momentum in early 1941. People had long been waiting for a bold and definitive act by him in response to the war but the actual programme for the *satyagraha* was oddly muted and heavily circumscribed compared to the great salt march or moments of civil disobedience which had gained Gandhi such international stature in the 1920s and 1930s. For many Congress followers, it was disappointing or confusing, not going far enough at a time of critical leverage against the state. Gandhi was tightly holding the reins of civil disobedience, trying to keep the restless public under centralised Congress control, in particular to restrain violence and keep the movement close to his own spiritual as well as temporal concerns. Gandhi was more contemplative about the subject of violence than ever, in the face of the war now taking place. He wanted to shine a moral light on the war, to hold up light to dark. 'The idea is to make all action as strictly non-violent as possible', Gandhi announced. 'How far I shall be able to present an example of unadulterated non-violence remains to be seen.' Gandhi called on certain specially selected individuals to make gestures that would lead to their imprisonment. The chosen *satyagrahis* gave inflammatory speeches in public places and gradually the movement opened up to other individuals. In January 1941 members selected by Provincial Congress Committees were permitted to step forward and to invite imprisonment by making peaceful protests like chanting anti-war slogans and after that came ordinary Congress members. Gandhi's tentative, experimental attempt to encourage the courting of arrests and peaceful individual *satyagraha* resulted in 20,000 arrests. Yet the movement was not a serious challenge to the Raj. High wages in the cities, driven up by war work, and the availability of employment meant that the crisis for the Raj was averted. For now, the peace held, but the foundations of the old order faced steady erosion.

Although the individual *satyagraha* may have been weaker and less dramatically effective than earlier Gandhian mass movements, nonetheless it did solidify and give form to a strong strand of anti-war feeling. The harsh sentence of four years' rigorous imprisonment given to Nehru by a District Magistrate in Gorakhpur was seized upon by anti-war demonstrators and proved counterproductive to British efforts. And a number of those who experienced imprisonment for political beliefs in 1940–1 would return to more violent anti-war action in 1942, when adherence to Gandhi's leadership would give way and his attempts at stage management and careful control would no longer prove effective.

*   *   *

One of the protesters in the hand-picked group selected by Gandhi in 1940 was the little-known wife of a senior Congress politician, Aruna Asaf Ali. She stood in the shadow of her husband but, like many middle-class and elite women in the politics of the 1940s, was becoming more actively involved in social work. Just before the war started, she had celebrated her thirtieth birthday. Her home in Old Delhi was a typical old *haveli* in Daryaganj, tucked away in the walled city, and in many ways at first glance she appeared the epitome of a courtly lady. She spoke in impeccable English and Urdu, could converse about art and poetry (Shaw and Ibsen were favourites), dressed in tasteful saris and hosted a number of the leading politicians, artists and intellectuals of the day, who would stay late into the evening at her home. Aruna, born into a Bengali Brahmo Samaj family, had begun life with the name Aruna Ganguly, and her father had run a refreshment room in Kalka, a railway junction town. Convent-educated and strong-willed from an early age, Aruna had left home to work as a teacher. Before long, she had met an unsuitable man and married him. Aruna's husband, Asaf Ali, was twenty-three years older than her, a Muslim and in the innermost circle of the Indian National Congress.

In 1940, Aruna was beginning to become caught up in the intensity of political feeling sweeping the country; she was coming round to the idea that more radical and revolutionary steps needed to be taken to eject the British. There was a generational division, with young people rallying to radical politicians, and this divide had started to make a rift in the Ali household, Aruna later recalled:

> With every rejection of Indian advice and opinion by Britain, anger and resentment against Imperialism blazed as never before. Britain's contemptuous and arrogant ignoring of the Congress offer to cooperate for defence of democracy was an intolerable national insult. Many men and women of the then younger generation were angry with the elder leaders' hesitation to embarrass the British Government.[16]

Her husband, Asaf Ali, had small, incisive features framed by dark round spectacles. He was a more cautious and introspective character than his wife and was more inclined to support the British in their war effort. To the annoyance of some of his colleagues in the Congress he made an appeal on the radio for political parties to band together and enter government. He wanted a national coalition that would back the war effort, particularly because he foresaw the rapid gains being made by the Muslim League. But Aruna was being pulled into a deep well of frustration and despair about the right course of action: should she follow Bose or Gandhi? Should Indians resist the British using revolutionary tactics or rely on Gandhian non-violence? Or should they co-operate in some kind of constitutional agreement and work with the British, despite all their dashed hopes and suspicions of the government's insincerity? Her dilemma was one shared by many educated Indians in 1940. World events dominated the headlines and, as in Europe, many intellectuals felt themselves to be taking part in an epoch-changing moment, in an epic period of world history which would shape future events.

When Gandhi hand-picked individual *satyagrahis* in 1940 to take part in the carefully calibrated protests, Aruna's name was on the list. By the end of the year she was imprisoned in Lahore Women's Jail for breaking the Defence of India rules as she had deliberately spoken out against the war in public. In jail she made efforts to educate her fellow prisoners about politics, relaying current affairs to the women and settling disputes between inmates, giving small gifts like combs and embroidery threads to the poorer women she came to know. Prison sentences had become badges of honour for Congress workers. They shared ideas, swapped stories about the warders, conditions and relative merits of different prisons, and drew legitimacy and pride from their detentions. Sucheta Kripalani, another wife of a prominent Congressman, remembered her own incarceration at this time: 'I had never been to jail before and I used to feel somewhat different. I would rather say I was suffering from an inferiority complex viz a viz the other Congress workers. So I was, therefore, very keen to go to jail as soon as possible.'[17] Aruna had a short spell in prison but it gave her invaluable thinking time. The course of the war was going to change her life irreversibly.

*   *   *

By the end of 1940, military commanders were demanding a new intensification of India's war effort. But the slow, unsteady start to the war in India and the failure to synchronise Indian and British needs, the failure to secure a people's war rather than emphasising imperial privilege and prerogative, left a lasting and bitter legacy. Many in Britain, not just Churchill and pro-imperialists, but even former supporters and allies of India's cause, could not square the circle and fathom the opposition to supporting the war. They were shocked at attempts across India to suborn soldiers, to deter recruitment, to refuse to contribute to the War Fund. When they did try to comprehend it at all, they fell back on culturalist assumptions about the Hindu and the Muslim, or on stereotypes of Gandhian non-violence. India had simply not grasped anti-fascism with both hands, it was too often believed, because it was too backward, irrational or undeveloped, or its people were too uneducated, superstitious or unable to see the international picture. The very real problems of ruinous inflation or the very obvious subjugation of Indian political rights were not seen by many British onlookers as strong enough reasons for resistance.

6

Bombed to Hell

Part hill station, part colonial plantation town, Keren, in present-day Eritrea, was 4,000 feet above sea level, perched in the crook of the Anseba River. It had a stunning, formidable position surrounded by a barren, rocky moonscape on all sides. The Italians who had colonised this part of East Africa in 1885 encouraged the locals to grow tobacco, coffee, fruit and other garden produce. Situated on the railway line and road from Asmara to Agordat, its connections and climate gave it a favoured position in the colony. Whitewashed Italianate villas and churches studded a landscape of red rocks and earth. By the start of the war there were about 9,000 local Eritrean inhabitants, and hundreds of Italian colonists including missionaries, priests and farmers. The town was a natural fort, easily defended and surrounded by immense mountains. The battle for this small town would take over six weeks and would involve troops from across the British Empire-Commonwealth, including Britons, Indians and Africans.

In early 1941, with the victories in North Africa behind them, the 4th Indian Division's next challenge was to capture Italian-occupied East Africa. In 1940, within six weeks Norway, Denmark, Holland, Belgium and France had fallen. Against this backdrop of unrelenting bad news, Indian troops were involved in some of the only heartening advances of 1941 and the Allies desperately needed news of a victory to lift morale across the empire. At the end of 1940 and into early 1941 the focus was almost solely on North and East Africa. Between December and early February, heavily outnumbered Indian troops helped to beat ten Italian divisions and the role of Indian troops in North and East Africa and the Middle East stood at the epicentre of the war.

Richpal Ram was from a village in Patiala, a princely state and traditional hunting ground for the Recruitment Officer. The forty-year-old was tall and thin with a prominent chin. Married with a young family, he was a lifelong soldier who had worked his way up from the ranks and hailed from a region with a long history of service. Men from his village came and went into the army, and he would have known men who had seen action in the First World War; he himself had only just missed participating in that war, joining the Indian Army in 1920. By 1941 he had only been abroad for four months, but as a *subedar* in the 4th battalion of the Rajputana Rifles, he was part of a battle-hardened infantry team. The 4th battalion had sailed for the Middle East just as war broke out and had arrived in October 1939. Things had been going very well for them. They had already taken part in the first offensive at Sidi Barrani on the Egyptian coastline in December 1940, a disaster for the Italians where the only major problem faced by the Allies was what to do with the vast numbers of prisoners of war after the victory. The battalion moved to Sudan and then on to the Eritrean campaign.

Richpal Ram and his men had reached Agordat, about sixty-five miles north-west of Asmara, by 1 February, as part of the mopping-up operation in the train of Italian defeats. They found the remnants of a deserted and defeated town in Agordat and while patrolling had heard the last Italians retreating in the distance, the sounds of their jeeps moving away and the lights receding. 'The gorge presented a scene of great disorder. Dead and wounded lay along the road, lorries still smouldered and great heaps of ammunition and supplies were dumped in the scrub.'[1] The 4th battalion spent their days in Agordat guarding the area and carrying out salvage from the twisted wreckage of battle, recycling tanks and other materials. One of the companies headed by Subedar Puranchand Ram had the most unpleasant job of pulling dead Italian soldiers from their tanks, but despite this, the mood was upbeat. Around them the men found numerous ammunition dumps, food rations and a fine supply of rum, brandy and Chianti, and Wavell sent his congratulations to the army for their 'spectacular advance' into Eritrea.[2]

On 7 February Richpal Ram and the rest of his battalion started out towards Keren, about fifty miles away, by foot and then by truck. They moved under the shadow of a mountain in the east,

Dologorodoc, nearly 1,500 feet high, crowned with a fort. To the west stood the forbidding Mount Sanchil, 1,000 feet higher. Between these two mountains stretched lower hills; the aim was for the men of the Rajputana Rifles to take three positions that night – nick-named Pimple, Sangar (from the Hindi for fort) and Tree Hill – and to help open up the valley, or at least prise open a place where a track could be laid. The men started to appreciate the daunting mountains that loomed ahead of them and the magnitude of their task; in places the rockface was perpendicular. The last company reached the foothills after five o'clock, 'very hot, thirsty and tired'.[3] There would be little time for rest as a few hours after arrival, as darkness fell, they began to move, along with companies of Fusiliers, Sikhs and Gazelle forces also at the scene, towards their objectives in the hills above.

Richpal Ram and their company were given Sangar, the highest of these hills, to secure and started their climb at about eight o'clock. In essence, they had to scale steep rocks in the dark in the direct line of fire from a well-prepared enemy positioned above them. Everything was on foot and there were no tanks and, as yet, no air cover. The shapes of these mountains in the dark were disorienting and forbid-ding as they picked their way through the darkness and scrabbled over the rocks, and they were about halfway up to Sangar when the situ-ation quickly deteriorated and heavy enemy mortar attacks, grenades and machine-gun fire blazed from all across the highest points. In the forward platoon, Richpal Ram's senior officer, Ivan Knowles, was badly wounded in the face – stretcher-bearers managed to get him back down the hill – and the men pressed on under Richpal Ram's leader-ship. Things went from bad to worse as his platoon lost touch with the other units, 'owing to lack of signallers and apparatus'. Behind the men, water and ammunition were being ferried by hand and by mule but the mules stumbled and suffered broken limbs, stretching the supply lines to their limits, and with little water, the troops felt burning thirst.[4]

There were about thirty men left with Ram under heavy mortar fire on the slopes of Sangar by midnight. Machine-gun fire rained down on them and, as they got closer, the enemy troops lobbed hand grenades. As they reached Sangar, the fighting became hand-to-hand and Richpal charged forward with his bayonet in the dark. Against the odds, the Indians won out and stood their ground on the hill. But although they had won this small sliver of land as instructed, remaining there was futile with such a strong Italian presence all around them. Over the course of the night, there were counter-attacks by Italian troops until there was a lull in the firing in the early hours of the morning as ammunition dried up. Taking his chance to retreat, as the sun began to rise over the mountains, Richpal Ram led his men out to safety by fighting his way out from encirclement with his bayonet. That afternoon, Richpal Ram and his remaining twenty-five men were spotted approaching the camp headquarters in the rain, dirty, hungry and exhausted. The men took stock of their losses: sixty-two men had been wounded, including Ivan Knowles, seventeen had been killed and ten were missing.[5]

Richpal Ram had little time to reflect on his night of battle in Eritrea. Across the valley, many other Indian and British regiments had been engaging the Italians (who were often actually North African local mercenaries) and facing heavy losses. Conditions were brutal. 'The corpses of course had been smelling to heaven since the second day of the battle; we tried to bury our dead, but explosions dug them up again, while the Italian and Indian and British bodies in the ravine in front of the Ridge just lay there, swelling', recalled Peter Cochrane, a soldier of the Queen's Own Cameron Highlanders who was also at Keren.[6] The men of the Rajputana Rifles were now faced with a second attempt on the steep hillside above them.

The men struggled to sleep the night before the new assault on 12 February. The mood was not good and there was low cloud in the sky. 'We had a miserable night because there were a few sharp showers of rain and a few mortar bombs which kept us awake', their senior officer reported, and just after midnight they heard that there was going to be a delay; the attack was postponed for another twenty-four hours and the tension mounted.[7] The enemy was estimated at two battalions but there were rumours that more were collecting up on the hills above them. Any earlier optimism about Italian desertions and fragility had dissolved after the first attempt. In the 4th battalion of the Rajputana Rifles, B and C companies had been fused into one new company – a reflection of the extent of casualties. Sepoys waited, joked and smoked while British and Indian officers shared a tin of beer in the officers' mess with the colonel, Frank Messervy, who had come to rally them.

Richpal Ram was in the advance platoon of his company as they started their second assault just after five the next morning as the sun began to rise. Once again his eyes were fixed on Sangar, transfixed by trying to capture the small scrap of rock, so narrow that it could barely hold more than a platoon of men. He had already held this place once for several hours, but as expected, almost immediately the company came under fire. The mortar fire exploding around the men was intense as Ram urged them on alongside him in the midst of the blasts: his company was taking the bulk of the shelling, clearly in the sightline of the Italian troops above who directed many of their mortars against them; the company 'became the target for every mortar attack in the area from the moment it set out'. The British artillery would fire 5,000 shells against the Italian troops that day but, in the words of their senior officer, 'it never seemed quite enough'.[8]

From the headquarters, a short distance away, nothing could be seen apart from the blast and smoke of explosions for over an hour. Occasionally Italian troops could be glimpsed through the smoke, rushing up the crest and hurling bombs at troops below them. While mortars exploded, men also came under machine-gun fire. Carriers and stretcher-bearers scrambled up and down the rocks, carrying up water and ammunition and carrying down messages and bringing in the injured. 'All runners who reached Bn. HQ [battalion headquarters] were without exception wounded and all men sent forward for any reason with ammunition or with messages went cheerfully and confidently.'[9] One Subedar-Major Tota Ram 'was indefatigable in his efforts' going up and down the ridge organising ammunition and water to try to supply the exhausted men struggling above.

There were few trees for cover and the men were stepping forward almost in the certainty of being killed. They had repeatedly been told to hold their objectives and that the eventual capture of Keren could unlock the whole struggle over North Africa. Naik Maula Baksh, just eighteen years old, from Jhelum in Punjab, advanced on his own with a machine gun, took two enemy posts then held ground and fired until he was killed himself. Richpal Ram also charged ahead, 'leading the forward platoon through intense fire with grim determination and complete disregard for his own safety'. The firing against them was heavy and accurate. Richpal Ram's battalion sent a terse message: 'Being bombed to hell' and requesting, once again, more artillery cover.[10] He was still pushing his men onwards, coming under fire and suffering further wounds as he died on the mountainside, telling his men as he lay bleeding and dying that they would capture the objective.[11]

The tattered company pressed on for the rest of the morning without Ram. They inched forward towards Sangar but were driven back again. Their lines were cut and they found themselves marooned again for the second time in a week. Around half past ten in the morning the men received the order to retreat. The shell-shocked men clambered back towards their starting point and began to realise their losses. In the words of one Commanding Officer, they had 'failed gallantly'.

In five hours of fighting that morning the 4th battalion of the Rajputana Rifles lost a further thirty-six men. One hundred and thirty-seven were injured and seven were missing. The men who were killed alongside Richpal Ram that day ranged in age from seventeen to their late thirties. Both Muslim and Hindu, they were drawn from a sweep of India stretching from the northern districts of Punjab down to southern Rajasthan. Ghulum Haider was seventeen, unmarried and from Attock in present-day Pakistan. Gheba Khan was nineteen and from Rawalpindi. Bhuja Ram was twenty-five and from Jaipur.[12] Many of their graves and cremation sites are marked in cemeteries in Sudan and Eritrea, where they can be seen today. And this was just a single day in the battle for Keren. It would be echoed across the mountain range and would involve soldiers from many other regiments and nationalities – including the Highland Light Infantry, the Central India Horse, the Baluch Regiment, the West Yorkshire Regiment and the RAF – and would doggedly continue over six weeks until the British and imperial forces finally pushed back the Italian General Frusci and his men and broke into Asmara in late March. The battle for Keren was an extraordinary feat of endurance and willpower, over six weeks of protracted and stubborn fighting in almost impossible terrain. The Allies were essentially trying to scale upwards into mountains, but from above them, the Italians had the advantage of being able to rain firepower down on the men, knocking them back off the slopes below, while, initially, the Allied troops had no air cover. It was such an extreme fight that Wavell considered calling off the entire attempt altogether and many considered the capture of East Africa impossible at this point.

Alongside the infantry, Indians employed as water-carriers, messengers, cooks and bearers died at Keren, among them a boot-maker simply named 'Ghafur' whose age, surname and provenance are unknown. There were at least 4,000–5,000 British and Commonwealth casualties in the battles to capture Keren, the turning point of the East Africa campaign.[13] One historian would later record that it was 'as hard a soldiers' battle as was ever fought'.[14]

On 7 April Churchill sent the Viceroy of India a letter congratulating him on the performance of the Indian troops, using language evocative of the nineteenth century:

> The whole Empire has been stirred by the achievement of the Indian forces in Eritrea. For me the story of the ardour and the perseverance with which they scaled and finally conquered the arduous heights of Keren recalls memories of the North West Frontier of long years ago, and it is as one who has had the honour to serve in the field with Indian soldiers from all parts of Hindustan, as well as in the name of His Majesty's Government, that I ask Your Excellency to convey to them and to the whole Indian Army the pride and admiration with which we have followed their heroic exploits.[15]

An effusive book of propaganda about the East and North African campaigns, *The Tiger Strikes*, which was circulated widely in India in the 1940s, declared: 'it is possible that history may mark this as one of the decisive battles of the world. It is a battle honour which all units, British and Indian alike, will treasure with particular pride in centuries to come.'[16] In fact, it has barely been remembered at all.

Back in Punjab, victories in North Africa were being publicly celebrated. Schools, colleges, government offices and some shops closed and marching bands paraded down the main thoroughfares of Lahore cheered on by flag-waving crowds. The British Empire-Commonwealth, paradoxically, was helping Haile Selassie's Ethiopian nation to emerge from colonial domination by the Italians, an accomplishment that was eyed with interest by Indian leaders. The politicians of the Punjab Legislative Assembly passed a unanimous resolution congratulating Wavell on his feats.

As defeat in North and East Africa eventually turned again to victory there was a determined effort in India to champion the role of the 4th and 5th Indian Divisions and their distinguished acts. The survivors, the injured and the dead were given a number of significant medals in the months to come. Richpal Ram was awarded the Victoria Cross posthumously, his citation recording 'great dash and gallantry'.[17] Two awards were given at the same time, to Premindra Singh Bhagat, the stoical officer of the Royal Bombay Sappers and Miners, and to Richpal Ram. They recognised two distinctive faces of the war: Richpal Ram represented the old traditional loyalties to the Indian Army, a man who had worked his way up as an officer from a humble village, spoke Punjabi and had served for two decades; the other was a highly educated, technically minded man who came from a more urbane and worldly background, more recently inducted into the army.

Newspaper stories and newsreels relived their exploits and heroism. The photographs of the famed Indian Victoria Cross winners appeared on collectible cigarette cards around the British Empire-Commonwealth and the Taj Hotel in Bombay printed their faces on menu cards. During the rest of the war, medal winners would be heavily photographed, featured on propaganda, sent on international tours to Britain and the USA. Back in India, once discharged from hospital, Premindra Bhagat Singh found himself fêted as a VIP wherever he went. The self-deprecating, gentle hero seemed just a little bewildered by his reception. He had lost hearing in one ear, been returned to India and separated from his unit. He would start at loud noises for some time to come. On his arrival back in Bombay in July 1941 the *Times of India* reported the scene:

To all who met him on his landing in Bombay on Saturday afternoon he was a picture of a dashing but a modest soldier. He was characteristically ill at ease with the press and reluctant to discuss his daring exploit which won for him the highest award for valour . . . Were it not for the small purple ribbon on his tunic, it would be impossible to guess from his self-effacing conduct that he has displayed a bravery

that makes the imagination reel . . . Indeed he might have been playing
golf instead of exploding land mines.[18]

Though individual acts of bravery were well appreciated, not everyone
was convinced by the storyline: the acerbic Ian Hay Macdonald, from
his magistrate's bungalow in Orissa, grumbled that Indian troops were
being celebrated more in the press than the British troops: 'Keren, for
instance, was really captured by the Cameron Highlanders, who now
have a hill there named after them, but from the papers here one would
think it was done entirely by Indian troops', he told his parents back
in Scotland.[19] There was pride among some nationalists in India that
the Indian Army was being celebrated in a global war. But among
the public, upbeat coverage of the victories in 1941 could not mask the
leakage of casualty numbers and rumours of trepidation and defeatism.

Two hundred miles away from Lahore, in the district of Barda
in the princely state of Patiala, Richpal Ram's wife – Mussamat
Janki – had not yet heard of his death. It would be several weeks
before she knew that her husband had died in Africa and had been
cremated there by members of his regiment. Nine months later she
would appear on the pages of newspapers across the world from
London to Australia. On a sunny November day, later in 1941, Richpal
Ram's widow was greeted with full military honours, cavalry and
marching bands and crowds of onlookers at the Viceregal Palace
in New Delhi. She was wearing full sweeping scarlet and yellow
skirts and heavy jewellery, and held her tiny daughter by the hand.
Mussamat Janki and her child had been looked after by a British
officer's wife who had helped shepherd the family around the capital
and purchased the special clothes for the occasion. There was a
distinguished turn-out including Wavell and the Commander-in-
Chief. In the forecourt of the Viceregal Palace the medal was
presented to Mussamat Janki and also pinned on the chest of
Lieutenant Premindra Singh Bhagat.[20] During the ceremony, the
citation was read out in Urdu and English. Lady Linlithgow bent
down to speak with Richpal Ram's child. Looking on were injured
Indian soldiers, dressed in dark coats and starched white pyjamas,
many with crutches and with limbs missing.

The award of the medal had a significant effect on Mussamat Janki's
status. The proud Maharaja of Patiala came from a family with a long

association with the army – his father had visited troops on the Western Front in the First World War – and the maharaja himself would later serve as a colonel in Italy, Malaya and Burma. This Victoria Cross had been awarded to one of his own subjects and he announced a grant of 500 *bighas* of land to Richpal Ram's family, a patch large enough to provide a comfortable income, while Mussamat Janki also received a special state pension of 525 rupees a year in addition to the usual widow's pension. Richpal Ram would become a Jat hero, his memory kept alive by members of his regiment and his name appearing sporadically in local history books.

For Premindra Singh Bhagat, the award of the medal had a very different effect. He was able to marry his sweetheart, Mohini. Back in Poona, Mohini's father, Colonel Bhandari, was finally won over by the persistence of the young couple and by Bhagat's new status as the first Indian Victoria Cross winner of the Second World War. They were married in Poona on 24 February 1942. Premindra did not return to the front and instead was assigned the task of using his iconic status, speaking on All India Radio about his feats and drumming up new recruits, touring rural parts of Maharashtra during the mid-1940s and encouraging and training more young men who came forward.

* * *

'British and Indians fought shoulder to shoulder, sharing the same dangers and discomforts and acquiring a remarkable degree of admiration and friendship for each other', a British major later wrote.[21] In the war diaries from North and East Africa there is little differentiation between British and non-British officers in the Indian Army. Battle in North Africa united the men, it erased petty tensions when they did exist and officers always pulled together at the critical moments. Propaganda aimed at an Indian audience such as the book *The Tiger Strikes* implied that the men had almost become indistinguishable and that race was now immaterial, with even the physical difference between men blurred in the conditions of war. While in Egypt, the book suggested, 'The British troops were so tanned by the blazing sun from which there was no shade that they became as dark as the Indians, while the way in which all fraternised made this encampment in the desert a friendly and happy place.'²² Yet such propaganda also unwittingly revealed just how much racial consciousness of skin colour and of difference still mattered.

Sometimes racial difference marred relationships between officers or created pecking orders and hierarchies within the more senior ranks of the military in the 1940s. Some Indian officers privately referred to petty acts of discrimination and long remembered snubs by their British counterparts, but this was compatible with maintaining close friendships and having positive feelings about the British as a whole. It is difficult to generalise on this question and as Major Kartar Singh remembered, 'The British people were very mixed – there were some who were very anti-Indian and some who were very friendly.'²³ Differences may have been more profound in some ways between officers new to the army (both Indian and British) who had been commissioned during the war, and those of the older sort of officer, who tended to be more attached to the traditional structures of the Indian Army before the immense changes of the 1940s. The new officers who had been rapidly recruited brought a fresh spirit to the army and often had more sympathy towards political campaigns for Indian freedom.

Indeed, many British officers shared and understood their Indian colleagues' nationalist aspirations. As one British sergeant of the Sudan Ordnance Corps wrote home from the Middle East, 'I have met scores of these Indian troops in Cairo and have had drinks with many of them and would do so again. If India was composed chiefly of these kind of blokes I would say they deserve Home Rule and be glad to see them get it.'²⁴ Nonetheless, for others, cordiality was not necessarily the same as solidarity. Differential treatment of Indians and Britons remained enshrined in the Indian Army's rules, and it was only midway through the war that Indian officers could sit on courts martial of British soldiers. The debate about courts martial revealed the stark attitudes of the British government – 'ICOs should not have power of punishment over white men', ordered Whitehall – but also reflected the differences of opinion between leaders in New Delhi and London on this question, with those in Delhi pushing for equality between officers, which was eventually allowed in 1943.²⁵ Command of important operations also remained a bugbear, with the most senior Indian officers feeling eclipsed by their British commanders.

The closer men got to the front line, the more the sense of racial difference and racism receded, however. In the heat of battle, the determination to defeat the enemy was an equaliser and the immediacy of battle erased many other considerations that appeared petty in the face of life or death. An officer of the Cheshire Regiment recalled a 'hellish' scene, when under heavy fire in North Africa, an Indian officer unknown to him risked his life to ascertain that his batman was dead: 'Throughout the rescue attempt this officer was as calm as though nothing particular was happening and I am deeply indebted to him for confirming the fate of my batman.'[26] Partly as a result of such encounters, throughout the duration of the war there was a drift towards more equality and shared fellow feeling in the army, and this was particularly experienced at the officer level, where glaring anomalies were erased. But camaraderie was never a reflection of a complete dissolution of identity.

Despite this, gaps in communication confronted officers and men. Emergency commissioned officers were fast-tracked and expected to grasp the basic rudiments of Hindustani (the Hind–Urdu hybrid lingua franca of North India) in a matter of months. This tended to be written in the Indian Army in a romanised typeface rather than in the usual Devanagari or Arabic scripts. Leave and promotion were tied to passing tests in Hindustani. The old guard of senior commanders prided themselves on their language abilities and a number could speak Hindustani with consummate skill. Wavell had not been in India for thirty years by the time that he returned in the 1940s so his earlier familiarity with Indian languages had faded, although his linguistic knowledge did aid his command of the Indian Army and later added strength to his leadership as Viceroy. Frank Brayne, the Indian Army Welfare Officer who had worked in Punjab for many decades, was an advocate of Hindustani in the roman script and was at ease in Punjabi. Field Marshal Slim was probably one of the most able to communicate directly and knew Gurkhali and Hindi. He was extremely conscious of the importance of language, 'the closest and the strongest link in the bonds between officer and sepoy', he wrote some years before the war, and even prized less successful efforts to try to learn the language as 'an effort to really understand' the Indian soldier, remaining

concerned about the diminishing linguistic skill in the Indian Army
in the 1930s and 1940s.[27]

Real proficiency in the language was a challenge even for the
linguistically gifted officer, particularly when listening to dialect, slang
and regional pronunciation. Among the ICS, too, the linguistically
versatile *pukha sahib* of Kipling's day, a man who had picked up
languages as a child of the Raj, had become more rare. Ian Hay
Macdonald struggled with learning Oriya and complained about the
difficulties in his letters home to his parents. A number of officers
crammed in their spare time, particularly on board ship and on long
journeys. During his military service, Clive Branson took opportunities to go into market towns and practise speaking Hindustani when
he first arrived, but the increased demands of war work, the diversity
of languages within India, the rapid changes of personnel and shifts
in location, all conspired to mean that among civilians and military
the linguistic versatility of the Raj was no longer what it once was.

Within the Indian Army, many of the British non-commissioned
officers were exceptionally dependent on intermediaries, primarily
havildars, who did the work of translation and interpretation for them.
This added to the abiding sense of a world 'lost in translation'. For
John Ffrench – who was Indian-born and had a long family connection
with India stretching back to the eighteenth century – the challenges
of speaking the languages still unsettled him, despite good relations
with his men.

> As a young British officer at the time I did not really know what the
> soldiers felt, my Urdu never being particularly fluent at any time. Even
> after four years with the same Company, whenever I spoke to them at
> muster parade, the *subedar* would always add 'sahib ke matlab hai . . .'
> (what the sahib means is . . .) I am not sure whether they really did
> not understand me, or whether the *subedar* was just putting his oar
> in![28]

Middle-ranking Indians, including those who acted as *havildars*, often
had halting speech in English. 'I was matriculate and I worked with
the British Officers also. But we were speaking slowly English, only
Punjabi English, you can say', recalled Major Dhatt.[29]

Sepoys did not have to be literate or have any knowledge of English on recruitment, although for many of them, the chance to learn literacy skills and English were additional attractions of the army. A number of officers recalled how soldiers studied from primers by lamplight after dark, took opportunities to practise their English and improved their ability to read and this could be rewarded by promotion and extra pay. In addition, as the recruitment pool rippled ever outwards into new districts, the sheer diversity of languages in the army was bewildering, and Hindustani would no longer suffice for communicating with Tamils and other southerners, speaking Tamil, Telugu and Malayalam. The army even briefly considered changing the lingua franca to English, and in African regiments officers changed from vernaculars to English as the language of command during the war. But in India, the chief training officer dismissed the idea as 'not practical politics'. The course had been set midway through the war and due to the lack of instructors, curricula and training manuals the emphasis remained on Hindustani as the medium of communication.

Despite the extraordinary assessment of the War Office that it would be 'obviously easier for ten thousand comparatively intelligent Englishmen to reach a reasonably high standard in a foreign language, than to instruct a million far less intelligent Indians',[30] in actuality, much of the linguistic flow was at least as effective in the other direction, with many Indian sepoys able to communicate in English within a short time. The Indian Army's language structures clearly functioned well enough for military operations and communication skills were sufficient enough for basic orders and military needs. But these slippages and misunderstandings of language rippled throughout the Indian Army in its later years.

But among the Other Ranks, more generally, it would be misleading to see war as a leveller. There were still important differentials of pay and conditions and when it came to food and sex, those two perennial barometers of social mixing, arrangements remained separate. One of the first tasks for the military commanders on the capture of the Eritrean city of Asmara, following the eventual fall of Keren, was the establishment of two sets of official racially segregated brothels, one for British troops and the other for Indians.[31]

Among sepoys, the time away from their families and the length of the stay in North Africa was starting to erode old ways of doing things and to change expectations of military life. In the desert all men seemed more equal. But this also meant more vocal demands for equal treatment. The sepoys started turning down cheap Indian *bidis* and asking for foreign cigarettes; they would not be fobbed off with lesser treatment, with bad equipment or poor-quality soap. 'The Indian is developing European tastes which he is requiring to be satisfied on British Army Standards', the commander of an Indian division overseas observed. 'He has quickly learned to appreciate the European cigarettes and demands his share of what is available of British stocks, claiming that any other distribution would show discrimination against the Indian.' Anonymous appeals from soldiers for better pay arrived at the General Headquarters in Delhi.[32] These sepoys had already sacrificed much for the war by 1941. Medals for fallen comrades were not enough to assuage opinion as maltreatment started to be challenged, standards were now critiqued and pay and leave allowance came under scrutiny.

*   *   *

Meanwhile, the fighting escalated in the Middle East and North Africa. In the spring and summer of 1941, Indian troops were playing a critical part in holding Persia and Iraq and seeing off an Axis puppet ruler, Rashid Ali. But earlier gains achieved with the help of 4th Indian Division, of which Richpal Ram was just one distinguished member, were being lost by late March 1941 as the see-saw battle between Rommel and the Allies went on: Benghazi was lost and the British imperial forces rolled back towards Tobruk. Until North Africa was finally secured for the Allies, battle went on backwards and forwards across the desert between El Agheila and El Alamein. The desert campaign ended on 4 February 1943 with the retreat to Tunis and the Tunis campaign that followed ended on 13 May 1943.

Large numbers of Indian troops were captured at Mechili in North Africa and taken to Italian POW camps. Among the Indian prisoners, Satyen Basu's capture in North Africa by German troops was frightening:

> Suddenly we heard somebody giving orders in German about 200 yards behind us. Then as if from nowhere, the whole convoy was smashed by a terrific firing from tanks and machine guns. In the night the fiery

streak of every shot passing through the air could be seen. It seemed to me as if somebody with a giant broomstick of fire swept the whole convoy off the ground.

He was soon reassured to hear a German soldier say, 'Indiano no enemy, Indiano friends.'[33] Taken to Italian POW camps, he had times of hunger and anxiety and laboured digging trenches in Naples, but he also recalled local generosity, ten-pound Red Cross parcels with tinned meat, cheese, milk, sugar, tea, fish and chocolates, and a thriving black market; he even managed to acquire a violin. Inmates in the camp argued vociferously about the politics of the war. Was Gandhi right? What was the Indian responsibility to defeat fascism in Europe? They also started putting on their own theatre performances: Gurkhas doing Indian dances to everyone's amusement, the men using tinfoil wrappings and Sikh *pugri* fabric to make costumes and saris, army carpenters making stage scenery. Compared to the experiences of some POWs who were held by the Japanese later in the war, these men had a palatable, even comfortable confinement.

About 15,000–17,000 Indians were taken prisoner of war in the campaigns around the Mediterranean. They suffered similar privations to their international counterparts – the monotony of incarceration and impatience while the war was being fought without them, the scrambling for precious foodstuffs, the moments of jollity and glimmers of hope. As with other POWs the particular camp, time and country of confinement made all the difference. The Indians were seen as particularly worth enticing into a fifth column by Axis leaders who recognised the propaganda potential of undermining the British Empire, as well as the attractions of gaining additional manpower. Attempts to suborn Indian sepoys and to use them as propaganda poster boys for the Axis were mildly successful, although limited to small pockets of men: a few thousand in Italian and German camps went over to the Axis in total and some were flown to Berlin and Rome. At a camp in Annaburg in Saxony (Stalag IV) several thousand were persuaded or pressured to join the Free India Legion by Indian activists living in Germany. In Italy, the smaller Centro Militare (India) trained up a select group of Indian saboteurs and parachutists. Axis leaflets showing smiling, well-dressed prisoners proclaimed in Hindi and Urdu, 'They have saved their lives and are living happily in the prisoner-of-war camps.' Just as in later years the INA's formation would be kept from public knowledge, this was top-secret information in the wartime British Empire. When the *Evening Standard* ran a picture of a Sikh named 'Chandra' in a German uniform with the caption 'an Indian quisling in Berlin', Leo Amery, Secretary of State for India, reined in the editor immediately.[34] Some men undoubtedly escaped and rumours of small bands of Indian POWs roaming around the Alps and southern France persisted for some time.

Italian POWs also flowed in the opposite direction in 1941, back towards the Indian home front. Thousands of the captured Italian prisoners from the Middle East and North Africa were shipped to India as POWs and disembarked at Bombay, where they were paraded through the streets in front of curious onlookers.[35] Conditions varied considerably. Germans were housed in camps in Purandhar near Poona, Satara and Dehra Dun while Italians were placed in Ramgarh, Bairagah near Bhopal and Poona. In Ahmednagar Elios Toschi, an Italian prisoner brought to India directly from the battlefields of North Africa, along with about 7,000 men captured at Sidi Barrani, Bardia, Tobruk and Benghazi, praised the camp organisation for the quality of the beds, bedclothes, cigarettes and mosquito nets. Nevertheless, life was monotonous and over time many of the men felt they were forgotten and became more desperate. Health was the most serious worry. At the camp at Ramgarh many succumbed to beriberi and typhoid fever, 'at an alarming rate'. The camp then turned into a sea of mud and was filled with mosquitoes when the rains started. 'The lorries, with the coffins covered by the Italian tricolour, drove slowly past our ranks.'[36] Several hundred Italians died while interned during the war in India, some from natural causes but the majority from illnesses caught while in confinement. For prisoners of war of all different nationalities, the war was characterised by a long, testing time of waiting in camps, longing for letters and hoping that their own news was getting through.

Within South Asia, opinions about the war in general remained diverse and depended very much on the location and perspective of the individual, his own economic prospects and the uncertain prediction of what course the war would take. Everywhere, however, South Asians wondered what the war was going to mean for the political future of their own country and how the war might be a way of leveraging freedom from colonial control. Some thought strategically about the possibility of higher wages and serving their families and communities by sending home savings. Few, though, anticipated the great economic devastation that was about to unfold back home in the subcontinent.

7

Money Coming, Money Coming

On the morning of 26 June 1941, a series of earthquakes shook the Indian Ocean for three minutes. The writer Sydney Ralli felt the ripples in Delhi, recording in her diary how the ground moving was more frightening even than war.[1] The worst-affected part of the British Indian Empire was the Andaman and Nicobar Islands. The long arc of tiny islands dotted in the Indian Ocean had, since 1858, been the site of the Cellular Jail, a prison for the most threatening political opponents of the Raj, convicts considered too dangerous to keep on Indian soil. The jail was a place of dread, with cells designed so that prisoners could not see each other, the sense of loneliness and isolation in the midst of the black waters underscored in every brick.

A very small community of British officials and their families, numbering less than one hundred, lived on the islands. They were in charge of running the penal settlement and overseeing the colony, which was increasingly populated elsewhere with less high-security prisoners who were allowed to farm and settle the land. Alongside this community lived the descendants of prisoners who had finished their terms, and migrant and indentured peasants from mainland India. Charles Waterfall had been in the Andamans since 1938, when he was appointed Chief Commissioner of the Andaman and Nicobar Islands. At the time of the earthquake he was nearing his fiftieth birthday. His had been a solid rather than stellar career and the posting in the Andamans was a mixed blessing. It took several nights by ship to reach the Andaman and Nicobar Islands, which were much closer to Burma and South-East Asia than the subcontinent. The Chief Commissioner's House was the single compensation for the isolation and the thankless task of governing the islands. Reminiscent of the grander homes in

Indian hill stations, part Swiss chalet, part English country house, it was a vast wooden-beamed building, with intricately carved gables and shaded verandas, surrounded by well-cultivated gardens. The house was situated on Ross Island, where the higher-ranking officials lived, which could be circumnavigated by foot in an afternoon, and so society was necessarily tight-knit. Equipped with swimming pools, ballrooms, squash and tennis courts, the Chief Commissioner's House had Italian tiled floors and was served by extensive granaries and a local bakery. The church had window frames of teak filled with fine Italian stained glass.

The number of prisoners in the penal settlement had been reduced to a few hundred and the jail was not full to capacity. The government had made attempts to settle less-threatening prisoners from other Indian jails on the island's land in exchange for their labour, in new efforts to tame and develop the landscape.[2] Every day at noon a cannon on Ross Island would boom, a reminder to the prisoners that they were not alone. In the late 1930s Indian politicians called vociferously for repatriation and the closure of the Cellular Jail and a serious hunger strike by 190 convicts on the island in 1937 had shaken, but not stalled, the administration of the penal settlement.

On the morning of 26 June 1941 the earth began to tremble on Ross Island. In a matter of seconds the buildings were uprooted and re-arranged. The ballroom floor was severed in two, the house caved open and tree roots punctured the tennis court. Elsewhere, on the archipelago the damage was extensive. 'For miles along the west coast north and south of Port Anson . . . the hillsides had slipped into the sea littering the beaches with huge boulders and uprooted tree trunks. It will be several generations before the hills are covered with jungle as before', Charles Waterfall reported after touring some of the damage. 'Parts of the coast appear to have sunk. All made ground has cracked or sunk. Port Blair harbour is believed to have become deeper by a couple of feet in several places.' The centre of the west coast had been hit the worst, 'trees fell, hillsides slipped, cracks opened in the earth, all huts collapsed and people had to hang on to tree stumps to avoid being thrown about violently'.[3] The Cellular Jail, however, still stood, its high brick arches and ramparts undamaged. The earthquake's timing was eerie. Some even saw it as a portent of impending doom.

That very same week that an earthquake shook the Andamans, Hitler attacked Russia. The brutal, unrelenting sweep against Russia in June 1941 would dominate the Indian news for months to come. For Indian leaders, who looked on with 'anxious interest', in the words of Nehru, the potential fall of the USSR was a sign of the changing world order, but also a threatening harbinger of fascism's real menace. The Congress Working Committee commended the Russian people for their 'self-sacrifice and heroic courage' and there was deep sympathy with the plight of ordinary Russians battling the Nazi war machine.

*   *   *

On the mainland, around the same time in late June 1941, a new ship-yard was opened in the eastern coastal port of Vizagapatam to great public excitement. Four thousand guests attended the inauguration festivities, priests said prayers and blessed the site and astrologers were consulted on the timing. Five kinds of jewel were buried deep in the concrete foundations where a berth in the shipyard would stand. Garlanded luminaries of the nationalist movement, most notably future president of India Rajendra Prasad, gave speeches extolling the enterprise and Prasad laid a foundation stone at the site. Gandhi sent a message of goodwill – 'May your enterprise be successful and may it be beneficial to the whole country' – while the renowned poet Rabindranath Tagore spelt out the dream with more precision: 'I hope the day is not distant when Indians shall sail the seas in their own ships flying the flag of their own country.' Commemorative brochures were produced to celebrate the historic moment.[4]

Midway between Calcutta and Madras on the Coromandel Coast, Vizagapatam had a burgeoning port, fed by new railways connecting the city to Madras and the eastern countryside of India, which was rich in natural minerals and coal. The sheltered natural harbour faced away from the open sea, carved out between two protective promontories. The port was a strategic asset in wartime as it was well hidden and the deep waters could hold large ships. Here, manga-nese from the interior, crucial to the making of steel and iron, was shipped, cargo steamers carried goods along the coast to Calcutta to the north and Madras to the south and workers sweated through the night during the war, loading and unloading coir, tobacco, groundnuts and cloth for export, and receiving incoming machinery and cloth.

The new shipyard was the start of a bold new venture. The owner of the site, the indefatigable industrialist Walchand Hirachand, had grand hopes for constructing a steamship, the first Indian-built steamship. The ships bringing and taking goods to and from Calcutta and Bombay had usually been constructed in Glasgow and Liverpool. Steamships, Walchand speculated, would make him wealthier still (he was already one of the wealthiest men in India) and also create a prestigious trophy for Indian industry.[5] Like many industrialists of the age he was not so much interested in waging war with the Germans or Japanese, as with making profit. The war presented opportunities to generate capital, to acquire technical assistance, to launch megaprojects and to found his own dream ventures. From the eighteenth century onwards British approaches to Indian shipping had been characterised by an unequal dualism, with one rule for British-owned ship companies and another rule for Indians. There were higher insurance rates and bars to Indian involvement in shipping, the deskilling of local crews, and outright resistance and dirty rate wars which drove Asians out of the business. War, many businessmen believed, would turn the tables. They eagerly hoped for new opportunities – unprecedented profits and the advancement of Indian heavy industry, and the chance to manufacture for the domestic market for which they had waited so long.

If the war had not really touched South Asia as yet, in the waters around India it had already started. The war in the East depended on shipping and shipping was the lifeblood of the empire. By March 1941, 643,198 imperial servicemen had moved through the waters of the Indian Ocean sea routes, many of these men in huge convoys, carrying troops in vessels that had been rapidly reconditioned and adjusted to accommodate men. Ships carried everything from coal and diesel to mules, petrol and tinned meat. India needed aeroplanes, cars, machinery and ships. The ability to sail commodities across the globe, either around the Cape or through the Suez Canal, had never been greater or more necessary.

Nor had it ever been more dangerous. U-boats had already started hunting in the waters of the Indian Ocean and raiders were soon laying minefields in the approaches to Indian ports. Attacks on shipping were an effective way of crippling supply lines. At least 385 Allied, British and neutral ships sank in the Indian Ocean over the next few years, many of them manned by Lascars. Indian businessmen waited anxiously to see if their orders would arrive, and both imports and exports suffered, while orders for new machinery could take three or four attempts. As fronts in Egypt and the Middle East became central to the ongoing conflict, India came under pressure to support the war by supplying manufactured goods to the expanding Indian Army and also the wider British cause. Channelling supplies from the eastern empire towards the Middle East was a solution to the pressures placed on Britain as the industrial and manufacturing pivot of the empire. After years of drawing on the empire for raw materials in exchange for manufactured goods, Britain now needed its colonies to provide ready-made products: guns, uniforms, paper, steel, leather boots, if not for export, at least for import substitution.

Government contracts soared in number and by the start of 1940 orders for manufactured goods weighed in at over £62 million. 'It is reported to me by persons of status that money is being spent like water in the name of the war', Gandhi wrote to the Viceroy.[6] Seven million garments a month rolled out of Indian factories and 3 million pairs of boots. Within three years, India would be producing as much for war supply as Australia, New Zealand and South Africa combined together.[7] Alongside government-run and protected ordnance factories, hundreds of trade workshops and railway workshops were subcontracted to produce spare parts, small machinery and tools. Private industries, particularly factories manufacturing chemicals, paint, paper, metal alloys, jute for khaki uniforms and canvas, all attracted increasing numbers of workers as the pressure to complete government contracts increased month on month; one paper mill owned by the Birla group, for instance, had soon tripled its output. By the mid-1940s India was churning out rifles and bayonets, machine guns and ammunition, artillery and shells, tractors and plating for armoured vehicles, anti-tank ammunition, boots, blankets, uniforms, camouflage and sandbags.

The impact on the ecology of the subcontinent was becoming evident as timber from the forests of Burma and from the north-east and central India was hewn into packing cases, ammunition boxes, railway sleepers and telegraph poles, leaving the natural landscape of the Burmese borderlands changed even before the ravages of war in the region. A few voices spoke up for the preservation of the forests but they went unheard. The war was about to unleash an unprecedented assault on the natural environment of the north-east and once road-building began in 1942, the region became more accessible than ever before. Private companies, often British- and American-owned, like Burma Shell, were given the rights to prospect for oil and minerals, and looked hungrily towards the Bengali river basins for exploration.

The economic boom was welcomed, especially after the long years of depression. Little wonder that G. D. Birla and his peers initially hesitated to support the Congress, and believed Gandhi was 'wandering in the wilderness'. Business leaders backed the war for the time being, demanding with candour 'a fair share of the additional demand'.[8] For a while, businessmen like Walchand and G. D. Birla threw themselves behind the war and when Churchill became Prime Minister in 1940, Birla telegraphed him to congratulate him. Pained by the increasing estrangement of the British and the Indians and concerned about the desperate fortunes of the Allies in Europe, industrial leaders attempted to straddle the middle ground, to mediate between empire and nation-alists. Birla pressed his old friend Gandhi towards a settlement with the British and told him frankly 'we are going the wrong way' when Gandhi initiated *satyagraha* in 1940.

Profits for war industries soared and time and again the roots of staggering post-war fortunes can be found in the 1940s. The larger Indian-owned companies could acquire licences, cartelise and buy out expatriate firms and concentrate wealth in ever fewer hands. Well-placed and canny operators like the *Marwari* Ramakrishna Dalmia, who had previously owned some of the largest sugar and cement companies in India but had not diversified, and turned his attention to finance. He established Bharat Bank in 1941 and was soon buying into flour-milling, sugar and jute mills, cotton textiles, civil aviation, railways, coal mines, electricity supply and newspapers. In Jamshedpur, the home of Tata Steel – India's iconic steel plant – towering chimneys smoked day and night. During the Battle of Britain, Tata Steel made a voluntary donation for the purchase of two Spitfires, so keen was the Indian-owned business to display its loyalty to the war effort. Alongside the larger companies, smaller firms stockpiled warehouses, chased contract opportunities and risked new ventures, often reaping profits on a new scale, while it soon became apparent that small work-shops and petty craftsmen could tap the new windfalls as well as the bigger players.

Indian laboratories started to make advances too and scientists could already trumpet the technical and scientific innovations generated by the war. Nearly 300 different drugs that had formerly been imported could now be made locally. Military and civil hospitals looked to the domestic market for everything from disinfectants to surgical instruments, hot-water bottles, bandages, rubber gloves and enamel dishes. 'An effective substitute for cod liver oil is now being made on an extensive scale in India', a cheery government circular declared, 'from the livers of sharks caught in Indian waters.'[9] In the hills of Conoor, amla berries were being grown, dried and pressed into vitamin C tablets for troops while a few specialist manufacturers in Calcutta sprang up making thermometers and new firms began retailing surgical instruments and dressings, morphine, codeine and caffeine. Vaccines were increasingly made in Indian laboratories rather than imported and scientists experimented with sera needed for the treatment of tetanus, diphtheria and jaundice.

For many people of far more modest means, wartime looked potentially promising too. The mega-cities, Bombay, Calcutta and Delhi, buzzed with a new energy while artisans, clerks and railway workers in small towns and cities looked forward to greater chances of employment, far preferable to the long hard years of the 1930s. Workers flocked towards the cities, and factory employment went up by a third. As one Lascar recalled at the start of the war, everyone was saying 'Money Coming! Money Coming!'[10] The rising prices of commodities could be matched, initially, by rising wages and the urban middle class – clerks, teachers, journalists and college students with more money in their pockets – mingled at new coffee houses and spent their money on new consumer goods, from gramophone records and bicycles to Singer sewing machines and machine-made saris. They went to the cinema to see K. A. Abbas's film *Naya Sansar*, or 'New World', which depicted a romantic young newspaper journalist, and appealed to the rising sense of radicalism among the young, urban middle class. More women entered the workforce, and in the cities the labouring poor manufactured munitions and cleaned tank parts and young men and women escaped family bonds by working at mines and brick-kilns, taking up seasonal work or adding to agricultural incomes. War workers were promised better conditions and higher pay and special access to increasingly costly cloth, food and medicines in return for their unswerving loyalty. This was all, at first sight, far preferable to the conditions of the 1930s, when it had been so hard to get a steady job at all and incomes had been precarious and uncertain.

The rising wages, though, have to be set against rising living costs. The boom in wages quickly proved illusory as the wartime economic pressure cooker in India started to boil. Demand was intense and shifts in the factories and war industries became harder, longer and more disruptive to ordinary life, and labourers had to be prepared to pick up day wages and to chop and change contracts. The usual mechanisms for negotiating problems between boss and worker also started to fail as the state could crack down on strikes using the Defence of India rules and managers used every trick in the book to keep mill hands at work, to keep the spindles turning and the engines humming twenty-four hours a day. But inevitably, the machinery started to run down and when the quality of materials declined, factory managers expected the same standards. In Bombay's textile mills, a worker who broke thread or tore cloth must pay a fine and all the workers had to improvise, ingeniously fixing up old machines and trying to meet targets against all odds. Bosses drove workers harder instead of investing in machinery – they could not update their machines or get hold of the spare parts even if they wanted to – and as a result factory workers literally risked life and limb. Industrial accidents were a common occurrence, and combined with the poor conditions in overcrowded new shanty towns or *bustees*, workers faced high risks of injury or disease.[11]

The cities began to swell in a way that was unprecedented, beginning an irreversible flow of workers from country to city which has continued to the present day. On the outskirts of cities *bustees* became visible, improvised structures of cardboard and cloth. In Cawnpore, the pre-war population of some 200,000 or 300,000 would nearly treble by the end of the war, driven up by wartime workers to munitions and industrial plants, although tellingly the number of hospital beds for civilians remained unchanged.[12] Resources were stretched under the pressure of these new populations, aggravating friction between communities struggling for access to the barest provisions. In Ahmedabad, where the textile mills churned out fabric for uniforms worn around the empire, there were some 380 hospital beds for a civilian population of 600,000. 'Nowhere in the world today', observed Daniel Thorner, economic historian and well-travelled Indophile at the end of the war, 'are there slums worse than the single-storey bustees of Calcutta or the multistorey chawls of Bombay.'[13] Factory workers in essential and government-controlled industries such as ordnance benefited from subsidised meals, but there was no simple trickle-down effect for those workers who served the war's industries and whose pay was consistently eroded by the inflation of real prices.

*　　*　　*

The war was being treated with a new seriousness of purpose as the administration intensified blackouts, air raid precautions (ARP) drills and internal defence. Delhi was plunged into darkness in summer 1941 and held its first complete blackouts: in both Old and New Delhi all street lights were extinguished or shaded and in Calcutta time was literally out of sync as the clocks in the city's municipal buildings, great monuments to ideals of Victorian industry and punctiliousness, were put forward one hour so that workers in the city's factories, making textiles and jute gunny bags for the war, could hurry home before the blackout at nightfall. As in Britain, air raid precaution workers patrolled the streets, looking for lights seeping out from between drawn curtains or blackout paper pasted across windows, and offering first aid and warning sirens in the event of the dreaded attack. The coloured lights of religious festivals were identified as a potential target from the air and worshippers were told to extinguish their lights as darkness fell, cigarette-smoking was banned in the blackout and traders and stallholders had to extinguish the small lights that illuminated their vegetables and other wares.[14]

Centrally disseminated propaganda was now targeted at the population in a variety of guises and languages. It was intended to show both the military might and preparedness of the country and to impress local people with technical wizardry. At the religious *mela* at Garhmukteshwar alongside the banks of the Ganges in the summer of 1941, big tanks were on show for the *sadhus*, devotees and pilgrims to admire. Displays of military hardware dubbed 'circuses' rolled through parts of the country that had 'seldom seen a soldier', part educational event, part rousing show of prowess, and exhibition trains and touring lecturers travelled the countryside with rolled-up maps and diagrams. Military and civil wings worked together to spread the word. Vans kitted out with loudspeakers and pamphlets, mobile cinemas and all manner of meetings and lectures toured from district to district while 44 million copies of a paper called *War in Pictures* circulated in twelve different Indian languages.[15]

The state was projecting a more sober and less lavish image than in the 1930s and a more serious effort to reflect the gravity of the global situation was urged on colonial officials by the military. There was a clampdown on parties and on alcohol sales in hotel bars and restaurants. Prodigious amounts of alcohol had kept Raj high society afloat during the 1920s and 1930s and whisky, beer and gin were favourites. The more high-class the establishment, the later it was allowed to stay open: in Delhi, at Hakman's Astoria and Davicos Restaurant at the Imperial and Maidens Hotels, parties went on until 2.30 a.m. on at least one evening a week and crowds listened to Russian cabaret artists and American jazz pianists. Officially, clubs in Delhi did not have the right to serve alcohol unless they had a special licence for dances or charity events; in reality, club-owners widely flouted such rules and drinking went on until the small hours. The rules had become increasingly elastic throughout the 1930s to the stage where a restaurant or hotel proprietor could get a special licence 'practically as often as he liked' but now, on army request, the normal closing hours would be ten o'clock.[16]

Shortages also played a role in dampening the nightlife. 'Only whisky and beer drunk these days,' complained Ian Macdonald, 'everything else substandard Australian import.'[17] Shortages of petrol and other commodities had begun to bite even for the elites. Yet these cutbacks still felt a little bit of a charade, a pantomime war which was not fully integrated into the thinking or behaviour of the Raj. As soldiers arrived from Blitz-battered Britain and saw the lifestyles of many British people in India they were amazed and angered.

Despite intensified attempts in 1941 to gear India towards war, the most important change that was taking place across the country was a silent, pervasive phenomenon. As the government printed more money and the purchase orders continued to flow, the economy looked, superficially, to be booming. But inflation was already outstripping rises in wages.[18] Ordinary villagers did not buy a vast array of goods and the price of a small number of consumable items was critically important, the basic stuff of life on which people depended: grain, kerosene and cloth. Disruptions to shipping, the dislocation of the economy and the prioritisation of military production meant that even if they had more money when they had sold their goods to market, villagers were finding that they simply could not get hold of the items that they usually relied on or that the prices were outstripping what they could realistically afford. All across India, people complained of weevils, shrivelled grain and admixtures. The warning signs about how risky and precarious life was becoming for the rural poor flashed again and again. Silver coins were disappearing from the market as high metal content was regarded as a form of security in times when money was becoming less reliable. The new rupee note, introduced ostensibly to save metal, was also a signifier of inflation and people instinctively rejected it in favour of the former metal coin. These telltale signs of people severely squeezed by economic circumstances were subtle, but widespread.

By mid-1941 the reality of the war, its severity and extensive reach were becoming clearer. The tentacles of war reached out slowly, grasping more and more territory. Germany overran Romania and Bulgaria and attacked Yugoslavia and Greece; in March 1941, 60,000 men from North Africa set off to defend Greece, including many thousands of Indians. But it was Operation Barbarossa, the game-changing moment of the war, when Hitler made a colossal push against Stalin's Russia, which resonated loudest in India. The war took on a new magnitude.[19]

Russia had long been part of a utopian hope as when Indians thought about progress and development, they looked to Russia for inspiration. Nehru had first visited Moscow in 1927 and the poet-polymath Rabindranath Tagore had also been an admirer. At a time when many Soviet crimes remained unreported, the leaps forward in industrial production and living standards had left a deep impression on Indian minds. The advance on Russia that summer shocked and divided people even further. Rabindranath Tagore, eighty years old and ailing, gave voice in a public speech, his last public statement, to

the agonies of seeing the world in conflict, and also the disillusionment with ideas of Europe as the heartland of mankind's progress:

> I had at one time believed that the springs of civilization would issue
> out of the heart of Europe. But today when I am about to quit the
> world that faith has gone bankrupt altogether . . . the demon of
> barbarity has given up all pretence and has emerged with unconcealed
> fangs, ready to tear up humanity in an orgy of devastation. From one
> end of the world to the other the poisonous fumes of hatred darken
> the atmosphere.

The feeling of a world cut adrift, of old ties severed with European
friends, persisted. 'Letters from across the sea have become painfully
scarce,' complained Tagore in a private letter, 'we crave mutual touch
with distant friends.'[20] On his deathbed later that year Tagore would
ask for the news from Russia.[21]

Indian communists now openly supported the war, and aligned
themselves with the war effort, alongside the anti-fascist Radical
Democratic Party. B. P. Jain, a member of the Radical Democratic
Party, remembered later how difficult the decision had been to support
the anti-fascist cause, how, over long hours in coffee shops and in each
other's houses, his colleagues had painstakingly assured themselves
of their position. They would continue to be ridiculed and sidelined
by opponents in other political parties for this unambiguous stance.
But despite their pro-war stance, the police and state administrators
continued to blacklist them and to view them with deep suspicion
because of their leftist views. B. P. Jain's friend, Vatsayan, who had
been writing anti-Nazi books, tried to join the army but was turned
down at first. For Jain, Vatsayan and other followers of the radical
politician M. N. Roy, taking a clear stand against fascism was not easy.
Often these men had studied in Europe and had a thorough grip on
global politics, and they saw, as Marxists, the political questions of the
day on a global canvas. But politicians opposing the war targeted them
as quislings, selling out to the imperialists. 'On this issue of war we
discussed and discussed and discussed to reach the conclusion that the
war had to be anti-fascist', remembered Jain. 'I would not have been
a revolutionary had I not stood up against the masses even at the cost
of my prestige, to fight fascism.'[22]

With the bombing of Pearl Harbor and the declaration of war in the East on 7 December 1941, India was about to be transformed. Tagore would not live to see the great changes to his home city of Calcutta. He died on 7 August 1941, just weeks before the Japanese began their lightning sweep through Asia. His funeral was marked by Bengalis who came out into the streets in their hundreds of thousands in a public outpouring of grief and respect, one of the greatest street spectacles ever witnessed in Bengal. There was a riotous element to the funeral: the body was manhandled as the crowds surged along; they threw wreaths and flowers from the roadside, climbed trees and telegraph poles to get a better view and the bier swept towards its pyre on a wave of shoulders, upheld by the people.

By this time, the focus of the war was still upon Russia and Europe, but the Japanese had been steadily advancing in China, and the threat of Japanese imperial ambitions for British rule in South-East Asia, across the Bay of Bengal, had been under-appreciated. Nobody suspected that Calcutta would soon find itself close to the front line of the war and that once the war came to Indian shores, the effects would be cataclysmic.

8

An Empire Exposed

In February 1942 George Orwell reflected on 'ten of the blackest weeks in our national and imperial history'. It is difficult to over-exaggerate how extensively the attack on Pearl Harbor by Japan and the American declaration of war rebounded in the British Empire, and how rapidly and dramatically it transformed India. In swift, uncompromising succession the Japanese toppled the British imperial presence across the arc of South-East Asia, from Hong Kong and Singapore to Burma and the Andaman Islands. 'With the Japanese army in the Indian Ocean and the German armies in the Middle East, India becomes the centre of the war,' Orwell continued, 'it is hardly an exaggeration to say, the centre of the world. For a long time to come, possibly for years, it may have to act as a supply base from which men and munitions can be poured out in two directions, east and west.'[1]

An extensive interconnected imperial world was now cut in two, as the eastern half of the British Empire fell under Japanese rule. The threat of invasion hovered over India for the next four months and the impact on the Indian home front was explosive. In the short term it undermined faith in the Raj's continued existence as many felt for a short, albeit acute, moment that the end of the empire had come and that the country was about to fall to the Japanese. In the long term, and more significantly as it turned out, the eastward shift of the war brought about a step-change in wartime production, as the mounting pressure to arm, equip and supply soldiers demanded a rapid milking of every available resource. The war was no longer in far-distant Europe. It had come right to the borders, forests and beaches of the state. It is no coincidence that 1942 would be a year of extraordinary dislocation and unrest in India.

The Japanese struck in a rapid series of manoeuvres. Landing on the northern coast of Malaya, and then pushing southward down the Malayan peninsula, they swept aside the hastily assembled defence forces. Worse still, the Japanese seemed to command not only the land but also the seas; the sinking of the *Prince of Wales* and *Repulse*, destroyed by Japanese aircraft in the Gulf of Siam, was both strategically and symbolically conclusive. As the new year approached Britain's grip on the East crumbled. Japan invaded Burma in December, Hong Kong had surrendered to them by Christmas and Malaya was in Japanese hands by 27 January. Britain had underestimated its rival in East Asia, a fact which was brought home most dramatically by the fall of Singapore, captured with shocking and brutal swiftness on 15 February 1942. The government was prepared for attacks, if not invasion, and believed a major attack on the east of India was likely. By mid-February the military was planning for the possibility of 'a major landing operation in Bengal or Orissa in conjunction with a campaign to secure the whole of Burma'. The Bengal Famine Inquiry Report would later describe how Bengalis boarded up their shops and vacated their houses, and how Calcutta witnessed a flow of people out of the city in the 'universal expectation' of an invasion of the province. The public mood in Bengal was 'extremely uncertain', with people unsure if Bengal would be in the possession of the Japanese within months.[2]

The army generals held their breath: 'The Japanese are in a position to carry out naval bombardment, submarine and air attack against the coasts of India now. This attack may extend as far inland as Digboi and Jamshedpur', surmised one military report.[3] They planned a demolition policy in case of invasion: all power stations would cease production, all utilities from power stations to oil refineries would be destroyed, wireless, cable and telegraph stations would be disabled and the ports of Calcutta and Chittagong dynamited. All river craft were to be collected and sunk or broken up, rolling stock and railway stock to be removed. Middle-class civilians suddenly were confronted by newspaper advertisements promising life insurance in case of death by air raid ('Civilian lives fully insured', the Hindustan Insurance Society promised), recruitment posters for the military and air force, advice on how to prepare first-aid kits and advertisements for air raid shelters and ARP equipment from hoses and pickaxes to shovels and stirrup-pumps. 'Be Prepared', one ARP publicity notice warned: 'Is your trench or refuge room ready? In the event of an Air Raid Take

Shelter.' Advertisements called for blood donors, there was a campaign against the wastage of paper and another to dissuade civilian passengers from using the railways, accompanied by large V for Victory emblems. 'Travel *only* when you must', ordered the notices. 'National needs must come first!'

*   *   *

The first of numerous hammer blows soon fell on the peasants of Bengal. The shorthand descriptions used, 'denial policy' or even 'scorched earth', do little justice to the realities of what this intervention meant for Bengali cultivators or fishermen. In Soviet Russia, retreating troops had been ordered to burn stores or supplies to prevent their use by the advancing enemy armies, and a similar, although not identical, tactic was decided upon by the War Office should eastern India and Burma fall to the Japanese. The military planners were mindful of how Singapore's resources had fallen into the lap of the enemy but took little note of the fragility of the Bengali economy and ecosystem. The demolition policy was planned for Assam, Bengal, Bihar and Orissa, but, ultimately, Bengal's experience of denial was the most extensive and pernicious. Why this scorched earth policy was initiated in late 1941 before signs of a definite Japanese invasion began is unclear, as is the decision to focus on two of the most prized essentials necessary to the life of the subsistence cultivators in East India – namely, rice stocks and boats. By contrast, large privately owned industrial plants escaped demolition or dismantling.[4]

'To deprive the people in East Bengal of their boats is like cutting off a vital limb', Gandhi declared in 1942, intuitively understanding the ways in which for East Bengalis their landscape and livelihoods interlocked.[5] In the densely populated Bengali delta, where richly fertile alluvial land was criss-crossed by waterways, boats were the principal source of transport for people and the goods that they produced. Fishermen relied on river craft to make their living but agriculturalists also relied on the waterways as the chief way for their produce to be moved on and sold. Rivers and their tributaries stretched across the delta like vital capillaries.

By the close of March 1942 the decision had been taken by the Governor of Bengal (under the pressure of military authorities who would have liked to see the policy more fully extended) to initiate the removal or destruction of boats in southern Bengal, below a line stretching from Chandpur to Kharagpur. Boats that could carry ten or more people were targeted and by the end of 1942, more than 20,000 of these country craft had been sunk, burned, requisitioned for military use or taken to 'reception' stations where many decayed and fell into disrepair. Some 20,000 other craft may have been hidden, while some owners chose to burn or sink their own boats rather than hand them over to government agents. At every stage the government was aware of the implications of this policy on cultivators. Gandhi sent his dedicated follower, Mira Behn, the British daughter of a naval rear-admiral – she had been following Gandhi since the 1920s – to report on the conditions along the coastal waterways of Orissa. She wrote back that the villagers were 'in despair . . . even for answering the calls of nature it is necessary to go in a boat'.[6] The Governor soon reported on the difficulties caused to local people once boats had been seized from fifty miles of coastline: trade in goods such as mustard oil and kerosene had 'virtually ceased', potters and craftsmen could not sell their wares onward downstream, fishermen could not set out their nets or sail out to the Bay of Bengal. In addition, the removal of carts and bicycles prevented even rudimentary land travel for some. 'Many fishermen have lost their livelihood altogether', Governor Herbert told Linlithgow, 'at a time of year when they normally expect to make their main annual profit from the *hilsa* season.'[7] On the other hand, rent-collectors soon had special dispensation and were issued permits so that they could move by boat. The pecking orders of the state were inscribed in wartime policy.

Denial policies created another lethal policy step towards man-made famine. The causes of the later famine in 1943 are still controversial and the role of these denial policies is still disputed. The Famine Inquiry Commission later made a direct and unequivocal link between the lack of available boats and the starvation of some river folk: 'the fishermen who had been deprived of their boats suffered severely during the famine. If it had been possible to provide them with boats from the reception stations they would have been less affected by the famine and the number of deaths amongst them would have been smaller.'[8] As one official, Alok Jha, who was working as an ICS officer in the district of Munshiganj in the heart of the river delta, recalled in his memoir:

> I hardly ever saw a large *balam* boat on the Padma or Meghna during my entire stay in Munshiganj in 1942–4 . . . No argument to the contrary will shake from me the conviction that it was this two pronged policy of denial – denial of rice and paddy by forcible seizure, destruction and removal; denial of movement of supplies by forcible destruction of boats and indigenous road transport – that caused the famine in Munshiganj.[9]

To many in Bengal it appeared that war was bringing devastation with or without a new foreign occupier, and that the incursion of an occupying force could not be more destructive than the defensive actions already being taken.

The Japanese forces came closest to India in April 1942 when Japan raided Colombo and Trincomalee in Ceylon on 5 April, aiming at the Eastern Fleet stationed there and causing damage to the port and the shipping supply route. By this point, in readiness for attack, Churchill had placed Ceylon under direct military control; the civil government, the Governor and Whitehall's Secretary of State for the Colonies were all put under military command. Forces including British and Australian brigades, Indian and East African divisions and aircraft carriers, cruisers and destroyers had all rushed to Ceylon, at the southern tip of the subcontinent.[10] India's eastern harbours were being bombed from the air and the Bay of Bengal was encircled by Japanese ships, cutting the vital links that sustained shipping and severing ties to South-East Asia. On 6 April Cocanada and Vizagapatam were bombed and along the eastern coast twenty-three merchant ships were destroyed. Corpses were washed up on Indian beaches and the widespread belief, both among the civilian populations and the military, was that Madras would be next. Troops, previously all moving westward towards the war in North Africa and the Mediterranean (quarter of a million had already been sent out of India), were now pulled back eastwards towards India.

India's defences were vulnerable. In late March and early April 1942, for a few critical weeks, it looked as though India would suffer an incursion by the Japanese. 'We passed full days and some anxious nights when scares of invasion called us from our beds', remembered the British General Bill Slim, then stationed in Calcutta. 'We know now that the Japanese never seriously contemplated a seaborne invasion of India, but at the time it loomed constantly over us.'[11] By 1942, Gandhi, according to the senior Congressman Abul Kalam Azad, 'inclined more and more to the view that the Allies could not win the war'.[12] As far away as Bombay, some families decided to evacuate and the government advised people to stockpile enough food for a week. The American Consulate advised American civilians to move to the west of the country. The Government of India and a number of provincial governments cancelled their annual retreat north to the cooler climes of Simla for the summer months and ordered the ICS to stay in Delhi and to forgo leave. Newspapers carried long lists of names of European evacuees from Rangoon and Singapore, about whom more information was requested.

Assaults further inland were not considered a serious possibility, as the Japanese supply lines would have been over-extended and the number of troops within India was already enough to provide significant resistance. Despite this, some officials panicked or gave voice to their own alarmist fears, sometimes in an attempt to galvanise the recalcitrant population into action. The Director of Civil Defence in the United Provinces even suggested in a public speech that inland towns such as Benares and Allahabad could face aerial attack.[13]

But the first crisis would not be in the south around Ceylon, as originally feared, but much further north in the inhospitable borderlands of Burma. The strategists had perhaps placed too much emphasis on sea power and underestimated the Japanese ability to wage war on land. The assumption that the Japanese would not be able to keep supply lines linked together over vast distances was proved wrong when two weak divisions of troops in Burma faced a Japanese onslaught.

Burma was an abundant source of timber, rice and cash crops and had gem, metal and mineral mines. Culturally and socially, it was linked to India in a number of ways. The last complete census in 1931 had recorded just over a million Indians living in Burma, about half of whom had been born in India, and the two economies were entwined and interdependent, with exports flowing in both directions and labour migration and capital investment coming from India.

Despite these links Burma was also surrounded by natural barriers, with some railways but few metalled roads and only three routes connecting it to India. It had scarcely been factored into the calculations of military strategists (with perhaps Wavell as one exception), and had its own peculiarities of history and governance that made it difficult to defend. Ruled as part of British India until 1937, it had recently become a separate colony administered by Burmese politicians under the direct control of Whitehall and, the system still in flux, fell outside the orders of New Delhi and was outside India Command, which was responsible for the protection of the rest of the subcontinent. As India Command tried to scramble ships and men back to India in early 1942, many of the Indian troops who had remained in India had had their units 'milked' and been deprived of officers and men for overseas service. The troops who were sent into Burma lacked training and equipment for jungle warfare, and had to mobilise rapidly and unexpectedly. 'No trained soldiers were left in India, only tattered remnants who often needed time in hospital, and always needed rest, retraining, new equipment.'[14] They were padded out with raw recruits of only four or five months' service.

Still, it took the Japanese from January to May to take the whole of Burma. It was a time of great indecision and anxiety among Burmese Indians, who sometimes hesitated before leaving, weighing up their options or listening to their managers who urged them to stay working in mines and plantations. At one point, 100,000 refugees were in the refugee camps at Mandalay, diverted from heading towards the escape route to India via Tamu. On 7 March Japanese troops marched on Rangoon and its defence was abandoned. On 29 March, the Japanese cut the Burma Road, the most important line of defence, which essentially meant the closure of access to China for the Allies. Once the Burma Road was cut and supply lines had been destroyed, it was clear that Burma would fall and the only option was retreat. On 12 May 1942 the monsoon burst, and as General Bill Slim recalled, 'from then on the retreat was pure misery . . . on the last day of that nine-hundred-mile retreat I stood on a bank beside the road and watched the rearguard march into India. All of them, British, Indian and Gurkha, were gaunt and ragged as scarecrows.'[15]

The chaotic retreat from Burma and the sufferings of refugees, especially those who left by foot over high northern passes, left indelible stains on the imperial reputation. For many people in the patchwork of complicated communities in Burma, people of Indian, British and Chinese descent, there had been difficult choices and painful journeys. Desperation cruelly showed up the differences between the wealthy and the very poor as bribes could not be paid, passages on the precious ships out of Rangoon could not be afforded, and cars and petrol could not be procured. At Magwe, Ramesh Benegal, an affluent Indian in Burma whose uncle was a tin mine manager, recalled, 'The scene at the airport was chaotic. The Japanese advance had been unexpectedly swift, and they were now only a few miles away, within field gun range and of course within fighter aircraft range.'[16] His mother and their eighty-year-old retainer and companion Madiman Datta managed to scramble onto a plane but the boys and men stayed behind. The poor did not have the resources to escape by plane, or to hire porters or to carry extra supplies when escaping on foot. Some Indian tea-pickers, silver miners, road builders and rice-mill workers, who already scraped by on subsistence wages, tried to blend into the Burmese countryside but for others the only hope was return to villages in India, often many hundred of miles away. Managers' attempts to keep labourers at work until the bitter end meant that many were discouraged from leaving at an earlier moment. Administrative confusion worsened their plight, and at one exit, local police charged a fee to let people onto their escape route.

British and Indians moved up from Rangoon into central Burma, with refugees often making multi-stage journeys, drawing on friends and family where they could, planning a route from the fragments of information and rumours around them, then moving up into the daunting mountains above. On the road out to Manipur, on mountains 5,000 to 8,000 feet high, barely clad and barefooted refugees straggled and died. Benegal Dinker Rao, a twenty-four-year-old graduate, and his friend, Mainmath, working in government service in Rangoon, plotted their escape carefully and managed to get their families away to safety earlier in the year than many others. But even so they still spent days of hunger in a trench:

plodding in torrential rain, we came to an abandoned cattle shelter with a half-torn thatch roof. We were too exhausted to walk any more. When we lay down in the slush, we realized that there was a half-bare woman and a naked child lying there moaning. But we were so tired that we fell asleep. When I woke up, I could not move because the child had its arms around my feet. To my horror, the child was dead. Both mother and child had smallpox. Somehow, God saved me from the contagion.[7]

From December 1941 to the following May, the refugees trudged into India and disorganised makeshift camps became swollen to bursting point around the north-eastern border. It has been estimated that 600,000 Indians fled Burma and that 80,000 of them never made it to their destination. The refugees battled leeches, mud and diseases, especially cholera and malaria. Insect bites covered their skin and most suffered with dysentery and diarrhoea. Separated families worried about their kin, sometimes not seeing them or hearing word of them again. Finally, exhaustion and starvation took hold of many. By May 1942, the weakest and poorest remained trailing behind, casual day labourers from rice mills and factories, with little surplus body fat or savings to buffer them. By July 1942 the refugees still coming out of Burma had been on the road for weeks and had not been able to find food. Some had become so emaciated that they verged on starvation.

Veronica Downing, a member of an old tea plantation-owning family of Assam, witnessed the arrival of the refugees as they reached the end of their terrible trail and a place of safety in the refugee camps near her family plantation in north-east India:

A Naga carried a white woman all the way who had just had a baby. No-one knew who she was but once she got to safety she and the baby quietly died . . . The refugees would go through incredible hardship – once they got to a safe place and no more momentum [was] needed they would just give up the ghost and die. The Manipur road would slip down, the rock was shale and would not hold a road. They would just sit at the slip and die. It was a great problem disposing of the bodies, especially in the tropics as it must happen within a few hours. I was rather shocked when I passed the hospital early in the morning on my way to the office and saw them unloading bodies. Graves would fill with water, the water level was so high. The only thing was to burn them in heaps to save firewood.[18]

On the Pangsau escape route, following the Namyang River to Lekhapani, reports of the refugees' arrival started in May. Indian tea plantation labourers, stationed there for road-building work, were used to help with the evacuation, often despite great reluctance on their part. Nagas and other members of north-eastern *adivasi* tribes worked as porters and built refugee camps. Among the Garo sick levels were rising, many suffered foot sores, and porters resisted helping the refugees, scared of contracting illnesses. As one report euphemistically put it, 'they were not working willingly'. The labourers' apprehensions were justified: at least twenty-three porters died of illnesses in one week on this route. Some of the mules suffered 50 per cent casualty rates as the tracks disintegrated under the pressure of elephants and mules, leaving only boulders and potholes. On 20 May daily air drops of food by the RAF began. Some of the forward camps were so foul and full of sewage that even exhausted refugees refused to enter them; human waste covered the floors, and bedding and mosquito nets were in short supply. The disposal of the dead was a particular problem: 'porters would not touch the dead and only occasionally could tea garden labourers be prevailed upon to do so'. Medical and liaison officers threw bodies into rivers or over precipices where they could, where this was not possible they carried out rough burials or burned them with kerosene.[19]

To the south, over the Taungup Pass, some 100,000 to 200,000 Indians attempted to escape to the East Indian port of Chittagong against a tide of petty charges from Burmese police for inoculation certificates and passes. One well-informed eyewitness suggested that casualty figures were 'infinitely greater' on this route than elsewhere, although verifying casualty statistics for the evacuee escape is fraught with difficulty, especially as some Indians turned back and tried to melt into the Burmese population.

Along the way there was evidence of long-remembered gestures of kindness and solidarity from Burmese monasteries, ordinary people and fellow Indians. Ramesh Benegal, who sheltered in a *gurdwara* with his family after they had abandoned their car, wrote years later, 'I will never forget the peaceful atmosphere there and the kindness showed to us.'[20] But refugees also suffered looting, robbery and extortion by the strong over the weak as the trek produced ruthless cut-throat competition simply to survive. In this crisis, some sepoys had deserted with their weapons, afraid of the Japanese onslaught, and rumours of aggressive acts of opportunism or desperation persisted. Some disorganised troops threatened people with loaded rifles in order to obtain food, or looted villages on their path out of Burma. 'A refugee, who said he was a sepoy, had taken possession of the stores at Shamlung and had 2000 Rs on his person. He was said by other refugees to be selling stores at extortionate prices.' Robbing of corpses or abandonment of weaker members of parties sometimes took place. There was, as in other moments of desperate refugee crisis, a persistence of class and caste differences and sometimes the rich could use their assets to insulate themselves by hiring porters or transport for carrying personal possessions, or buying favours. Indian traders and merchants left with their life savings, and carried large wads of cash or jewellery, and sometimes became targets along the route. Occasionally, justice was served. After the theft of over 20,000 rupees from a *Marwari* trader in a refugee camp, soldiers found the offenders and captured them on the road. Another prosperous Indian family trying to get away had to watch as their father was knocked unconscious and robbed but the assailants, a party of poor Indians, were apprehended and sent to base under escort.

Further down the line, at Asansol in Bengal, a young and thoughtful British nurse, Angela Bolton, who had trained as one of Florence Nightingale's Queen Alexandra's Nurses in Britain and had reached India in 1942, was working long hours in a General Hospital for troops, both Indian and non-Indian, who were housed in separate wards on different sides of a corridor. Over the spring and summer of 1942 she saw the ramifications of the war, and the story of the fall and recapture of Burma inscribed on the bodies of men, while nursing British, Indian, West African, Chinese, American and even Japanese casualties. Men arriving at the General Hospital told depressing tales, many of them sick with malaria from their long trek. 'British, Indian and Gurkha troops, distinguished solely by the identity discs around their necks – we never knew their units – shared a brotherhood of emaciated raggedness.'[21] Throughout the month of May men died daily. A melancholy mood pervaded the hospital, its staff and patients:

There are now sixty-five patients in the medical ward. My heart sinks when I see yet another casualty brought in on a stretcher. All these deaths are having a bad effect on the morale of the rest of the patients in the ward. The dramatic treatment of wringing out sheets in a tin bath of ice-water and wrapping them round the patient in full view of everyone (there is no room for screens even if we had them) must be having a depressing effect on the others as it is frequently followed by the death of the patient. Can the heat get any worse? It is said it will be even hotter next month before the monsoon rains.[22]

In the sudden evacuation from Burma, military men received scarcely better care than refugees. There was a scramble to try and prepare beds, hospitals and rest camps and to organise transport. Sometimes only airlifted as far as Dinjan in Assam, the less serious casualties went onward by ordinary train to Dimapur and further along the tracks towards northern and eastern India. Exhausted and filthy Allied troops, even if not badly injured, could be seen by other passengers, on stations and passing through the towns. Villagers, who watched these soldiers coming back from the front looking bedraggled and sick, drew their own conclusions about the progress of the war. Some fellow passengers gave out water, fruit and snacks to men who had exhausted their rations, passing goods up through the bars in the windows to the fatigued soldiers. Onlookers talked to each other about what they had seen and rumours spread.

*   *   *

The Burma retreat, and the differential treatment of refugees, shocked the nation. The effects of the British rout could not be screened from the public. After his harrowing escape from Burma as a nine-year-old with his family, Dr Krishnan Gurumurthy recalled the relief on reaching India, and the ensuing long journey southwards from Calcutta:

It took about ten days for us to reach Madras. The train wended its way slowly, partly because of the over-load and partly because it stopped frequently in all major stations. At every major station, people from the villages flocked to the train and showered us with delicacies, fruits and beverages. The affection shown to us by Bengalees, Oriyas and Andhras en-route was touching. At that time in the year 1942, the fervour of patriotism and freedom from British Rule was such, everyone was vying with each other to do their bit for their fellowmen.[23]

Lending a hand to the refugees from Burma became a nationalist cause. And among the refugees, the idea of Congress as a protector had taken root:

> Fantastic rumours spread among the evacuees; it was said that Gibraltar had been taken and that the Japanese were advancing so fast on the Manipur road they were being machine gunned by their own planes. Indian refugees were told in Burma that a Congress organisation would feed them en route. They frequently asked where this was.[24]

The faith in the Congress to provide protection where the British state had failed to do so is a telling insight into the loss of faith in the Raj.

People had high expectations of support and protection from Indian politicians. Many of the South-East Asian refugees from Malaya and Burma had family roots in Madras Presidency. They had been arriving in large numbers at short notice throughout the early months of 1942. Inflammatory reports reproduced in local newspapers were blamed on the tales told by refugees from South-East Asia. Local newspapers faced government censure for churning up panic, sounding defeatist or reproducing enemy propaganda. In truth, though, much of this news had been circulating regardless of the newspapers, filtered through the networks of refugees and soldiers who passed on smatterings of information from across the Indian Ocean.

Refugees arriving in India urgently needed to find an Indian foothold. The survival strategies and rehabilitation of the Indian refugees from Burma, Malaya and Singapore varied and depended heavily on their previous education, connections and class. Some of the businessmen, *Marwaris* and *Chettiars*, with close links to the commercial interests of Indian business magnates, championed their cause through Chambers of Commerce and other public organisations. In Assam and Bengal, refugees benefited from the lobbying and activism of an Indian evacuees' relief committee with no less than G. D. Birla at the helm. This organisation worked closely with the provincial Congress committees, and lobbied central government for compensation for traders who had lost orders and stock, had had property requisitioned or warehouses and stores damaged by the Japanese or the retreating Burmese government.[25] Other organisations working for the displaced included the Burma Indian Association and the Federation of Indian Chambers of Commerce and Industry, and the Muslim League urged its committees to assist Muslim refugees coming from South-East Asia. These committees also articulated the hardships of the refugees and called for preferential treatment in the allocation of government jobs. Ramesh Benegal's brother, who had been hospitalised with lacerated feet for a number of weeks after his trek from Burma, eventually took up a senior position in the Ordnance Department of the Government of India.

A number of other refugees, however, continued to face visible hardship and destitution. Many urban shopkeepers and merchants from Burma could not adjust easily to agricultural or manual labour. In Madras, some 200 evacuees from Burma employed on aerodrome construction complained about the work they were doing breaking metal in the searing summer heat.[26] It was estimated in May that in Madras alone, 15,000 evacuees from Burma had no employment at all. They faced 'acute distress' and it was suggested by the government that public works under the famine code, which provided for state intervention in extreme conditions, might be needed to ensure their survival.[27] Only a small number had received any government grants even by early 1943, and the interpretation of the welfare rules had been 'over-strict'.[28]

*   *   *

India's war had now become a global concern. Chiang Kai-shek, the Chinese nationalist leader, had arrived in Delhi in February 1942 to talk to Nehru, Gandhi and Jinnah to much excitement in the press; those who supported the war hoped for mutual co-operation between the Chinese nationalists and Indians, other onlookers thrilled to see Asian world leaders in conference, glimpsing a foretaste of future post-colonial Independence. Leading Bengali politicians, headed by Fazlul Haq, signed a letter and called a meeting 'to express the enthusiastic admiration of the people of Bengal for the people of China' and calling for Indians to show 'the same spirit of determination and fortitude in adversity as have the people of China over the past four and a half years'.[29] One-third of the world's population should stand side by side, the advocates of Indo-Chinese solidarity proclaimed. Chiang Kai-shek was making a bid to reconcile Indian leaders to the war effort, believing the future of China, and his own leadership of China, depended on an Allied victory which now hung in the balance. But he found his five-hour conversation with Gandhi on 18 February disappointing. 'My expectations were too great, but perhaps the pain of being ruled by the British has hardened his heart . . . he knows and loves only India, and doesn't care about other people and places.'[30] There was mutual incomprehension between the two men, and Gandhi's non-violent principles could not be squared with the Chinese war leader. Indian nationalism was now, in any case, outstripping any other forms of pan-national solidarity or cosmopolitanism that had been more ascendant in the 1930s. The emphasis was narrowing to a simple but powerful message, that the empire had to be swept aside, although the form of politics that would replace it was still highly uncertain.

Gandhi mentioned Burma repeatedly during these critical months and his speeches and writings became uncharacteristically angry. His new determination to see the British quit India can be directly linked to the fallout from Burma. 'Hundreds, if not thousands, on their way from Burma perished without food and drink, and the wretched discrimination stared even these miserable people in the face. One route for the whites, another for the blacks! Provision of food and shelter for the whites, none for the blacks! And discrimination even on their arrival in India!' an irate Gandhi told American journalists from *Time* and *Life* magazines. 'India is being ground down to dust and humiliated, even before the Japanese advent, not for India's defence – and no one knows for whose defence. And so one fine morning I came to the decision to make this honest demand: "For Heaven's sake leave India alone."'[31]

9

Urban Panic

There was a scramble now to put India on a war footing. A young Quaker volunteer, Richard Symonds, who had experience of the Blitz in London and was now living in Bengal, recalled how 'with a strong sense of urgency' he helped to set up air raid shelters, dispensaries, fire-fighting units, first aid posts, ambulance services and information points for those whose homes had been destroyed. He gathered thousands of volunteers armed with stirrup-pumps and buckets:

> The greatest danger of conflagration was in the vast *bustees* or shanty towns inhabited by the migrant population. During the day the men were out at work and their wives were too shy to volunteer, so we mainly recruited the prostitutes who were delighted to come forward and when I came on inspections, would greet me with the cry, 'Long live commander.' Why the Japanese did not continue the bombing is difficult to understand, for though the damage was small, the disruption was great.[1]

Panic had gripped people who rightly feared that the country was about to fall under attack, that their property and land were not safe and that their subsistence livelihoods would be subject to the predation of either an incoming conquering force or a military backlash against Japan.

At this critical juncture, some Congressmen also took part in civil defence, raising their own People's Volunteer Brigade to carry out parallel functions. Bhulabhai Desai, a famed lawyer who would later defend the accused of the Indian National Army in their trial, presided over a civil defence committee, discussing air raid precautions in Bombay.[2] Gandhi also had to face the issue of what to suggest in the occurrence of invasion. He called for calm and equanimity. 'I would not like it to be said of us as a nation that we run about like madmen on approach of slightest danger ... while I was and am against Congressmen joining ARP I have never thought of or suggested that Congressmen should leave points of danger or fields of service.'[3] Elements of Churchillian rhetoric seeped into the speech of British and Indian leaders alike. Jinnah even paraphrased Lord Nelson: 'Islam expects every Mussalman to do his duty by his people and by his nation', he declared in March 1942.[4]

In Vizagapatam, Walchand's shipyard was standing empty, as it would do for several years, the local workers having abandoned their work and fled inland. Walchand had failed to foresee, along with many of the British imperial administrators, the vulnerability of India's eastern coast. The speed with which the Japanese now seized territory in South-East Asia and drew closer to the Raj's borders and coastline surprised Walchand, and overnight his shipyard became moribund. As the Japanese advanced in Burma and South-East Asia, the blue bay of Vizagapatam looked exposed, and the atmosphere changed to one of apprehension.

Parents, as anywhere in the world, fretted about evacuation and securing the future well-being of their young. The evacuation of children in Britain was organised by the state, but in India people made their own arrangements, drawing on the resources of large, widespread extended families. The writer Kamala Das remembers in her memoir of childhood how she was sent away from her parents in Calcutta to live in a family village in Malabar, a strange and disconcerting adjustment at first. A schoolgirl from a prosperous family, Sulochana Simhadri, remembered the foreboding atmosphere in the Vizagapatam of her childhood, the blackouts, rations and panics, which now bore some resemblance to the British home front:

We were scared of war as we are afraid of bombing by enemy countries. We used to live near the sea coast of Visakhapatnam. Defence services used to have coastal batteries, anti-aircraft guns and searchlights. Every week they used to practise firing into the sea. We used to watch as we were close by and get scared. We had training in Air Raid Precautions ... They used to signal by a siren warning so that we could take shelter. Sirens used to be short and

long, three or four times quickly. We used to keep food stored in
small boxes and also we used to keep large torchlights. We dug
trenches in our house deep in the garden and covered with planks
and palm leaves. We used to take packed food and go into [the
trenches] when we heard the siren and come out when we heard
the long signal that meant we were safe. So many houses had been
taken [requisitioned] to keep the army close to the sea. Soldiers used
to march in front of our houses. Our parents never allowed us out
of the house to protect us.

We had blackout throughout the city. City lights are covered with
black cardboard domes. No light to be seen in the night. In the houses
also we covered lights. Sometimes when air raid warning comes army
used to cut off power so that enemy planes cannot see. They used to
put searchlights into the sky whenever is needed.[5]

In April the government ordered Walchand to dismantle his prized
shipyard for fear of aerial attack. He was left with thousands of pounds'
worth of teakwood in the yard, which he was unable to transport to
Bombay. The industrialist's company initially rented a plot in the
neighbouring village of Anakapalli and constructed temporary housing
for labourers. But workers were in short supply, either fleeing bombing
or taking on risky but lucrative work on new Allied construction
projects. When the shipyard in Vizag was closed, the Scindia company
constructed a replacement yard at Mazagaon in Bombay, transported
employees and railway-wagonloads of materials across central India
and commenced construction there instead.

All was not well with the Indian war effort. People could justifiably
point to the lack of shelters and there were no proper arrangements
to protect people in the event of aerial bombing. Thousands of pounds
were allocated for the construction of a state-of-the art reinforced
shelter under the Viceroy's House. A handful of elite administrators
dug and installed Anderson shelters in their bungalows, but for the
population at large such protection was never a possibility. The Secretary
of State for India, Leo Amery, was asked in the House of Commons
about what kind of protection was available for Indians and had to
publicly admit that people were making do with trench shelters. 'In
the main', he told his fellow politicians, in the case of aerial bombardment, 'resort will probably be had to dispersal of the population from

crowded areas to temporary camps.'[6] It was just simply, in the words
of one official, a 'physical impossibility' to construct deep shelters to
give protection from bombs and the cost of reinforcing the structure
of private dwellings was 'prohibitive'.[7]

Air raid precautions now absorbed much time and money, particularly in eastern India but also in all the major cities. Paying people to
come out as air raid wardens was proving one way to make the service
function. ARP profiteering was not uncommon, and as with other
police functions, the opportunity to impose fines on people came with
added advantages. In Cawnpore the recruitment of ARP wardens was
proving 'peculiarly difficult', and in the Central Provinces and Berar,
the response to the call for wardens was 'poor in the extreme'. In
Ranchi it was explained that it was difficult to get ARP volunteers
because local people had heard that if you signed up you might be
sent to the front in Europe and even those voluntary personnel who
did join 'almost invariably declined' to sign anything on paper. In
Raipur a Deputy Commissioner issued personal letters to fifty people
inviting them to work as wardens and only three replied.[8] In Parliament
Amery continued to answer questions on the subject of the protection
of Indians and confidently assured his audience that 'there is abundant
willing co-operation from the general population with the work being
done', although he knew as well as anyone that in reality this was far
from the case. By the end of the year, not a single province had met
its target for recruiting air raid wardens.[9] Fire-fighting equipment was
substandard and years out of date; in Bombay the fire service resorted
to retrieving some hoses dating from 1859 from the local museum.
Many factory shelters in the cities were stinking, filled with rubbish
or used as latrines. These pits had little appeal to factory workers who
were ordered to stay in them during air raid warning signals but were
unable to join their families or to bring them into the shelters. Many
people were suspicious of official information about potential air raids,
and preferred to listen to rumour: 'Don't believe what people tell you
about what happened in Burma', instructed one pamphlet issued for
factory workers. 'You can get absolutely true and reliable news from
the factory news bulletin or broadcasts.'[10] The priority was to keep
these men at work.

*   *   *

Japanese civilians living in India now joined the inmates of POW camps. The police seized a Japanese follower of Gandhi, who had taken the name Keshav. He had become a Gandhian follower in 1935 and remained in India, living the life of a devotee in Gandhi's ashram. The police turned up with no warning and seized him in front of Gandhi, much to the Mahatma's repugnance.[11] A local Japanese manager of a steamship company in Bombay, Hirozi Uemura, hanged himself, and was widely suspected of leaking information about the schedule of ships leaving Bombay harbour.

Some 3,000 Japanese civilians captured in Singapore, including women and children, were also arriving in India by the end of the year. A large camp was set up in the grounds of the old Mughal site in Delhi, Purana Qila, housing 2,115 Japanese in basic tents, exposed to Delhi's extremes of heat and cold, susceptible to beriberi, dysentery and other diseases. One hundred and six died, including nine children, and a number of women, despite earlier protests by the Japanese government about the inadequacy of their accommodation. This incident (although well hidden from public view at the time) embittered relations between the two imperial enemies in the East even further, prefiguring Allied treatment at camps like Changi in the Japanese-occupied areas later in the war.[12]

There was ambivalence among many Indians about this new 'enemy'. A number of Indian intellectuals had long taken an interest in Japan and the Japanese, particularly since the defeat of Russia in 1905; Japan was the country which proved, in the eyes of many, that Asians could 'modernise' and 'develop', that Asians could rise to the military challenge and equal European firepower, or aspire to a form of global modernism. For some, there was a mythic, though as it turned out largely ungrounded, sense of solidarity with the idea of Japan, expressed, for instance, in the paintings of Tagore's nephew, Abanindranath Tagore, that had been influenced by Japanese landscapes and calligraphy. Others believed in a form of racial solidarity, again perhaps more imagined than real, but pervasive and persuasive nonetheless. 'When I went to Japan, the Japanese treated me on terms of equality; they looked after me right royally in smart high-class tourist shelters like the Imperial Hotel; wherever I went out I was entertained with honour and respect', remembered Walchand Hirachand, a number of years later.

In England on the other hand every hotel I went to would be found 'full up'. Big merchants and industrialists had no desire to invite me to their homes. Even in America, hoteliers would tell me that they 'didn't allow blacks'. So what sort of feelings are men like me going to have about people like those?[13]

In India, among those who heard Subhas Chandra Bose's first broadcast in February 1942, there was an exhilarating thrill of a new world order which might challenge the hegemonic power of Europe over the East that had shaped life since the eighteenth century. 'This is Subhas Chandra Bose, speaking to you over the Azad Hind Radio. For about a year I have waited in silence and patience for the march of events and now that the hour has struck, I come forward to speak.' Bose chose to speak out publicly for the first time since he went underground because of the wave of Japanese victories. 'The fall of Singapore means the collapse of the British Empire, the end of the iniquitous regime which it has symbolised and the dawn of a new era in Indian history.'[14] Bose remained convinced at this point in the war that the Axis powers would help to liberate India by initiating a new world order and gave strong voice to this view:

> The Tripartite Powers – Germany, Italy and Japan – through whom this consummation will be brought about, are accordingly our natural friends and allies. It is the blackest lie to say that these Powers constitute a menace to India. From my intimate knowledge of these three nations, I can assert on the contrary that they have nothing but sympathy and goodwill for India and for Indian Independence.[15]

Like a deus ex machina, Bose's appearance at the critical hour and his cry of faith, unity and discipline was a reassuring godsend for many in the uncertain and threatening days of 1942. Although much of the population at large still felt uncertain about what invasion might entail, he simplified the political task ahead and reduced it to one basic mission – the ejection of the British – and persuaded many Indians that they did not have the same reasons as the British to fear the Japanese. Instead, he encouraged his listeners to relish the breakdown of the old status quo.

When local people did become fearful about the threat of invasion, as rumours of imminent Japanese attack grew more plausible and realistic, panics were localised, and failed to connect with British orders and commands. There was a gap in communication between the government and the public and people made their own arrangements, without reference to the orders emanating from the District Magistrate or local police. The Blitz spirit of wartime British cities, the cheerful if mythic ideal of community united in resistance to the enemy, was entirely absent. Instructions and pamphlets told factory workers how to conduct themselves in a shelter: don't crowd out space, obey your shelter marshal, do not leave until he gives the word, 'Try a little singing. It will keep your spirits up.'[16] But these instructions and models had been directly imported from blitzed London and had far less resonance among the Indian population, already struggling with more pressing daily concerns of subsistence amidst rampant inflation.

This elusive but significant feeling of a war not properly understood or appreciated troubled the imperial administrators throughout the 1940s in India. Accompanying this was the attempt to emulate tried and tested methods from the British home front, to export diagrams, manuals and handbooks directly to the Indian public with the concession of translations into local vernaculars. The problem, mused one official, was that the material coming from Delhi was 'very academic'. Euphemistically, he cited the 'different' conditions of India, without putting his finger on the vast iniquities of income and living standard.

> I retain an uneasy feeling that our system is too much an attempt to copy methods which have proved effective in 'blitzed' British cities (which are inevitably copied very badly) and that with the material at our disposal and our conditions we want something rather different, possibly a more diffused effort with a greater concentration on the prevention of casualties.[17]

Ian Hay Macdonald, now engaged in ARP work, wrote to his parents, 'It is all based on British experience – many think that a far better model would be the Chinese cities, which have been bombed, as they are much more like Indian towns.'[18]

Gradually more expensive air raid equipment was produced and large buildings in Calcutta were requisitioned as shelters. The government used films, light shows, puppetry and loudspeakers to educate the public. But despite this, protection remained extremely patchy and was most effective in places attached to essential services and industries.

People fled inland, away from the eastern coastline. *Marwaris* and other business people had been the first to leave, pushing up rental prices and creating a small rental boom in the lush lands around Conjeevaram and Chittoor. Government officials sped to the hill resort of Ooty. Local administrators and officials, told that they did not need to stay on the spot if the city was endangered, fled. This sliced through all sections of society in several eastern port towns too; over half of the total population of Vizagapatam had gone by the end of January 1942. Madras was particularly chaotic and lost 20 to 30 per cent of its total population, initially women and children, and later on the men. This steady flow of migrants continued into February and early March, when the government advised people to leave Madras 'as soon as they conveniently could'.[19] Then in early April, there was a day when the Governor believed that the Japanese invasion had actually commenced, having been told by Southern Command that 'a large Japanese force was on its way to South India', and called for a public evacuation of all remaining non-essential residents in the city. The whole administration except for a skeletal staff and the greater proportion of the city packed up and left. Convoys of vehicles, bullock carts and people trudging on foot away from the city stretched many miles inland. There was chaos at Central and Egmore Railway Stations where people converged, trying to get aboard specially commissioned trains. In just one day on 8 April, railway tickets to the value of 50,000 rupees were sold in Madras, before it was announced that the trains would actually be free of charge. Businesses packed up wholesale, and removed their entire stocks. Many people had family or ancestral villages to flee to, and Vellore, about ninety miles west of Madras, was a popular destination, but government-operated refugee camps also sprang up in at least six places on the outskirts of the city, housing several thousand between them. The Governor, Arthur Hope (who remained behind in the beleaguered city), reported on the panic that afflicted Britons and Indians in equal measure as people as far afield as the hills of Ootacamund 'gave way to sheer terror'.[20]

This debacle compounded the sense of an administration no longer in control of the fate of the people, and the Congress inevitably seized on this 'astonishing exhibition of panic and incompetence in Madras'.

For those who did remain in the city, food supplies ran low and milk was in desperately short supply. Government advertisements for emergency co-operative shops ran with the less than reassuring headline 'Madras Will Not Starve!' Regulations extended across the city, to try to secure air raid precautions, food supply and public health. The animals in Madras Zoo were taken out one by one and shot dead on government orders, in the apprehension of wild animals roaming the streets of a bombarded and desolate city. Even the cremation of the dead was now controlled and had to be completed in the morning, so that the flares of the pyre did not attract the attention of enemy pilots.[21]

Gandhi, who suggested evacuation to villages as the best protection from bombs, also encouraged the flight inland from the coastal cities. People fled to the relative safety of West and inland India, often finding housing with distant relatives. Towns and cities along the eastern coastline became desolated for a time. Chittagong was described by Field Marshal Bill Slim, now plotting his recapture of Burma, as a 'melancholy place':

> It had not been badly knocked about, but the light bombing it had suffered had driven out a large part of its inhabitants. Those who remained, the poorest, were menaced by approaching famine. The railway workshops, formerly the chief industry of the town, had been dismantled when it looked as if the Japanese would advance into Bengal and even the roofs had been removed. The docks, whose demolition had been stopped just in time, were a brighter spot. Under the energetic drive of Hallet, the naval officer in charge, and of some devoted civilians, the quays were beginning to show great activity. In peace, Chittagong must have been one of the most attractive of the larger towns of Bengal; now, its general air of neglect, stagnation and apprehension was depressing.[22]

*　　*　　*

As Malaya and Indochina fell to the Japanese, the Indians of South-East Asia, caught between rebel and imperial armies and living in archipelagos with complex ethnic mosaics, had to make rapid decisions. Many of them had been away from mainland India for generations. Some had scratched a living on Malayan rubber plantations or grown rice, while others lived more comfortably in Singapore or Hong Kong as moneylenders or traders. Different Indian communities looked to

India as 'home' to varying degrees. The Japanese challenge to white superiority initially looked bracing and dynamic, drawing together Burma, Indochina, Malaya, Hong Kong and the Philippines into one Asian bloc, but, as the historian Sunil Amrith puts it, 'The sense of possibility that many Asians felt in the first flush of Japanese victory soon soured'.[23] Now, as the Japanese armies swept forward, Indians in South-East Asia became vulnerable to forced labour, to the predations of hungry armies on the march and to aerial bombardment. The realities of life in wartime, as the old imperial system crumbled and gave way to a new one, splintered the economy. Some workers fled upcountry or into interior jungle. Often they were cut off from their old markets or family connections across the Indian Ocean, and the future soon looked uncertain. A great question mark fell over the future citizenship rights of Indians in South-East Asia. Compared with other ethnic groups such as the Chinese, who suffered very heavily at Japanese hands, many Indians had a strategic advantage. Some positioned themselves successfully as local agents for the new power, whether driven by ideology or by hunger. This could be a matter of life and death; access to food was easier for pro-Japanese Indian Independence Leaguers in Singapore and Malaya and they soon started to control rations and passes. They could intercede with Japanese officials and take forward petitions and complaints. As in Burma, decisions to flee or stay turned on contacts and swift calculations. Building strategic alliances with the invading power was simply a matter of survival in some cases.[24]

The Indian Ocean was not an abstract geographical feature for those Indians settled along the coastlines of eastern India; oriented outwards, to the sea, the ocean was the source of life: it sustained daily life for fishermen, and was the gateway to South-East Asia for traders. Many of the Indians living in Malaya and Burma were drawn from trading communities scattered around India; they had sailed around and along the coastline, selling, buying, marrying and visiting kin. Other Indians had investments and business interests tied up in Malaya, Thailand and Burma. A number of districts depended heavily on remittances from kin employed overseas in South-East Asia and these chains of remittance were now dramatically severed. The sweeping Indian Ocean network was broken.

Occupied South-East Asia was a strange twilight world for Indians caught between two imperial masters, and a world in which political allies could be fickle and the borderline between the Indian Army, the INA and civilian life was sometimes surprisingly porous. Sepoys went undercover as waiters, porters and merchants. 'Numerous cases are coming to light of stragglers from Burma who maintain that they have never actually been prisoners in Japanese hands but who have spent varying periods in enemy occupied territory before returning to India', said one War Office report.[25] People darted between borders and in and out of the employment of the army; some soldiers deserted the Indian Army in Burma or became separated from their units and returned home as civilian refugees, only to turn up at their regimental centres again after many months.

The strength of the INA was undoubtedly built on the bedrock of local support from Indians resident in Malaya, who provided money and thousands of men for the cause and had already established a powerful Indian Independence League. The Indian National Army was forged at Farrer Park in Singapore just days after the fall of Singapore, and its existence was formally proclaimed in April 1942. Although the core of the INA constituted soldiers captured by the Japanese in Malaya, and these men were promoted as the INA officers, ultimately – once Subhas Chandra Bose took over the INA's leadership – up to half of the 43,000 foot soldiers of the INA came from the local Indian population of rubber plantation workers, paddy cultivators and merchants, including Tamils, Punjabis and Orissans.

Among the Indian population of South-East Asia, in mosques, temples and *gurdwaras*, in marketplaces and public halls, Indians – living in tight-knit communities – weighed up their options. Rumours spread about Japanese brutalities in prisoner-of-war camps, of the conditions at the front, of the factions in the first INA, under Mohan Singh, which was fragmenting into acrimonious schisms. Relationships faltered under suspicions and accusations. Although starvation on the scale of Bengal did not take place, malnutrition and extreme deprivation were common as well as the extreme conditions of forced labour on the Thai–Burma railway.

In some cases, Indian Army soldiers felt heavy pressure to join the INA against their will. Others took shelter when and where they could, or decided to leave the army altogether and to attempt to find stability as civilians in the complex conditions of Japanese-occupied South-East Asia. Personal bonds or circumstances could drive people into unusual alliances. One Mr Govindasamy, a Tamil sepoy in Singapore, deserted and found work with a Chinese merchant. He was taken in as a member of the family, living and working in the shop. Despite pressure to join the INA from his Indian friends, Mr Govindasamy sympathised with the Chinese and their sufferings, ultimately joining the Chinese-led resistance army, often carrying messages for them and eventually losing a leg. He was able to dodge detection, living in hiding in the jungle, carrying out guerrilla attacks on bridges, roads and railways.[26] Sepoy Abdul Matlab of 2/16 Punjab Regiment opened a tea shop at Serembam Railway Station and was earning his living there, and managed to avoid arrest by the Japanese or forced recruitment to the INA, attempting to carve out a peaceful existence in the midst of the war.[27] In many ways, Indian soldiers often felt far more inner conflict about joining the INA than the local populace, who solidly backed Bose, to the extent that one officer recalled that when he reached Bangkok at the end of the war, 'If you did not greet local Indians with "Jai Hind" they would not accept you as an Indian and they would treat you as a foreigner.'[28]

South Asians reproached the British for protecting their own welfare and securing escape routes for their own women and children first, an accusation that echoed across the press and in the chamber of the House of Commons, where Amery was challenged in Parliament on the matter. Muslim Leaguers who had remained relatively sympathetic to the British war aims recoiled at the 'shameful discrimination against Indian nationals' who had been arriving in their thousands daily, 'penniless and foodless'.[29]

What was the substance to the rumours? While discrimination was not all-encompassing or simplistic, it certainly existed and left a bitter legacy among those who experienced it. At certain crucial bottlenecks when leaving Burma, Europeans had been prioritised, accessing safe passage away from the Japanese and leaving Indians stranded. For instance, in Burma, while the Tamu–Palel Road had been closed to Indians, the British had been able to get through. In the administrative chaos the government had tried to prevent refugees from taking perilous paths, closing routes or redirecting them away from life-saving exit points. The chaotic scenes at the port of Rangoon became emblematic of a two-tier system based on racial privilege, as Indians were denied spaces as deck passengers. Despite this about 70,000 did make it onto the steamers. 'We left for Rangoon sometime in the end of

January 1942', Dr Krishnan Gurumurthy, the son of a Burma Railway manager, remembered:

> With great difficulty, my father managed to get steamer tickets to Madras. On the appointed date, we went to the Rangoon port to board the steamer and at the last moment fate again played its tricks. Just as everything was seemingly going well, we were denied entry into the steamer. By that time, the Japanese had advanced to the outskirts of Rangoon City, and the then British government thought that only the lives of the British and Anglo-Indians were worth saving and allowed only them to board the steamer. The rest of us were thrown out to fend for themselves.[30]

At root there was a colonial mentality upholding the layered hierarchies on which the imperial system in Burma depended. It underpinned 'the entire system of social relationships', concluded one credible observer, Martin Hillenbrand. Hillenbrand was a young American consular official in Rangoon at the time and kept a personal diary, 'full of anger' at the debacle. In a sober report to his superiors he noted:

> As one who witnessed the process of civil evacuation in Burma, the writer could not help noting that underlying the motivation of British evacuation officials was a concern pre-eminently for the safety of Europeans, secondly for the safety of Anglo Indians and lastly, for the safety of Indians. This was perhaps only natural since many of the officials engaged in evacuation work had their own families, relatives and personal friends to worry about.[31]

Compounding the sense of injustice, British welfare payments to non-Indian refugees in camps were paid at a higher rate, charged to the UK government directly.

At other times, discrimination was more coloured by class. Personal wealth and the ability to pay for fares on aircraft trumped skin colour, with wealthier Indians able to secure routes on aircraft and steamers. The Government of India considered an investigation or publishing a report into the question of discrimination in evacuation policy, but this was dropped once Linlithgow recognised that the findings would be potentially inflammatory rather than reassuring.[32]

The historian Indivar Kamtekar has made the argument that the 'credibility of the state' collapsed in early 1942 in the face of near invasion, and it is an argument worth reiterating. 'Though only a few voices are audible, mentally we can hear the chorus: invasion is imminent, the Japanese are coming, the British are set to flee . . . Who were the Japanese, these men who could humble an empire that had seemed all powerful? What awesome powers did they have?'[33] The approach of the Japanese was both concrete and illusory; it had repercussions on real resources and on the national psyche, the latter no less significant than the former. Real stories, mingled with half-truths and exaggerated rumours, reflected the loss of faith in the Raj as a plausible form of authority. Even if the Raj had never been actively *liked* in the past, at least it could be relied upon as a coherent administration, one that would keep its inhabitants reasonably secure from military incursion and underwrite the validity of currency and savings. Now, there was a widespread loss of faith in even the most basic functions of the imperial state.

10

The World at the Door

In 1942, new types of people arrived daily in Indian stations and ports; refugees, fresh recruits from Europe, Australasia and North America, even survivors from shipwrecks arrived on beaches. War and displacement were intricately interlinked. People decamped around the British Empire, often establishing new homes multiple times, trying to piece together some security, to find jobs and make a new life for their children. Flight was both forced and unforced and it was long- and short-term. It encompassed all the technical and legal categories of people who had moved – 'refugees', 'displaced persons', 'the stateless', 'expellees' and 'evacuees', as well as a great many more who never fell under these systems of categorisation or control, who escaped out from under the radar of the state. The refugee movements from Burma constituted the largest concentration of incoming people to India, but as the British Empire east of India collapsed there was a significant flow of people, of numerous ethnic, religious and national backgrounds, into the country. Many of the people who lived in India for a time in the 1940s have remained elusive in the historical record. This mass migration was also part of a wider story of population movement, death and dislocation during wartime and the long separations of families who did not see their fighting men for many years on end. The sight of new and quite distinctive people arriving in Indian ports and cities added to this sense of a state losing control of its population.

People arrived from South-East Asia but also from other parts of the world shattered by war. 'Few people realise that destitute people have been flocking here not only from the far east but also from the near and middle east', reported the Indian *Telegraph* in 1942:

There are also large numbers from the Balkans largely Greeks. The threat of war drives others from Persia, Somaliland, Djibuti and Aden. They include French, Austrians, Rumanians and Canadians. There are also numerous Anglo-Chinese, Anglo-Burmese and Anglo-Malayans. Many of the European refugees although holding British passports cannot speak a word of English.[1]

India had been a hub for pilgrimage and trade for many centuries; now it entered a new era of cosmopolitanism in the 1940s. These newcomers added to the challenge to uphold the prestige of the Raj, as the arrival of poor or destitute refugees from around the world symbolised the loss of imperial territories. They also held up a mirror to the fabrications of the Raj: colonial prosperity clearly did not depend on white skin, as Europeans could also be intensely vulnerable, fall into poverty and become victims of war.

Thousands of those who arrived in 1942 had come from war-torn Europe and the Middle East. About 600 Maltese arrived in India. They had travelled through Turkey, escaping their besieged island, which was caught in a protracted struggle between Allies and Axis. On the outskirts of Coimbatore, men and women cleared forest to make room for tents housing thousands of refugees from Greece and Malta, later sheltered in barracks in the grounds of a local college. The police surveilled 'Iraqi beggars' who had come overland, escaping the upheavals in the Middle East. The Muslim League even passed a resolution in support of Muslim Kazaks, arriving destitute from Soviet Russia.[2] Vast upheavals of population accompanied the Second World War on every continent and for some in Europe, India, despite all its own difficulties, looked like a potential safe haven, protected from the worst extremes of war on the European continent.

Around 10,000 Polish nationals found asylum in India, escaping from the cleansing policies of both Soviets and Nazis. Over 5,000 of the Poles were children who had undergone harrowing ordeals in the Soviet Union. Some had been the victims of earlier Soviet deportations to gulags in Siberia, Kazakhstan and central Asia. Aged between two and sixteen, most of the young had been through terrible hardships, orphaned or separated from their parents. Many had skin ulcers, rotten teeth, whooping cough and other afflictions. Evacuated under an Allied agreement with the Russians, via Ashkhabat in central Asia, and onwards to Tehran, some had managed to pick their way to safety; one seven-year-old boy, exiled to an Uzbek farm, carried his little sister on his shoulders over many miles after his parents had died of typhus, in order to reach the Red Cross evacuation point. Once picked up, most travelled in convoy trucks overland through Quetta and present-day Pakistan, then onwards by rail. On their long and difficult journeys, they received an unexpectedly warm welcome in India. 'In spite of their shaved heads and ill-fitting, tattered clothes, the children made a good impression, arousing genuine sympathy', reported the wife of the Polish Consul General to the Polish Red Cross. 'At many stops on their way to Bombay, local people greeted the children at the stations, treating them with sweets, fruits, cold drinks and toys.'[3] Their home for the next four years was a children's camp at Balachadi near Jamnagar, part of a princely state on the Kathiawar peninsula of western India. Maharaja Jam Sahib had opened his doors to the children, funding the camp and acting as a jovial father figure to the Poles in India.[4] He placed the camp in the shade of his own summer palace, close to the coast. The children found themselves living in ordered barrack-style camps in barely inhabited scrubland.

The orphans soon began to adapt to their new surroundings, and aroused considerable interest. Physically they had suffered terrible attrition and the *Times of India* reported how 'In spite of the abundance of food in the camp, the children remember the days of hunger during the war, and, unable to get rid of their fear that there might be no food the next day, they often hide bread or fruit under their pillows'.[5] Although now well fed the children remained vulnerable, prey to the spike in Indian summer temperatures and the dangers of malarial mosquitoes, and over 80 per cent of the children contracted malaria in the camp in 1942. Life was basic, regimented and mundane; there was little for the children to do other than to explore outside and climb trees. Polish religious and military leaders who staffed the camp lost little time in setting up schools, religious services, scouting groups and clinics. The children performed folk dances and Polish songs, encouraged to keep alive their cultural traditions, stitching folk dresses and braiding their hair with flowers.

Another large Polish refugee camp was also being constructed, hundreds of miles away, at Valivade near Kolhapur, this time for adults, including some families with children that had managed to stay united.

The Government of India hurriedly knocked up the camp at the lowest possible cost, under pressure to take Polish refugees against its own wishes. As Linlithgow had put it in a terse telegram: 'Take this number [of Polish refugees] despite difficulties. No guarantee in good all year climates. Old buildings e.g. disused barracks may be available, but if new required, because of materials shortage, we can guarantee only mud huts or tents or other accommodation below standard previously provided for prisoners of war, internees and evacuees.'⁶ Linlithgow, ever sensitive to the projection of imperial grandeur, was nervous about the diminished status of Europeans in the eyes of locals, and suggested that Poles should not come to India partly on the grounds of the 'humble' locations they would have to be housed in, such as refugee camps, convents and mission schools. The refugees unsettled the conservatives of the Raj as impoverished white Europeans on Indian streets became another visible sign that the white man was not invincible.

*   *   *

In the Andaman Islands, the Governor's difficulties had already begun. By the close of 1941, and the attack on Pearl Harbor, it was widely known in Delhi that it would be almost impossible to hold the Andamans from the Japanese and an evacuation plan was ostensibly put in motion for the islands. As the war tilted eastwards and the Japanese made their advance through Asia, this sleepy backwater was now under the threat of imminent invasion. The Governor, Charles Waterfall, was in a tight spot but heard little from Delhi. The Government of India would have gladly been rid of the responsibility to defend the islands altogether, but attempts to have the islands fall under a different area of command, so that they would be beyond the responsibility of Delhi, were rejected. As Waterfall waited patiently for ships to arrive throughout December, officials in New Delhi apologised for leaving him 'without news since the outbreak of the Japanese war'.⁷ By now shipping had been so badly disrupted that stocks of imported goods had started to run low on the island. The islands' supply officer, and Waterfall's friend, neighbour and right-hand man, Major Alfred George Bird, was seriously concerned about the need for 'brown sugar, salt, dal, wheat, flour,

rice, ghi, mustard oil, chillies, tamarind, tea, jam, pepper, cumin, cori-
ander, tinned meat'.

When Waterfall did finally hear from Delhi, the news was not
comforting. 'General staff do not consider Islands in imminent danger
of attack but air raids are likely', he was told, disingenuously; there
was no further suggestion of a plan to defend the islands: 'Government
of India have no doubt you and all concerned will do your best in
difficult circumstances and you have their full support in all reasonable
measures you consider necessary.'[8] On Christmas Eve Waterfall wrote
a letter to Delhi reporting on the evacuation of women and children.
Fifty-three children and thirty-three women had already sailed for
Calcutta. He was anticipating the worst. 'The settlement is quiet but
nervous. The convicts have so far behaved well. Our most serious
anxiety for the time being is shortage of supplies.'[9] He was optimistic
that lives would be saved if air raids took place; there was an air raid
scheme on the islands and people had been dispersed away from the
only real town centre.

> Property, of course, would be another matter as most of the buildings
> would burn like fireworks or collapse like a pack of cards. All the
> crowded parts of Aberdeen have been thinned out by sending those
> who can get away to distant villages. Convicts too, who are not required
> to work in headquarters have been moved to barracks in out stations
> . . . We will do our best to hold on but as you know we are woefully
> weak especially in equipment.[10]

The first air raids took place from 24 February and lasted for two days.

Over the following weeks, throughout January and February, ships
slowly made the return journey from the Andamans' Port Blair to
Calcutta, taking with them British and Indian officers, their families
and more junior officials. But what to do with the prisoners on the
islands? Shackled and kept on the lower decks, many of the prisoners
from the Cellular Jail were also evacuated back to mainland India as
the government feared that the prisoners would be a gift for the
Japanese if, and when, the invasion took place. After much indecision
and mixed feelings about where to send the prisoners ('Is Africa at all
a possibility?' scribbled one senior civil servant in the margins of a
document), ultimately the government shipped 171 of the 342 prisoners

back to Calcutta secretly and took them on to jails in central India. The prospect of these prisoners being shunted from dockside to police van, or shackled prisoners in transit being spotted by a passer-by, preoccupied the ICS officers who were deciding on their fate. As an officer in Bengal put it, 'If these prisoners were marched in handcuffs openly from the ship to the place of detention, there would be a sensation and nothing could prevent a crop of rumours.' A coded telegram was used to instruct the Government of Bengal to try to keep this matter as 'unostentatious as possible', and to ensure that 'contact with or exposure to public [was] avoided'. It was to be kept secret, completely out of the newspapers.[11]

Alfred Bird and Charles Waterfall waited behind on the islands. Before they could board one of the last ships, the Japanese captured the Andaman Islands on 23 March 1942. In India, officials lost contact with the Governor and admitted in a public statement that they feared for his welfare and did not know if he was 'dead or alive'. Waterfall had in fact been taken captive by the Japanese and would be a prisoner himself until the end of the conflict.[12]

*   *   *

Twenty-four-year-old Bhajan Singh was one of these top-secret secur-ity prisoners sent back to mainland India from the Cellular Jail in February 1942. He was not only a prisoner but also a former soldier, a sepoy of the Central India Horse, recruited from a typical Sikh agricultural tract in Punjab. Among the prisoners on the Andamans who had been convicted for civil crimes, like murder, lived these military prisoners, described by one official as 'lost sheep', convicted by court martial and sentenced to transportation. Convicted for mutiny in Trimulgherry, South India, and sentenced to transportation for ten years (he had already served two years in the penal colony), Bhajan was heavy with regret. He may also have been feeling relieved to be back on the mainland. Above all, he dreamed of reprieve and of being allowed to rejoin military service. Bhajan Singh was remorseful, lamenting his crime as a 'foolish act' of a 'young man'.[13] Piqued at not getting promoted, he had failed to carry out transfer orders when stationed in July 1940 in the Deccan with the Central India Horse, 21st Cavalry. He claimed he 'was partially under the influence of liquor, and had no idea that his act amounted to Mutiny'. He also regretted having 'joined bad company . . . thus being led astray'. His crime was refusing orders.[14]

Guards bundled Bhajan Singh and his fellow prisoners into vans on arrival in Calcutta's port and they were taken to the Presidency Jail while train arrangements were made. Within days they boarded the Bombay Mail for central India. They had been in transit for about a month, and while preferable to the isolation and eerie strangeness of the Andamans, the Central Provinces must have still felt a long way from Bhajan Singh's home village in Amritsar in Punjab. And there was little prospect of any visit from a family member. On hearing of his 'delinquencies' his father, Bhuta Singh, in all likelihood a former soldier himself, had disowned him. Bhajan Singh's mercy petition, written from Nagpur Central Jail, conveys the angst of the young soldier who 'came from a thoroughly Loyalist family and feels very ashamed of himself'. To further reassure the Crown of their loyalty, his father immediately on hearing 'the bad news' had his younger son, and nephew, enlisted for active service. This was a family with long-standing ties to the Indian Army that had 'rendered loyal military service during the great war'. Singh's great hope was that, at a time of expanding recruitment and war overseas, he could implore his way to freedom. His conduct in jail had been 'good' and 'quiet', unlike others who were considered violent or had turned to hunger strikes.

> Your petitioner further assures Your Excellency [his petition continued] that should your pardon be extended to him, that he is prepared to show his loyalty, and atonement for his faults, by immediately proceeding on Active Service anywhere out of India, and further swears to be loyal to the Crown for ever after . . . your petitioner feels that he could be of better use in this world by fighting for the cause of freedom, and is prepared to die for his King . . . give him another chance to show that his above request to fight once more is no idle boast. For this act your petitioner will be ever grateful.[15]

The letter was signed in Urdu in blue ink and the assistant jailer read aloud a translation to Bhajan Singh.

Bhajan Singh's timing was fortunate. Both the fall of the Andamans to the Japanese and the growing need for trained young men in the military worked in his favour. He had won the sympathy of the jail board, which recommended that sepoys like him might have learned 'wisdom' and be better returned to service than kept in detention. In addition, and decisively, there was growing pressure on heaving Indian jail populations; the government did not want the cost or the inconvenience of military prisoners in its keeping and preferred it if they were returned to the Indian Army where, many of the men pleaded, they rightfully belonged.

Military prisoners added strain to the civil jails, which were already struggling under the weight of the arrests for civil disobedience. Jails in Bombay were 'desperately overcrowded' owing to the civil disobedience movement and had 15,800 prisoners in a space allotted for 11,700. Even the extensions to jails started to overflow. Prisoners from the Indian Army added pressure: 'the number was reported in October last to be of the order of 400 but it is believed to have nearly doubled since', recorded Bombay's provincial prison governor.[16] This reached a crisis point in 1943 when a peculiar and virulent epidemic swept through Belgaum Central Jail, in present-day Karnataka, killing an unspecified but significant number of inmates. 'An alarming proportion' of the attacks proved fatal, and the disease was never identified, although it was attributed to overcrowding.[17] This was a turning point. The war effort could not spare healthy military men any longer and the provincial and national governments demanded to be spared the cost of maintaining them in their own prisons. In 1943, two new military prisons were established for those 'whose ultimate return to the army is considered worth attempting'.[18]

*   *   *

With half of the prisoners evacuated, by February it was clear that the Andamans were lost. Everything of use was pulled out as quickly as possible: mules, lorries, ammunition, fuel and electrical equipment. Harbours were mined, mills and airstrips destroyed. Government servants left on the HMS *Maharaja*, which plied back and forth to Calcutta, but also by BOAC aeroplane and motor boat. A handful of British and Indian officials waited behind, alongside the remaining motley population of local cultivators and former convicts. On 22 March ships were sighted off the coast and on the 23rd the Japanese landed on Ross and Snake islands. The Japanese occupation was swift and initially bloodless; a single cannon shot was fired, the police station was disarmed, Japanese sentries were posted at strategic points, and the remaining British officials taken back to Ross Island, a pitiful shadow of its former self. In a grand if reckless populist gesture, the Japanese invaders opened the doors of the Cellular Jail and the prisoners were allowed to go free. However, the prisoners immediately started raiding villages for food and women, and the Japanese shot at these free prisoners within hours of their release. Ten thousand Japanese soldiers now occupied the islands.

Ambivalence and silence still fall over the Japanese occupation of the Andamans, partly because of a shortage of archival sources and partly because of the contested and controversial nature of the Japanese presence, in which some local inhabitants became actively aligned with the occupiers, while others suffered torture and repression. Some entrepreneurial individuals ingratiated themselves with the new regime and became important functionaries, sitting on committees and having access to goods and to Japanese language classes. They worked with the Japanese to maintain rice cultivation and to make the relationships between Japanese and Indian more functional. At the same time rumours of horrible tortures spread, and labourers were compelled to labour on airstrips and in the docks. The public execution of a young man, Zulfiqar Ali, who had fired at Japanese soldiers when they chased local chickens in the village of Aberdeen, chilled the local onlookers, who watched his bones being broken before the firing squad. One witness later recalled how as a child he was 'fascinated with the way a Japanese soldier could throw about Zulfiqar, almost in the manner of the *dhobi*, the Indian washerman, pounding clothes'.[19] Another notable act of brutality, the public execution of Waterfall's friend and colleague Major Bird, was also watched with horror by the locals, who had warmed to the British official, who spoke fluent Hindustani, and had nicknamed him Chiriya, after his surname. Brought to the public square with a sign reading 'traitor' hung around his neck, after a public demonstration of vicious body blows, his head was severed by one blow from a sword.

The Japanese had also been optimistic about pan-Asian solidarity but these hopes fizzled out quickly once dealing with the complicated, eccentric local community, which was accustomed to habits and patterns of British imperial rule. The Japanese frustrations grew as Allied air raids increased in success and intensity and cut supply lines from South-East Asia, making it harder to feed the population and the occupying army.

The Andamans occupy a special place in colonial history as an island penal settlement. Ultimately, it was the only place occupied in India during the Second World War.

II

Thirty Months Too Late

The general feeling by now in India was one of despair and disen-franchisement, of political stagnation and lack of freedom to determine decisions. The complete breakdown of trust was threatening the continued existence of the empire, potentially the whole war effort. A political response was needed, and politicians in London, grasping the gravity of the situation, reacted at last. Sir Stafford Cripps, the independently minded lawyer and Labour politician, had completed a world tour in 1940, including the USSR, China and India. He had a reputation for robust fair-dealing, his personal star was rising and he volunteered to try to settle the constitutional crisis and broker a deal between Indian politicians and the British government. He arrived in Karachi on 23 March 1942. Although the Cripps Mission has generated much attention ever since, significantly at the time of Cripps's arrival in India he was not greeted with much fanfare or anticipation of success.

Jaded by the tumultuous changes of early 1942, the Indian public response was wary. This austere member of the British War Cabinet did not capture the public imagination in the way that would be necessary to turn the tide of public feeling in 1942 (and in contrast to the Cabinet Mission Plan of 1946, which Cripps also led and which would at least draw on the euphoria of war's end and demobilisation, although it too ultimately failed). The diplomatic effort was a contingency measure born out of the particular crisis that the British Empire faced in early 1942.

The week of Cripps's arrival in India, he was competing for space in the newspapers with many other headlines: Soviet advances and fierce fighting on the Russian front; the increased tempo of the air war in the Far East; and recent news of intense battles over Malta and

British bombers over Essen. *The Statesman* of Calcutta was running stories that week entitled, 'If Britain Is Invaded' and 'America Wakes up to Total War'. The very week Cripps arrived in India, Vizagapatam was bombed. Bad news flowed from Burma, including the reports of selective evacuation of white people and the vague promise of a government inquiry into the matter at some point in the future. Stories of Indians refused entry to bomb shelters also circulated in Calcutta. Something had to be done to show British goodwill towards India. But Cripps's mission was not built on a groundswell of support for reconciliation and co-operation with the British. He met hand-picked senior Indian politicians, but he did not consult widely, unwisely leaving major industrialists and businessmen like G. D. Birla absent from his itinerary. This gave the impression of trying to secure a fait accompli. The Congress remained cagey about intentions and deliberately minimised expectations. 'As everything is nebulous about Sir Stafford Cripps's proposals, nothing can be said but the Congress Working Committee will give its thought to them if they are worth considering', Abul Kalam Azad told reporters. 'The whole business will be finished soon if nothing substantial is immediately granted.'[1]

In Britain too, the expectations for Cripps's prospects of success were suspiciously low and built on the idea that the mission was born out of necessity rather than goodwill. Orwell noted in his diary that people in Britain, both the ignorant and the well-informed about India, were 'gloomy' and 'pessimistic' about the chances of full Independence for India even before Cripps set foot in the subcontinent. Orwell would later describe the whole affair as 'a bubble blown by popular discontent'.[2]

Cripps had a cordial pre-war relationship with Nehru, but in the intervening years, the gulf had continued to widen between British and Indian perspectives on the war. And now Cripps had staked his own ascendant reputation by attempting to make a deal in India. He was careful to distinguish himself from Linlithgow, moving out of the Viceroy's Palace, and joking amicably with Gandhi in front of reporters. The prospect of reconciling the British and Indian nationalists was picked up on by the Japanese and even featured in propaganda dropped in leaflets on the eastern theatre: 'Sir Stafford Cripps is no angel!' one leaflet proclaimed.[3]

There was little risk of a Cripps–Congress front countering the
Japanese, however. The unforgiving editorial verdict in one Indian
newspaper was closer to the mark: the mission had come thirty
months too late.

The arguments over the details of what exactly was promised and
why it was rejected still rage on. Even basic clarity about the diplomacy and what was on offer could not be achieved, then or now, and
the charges of propaganda-friendly gesture politics, rather than a real
attempt at solving the problem, persist. Once a proposal to give more
power to Indian politicians was announced the vernacular press
remained lukewarm, commenting on 'jarring elements', 'significant
gaps' and 'complete dissatisfaction' with the plans. 'The proposed
transfer of all power minus defence will be like playing Hamlet
without the Prince of Denmark', announced the *Bharatadevi* of
Madras. 'The sooner the British government shed the distrust
complex, the better for all concerned.'[4] The impression among the
public was that something akin to dominion status could have been
achieved mid-war, but only with the defence portfolio withheld. But
as the legal, economic and social structure of the Raj was at that
moment completely dominated and geared to defence, it is little
wonder that this offer rang hollow and could no longer satisfy
Congress under the radically transformed conditions of war. In
addition, the threat that any province might be able to opt out of a
new constitution risked the fragmentation of the centralised Indian
state. A strong, centralised state had long been the ultimate Congress
vision and prize.

Under the Defence of India Act, defence and power had become
synonymous in India. Truly non-violent Gandhians could hardly take
part in leading a warring state. Other Congress leaders could barely
see the advantage of falling in line with the Allies, when the Japanese
looked likely to win in any case, and they were unwilling to be jointly
responsible for the economic and social fiasco unfolding in India. To
put it plainly, supporting the Allied war effort had simply become too
politically unpopular and risky in India. In a public radio broadcast,
as he admitted failure and prepared to leave India, Cripps also conceded
that the plan faltered on the 'wrangle over defence'.[5] Both the mission's
rationale and its failure can be explained only by the daily drama of
war in India in early 1942.

This was a decisive turning point. Coercive measures to ensure success against the Japanese could now be sanctioned without hesitation. As far as Churchill was concerned, Indians had turned their backs on collaboration. 'We can now go ahead with the war with a clear conscience', Amery noted in his diary; political collaboration had been attempted and found impossible, so from now on the government could focus on extracting resources for the war effort without compunction.[6] Churchill continued to demonise Indians, championing an unbending diehard imperialism and showing an irrational and offensive hatred of the country. He cheered at the growing signs of division between Hindus and Muslims and declared he would 'sooner give up political life at once, or rather go out into the wilderness and fight, than admit a revolution that meant the end of the Imperial Crown in India'.[7] From now on, the government would sideline any resolution of the political question as an irrelevance while prioritising victory at all costs. The war was being imposed on India without consultation or further negotiation, disconnected from indigenous sentiments and priorities, reversing years of hard-won stakes in the political system. To more and more people the costs of defeating the Japanese seemed higher than the gains.

★   ★   ★

Relationships between Hindus and Muslims continued to deteriorate. This was Jinnah's moment. 'The war which nobody welcomed', he would later say with candour, 'proved to be a blessing in disguise.'[8] Piqued at the start of the decade by the Viceroy's attentiveness to Gandhi's views, by 1940 Jinnah was equally frank about how he had been 'suddenly promoted' in the eyes of the British.[9] War was exacerbating the divisions between different ethnic groups in the country, with the ever-increasing alienation of Muslims from the Congress nationalists. The earlier failure of the Congress to fully articulate an inclusive vision of Indian nationalism, particularly during the enthusiastic heyday of the Congress ministries in 1938, was now rebounding on the movement. The resignation of the Congress ministries in the immediate crisis following the declaration of war in 1939 had been announced as a 'Day of Deliverance' for Indian Muslims and Jinnah had taken every opportunity since then to reiterate the perceived threat of Hindu domination and a Hindu Raj should Congress come to power. He was carefully welding together a coalition, appealing across diverse regional leaderships to try to bring the Muslim majority provinces into the Muslim League fold, courting the loyalty of landowners and spiritual leaders or *pirs* who could steer their followers towards the league.

The sharp upswing in support for the Muslim League was noticeable in the streets of many small towns of North India: in the strings of green bunting and green and white flags, the pictures and images of Jinnah installed in modest homes, the Muslim League National Guards in uniform parading through towns, and the scale and theatrical flair of rallies and demonstrations in support of the league. A new and virulent support for the league was also becoming obvious in the Urdu press. Manzoor Quraishi, working for the government as an ICS officer, was troubled by a visit in 1942 from his younger brother, who was a student at Aligarh Muslim University, an institution where Quraishi had also studied several years earlier: 'From his talks, and to my shock, it looked that the entire atmosphere of the Aligarh Muslim University Campus had changed completely by 1942 to become pro Muslim League and Pakistan.'[10] Another sign of Jinnah's rising star was the fanfare now accompanying league processions and rallies, and their new scale. The league could now summon thousands onto the roadsides, often with the accompaniment of musicians, camels, horses and armed bodyguards, illuminations and loudspeakers. New calendar dates challenged the older rituals of the Congress: Jinnah's Birthday and Pakistan Day now rivalled the birthdays of Congress leaders and the annual festivities that accompanied them. Jinnah was welcomed in Quetta, one government source commented, like a 'royal potentate'.[11]

Jinnah was not the only one to benefit from the rising tide of public fervour, however. Everywhere a new militarism, and the protection of militias and clubs, was becoming commonplace. The link to wartime conditions was explicit. 'In view of the grave world situation and its possible repercussions on India,' noted the Muslim League Working Committee, 'every community is organising its volunteer organisations for the defence of its life and property.'[12] Everywhere, a new martial spirit was entering public spaces. From communists to Hindu nationalists, Khaksars to pseudo-ARP groups, there was a rapid and noticeable flowering of associations and clubs which championed self-defence, drilling and self-discipline.[13] Women and men drilled with flags, *lathis* and daggers, wore distinctive uniforms and badges, sang songs and staged public dramas and lectures. Historians have noted the uneasy similarities with some of the European expressions of fascism, particularly the acceptability of violence as a political method and the global turn towards a new rhetoric of death and sacrifice in the context of war. This also meant that real servicemen and pseudo-soldiers could blur in the crowd. 'In Bombay, I remember in those days, due to this war, military clothes and military uniform were available', recalled Ram Krishna, a Punjabi Congressman and post-Independence chief minister of the province. He donned a uniform in 1942, 'then boarded a train and left for Punjab'. In this case, Krishna was evading the police as a fugitive, but his comments are suggestive of the ways in which civil and military appearances could be deceptively similar in 1940s India.[14] On *maidans* and along main thoroughfares political militias, armed groups and party functionaries could be seen at public gatherings, fired up by evocative slogans and extolling their leaders. In the vanguard stood lawyers, bureaucrats and shopkeepers, members of a new urban middle class in India. Men much like my own paternal grandfather, a modest Muslim *zamindar* who had diversified into shopkeeping in the North Indian city of Bareilly and gained a government licence for the distribution of radio sets and gramophone records, and was benefiting from increasing pockets of urban prosperity in the 1940s. He hitched his own star to the rising fortunes of the Muslim League. Many others in this new urban middle class looked to other organisations which might assist them to seek and win contracts, protect their families and secure their access to increasingly protected and rationed goods and foodstuffs. All kinds of leaders, lowly and mighty, with aspirations to rule in the new and unforeseen India that would follow the end of the war, made contingency plans by organising volunteers or by quietly stockpiling arms. Princely leaders in states like Patiala and Bhopal, for all their vocal support of the British war effort, also simultaneously realised the need to protect and defend their own territorial interests in the event of a political breakdown and started to amass armaments and to encourage local militias.

In this sense, the rise of politically divergent movements, from the
Muslim League and the communists to the Indian National Army,
was entirely consistent with the public mood. These activists shared
many more features than is initially apparent. Men wanted to act,
stirred up by the uncertainties of the war, the loss of credibility of
the British state and the weakness of the Congress leadership at a
critical moment. Parallel Home Leagues and Civil Defence Units
mirrored and mimicked those formed by the Raj. They drew on many
of the same technical vocabularies and ideas as the military by emphasising muscle-power and masculinity, the protection of families and
the safeguarding of homes. For many Indians in the 1940s these organisations presented the possibility of influencing constitutional outcomes
that hung uncertainly in the balance. In the 1920s and 1930s, Gandhi
had often been able to seize the initiative at a crucial moment and
marshal politics into his non-violent movement. Yet Gandhi continued
to advocate *ahimsa* and in the eyes of most people this seemed an
ideology at odds with the realities of the new world order. But confused
and weak, the Congress was one step behind the public, unable to
assert party authority and soon to be banned altogether.

*   *   *

In the meantime, for government loyalists, especially the princes,
support for the war effort was paying off handsomely. Reaping the
benefits of state subsidies and government orders, they found their
balance sheets healthier than ever. Cities like Bangalore, Jaipur and
Rampur boomed, as new factories sprang up, turning out specialised
war materials. Gandhi's home state of Porbandar supplied cement
to the Allies, Baroda manufactured cotton textiles for uniforms, and
Hyderabad invested in chemicals, fertilisers and cement and had a
Bren-gun factory. A number of princely states doubled or even tripled
their economic growth during wartime; in just one year of the war,
1943–4, over five *crores* of industrial capital flowed into the princely
states.[15] Maharajas who had already pioneered developmental projects
and public works in their states in the 1920s and 1930s found
themselves well placed to court wartime investment. From the 1940s,
there was surplus that could be ploughed back into loans to other
princely states and into Government of India securities, generating

yet more profit. Much of Bangalore's infrastructure was a result of the war, and whole new areas of the city were being redesigned and electrified.

Both the USA and the UK turned to these 'loyalist' strongholds as safe havens for wartime ventures, and the profits continued to flow in. Mysore was particularly fêted for its developmental success, and was featured in *Life* magazine as a 'bright spot' in India, 'cleaner and more attractive than even most US cities'.[16] Mysore workers mined Kolar gold, produced iron and steel, and factory workers made paper, glass, porcelain, dynamite, Bakelite, soap and silk products.

Striking public works and building projects appeared on the skyline of some of the princely states. In Mysore, the German modernist architect and Jewish refugee Otto Koenigsberger designed geometric, domed pavilions and other public buildings for the Dewan. In Jaipur, the maharaja was warned by the Viceroy to slow down his beautification of the city; the Viceroy thought it unseemly in the age of wartime austerity. But the princes and their courts were not the only beneficiaries of the boom, and even traditional craftsmen could adapt rapidly to the changed conditions of war. The traditional gemstone cutters of Jaipur were soon cutting synthetic gems and supplying them to the Allies as sights in weaponry. But there was ultimately a new gulf growing here, as elsewhere, between those profiting and those being used as cheap labour towards the war effort. Trade unions emerged and strikes faced swift repression. The princes in states such as Mysore and Travancore also levied labourers into state labour units (30,000 men had been allotted by the states to civilian labour corps by mid-1942) and thousands of men and women soon started heading northwards towards the aerodromes and roads of North and East India to work on wartime mega-projects. The status and autocratic privileges of the maharajas would struggle to survive this transformation.

* * *

By midsummer, with the failure of Cripps to deliver any meaningful rapprochement, the frustrations and tensions between the Indian National Congress and the British rulers reached incendiary levels. Nehru admitted he was 'worried and distracted beyond measure'. The Governor of the Central Provinces described Gandhi as 'the Hitler of

India' and called for his 'deflation', while the question of when and where to deport the Congress leaders was recurring as a prominent theme in government deliberations. Gandhi's secret deportation and the risks concerning his ill-health were freely discussed. Should he be taken to Aden, to East Africa or to a secret location in India? 'My own leaning would be to put him in an aeroplane for Uganda', Leo Amery wrote, almost unashamedly wishing for the Mahatma just to vanish from sight.[17] Serious investigations with the Colonial Office explored the possible arrangements for banishment of Congress leaders to East Africa, although this plan was always more keenly supported by London than by the men on the spot in India who perceived the potential for fuelling rather than dampening nationalist feeling. Ultimately, the fact remained that retaining popular support for the war and denying the legitimacy of the Congress had become irreconcilable positions.

The first months of 1942 had seen India's old imperial equilibrium thrown into turmoil. The superficial compact between Indian political leaders and the British was shattered, as the sovereignty of the country was sacrificed in the name of war. The public looked on as foreign troops arrived at their ports, goods and land were appropriated in the name of defence and the physical resources of the country were placed at the services of the military. Aerial bombardment became a realistic threat along the eastern coast. Ultimately, the official casualties from air raids in India were 3,521 people, including 1,432 killed: a minuscule number of global wartime casualties but enough to cause widespread panic in major cities.[18]

By mid-1942 government documents alluded routinely to 'abnormal conditions' and the 'abnormal situation' in India. Officials sweated it out in the ministries of New Delhi and the provincial capitals, from Lahore to Madras, banned from retreating to the hills for respite from the fearsome heat and equally unable to evade the rising political temperature. This rapid transformation was changing the ordered relationships that underpinned the Raj: between communities, within cities and villages, exacerbating differences of political affiliation and ethno-religious expression, and accentuating differences between the wealthy and the poor. Once the failure of Cripps to deliver any meaningful progress on Independence became apparent, the Raj forged ahead with wartime priorities while relying on a diminishing and pragmatic partnership with a small wedge of society – mill owners, factory workers, princes, military families, large landowners, the bedrock of sepoys. But even these apparent accommodations with so-called loyalists were fraught with contradictions and ambiguity. Paradoxically, the increase in foreign troops to India in the summer heat of 1942 would add to the dissolution of authority.

12

Welcome to Bombay

Throughout 1942, British and American troops poured into the country. British regiments had always been stationed in India from the earliest days of British rule in the eighteenth century. This was something different: a great wave of incoming soldiers, fresh to the country, unfamiliar with local languages, conscripted and sent to Asia not of their own free choice, often resenting their posting and longing to be fighting the Nazis instead. In the past British regiments had cracked down on locals after insurgencies such as the 1857 uprising. This time of course their primary purpose was not internal security, although as resistance to the war intensified, they came to be used as a way of exerting control over domestic disturbances too, further muddying their mission and purpose in the eyes of both British soldiers and locals. They had come to secure the empire against Japanese invasion. American GIs with the mission of 'saving China' from the Japanese found themselves in alien and unknown landscapes, dealing with Indian traders, merchants and craftsmen, trying to thrash out a war plan in a densely populated, and unfamiliar, part of the world. Many more men came to India than would actually see fighting on the fronts of Burma.[1]

Behind the fighting fronts lay long supply lines and complicated chains of men (and increasingly women too) in non-combatant roles: manning the aerodromes, supplying, equipping and feeding the juggernaut, carrying out training, planning strategy, and running hospitals and clinics. The formidable range of activities needed to service a total war had to be rapidly assembled within India, and the military commanders started to reconfigure the state, acquiring land and food, clearing villages, and recruiting local labour. The creation of an Indian war front was starting to impinge on lives all over the country, not simply in the big cities.

★   ★   ★

In Calcutta, Bombay and Karachi locals suddenly saw soldiers everywhere, ferried by rickshaw drivers, shopping in the marketplaces for trinkets and souvenirs to send home, taking photographs of the Taj Mahal and other tourist spots, holidaying on houseboats in Kashmir and visiting tribes up in the hills. Arriving in India after long and cramped journeys, these young soldiers often knew precious little about India and were pale and nervous in the face of the disarray that greeted them in the dock areas of Bombay. Officers warned new arrivals against tricksters and fraudsters, shoe-shine boys and snake charmers. A pamphlet issued by the Bombay Hospitality Committee, *Welcome to Bombay*, instructed soldiers to 'AVOID exposure of your head to the sun before 4pm; eating over ripe fruit or fruits not protected by skin; drinking water from a street fountain; walking bare footed; drinking intoxicating drinks during the day, especially spirits; soft drinks from marble stoppered bottles; patronizing beggars, mendicants, fortune-tellers and curio dealers'.[2] Old hands who knew the city teased and frightened the younger ones who often had rarely left their own local counties. The men, uncomprehending and stunned by the sights of poverty, resorted to clichés about the city. The communist (and later history professor) John Saville, who had many Indian friends in London and was probably more worldly than most, having studied at the LSE and read extensively about the empire, still found Bombay 'frightful and frightening' on arrival:

> The buildings in the centre were I suppose what might be called classic colonial architecture and this was the area of large shops including salesrooms of very expensive cars. The contrast was striking and un-pleasant between this administrative, residential and shopping district and what seemed to be the rest of Bombay – filthy, smelly, the streets full of rubbish and the native Indians looking half-starved.[3]

There was a disjuncture between the imagination of the exotic East and the men's first experiences in Bombay. Strikingly similar motifs run through memoirs of soldiers remembering their arrival in Bombay. An American GI named Tom Foltz recalled:

> I was only 19 when I arrived in Bombay. The sights, sounds, smells, poverty and the life of the average Indian in those days were quite overwhelming to me . . . The minute we left the dock area, the smells and sounds of this foreign land simply overpowered us. The crush of humanity, overwhelming poverty and grime, the squalor and appalling smells of the everyday living conditions these people endured engulfed us. We had never experienced anything like this in our lives. Such would soon become commonplace for us.[4]

Clive Branson, a committed communist, poet and vocal opponent of British rule, who also arrived in India with the British Army in the spring of 1942, recorded in his diary: 'We went by train from Bombay to a camp outside Poona. Everyone was filled with amazement at the appalling conditions in which the people live – this has been the subject of many very lively discussions since.'[5]

This initial sense of shock was common. The 'real' India was a contrast to the jolly, sanitised newsreels which troops had been shown prior to their departure, in which they had been promised tropical fruits, constant sunshine and cheap shopping. One journalist thought Americans expected to find Hollywood's oriental fantasylands: 'The Americans, accustomed to see India through Hollywood's cameras as a fabulous land peopled by maharajas and elephants were appalled and sickened by the stink and poverty of the place.'[6] On arrival at Bombay, troop ships stayed in port and men often slept on board the ship at night awaiting their onward orders, and passed evenings playing cards or reading. But in the daytime, after cramped weeks at sea, men shopped, toured local sights or sought out alcohol or company at canteens. Brothels did a brisk trade; Bombay was notorious for a red light district in which 'the women display themselves behind bars rather like goods in a shop window or animals in a zoo'.[7] The fear among the population at large of single men looking for sex with Indian women was to become a prominent and recurring theme for the rest of the war.

Bombay was a transient place that troops passed through, en route to other camps and training centres. Matching up the timings of troop-ship arrivals with onward train connections to military camps around India created a logistical bottleneck, and meant that troops often had to linger for a few days or weeks. Over the duration of the war, the facilities for troops in Bombay and the other port cities improved. Volunteers, often British memsahibs, began to start up canteens, hostels and rest rooms with magazines and newspapers, games like billiards and table tennis and services like mending and stitching for troops. Greens, opposite the Gateway of India, was one of the largest and the most well-known hotels for troops in Bombay. Many also stayed at the Salvation Army hostel, the Wesley House Institute and the Sir Alwyn Ezra Services Canteen, whilst the Seamen's Institute offered dances and socials and the Shandy Tavern, refreshments, darts and billiards. Nearly all the major cinemas admitted sailors and soldiers in uniform at concession rates, and cinema owners noticed that their usual Indian clientele began to drift away, replaced by the troops. Men in uniform filled local cinemas like the Regal and the Eros playing *The Wizard of Oz*, *Casablanca* and *Gone with the Wind*. Photography burgeoned as a popular hobby among those soldiers who could afford it. Entrepreneurial locals also responded to the thousands of foreign soldiers passing through Bombay each year. *Gharry* and taxi drivers organised guided tours to the Elephanta caves and to Juhu beach. The seeds of nascent tourism industries took root in many wartime beauty spots.

For most ordinary young men in Britain who did not have family connections to the Raj and who had come to adulthood in 1930s Britain, the empire was a remote and little-understood place, either part of royal ceremony and pageantry or a site for action adventure and heroic deeds in comic strips and films such as Alexander Korda's fantastical 1938 tale of derring-do on the Afghan border, *The Drum*. Latterly, wartime newsreels in the UK had emphasised 'a devoted empire coming to Britain's aid at a time of peril' and depicted both the selfless help of the British Empire and also the way that the empire itself was becoming developed, modern and sophisticated under British tutelage.[8] It was a shock for British servicemen to see the slums of Bombay or the poor on the streets and they had to make sense of the British imperial 'civilising mission' anew. Officers struggled to maintain their men's morale in an environment where local shopkeepers and people seemed indifferent or openly hostile to the military presence. A mutual undercurrent of apprehension and suspicion marked many initial transactions with shopkeepers. As one official perceptively remarked, 'the imperial motif alone' was not going to be enough to preserve morale.[9] School textbooks had taught many British youth about the benefits of imperial rule for India but now many began to doubt this when faced with the evidence before their own eyes.

American servicemen were even more confused by what they saw than their British counterparts and the US military tended to encourage ignorance of politics. 'The political situation in India is not easily understood and a short stay in India is not long enough to be informed about it', cautioned a handbook for soldiers arriving in India from the USA.[10] GIs were warned against discussion of local politics, and their command strenuously tried to avoid GIs becoming caught up in Britain's domestic conflict in India in 1942. Yet there was osmosis of information and knowledge; Nehru was starting to appear in American publications and his autobiography was published in the USA for the first time in 1941. The energetic diplomat and democrat Louis Johnson, sent to Delhi by Roosevelt, became a lifelong friend of Nehru and spoke out blatantly in favour of Indian Independence, much to the irritation of the Viceroy.[11]

In the trail of troops came foreign correspondents and press photographers. Alan Moorehead, the razor-sharp *Daily Express* correspondent, arrived in 1942, on the eve of the Cripps Mission, to find a weary Viceroy who 'left me with an even stronger feeling of pessimism than I had when I arrived'.[12] The American journalist Louis Fischer was in India from May, and spent many hours with Gandhi during a stay at his ashram. Indian political leadership was courting favourable international press coverage in an unprecedented way, much to the chagrin of the British Raj. But much of this coverage was dictated by the pace and concerns of war and necessarily sanitised some of the less palatable aspects of the unfolding social context in India. Photospreads of the Burma campaign became more prominent in magazines but food shortages or denial policies rarely featured in press photography until famine made them inescapable. Privately foreign correspondents railed against the red tape, inefficiencies and stooges of the Raj, finding the imperial system antiquated and challenging to navigate.

The presence of so many recently arrived British and American troops divided Indian politicians. It was hard to explain to the ordinary villager why Indian youth had been sent abroad to defend the Middle East and North Africa and yet foreigners had come to defend India, especially when the threat of sexual predation by 'outsiders' was a prevalent fear. A draft of a resolution demanding that the British 'Quit India', which bore Gandhi's imprimatur, was presented to the Congress Committee on 27 April 1942. At its core was a strong statement about the presence of foreign troops in India, declaring them 'harmful to India's interests' and 'dangerous to the cause of India's freedom' and demanding their immediate withdrawal. The ambivalence at the heart of the Congress about the purposes and morality of the war was never far from the surface of such debates. Nehru, troubled by the idea of people harassing foreign troops engaged in war with fascists, insisted they should be able to stay in India undisturbed by nationalist protest for the duration of the conflict and had the clause removed. Gandhi consistently argued that soldiers should be expelled from Indian soil and continued to make complaints about their presence; his own spiritual commitment to *ahimsa* seemed to strengthen daily, alongside his disgust at the flagrant spectacle of warfare. Nonetheless, American and British soldiers were embedded in India, some for many years to come, and contacts with local people began to flourish, as they built aerodromes and installations, procured services on the camps, and employed builders, washermen, cooks and contracted for goods in the marketplaces.

Labour was astonishingly cheap for the military. And soon people found that they could get jobs at bases and aerodromes at wages that completely outstripped local rates. American soldiers and airmen in India often had their own 'native bearers', locally recruited man-servants who swept, dusted, polished shoes and, fetched and carried tea and snacks, thus helping, as one GI magazine joked, 'make a perfectly lazy man out of a soldier'. The cost of hiring a local boy as a personal servant was so cheap that even ordinary GIs could afford it. As Douglas Devaux of the US Air Force, flying out of Dum Dum, remembered:

A young Indian boy, about 12 years old, turned up next morning and asked for a job taking care of the tent: sweep it, put things in order, shine our shoes, and general cleaning. He said he would be our bearer.

'How much?' we asked. 'Sahibs, a rupee a week, each,' he replied. A
rupee was 35 cents. Melvin and I hired him. He called himself Abdul
Kali and we christened him 'Kelly'.[13]

Soldiers gave their servants comical nicknames which bore little
relation to their real names. 'Our bearer's name is "Smokey." We've
forgotten why we call him that, but there are no objections, since
his real name is "Pabitra Mondel"', another soldier wrote. 'Aside
from his regular duties, Smokey spends most of his time learning
GI ways.'[14] General Lewis Pick, the Chief Engineer who oversaw
the construction of the Ledo Road in the later years of the war,
had three servants who waited on him in Assam. A photograph of
the general's departure from Ledo shows the three men, wearing
dhotis and barefoot, standing solemnly in front of a heavily garlanded
car. In the British Army, officers had also long relied on bearers.
Field Marshal Slim spoke warmly of his 'faithful Gurkha orderly,
Bajbir', who woke him every morning. It was not unusual to be
brought a cup of tea in bed or for servants to shave men in the
morning.

Some of the relationships between bearers and their soldier-sahibs
developed paternalistically as they grew to know each other.
Sometimes soldiers were invited back to local homes and introduced
to families, or the soldiers helped pay for the cost of weddings or for
the education of young children. For most of the people who worked
as servants on airfields, at barracks and bases, the job gave them
opportunities to learn some English and to earn inflated wages. For
the most entrepreneurial, contact with the bases was even more
lucrative: an opportunity to act as guide, procurer of alcohol and
women, interpreter and general right-hand man. Some of the bearers
participated in drinking games and it was not unusual for a soldier
to swap roles with a servant, dressing in his clothes while he donned
military uniform. But on other occasions servants were the butt of
the jokes, shouted at or even abused, given 'unprintable' names.
As the *Hellbird Herald*, an American propaganda news-sheet, summarised
it: 'Ever since the beginning of the present "invasion" of India by GI
Joe, the native bearer has been a source of wonder and amusement
. . . He affords one of the few amusements readily available in this
part of the world.'[15] Soldiers often did not take their bearers seriously,

laughing at their mannerisms and habits although physical violence was strongly discouraged and could result in a soldier being disciplined. The acquisition of a personal servant by regular troops was rare in other theatres of war; it was seen as one of the perks of the jobs and a way to dodge some of the service hardships of India. Of course, it also contributed to the sense of India as a particularly peculiar site of war.

*   *   *

As foreign troops continued to pour into the country, prostitution in Indian cities steadily increased in prevalence and visibility. The threat to women of sexual predation by soldiers is one of the less well-known and yet most lurid features of the 1940s, at least as it was experienced through the eyes of Indian onlookers. The increased demand due to the new migrants to the cities and the growth of wartime production and military spending power drew more and more women to working in prostitution. The vast differential in the purchasing power of the foreign soldiers combined with the geographical context of war to produce a cocktail of supply and demand; troops could not easily go home for many years and took their leave in local towns and cities. India Command's consultant venereologist, Eric Prebble, assessed the Military Police as 'completely inadequate to deal with the situation' and local police shied away from disciplining foreign soldiers. 'Pimps and touts abounded wherever the troops were stationed or on leave', and taxi and rickshaw drivers and men employed in the cantonments acted as middlemen.[16] Troops of all nationalities saw the brothels as tacitly sanctioned, even if technically off-limits according to the rule book. By the end of the war, Calcutta would have some of the highest rates of venereal disease in the world, exceeding the rates in other theatres. This would be a source of tension and potential conflict with civil authorities until 1945, adding considerably to the alienation between the civilian population and the imperial state. It was also a military concern, as so many men needed treatment and hospitalisation, challenging resources and removing trained men from active duty.

War, many argued, was bringing India to the brink of moral degradation. This opinion was fuelled by a prurient and often wildly

exaggerated notion of western sinfulness, sexual amorality and lustful-
ness. This idea had a long lineage, and derived from far older notions
of Indian respectability dating back to the nineteenth century. The
chastity of well-behaved Indian women was stressed by some nationalists as a contrast to the flesh-pots and strumpets of the West. 'Egypt
is now full of ATS girls and British officers are enjoying shameless
pleasures with nurses', wrote one Bengali assistant surgeon. 'They
will win the war with merry-making.'[17] In the subcontinent, the idea
took hold that Indian women were being brought into disrepute
because of the sinful foreign soldiers, and this often carried a dark
undercurrent of extreme nationalism and a fear of miscegenation or
the blurring of racial boundaries. This was an evocative and potentially
explosive undercurrent in the context of deteriorating Anglo-Indian
relations and one that would be turned to repeatedly in the months
to come.

The darker side of this was the fear among villagers, particularly
those living close to army training grounds or aerodromes, of local
women suffering rape. The Governor of Madras, Arthur Hope,
complained to Linlithgow of 'the genuine feeling that the troops, both
British and Indian, will rape any women they can get hold of' and
that he had heard this sentiment 'everywhere'.[18] Some soldiers occasionally but undoubtedly did make sexual attacks on women and such
incidents reverberated far beyond the locales in which they took place,
becoming the subject of more generalised fears and rumours and
adding to the 'deep-seated feeling' that soldiers were 'savages' and 'not
respectable'.[19] Gandhi distilled this mood into words, entangling his
own deep-seated ideological objection to the increasing presence of
troops of all nationalities on Indian soil with the perceived threat to
women.

The behaviour of troops, white or brown, has become a public scandal.
Even respectable and well-known women are not free from danger . . .
The instances of looting in the open are too common to be decently
challenged . . . I get almost daily complaints of such cases . . . No
wonder. Full-blooded soldiers not on duty find vent for their exuberant
physical energy by taking liberties which cannot be allowed in a society
not used to such conduct.[20]

The insinuation of sexual threat was only lightly veiled, and unusually inflammatory for the Mahatma, once again reflecting his particularly acerbic tone in early 1942. The heightened threat to Indian women generated by the presence of soldiers would continue to be an emotive motif for many years to come.

*   *   *

'Where there are Americans prices become Prohibitive. They certainly get colossal pay and live much more luxuriously than British troops do.'[21] The Indian civil servant Ian Macdonald liked to use his letters home to complain about his circumstances and to let off steam. But many British administrators around the empire who feared and admired Americans in equal measure would have shared his sentiments. The newcomers were transforming the Raj. The purchasing power and superhero stature of the American GIs made much of the Raj look fossilised and diminished. The old hands of the Raj struggled to adjust in many cases, disorientated by the rapidity of the changes that were now overtaking India. In the clubs of Simla, the rumours of increasing American designs on South Asia, the strength of American imports and the sexual irresistibility of American men all mingled together to create profound wariness about the new allies.

Raj officials were also riled by American exhortations to democracy and their implied support for freedom from British imperialism. Americans publicly stressed their own commitment to freedom for colonies, emphasising their difference from the British rulers. Indian newspapers ran a series of full-page advertisements designed by the Office of American War Information in late 1942 and January 1943 under the clunky title 'America Fights for Freedom'. These pictured episodes in American history and folklore, including the Declaration of Independence and the freedom of the Philippines from American rule. One poster, under the Star-Spangled Banner, carried the pledge that 'the people of America, through their president, have reaffirmed the right of all men to freedom' and 'the American people will not permit these freedoms to disappear from the earth'. Propaganda directly invoked the Atlantic Charter of 1941 in which the Allies had stated their aspirations for post-war freedom and self-determination. Readers could even apply for a free, fully illustrated copy of the life of President Roosevelt from the Bombay office. The Government of India expressed fury when these adverts appeared in Indian vernacular and English newspapers and quickly pulled them from circulation.[22] Nevertheless, managers at the Tata steelworks irreverently displayed them under the glass surfaces of their desks over the months to come.

Behind the rhetoric, there was a great deal of ambivalence about Asian decolonisation in Washington, and much more shared feeling between Churchill and Roosevelt about the need to prioritise the war above all other political considerations in the immediate term. And on the part of Indians there was no simplistic belief in America as a liberating power. In particular, America's own internal race issue and the blatant subjugation of black citizens drew comment and reprehension from a number of south Asian politicians. 'You have yet to abolish slavery!' Gandhi reportedly told one American visitor.[23] Ultimately, as many in Asia found, American demands for wartime resources might quickly start to resemble a form of neo-imperialism. But in appearance at least, the arrival of the Americans in India seemed to signal the possibility of a new world order.

There was also a yawning difference of class and sensibility between the old India hands and the British Tommies now arriving daily. Many of the imperial administrators in India had family connections with India that could be traced back several generations, had themselves often been born in India and more often than they cared to acknowledge had Anglo-Indian ancestry, and knew the local languages. The incoming junior ranks from Britain, and later America, often had no prior knowledge or interest in the subcontinent and would have preferred to fight the Germans in Europe. Mutual exasperation and frustration divided the old sahibs and the new Tommies. Soldiers fresh from training in Britain, painfully conscious of leaving families behind in a Britain vulnerable to bombing and conscious of conditions on the home front, found the high life led by some of the Raj officials shocking, perceiving a lackadaisical attitude towards war and an antiquated way of doing things. They felt the sharp end of Raj snobbery and disliked the elitism, etiquette and pecking orders that defined cantonment life. These conscripts had neither chosen to come to India nor elected to join the army and were repelled, on many occasions, both by the Indian resistance to the war effort and by the ruling men and women of the Raj:

There is no war here on Sundays! They will not realise there is a war on. It is exasperating and disgusting. Last night I went to the club here. The last time I was in it was 1934 and there was not the slightest change – memsahibs in evening dress, sahibs, God help me! in dinner jackets, same cackle about anything but the Jap who is right at the door.[24]

This was all well known by the War Office and also by the India Office, which surveyed the men, read the censorship reports and summarised the feelings in the ranks:

The British Tommy hates the East. He hates the dirt, the heat, the discomfort, the lack of home amusements and the dislike with which the Indians appear to regard him. He does not understand Indian politics. To him it appears foolish to fight for a country that does not want to be helped and from which we are clearing out after the war.[25]

On another occasion, the War Office reported, 'The British soldier himself is convinced that India is not ready for self-government and illustrates his contention by pointing to the lack of roads and the almost complete absence of education, hygiene and all the other distinguishing marks of civilisation.'[26] Men complained about the postal system and the lack of contact with their wives. Aware of the presence of Allied soldiers in Britain, men had anxieties about the fidelity of their wives and disquiet about what kind of home life they would be returning to. 'Men are nervous about their womenfolk and consequently resent the presence of Allied troops in Britain and hate hearing about them.'[27] The War Office requested that information about the Allies stationed in Britain should not be broadcast to soldiers in the East, as it was so unsettling for men stationed in India. Men in India heard rumours about affairs between British women and enemy POWs, and dalliances with Allied troops. They also worried about their job prospects if and when the war ended, believing astutely, as it turned out, that men stationed in Europe, closer to home, would get the plum pickings.[28]

Yet the Raj itself was undergoing seismic change and was not as static as many imagined it to be. Across the subcontinent women started to work. The Raj was mobilising towards the war effort and some of the genteel ladies scorned as memsahibs began to live more intrepid lives. The Women's Auxiliary Corps (India) – WAC (I) – was rapidly raised in 1942, and women worked in anti-aircraft direction finding and plotting, parachute inspection and packing, as cipher clerks and operators, as well as in more traditional roles of catering or house-keeping duties. Although treated patronisingly by some of the menfolk, and barely remembered by history, these women plugged the gaps in skilled labour and performed urgent and essential tasks. Qualified women also worked as intelligence officers, translators and radio mechanics. The formation of the WAC (I) has parallels with the raising of women's militias, guards and units in many places around the world during the Second World War. Indeed, it was modelled on the British Auxiliary Territorial Service. British and Indian women could join on equal terms and the plan to give Indian and British women equal status caused consternation in Whitehall as, technically, Indian women officers might be able to command white men and this was seen as potentially inflammatory for white Tommies.[29] The fact that the Government of India backed the plan is evidence both of the changing racial climate and also of the desperation of the state to keep the war effort on track at a time of skilled labour shortages.

Sydney Ralli had now left her home in Karachi (the house had been requisitioned along with so many others and she had sent her children up to Simla) and volunteered in the typing pool at the General Headquarters in Delhi. She was struck by the 'blowsy' haircuts, fashions and double Dutch of the other 'cipherettes' working there: 'The Anglo Indian girl, most efficient in charge of the typists, had cultivated quite a realistic American accent. She typed mostly figures with speed and accuracy yet she had the longest nails for a working girl I've ever seen.' Initially unsettled by the way the women gossiped over their desks, Ralli gradually adjusted to the work, but disliked sending out death notices to the families of Indian soldiers: 'I felt dreadfully inhuman setting out telegrams to families that so and so had been reported missing. I felt that there should be some scheme of sympathetic district visitors to break the news.'[30]

On the other side of India, Veronica Downing, the British planta-tion owner from Assam, exchanged a life of riding, tea parties and pig-sticking for war work and worked as a coder with the Enigma machine at the RAF air base established close to her plantation. Her secluded existence at the plantation was radically altered by war work and she had never even been in an office before. She was friendly with the American, South African and British pilots stationed at the airfield and also volunteered at the American Red Cross canteen when the base was taken over by the US forces. She remembered: 'It was entirely a man's world. All I heard talked about was boost (aeroplanes), fragmentation (pieces of exploded shells), skies, the men's misdemeanors and, of course, mostly aeroplanes. Somehow one grew to love them.'[31] The social world of the Raj was being transformed as the annual summer visit to Simla was restricted, women's husbands joined the services and wives joined the number of civil and military organisations that were being established to support the troops: the Women's Auxiliary Corps, the Women's Volunteer Service, St John Ambulance, the Red Cross, and other blood banks and volunteer aid detachments. In hospitals a number of memsahibs took up tougher and bloodier work as volunteer nurses with the Auxiliary Nursing Service, also raised in the midst of the emergency of 1942, showing incredible reserves of stamina and commitment. They worked intensely long and difficult shifts in military hospitals and were among the first white women nursing sepoys, a radical departure for the colonial state.

In Delhi, jeeps roared along the streets, men in uniform filled the cinemas and, the colonnaded Imperial Hotel became for a time the American Headquarters – genteel afternoon teas were now accompanied by men in uniform poring over maps. The American presence, combined with the great threat of Japan, injected new urgency and efficiency into the military operation in India. Everything moved up a gear. 'American generals jostled for space with Chinese admirals, British air marshals and Indian administrators',[32] William Slim said of the scene in the corridors of power in New Delhi.

As everyone waited for the next chess move in the war, men took every chance they could to go sightseeing, to visit shops and markets, cinemas, dances and bars, using the services of tailors, rickshaw pullers and taxi drivers, hotel and canteen owners. Chinese restaurants gained popularity, becoming favourite spots for foreign soldiers; Chinese merchant sailors jumped ship in Karachi to establish lucrative canteens. Dances and parties promised 'girls galore' and 'Louis' Jazz Band' played Delhi 'in good old Yankee "Jumpin' Jive"' style'.[33] Street hawkers sold black market cigarettes, Old Gold, Luckies, Dominoes and Chesterfields, stamped 'compliments of the Red Cross'. The Grand Hotel in Calcutta was a place where you could 'Forget the War!' with Teddy Weatherford at the piano in the American Cocktail Bar, Chinese jugglers, raffles, quizzes and 'hand-picked dance hostesses'.[34]

The big cities started to look and feel different. New goods came into India, despite the wartime food shortages and shipping problems. For those privileged few who could afford them, sparkling new goods had great allure. Fridges, air-conditioning units, cars, tinned foods and new kinds of medicine suddenly appeared on the market. 'I don't like America much but they know how to tin food, an art which the Australians have not yet mastered', wrote Ian Macdonald.[35] By 1943, America was exporting cosmetics, cars, radios and fridges. Some of these items were offered as prizes in raffles for the War Fund or at fairs and circuses. In Karachi, a Coca-Cola plant was in operation from 1942, producing bottles of fizzy pop. An American firm, Remington Rand, had a virtual monopoly on the supply of typewriters to government offices (a product indispensable for modern government and for modern warfare) and a factory in Calcutta provided the spare parts, while Volkart Brothers monopolised air-conditioning units.

These items became prestigious symbols of modern living, changing the appearance of homes. The fridge in one affluent Indian household had to be moved out of the kitchen as the cook and servants' children kept opening and closing the door to take out ice, marvelling at it.[36] Bicycles were becoming increasingly prevalent and some women rode them more than ever before. But at the same time, some administrators with cars were taking to horseback to tour the districts as the petrol shortages had become so severe. A number of wealthy families abandoned their cars altogether. Before his incarceration Nehru took to riding an Indian-made bicycle in response to the petrol shortages.

Hollywood and Bollywood had been in competition for Indian audiences since the 1930s. Now posters and magazines showed curvy ladies with puckered lips. The expansion of the war brought fantasies of Hollywood glamour and sex into Indian cities and to Indian troops on a far greater scale than ever before. One consulate considered glossy prints of American army pin-up girls, in bathing suits and tight outfits, known as 'girl art', too sensitive for local sensibilities in the Middle East, but they were in wide circulation among Indian troops. 'The Office of War Information has been supplying sets of pictures that are definitely on the spicy side', noted the Consul in Karachi.[37] In collaboration with the British administration, five magazines in eight different Indian languages published these pin-ups, which were aimed at the general population as well as at the troops. After consultation with the Government of India, it was now policy that 'pictures of pretty American women can and should be used extensively in India' (in contrast to the Middle East where this was warned against) and 'lively' images were offered for public consumption, although nudity or semi-nudity were strictly taboo.

Americans also carefully considered the growing popularity of Hollywood cinema, keen to use soft power to create support for war aims, literally using 'the legs of Dietrich or Garson' to try to garner support for the war, in the words of one official. Images of women and promises of sex, whether real or imagined, were hitched firmly to the war effort. The Raj had to jettison, or at the very least reformulate, the old ways of protecting the prestige of white women.[38]

For the vast majority of inhabitants of South Asia, this was a world disconnected and alien to their own but one which was starting to impinge on their own resources: beneath the glossy exterior was the hard, material reality. Supporting such an extensive military presence required land, property and food. The war could not be based in India without infringing drastically on the everyday world of its inhabitants. This was a world soon occupied and transformed by the building of roads and aerodromes, by requisitioning, and, most devastatingly of all, by the demand for food.

13

Plantations and Paddy Fields

The directors of the British-run tea industries in Calcutta sent out telegrams to their plantation managers in early 1942. These managers lived on large remote hill farms in north-east India, overseeing great swathes of tea-growing territory, vast acres of emerald land chiselled from the north-eastern hills. Now the war was coming to the tea terraces. The planters had been requested to take labourers from their tea plantations to be used as manual labour towards the war effort. From 6 March 1942 planters started to arrive with labour gangs in tow at Manipur Road Station from where they would travel towards Burma. One plantation manager, Colonel Pilcher, who accompanied the workers harked back in time for an analogy:

> The journey from mid-Assam to Manipur Road by rail on that date was somewhat reminiscent of mobilisation in August 1914; every wayside station had a contingent of tea garden labourers waiting to entrain, each man was equipped with a hoe, two blankets, sufficient food for a fortnight, and the inevitable hurricane lamp. There was a large send-off party of wives and relatives who waved and cheered as the train pulled out.[1]

These labourers were being sent into the mountains of the Indo-Burma borderlands, to build one of the three major roads which would be hacked out in the 1940s in order to create a link between India and Burma. Although controversial, a number of military commanders considered these roads critical in allowing the Allies to circumvent the Japanese attack to the south and traverse hostile jungle terrain in order to enable soldiers to re-enter Burma and ultimately recapture it. Just as refugees and soldiers were fleeing the Japanese, tea labourers were being sent back in the other direction: towards the enemy.

Life on tea plantations was tough, regimented and heavily disciplined. The tea estates had a reputation for low wages and the plantation managers had become nervous about increasing numbers of strikes during the early years of the war. Tea was an exceptional industry and had been protected as a virtual British monopoly; nearly all of the estates were in the hands of British companies. The plantation owners had a firm grip on their labour in Assam and a long history of employing the Indian 'coolies' in semi-servitude. Managers on tea plantations had a reputation for beating workers and squeezing them for long hours on subsistence pay. Nightwatchmen kept the tea-pickers on the plantations at night, workers had to ask for permission to leave the plantations and sometimes had to seek permission even to marry. But, for all its hardships, work in the tea gardens followed set patterns and routines. Now thousands of men were sent forwards as semi-indentured labourers to work on roads where the conditions were unknown and the expectations uncharted.

In early 1942, the work gangs on the border roads faced unprecedented dangers and a strange new landscape. As Indian, Burmese and European refugees fled the Japanese invasion, the road builders were pushed across the border back into Burma. They were put to work widening the mule-tracks that now had to be rapidly expanded into viable roads. Tea-pickers now quarried stone, built petrol storage depots, cut into the mud and rocks and widened the road with their bare hands. Pickaxes and hoes were the only tools, and long parts of the road to Tamu were cut entirely by hand. The track rose to 4,000 feet in places and all rations and water had to be portered up to the work parties. There were not even basic tarpaulins or shelters for the workers, who slept on the ground.

The work was hard and tedious. The road was prone to landslips and rockfalls and a rainy mist often hung over the workers. Occasionally a Japanese reconnaissance plane would circle overhead. By late spring the rain was falling in steady streams on many days, creating a mud slick. The workers were terrified of being stuck there in the monsoon rains or of being attacked by the Japanese. Some of the porters were Manipuri and Naga hillsmen, who were regularly loaded with 40-pound packs. Naga porters also evacuated sick soldiers on stretchers from

Burma, carrying them down to the railheads. Others laboured under compulsion: convicts from the Imphal Jail were forced to carry heavy loads for hundreds of miles along the mountain trails, escorted by guards.

In April 1942, the tea workers on the Manipur Road, nearly 200 miles from Dimapur and much further away than had originally been agreed, became deeply worried. Short of food, cut off from their families and with an alarming number of them falling sick, they became scared and angry. Bedraggled refugees talked to the labourers as they passed back down the road towards India: 'A constant stream of demoralised refugees was meeting and passing the labour marching in and all sorts of depressing rumours were rife.'[2] Corpses and bones glimmering in the mud told their own grim stories on some stretches of the road. 'Every few yards one sees a pathetic-looking bundle of clothing and nearby a human skeleton – mute reminders of the suffer-ings the refugees had to undergo.'[3] Rations fell short of promises and, already undernourished and stunted, the labourers began to lose weight. Even to the untrained eye the men looked 'under nourished and weakened by fever' and labour gangs had to be large enough to allow for the high sick rate.[4]

As the gruelling work on the road pushed on into late April, the labourers started to fear that they would never be able to leave; they were completely isolated on the road, cut off from home without road or rail transportation. Desertion was not an easy option, as any fleeing workers faced a dangerous journey back through the hills and the complete loss of wages. That many did decide to leave is telling of the perils the road builders encountered if they stayed. By early May labour was, in the veiled terms of one of the tea managers, 'very jumpy' at the forward end of the road. Outbreaks of cholera and cerebral meningitis, dysentery and malaria, had broken out in the camps and there were 'definite signs of unrest' among the labourers. The original request had been for six weeks' work and some had now been working for twice that long. The workers insisted they wanted to inform their relatives of their whereabouts. Rumours were also rife about the future security of tea gardens.

When the work parties trekked back down the mountains to recu-perate, many of them were sick and under 'tremendous strain'. Resistance broke out in the railheads of Imphal, where refugees had been passing in their thousands. To add to the woes of the local people, the Japanese started bombing raids. Deaths were small in number but panic ensued. During bombing raids on 10 May about twenty refugees in the camp at Imphal were killed, along with Mrs Shaw, the woman who had been overseeing the running of the camp. Buildings and houses were destroyed, cattle were killed and vehicles smashed. The Indian camp nearby at Korengei was undamaged but the attack sparked an exodus of 10,000 refugees, walking against the tide of incoming soldiers. A breakdown of law and order followed and protests broke out on the streets. Prisoners in the local jail (from which workers had been recruited for road-building) escaped and went on a campaign of looting and arson. The targets had been carefully planned, to do maximum damage to the road-building plans. Public Works Department officers had their quarters completely stripped and Indian Tea Association trucks were unable to move; lorry keys were stolen or the batteries shorted to sabotage them. Clerks, postal workers and sweepers all fled, the post office closed down and for a number of days there was no receipt of mails, telegrams or news.[5]

The tea-plantation owners fully realised the Japanese threat posed to the empire and the vulnerability of their own plantations. They could not risk the hazard to their own workers, and needed to continue to produce tea for consumption back in war-torn Britain. Once the crisis of invasion or bombardment had been averted in 1942, they suggested a new plan to the government, 'the shadow force labour scheme'. With their expertise in recruiting and managing labourers, they would provide the work parties needed for road- and aerodrome-building by employing new workers from around India and marshalling them into levies. This would keep down wages and keep up the supply of men. Every tea estate in North India agreed to supply one labourer for every ten acres of estate and the industry created a steady force of 75,000 to 90,000. These men and women constructed buildings, quarried stone and built the aerodromes that were starting to transform India's borders and landscape. They would also be the backbone of labour on the Ledo Road, an even more drastic and treacherous project which would commence later in the year: a 500-mile road switching back through the mountains of northern Burma designed to link India and China, and to provide a supply route to the beleaguered Chinese nationalists.

*   *   *

The villagers living near Chakulia in present-day Jharkhand heard by the beating of a drum that their paddy fields were being seized. The District Magistrate sent messengers, beating drums, to announce their eviction. For the villagers, strange things had been happening for the past six months as foreigners arrived with vast aeroplanes. The locals worked for them, at first carrying and breaking rocks to construct the airfields, then building bamboo huts or *bashas* where the pilots, navigators, flight engineers, wireless operators and ground crew would live or pumping chemicals into the air to kill mosquitoes and flies. Some of the villagers had become involved in selling opium and *ganja*, and there were always rumours about which women were visiting or being visited by the men. The pilots joked with the villagers and paid them well and at first it seemed a promising sign that the foreigners had come. But many of the foreign men were sick with malaria, and now some of the villagers also fell ill with cholera. Military inspections had followed; strange doctors and visitors had been to the village and to the neighbouring airfields, looked at the wells and waded out into the low-lying paddy fields.

The military had decided that the only way to protect the health of the air force men stationed at the airfields was to destroy and drain paddy fields within a half-mile radius of the aerodrome, which were harbouring deadly mosquitoes and flies, and to evict the local people who had cultivated these fields. The local Indian government obliged, invoking the Defence of India rules. 'Signatures of as many villagers as possible should be taken on the requisitioning order', instructed the District Magistrate, Arthur Kemp, from Singhbhum.[6] Over 500 acres of paddy fields were taken over, amounting to 15,000 *maunds* of paddy.

By March 1942 plans had been laid to build 215 new airfields in India. Provincial governments jockeyed to demonstrate their readiness to make land and materials available: 'Bengal is as flat as a billiard table and given the requirements of the airforce, it is a simple matter to construct hard earth runways to meet the present emergency', wrote the Governor of that province, promising to cement relationships between the RAF and his Public Works Department.[7] By the end of the war some 122,000 RAF personnel, 13 per cent of the RAF's total strength, would be in India. Commanders viewed air superiority as a vital ingredient in winning back Burma and South-East Asia. Fifty-seven Hurricanes in crates arrived for assembly in Karachi and were pulled through the city like modern-day juggernauts. Scattered throughout agricultural land in East India, Royal Indian Air Force (RIAF) and USAAF pilots stationed at these aerodromes in Bengal and Bihar lived in a bizarre and demanding environment. Their quarters were extremely spartan, illness was rife and there was little to do in between sorties although ground crew worked long hours and leisure time was scarce. The rapid building and equipping of aerodromes in Bengal and Bihar was to support flying reconnaissance missions over Burma, or the notoriously lethal trans-Himalayan route, 'the Hump', keeping China stocked with essential supplies. Later, these planes would bomb and mine in South-East Asia and Burma. In order to disguise these airfields and to prevent them from being wiped out by aerial attack, numerous airstrips were scattered throughout different districts, in particular Midnapore, which would soon, perhaps not coincidentally, become notorious for an uprising against the Raj.

By July 1942, barely a province of India escaped requisitioning. Central and eastern India were hit hardest. Whole villages and hamlets might be evacuated overnight to make way for aerodromes. In addition, the armies had other demands: for storage space, factory provision and housing. The police seized bicycles, cars and lorries and even took over mansions in prime locations of Bombay and Calcutta and cleared them for offices or depots. In United Provinces they took farmers' carts. In Satara district 6,000 villagers were ejected; as in Midnapore, it is likely that the later strength of rebellion in 1942 in Satara was connected to this fact. In Manipur, tea factories, lorries, cattle and schools had been co-opted and in Central Provinces there had been 'considerable acquisition of land' amounting to some 13,500 acres. In Bihar, on occasion, military authorities stepped in ahead of the local police and took land by force, and ultimately some 25,000 acres were used for aerodromes and defence installations there.[8] From Punjab a letter reached a sepoy in the Middle East complaining about the requisitioning: 'All the land of the village has been acquired by the Government and numerous factories are springing up here. It is a troublesome thing for us.'⁹ The Famine Inquiry Commission, looking back at the war in Bengal, estimated that 'more than 300,000 families were required to evacuate their homes and land. Compensation was of course paid but there is little doubt that the members of many of these families became famine victims in 1943.'¹⁰

The sudden disruption entailed by this requisitioning is rarely factored into accounts of the 1940s in India. Furthermore, managing requisitioning and 'denial' policies – in essence, taking control of others' property and warehousing it or commandeering it on behalf of the government – opened up a number of loopholes for profiteering or corruption by the firms and individuals paid to carry out the work. In Bengal a contract worth 1.5 *crore* rupees was offered to Mirza Ahmad Ispahani, a prominent businessman, Muslim Leaguer and friend of Jinnah's, for the removal of extra paddy stocks in 1942. When other Bengali ministers objected to one of their leading opponents winning this contract, a compromise was reached by which Ispahani was given one district, and the other two districts were divided between four rival firms and their purchasing agents.¹¹

Throughout the 1940s the Ispahani firm, among others, would win lucrative, exclusive contracts for forcibly collecting and warehousing rice stocks. Agents were employed to seize stocks in 'denial' districts, but extended their work beyond these limits, seizing grains and moving freely around districts in order to get access to farmers' stocks. These agents leaned heavily on reluctant cultivators, harassing them and forcing them to sell on terms set by the government. Accusations of profiteering, although unproven, increased and would linger long after Bengal descended into deadly food shortages.

The law demanded that cultivators should receive compensation on the spot and that they should be assisted to find new land for cultivation when fields were seized. In reality, this was an idealistic hope. In Bombay, the government was still considering plans to give 'doles to infirm and aged evacuees' long after actual eviction had started.¹² This was the combustible fuel firing popular anger in 1942. Compassionate District Magistrates, conscious of the problems the villagers faced, put their foot down on occasions, in one case intervening when a village had been forcibly relocated and was now facing eviction again for a second time. Decisions and requests did not go unchallenged by civil authorities; District Magistrates always had to balance the needs of the war with the pressures of anti-British agitation and the risk of rebellion. And the men on the spot had a difficult task carrying through orders from above, often feeling torn by their sympathy for the people affected by new policies. The official in charge would later describe the job of removing rice stocks for Bengal's 'denial policy' as 'a completely heartbreaking job' but one that he had to carry through nonetheless.[13] Requisitioning was also extensive in wartime Britain, but in India it was simply of a different order as people already lived at bare subsistence levels.

Requisitioning hit a range of different people, from urban elites to peasants. The military establishment required houses and apartments in downtown Calcutta and Karachi. Clerks, schoolteachers, managers and lawyers all saw their bedrooms occupied by men in uniform or had to make way for military stores. Poorer 'middle-class' Britons, probably those involved in trade and business, and Anglo-Indians had been turned out of a large block of flats, Karnani Mansions. One government report admitted that requisitioning was causing 'serious hardship', and the American Consul also regretted the 'considerable inconvenience' to people in Calcutta, although this hardship of being made to move out to alternative residences, or being squeezed into rooms in cramped apartment blocks with numerous family members, was relatively mild in a city which was also beginning to experience famine.[14] When the members of an important central government investigation on public health carried out their research, their chairman, Joseph Bhore, decided that they simply could not tour the country to collect further data due to the shortage of accommodation in major towns and cities and the restrictions on railway travel. Rail passengers had seen repeated ticket rises and were forced off some passenger lines altogether.

In Calcutta, requisitioning disrupted extended families, even the well-off, and their servants and staff. The ports were crammed with ships, every *godown* (warehouse) space was packed and local factories and properties were requisitioned for storage space. Workers suddenly learned that they had been replaced when the military took over their mills. Workers of the Craig, Anglo India and Reliance jute mills went on strike against the requisitioning of their factories. When offered alternative shifts in neighbouring mills, the men refused: 'The position has been complicated by the recent bombing and by some shortage of labour, both skilled and unskilled, mainly owing to heavy military demands', reported the Governor.[15] Walchand Hirachand railed against the requisitioning of ships that he owned when twenty-four were seized with no terms for compensation: 'Here we are at war and a few petty Indian owners demand certain terms', retorted a British shipping journal, advancing the argument that complaining about requisitioning showed a meanness of wartime spirit.[16] The industrialists usually knew how to play the game, though. and lobbied hard against requisitioning when it threatened personal interests. G. D. Birla, a favoured industrialist of the Americans during the war years, had orders to acquire his own private property in Birla Park, Calcutta, rapidly rescinded. The army wanted Birla Park, the Calcutta Chamber of Commerce complained, because it was 'beautiful', despite having already been offered land of a comparable size. The Birla Brothers dashed off a pointed telegram to the supply department: 'American Army HQ trying to requisition our house Birla Park which is occupied by family members including ladies. Is also required for our business which [is] executing huge war orders . . . Unable [to] understand why we are harassed. Request your immediate kind intervention''[17]

Similarly, the industrialist Ramakrishna Dalmia fought a successful campaign to avoid requisitioning of his own private property, refusing to sell it to the British authorities when they made him an offer. Once again, those with the right social capital or those perceived as loyalists tended to be able to manoeuvre their way through the minefield of new security legislation and regulations.

Despite all this, many officials believed India was still too slow in changing into a base for total war. A number of strategists proposed inventive new ideas about how to maximise production. In August 1942, Henry Grady, a Californian diplomat, later the first American Ambassador to independent India, toured the country with a committee of economists and technical advisers. The team met with Indian workers and manufacturers, inspecting munitions factories, workshops, depots, shipyards and industrial plants. He spent two days touring Tata Iron and Steel in Jamshedpur, and crossed the country from Cochin to Calcutta. He met hundreds of people, from Walchand Hirachand and Birla to the shift-wage workers manning textile and munitions factories. The conclusion was damning. India was simply 'not organized on a war basis', Grady concluded. He argued 'a much larger army' could be recruited from among the local people, and his report called for 'urgency' in increasing Indian production, and railed against the 'totally inadequate' docks and ports and the 'seriously overburdened railways'. In Bombay the docks were overcrowded to the point of gridlock, with 200 ships waiting to unload or be repaired in May 1942, and 'prompt' and 'drastic' steps were needed. Communications were also inadequate and conveying messages by telephone or telegraph involved very long, frustrating waits, as many a foreign correspondent would bitterly testify.

With prescience, the report warned of the potential for rice shortages in the future, now that rice stocks from Burma and Indochina had been cut off, and criticised the lack of price control. Like many others in 1942, Henry Grady noted the potential for famine (using the actual word) without giving the issue more than passing interest. (He was not the first: Gandhi had already pointed out in April 1942, 'Bengal is suffering from famine'.[18]) Taking a purely technocratic and politically neutral line, the Americans urged a step-change in war production and more opportunities for Indians to manufacture and produce the materials vitally required for the war. Anyone who read it, however, could see it was also a censure of Britain's failure to fully extract the most from its colony; it could be read as an implicit criticism of British rule. Yet, it was also a command to squeeze India's people and resources much harder. The Americans had arrived and meant business.[19]

The quick, well-connected and enterprising traders and manufacturers sensed the possibility of profits. Vast numbers of men needed provisions. Those who had already established themselves as reliable contractors or purveyors for the British Army and Indian Army in the past, who had usually supplied food and basic provisions on more modest scales, now found themselves well placed to supply goods at previously unimaginable volumes. Small-scale military contractors, based in specific regions, could transform themselves within weeks into giant all-India suppliers. If they were fortunate they could secure almost exclusive rights to supply soap, boots or tyres with little oversight of

charges or profits. In Lahore, some family businesses boomed on an
unthinkable scale.

> We were called purveyors to the British Army. Whatever they needed by
> way of clothing, food – nothing to do with army hardware – boots,
> uniforms, food, canteens, what they required, consumables. And this was
> spread all over India, because the Indian Army was spread all over India,
> especially during the War, when the Indian Subcontinent was a big theatre,
> feeding both the Middle East and the China theatre. Lever Brothers came
> here and set up their factory and we were linked up with them,

recalled Syed Babar Ali many decades later, whose own family business in Lahore had begun as a traditional military contractor.[20] 'We
were buying soap and other Lever Brothers' products for the army,
not in wagon loads but in train loads.' A number of these Punjabi
contractors looked increasingly to the Muslim League as a way of
securing their own provincial commercial power base.

Many people attempted to find employment or to secure contracts
with the US forces by using their previous track record as suppliers
to the Indian Army. M. N. Chakraverti, who described himself as an
engineer, contractor and general merchant, was a registered contractor
to the British Army at Fort William in Madras and wrote to the US
forces offering to sell them fresh fruits and vegetables in East India.
Others made donations to the Allies in the hope of securing supply
contracts, such as the battery manufacturer Nalini Choudhury, who
was already supplying the RAF and sent a hundred rupees to the
Americans to support their Defence Fund. Initially decisions on
American supply were taken from Delhi but this responsibility was
soon transferred to Calcutta, where contracts could be more responsive to the needs of the army that was concentrated there.[21]

Other negotiations for supply continued to be made locally with
contractors and suppliers directly, for everything from textiles and
blankets, uniforms, shoes, equipment, paper and printing, to building
materials and major raw materials such as metals, coal and minerals.
These purchases would be paid for by India under the terms of reverse
lend-lease.[22] Multi-layered accommodations, agreements and convenient
quid pro quos emerged on both sides. Indian contractors and suppliers
recognised immediately the opportunities on offer. Gandhi, unusually,

was dragged into a commercial controversy about whether it was legitimate to sell homespun blankets to the army, and made a statement to clarify that it was permissible to trade products like rice and blankets with the Allies although it was a matter of conscience for each trader.[23]

Some potential contractors made accusations of foul play against their rivals: an anonymous 'wellwisher to the allies' informed the American Consulate that a shoemaker and tailor at a US Bengali base, A. A. Qureshi, was acting as an enemy agent but, after investigations, nothing incriminating was discovered. Another unsolicited letter from a former Indian police prosecutor, backed by a member of the Bengali Legislative Assembly, warned the Americans that Hindu policemen were failing to prosecute thefts of American supplies. In another case a shoe contractor, Shankar Ram, was accused by a rival supplier in a letter to the Americans both of political involvement in the 1942 Quit India movement and of overpricing his stock. The implication was that he should not be given the military contract if he had been involved in the anti-war Quit India campaign. Noticeably, the investigation into these allegations ignored the issue of 1942, and only sought to find out whether the shoes were being sold at the right price: it concluded that the rival's charge was baseless.[24] The urgent need to scramble resources for the war, to feed, clothe and supply an army at a time of great peril, had transformative effects on the fortunes of some local people.

Business for hotels, canteens and restaurants boomed. As members of the services reached the cities, these became packed with RAF, RIAF, army and naval men. Many complained about the shortage of suitable urban accommodation and the cost of rents. Senior military staff and large numbers of civil personnel all put pressure on the hotels and apartments, driving prices to record levels and placing hotel beds at a premium. One beneficiary was Mohan Singh Oberoi. Still establishing himself in the hotel business in the late 1930s, he had the chance to lease the Great Eastern Hotel in Calcutta at a cheap rate. Bad memories lingered, and the hotel was remembered as the place where a cholera epidemic had wiped out a hundred guests in 1933. The place was shabby and unloved. Oberoi's timing could not have been better. He took it on at a reduced rent of 7,000 rupees a month, spruced up the place and refurnished it. Then, in his own words, he 'improvised' 1,500 beds for the troops at ten rupees per head for board and lodging.

> The British Army was frantically trying to find accommodation . . . Taking over a cholera-ridden hotel had been a landmark in my career. The fact that I converted it and helped the Army in the time of stress and difficulty had come to the notice of the government . . . From now on my good luck was assured and gradually I went on increasing the scope of my activities with, I hope, benefit to many and much fulfillment to myself. Everything I did prospered.[25]

By the end of the war, Oberoi was managing hotels in Rawalpindi, Peshawar, Lahore, Murree and Delhi. He began to dream of building his own hotels across Asia. The foundations of the hotelier's luxury chain were based on a fortune of war, an entrepreneurial ability to seize a chance in the new circumstances.

*   *   *

The indefatigable Walchand Hirachand now decided to capitalise on the sudden availability of American finance and expertise. Walchand, frustrated by the progress of his shipbuilding, had decided to move into the production of something even more alluring and just as crucial for the war effort: aeroplanes. He formed a partnership with William Pawley, president of the Inter-Continent Corporation of New York and a director of China's Central Aircraft Company, and within seventy-two hours of Pawley's arrival in India, the two men agreed to set up an aeroplane factory together. They secured 4 million dollars' worth of orders from the Government of India and the Chinese nationalists, and the Maharaja of Mysore donated a vast patch of barren scrubland seven miles east of Bangalore. The Hindustan Aircraft Factory was born.[26]

Labourers cleared cobras and termite nests from the barren land, built their own kiln for brickwork, and within three weeks an airstrip and outbuildings had been established. The building work went on day and night, made possible by electric lighting. A group of American technicians and their families stayed in Bangalore throughout the war working for Hindustan Aircraft and at least 300 Indian engineers worked on building India's first planes. The first Indian-built aircraft, a Harlow, took to the skies in July 1941. The factory manufactured over 100 planes, used to transport troops around the subcontinent and across 'the Hump' to China. American and Indian capital (both private and later state investment and control) delivered Indian-made planes to South Asia.

The RIAF, like elsewhere, was the most glamorous of India's armed forces. Well-educated young men applied in large numbers, celebrated in the posters as 'a splendid band of courageous and enterprising youth'. The recruiting posters beckoned men who wanted to fight but 'equally importantly' to serve India after the end of the war; the air force promised 'thrills, adventure and a career' and 'free training for your post-war job'. The wartime state was again promoting the development of India, and the potential for acquiring technical expertise, as a way of attempting to harness the educated middle class to the war effort. Well-heeled young graduates, who had often thrilled to the exhilaration of flying in amateur flying clubs, started applying to the RIAF. They were promised world-class technical training and the chance to be in the vanguard of civil aviation at the end of the war. Schoolboys cut out pictures of the Hurricanes, Vultee Vengeances and Spitfires published in magazines. Cecil Beaton photographed the dashing student pilots training on the North-West Frontier. In Britain, too, Indian test pilots like P. C. Ramachandran looked as handsome as Bollywood stars as they posed with cigarettes and mugs of tea after their flights.[27]

On the ground, things were more fraught. It took time to train enough Indian technicians and the spare parts, batteries and communication sets had to be cobbled together. And the RIAF did not share the glory of the RAF. Mechanically minded men yearned to get their hands on a real fighter plane and educated men were frustrated playing second fiddle as ground crew: 'the feelings at that time were such that the RAF did not "want" us IORs [Indian Other Ranks] to be anywhere near the workspot. In clear but blunt terms we were told that we would only be a hindrance in the hangars. Hurricanes, Spitfires, Hudsons, Wellingtons and even Dakotas were kept out of our reach.'[28] Some Indian pilots felt that they were treated as second-best to the RAF.

Indian women in the WAC (I) joined the plotting rooms, meteorologists and radio-location teams. The mechanics, engineers and technicians of modern Indian flight would serve the airlines of independent Asia, PIA and Air India, once the war was over. Flight had never been so crucial, not solely for bombing sorties and reconnaissance over South-East Asia but also for the sheer movement of people from A to B. Military commanders performed logistical wonders. Wavell was flying to and fro across South Asia, the Middle East and Europe at an astonishing rate, making several changes of aircraft and barely escaping with his life from crashes on several occasions. Senior officials, but also nurses and Red Cross girls, hitch-hiked, catching lifts on military planes as if they were buses from Karachi to Bangalore or from Assam to Calcutta. Crashes and collisions were frequent and often fatal (Subhas Chandra Bose later died from a quite typical wartime incident when his plane crashed) and in India the remoteness of airstrips, the Himalayan mountains and the heat all added to the delicate operation of keeping the planes in the sky.

Requisitioned civilian aircraft could be rickety. Fifty pilots and air crew lost their lives and over 700 others were in associated incidents and accidents. 'The weather was frequently very dangerous for ordinary flying not to speak of dive-bombing with deep sucking downward convectional currents over the fairly high hills between Burma and India. The snow white towering Himalayas to the north were equally menacing vying with the beautifully red Jap flak coming from the target below.'[29] When Allied bombers crashed, the censor often suppressed the news, but the mangled wrecks made popular attractions. The wreckage of a plane in a paddy field near the railway station of Burdwan in Bengal pulled in crowds large enough to merit noting in provincial correspondence to New Delhi.

This was all wondrous to villagers. The majesty of the shiny planes was certainly used as a way of trying to inspire, impress and threaten. In the centre of Madras a strange window display stalled passers-by. A German bomber, shot down in Britain, had been sent to Madras for exhibition and was placed behind a large shop-window frontage in the central shopping mall.[30] Princes lined up to pledge money towards the construction of fighter planes. The Assam war fund raised £20,000s for the production of an 'Assam Bomber'. Naming the planes after places and princes was one way of buying into the dream of aviation. The Nawab of Bhopal, a mechanical enthusiast, gave out solid silver medals imprinted with four-prop planes to civilians who helped out with war duties. In cinemas, Movietone films showed Hurricanes looping through the clouds, and the surreal sight of the fields from the air. Flying aircraft low over the pastoral folk grazing their flocks on the Indo-Afghan border was, by the 1940s, an old tactic for both impressing and intimidating them.

In the summer of 1942 Linlithgow announced a 'morale-boosting' tour around the country, visiting Madras and the sites of coastal bombing. The Raj continued to attempt to boost morale by drawing on the ceremonial trappings of statehood. On 12 June, the King's brother, the Duke of Gloucester (and in Amery's view 'the most soldier-like in appearance of the Royal Family'), arrived in Delhi for a month-long state tour, intended as 'a real tonic to the loyal elements everywhere in India'. The duke made a demanding month-long whistle-stop tour of all the major cantonments and towns. He visited the Taj Mahal and reviewed American, British, Chinese and Indian troops outside the Viceregal Palace, while convalescent Indian troops, some with crutches and missing limbs, looked on.[31] But this was ceremonial puff, which had little resonance for local people or indeed for some of the troops that the tour was intended to encourage. Clive Branson, stationed in Galonche near Poona, was one of the soldiers to be reviewed by the duke and expressed his fury in a letter home:

> This parade is a purely bull-shit parade. It will take several days to polish boots, brasses, etc. It will take days and nights for some eight Indian tailors to alter, clean, press, etc. etc. clothes for white sahibs to wear like bloody waxworks. The Indians, of course, will not be on parade, the lucky fools . . . nothing more could help the enemy more by undermining morale.[32]

Even Linlithgow and the Heads of the Defence Services grumbled after standing in the furnace of Delhi's mid-June heat on tarmac for three hours waiting for the duke's plane to arrive. Soldiers were becoming frustrated by the long waits before action, and soldiers and civilians alike shared scepticism about the emphasis on viceregal and royal ceremony at a time when the dangers to India's borders felt tangible.

*　*　*

The war was not completely unwelcome. As mentioned earlier, depending on wealth, region, occupation and status the war's effects were variable and for some they were a boon. In the Hindi novel *Aadha Gaon*, the traders and weavers in the village of Gangauli want the war to continue, as their profits are accruing. As with the larger companies, *zamindars* who diversified into selling consumer goods, from gramophone records to opening shoe shops in United Provinces and Punjab, often reaped the rewards. Wages were still being driven upwards and there was plenty of work available; men who had been working in mines and collieries could find comparatively easier work overground, in the construction of roads and aerodromes. Workers in the jute factories of Calcutta, turning out the hessian gunny bags, were working round the clock. In Bombay and Ahmedabad workers did back-to-back shifts, working for sixteen hours or more at a stretch. Factory labourers resisted opening the factory doors to migrant labour from the neighbouring provinces.

But increasingly when they took their pay home at the end of the day, workers found the market emptier than usual, with less for sale, in both quantity and quality. Bags of rice and lentils mixed with stones or rough grains, sold at higher prices than the previous month; stores had empty shelves; stalls displayed less and scrawnier meat. The Faustian pact of war work was becoming apparent. By the second year of the war, prices had gone up over a third in real terms. By August 1942, General Raymond Wheeler, the deputy commander in South-East Asia Command, could report to his senior commander, Joseph Stilwell, 'that the US forces were practically living off the land in India'.[33]

14

Living Dangerously

Back in Britain, a small committed cadre tried their best to bring the Indian cause to public attention. Krishna Menon was forty-four years old and a councillor for St Pancras. He was the lodestar of the Indian Independence movement in Britain. He stood behind campaigns to lobby, cajole and shame the political establishment into granting Indian Independence and was the driving force behind the India League in London. The offices of the India League, at the top of a dingy stair-case above a shop on the Strand, consisted of two small rooms. The front room doubled as a print shop, stuffed with printing machinery and tottering stacks of magazines and papers, the cheap pamphlets that Menon sold at the endless rounds of lecture meetings he addressed. In the back room, Menon could be found behind a sham-bolic oversized writing desk, overloaded with books and papers. From here, he wrote newspaper columns and pamphlets, arranged meetings and speaker tours, planned demonstrations and protests. Volunteers and sympathisers, many of them women, tiptoed around him. This was the epicentre of the movement for Indian Independence in Britain and the channel through which the actions of the Indian National Congress back in India were filtered and publicised.[1]

In February 1942 Krishna Menon's frenetic activities for the India League reached a new fever pitch of intensity. He began a tour of all the major cities of Britain, voicing the need for Indian freedom. 'India faces the gravest moment in all its seventy centuries of history', he told a large mixed Indian and British crowd in Glasgow. One hundred and fifty people stood in the audience, among them students, peddlers, workers from munitions factories and merchant seamen.[2] They had paid sixpence to hear him. In Cardiff and Birmingham the crowds included Africans, West Indians and Chinese workers alongside whites.

In Dagenham a week later, factory workers, members of the Workers' Educational Association, gathered to hear him speak at the local public library. When asked by one about the threat of Japanese invasion in India, and the risk of Indians preferring Japanese rule, Menon shot back that the question was like 'asking a fish whether he wished to be fried in butter or margarine'.[3] What India wanted was Independence, and, he argued, the country had been left defenceless and without the motivation or ability to resist invasion without a truly popular government.

While Menon toured the country, trying to garner support for the India League, the security services were on his tail, tapping his phone calls and sending detectives to take notes from the back of his meetings. MI5 also tried to ensure that Menon was enlisted in the military as a way of eradicating his troublesome presence. 'It is time that the machinery of the law was put into operation to compel him to take up National Service', one MI5 officer urged. 'He is a first class wangler and will strain every nerve to avoid his obligations.'[4] The attempt to enlist Menon floundered because of his age and ill-health. In any case, he was already doing war work as an air raid warden in his borough of St Pancras. He earned notoriety and admiration from the locals for his punishing hours on the streets and his apparent obliviousness to the bombs of London, apocryphally at one point emerging unfazed from his office after a bombing raid with fragments of glass stuck in his hair.

*   *   *

By June 1942 the direct Japanese threat to India was passing. India was starting to release troops again, and sending men to North Africa to assist in the fight against Rommel; Tobruk fell on 21 June and by late July there was stalemate at El Alamein. But by the end of the summer, British authority in India was unravelling. The exodus from coastal cities, the fall of Singapore and the raids on Ceylon, threats of invasion with little real concerted strategy to explain how Indians would resist the Japanese, the general panic and above all the sight of refugees from Burma on the road and the stories of the two-tier refugee system all conspired to fundamentally damage the reputation of the Raj to a point where it looked beyond repair. As the historian

Indivar Kamtekar has suggested, 'the state seemed to be announcing its impending demise'.⁵ The withdrawal of savings from post offices and the widespread hoarding of small coins in preference to notes indicate the scale of uncertainty and distrust of the state. In the summer of 1942, as the threat of invasion receded, workers started to drift back to their factories in the cities from their rural homes (although often leaving families behind in the villages) but now the threat was a political one and the overriding question was whether the Raj could ever come to some form of settlement with the Congress.

Internally, the Congress was in factional disarray, trying to decide whether to launch street action and civil disobedience against the Raj. On 14 July the Congress Working Committee at Wardha passed a resolution calling for complete Independence, with Gandhi moving towards a more confrontational stance than he had ever taken. All summer, as the heat rose and the monsoon broke, the tension and speculation over the future of Gandhi and his movement reached boiling point. The government dithered about pre-emptive arrests and weighed up whether to send the Congress's senior leadership out of the country altogether. Uganda and Aden were potential destinations. The Governor of Madras wrote to the Viceroy in July in typical vein about Gandhi, 'the villain of the piece': 'If the movement comes to anything I would suggest arresting him at once and deporting him to Mauritius or Kenya, and prohibit any reference to him in the press. If he fasts let it not be known; and if he dies announce it six months later.'⁶ Yet within the Congress the path was not clear; the right-wingers became split and the communists and the Congress Socialist Party stood on opposing sides. Nehru felt the issue acutely. He had great sympathy for the Allied forces in Europe and wanted to back an anti-fascist cause but the failure of Cripps, and the ongoing suspicion that the mission had been an insincere set-up, forced a polarisation of opinions.

The uncertainty over a Japanese invasion stood at the heart of the indecision about commencing the Quit India movement in the summer of 1942. For a time in early 1942 Gandhi had believed that India would fall to the Japanese.⁷ He calculated that it was better to wrench Independence immediately from the British than to fall into fascist hands, perhaps even with the consent of the disgruntled Indian public who watched Bose's every move with the glee of a cinema audience. Gandhi was alienated by the ugliness of war and its transformative effects on the Indian landscape: the killing of cattle for beef rations for troops and the reports of assaults on village women that circulated widely. Earlier in the year when the Chinese leader Chiang Kai-shek had met Gandhi he had been struck by his obstinacy. Everywhere under conditions of war, positions had calcified. Now, Gandhi's statements became unequivocal and more clearly marked by ideas of race than they had ever been. It was time, he announced, 'for the British and the Indians to be reconciled to complete separation from each other'.[8]

Ironies abounded. Communists, once so feared by the government that they had been banned, but now a rare and much-needed government ally, were legalised in July, released from jail and bans on their publications lifted. Among other nationalists, the question of how to proceed was still causing heartache and wide differences of opinion. Old colleagues, husbands and wives took up different places on the political spectrum and anguished discussions divided former political allies.

The Congress activists Aruna Asaf Ali and her husband had a difference of opinion. They had been travelling the country, taking part in meetings, discussing furiously whether or not to start civil disobedience. She argued the need to launch a concerted protest; he was more circumspect and cautious about the new demand for civil disobedience which was building a crescendo. Ironically, it was he who would be arrested alongside other Congress leaders. The government would come to regret leaving his wife off the list.

In the early morning of 9 August 1942, the government pounced. The mass arrest of Congress leaders from the Congress Working Committee in Bombay that morning was swift and well anticipated. As in the past, news from government had seeped into Congress circles with ease, through sympathetic police and officials passing on the word. Abul Kalam Azad heard about his own imminent arrest from a friend of a friend in the Bombay police. Aruna Asaf Ali recalled the police arriving at her home that morning: 'My husband and I were not in the least surprised when, in the early hours of 9th August, the police knocked on the door at the flat where we were staying. When they announced Asaf's arrest, I asked, "What about me?" "There is not [a] warrant for you, madam" I was told.'[9] The arrest was impeccably civil although menacing and a train was waiting at Victoria Terminus in Bombay to take the arrested leaders on to where they would be detained. 'The whole place was swarming with CID plain clothes men. We could not enter the platform', remembered Sucheta Kripalani, who, like Aruna, was the wife of a jailed leader and was also in Bombay that day. 'I think Aruna was the only lucky person who managed to get into the station. So we returned. The whole city was in turmoil. Overnight I was thrown into a larger role than I had ever played.'[10]

The Congressmen feared deportation to another part of the empire but after deliberations about a secret extradition, Linlithgow had decided to imprison the Congressmen at Ahmednagar Fort in central India. Abul Kalam Azad, who had also been seized that morning, saw Aruna on the platform and later recalled, 'As the train started to move she looked at me and said, "Please don't worry about me. I shall find something to do and not remain idle." Later events showed that she meant what she said.'[11] From every window of the train carriage the faces of the detained peered as the train pulled out of the station and receded from view. On board Asaf Ali breakfasted in the dining car with Nehru, Azad, Patel and the rest of the Congress High Command. The atmosphere was one of forced jollity.

> Each ordered what he desired, some had eggs, poached, fried or boiled; some had toast with coffee or tea, but the majority had only fruits and milk. As we passed station after station we found the platforms guarded by the police, with not even railway staff or porters on the platforms. Occasionally we caught sight of some railway officials in their black coats, stealthily peering from behind trellised screens or glass panes of office doors.[12]

These would be the last members of the public they would see for three years.

The guards took the Congress Working Committee to Ahmednagar Fort, a fifteenth-century circular fort with thick black walls of hewn stone, with twenty-four bastions and one gate. An immense curtain wall stretched upwards for 80 feet. Asaf Ali, Nehru, Azad and the others negotiated the steep steps and walkways into the more modern barracks in the interior of the fort. Around the fort ran a deep moat, which could be crossed by a suspension drawbridge. As far as the eye could see, rocky scrubland stretched to the horizon. Parts of the fort were crumbling but it had a reputation, centuries old, of impregnability; the Mughal emperor Aurungzeb had died here in 1707. For the next three years, without a radio and with only a handful of visitors, this would be Asaf Ali's prison.

In the meantime, his wife was taking matters into her own hands. Alone, she felt in a quandary. Unclear how best to vent her opinions, separated from friends and family, she kept repeating to herself, 'What should I do?' Crowds, hearing of the arrests, had started to mass on the streets, and the police had to erect barricades. Beaten back by police batons, and fired on with tear gas, a demonstration in Bombay deteriorated into violence. That day was a psychological tipping point for some of the Congress leaders, recalled by many of them in the years to come. It became part of national lore in Independent India. The sight of police violence against protesters who had heard of the arrests and attempted to get close to the train station fuelled anger. Like many others, Aruna was incensed by seeing gas attacks and *lathi* charges in Bombay. At a public square in Bombay, Gwalia Tank Maidan, where a Congress flag-raising ceremony had been scheduled, she found herself propelled forward to leadership, raising the Congress flag and heading a procession. The conflict with the state had reached boiling point. Thirty-three people died from police gunshots in the first four days after the arrests in Bombay.

By simultaneously arresting prominent Congressmen all over the country the government believed it had cut off the head of the movement. But trouble bubbled up everywhere from unexpected sources, linking together middle-class nationalists with villagers and workers in a surge of anti-state sabotage.

*   *   *

The Quit India movement has been heavily mythologised and celebrated by successive post-Independence governments in India, and often lauded as part of a linear progression towards Independence, chalked up alongside the movements of the 1920s and 1930s. The actions of freedom fighters have been well catalogued and their heroic actions tabulated by nationalist historians. However, in a number of ways it was distinctive when compared with many earlier movements that Gandhi had spearheaded. Most obviously, Gandhi was absent due to his imprisonment and was not commanding events. Younger members of a new generation, teenagers and students, stood in the vanguard and outran the constraints of their parents and elders.

There was a groundswell of anti-state feeling in the country that was outstripping the control of Gandhi; it was amorphous, without a centre, driven by youth and peasants who were disenfranchised and furious.[13] In the early weeks of August students stopped going to school and college (attendance in Bombay dropped to less than 20 per cent) and joined sit-ins, strikes and marches in their thousands. A sixteen-year-old girl, Chitra Mehta, was sent away by her Congress-leaning family to stay with more politically aloof relatives in order to try to keep her away from joining the movement, while she finished her exams.

> Whenever I used to open my study books I could not see anything but hazy black circles. At last the inner conflict proved too much for me and I was laid up with high fever. For about fifteen days I was in bed. Then I wrote a letter to my father telling him that under the prevailing circumstances I would never be able to study.

Chitra Mehta's account gives a sense of the intoxication of the hour, the sheer adrenalin and elation that were driving young women like herself to disobey their families and to take personal risks. 'I would go mad if I tried to keep out of Freedom's Battle', she wrote.[14] It was an intensely exhilarating moment for many young people. Interception of correspondence in Bengal was described by the censor as showing 'women often worked up to a fever pitch of emotion'.[15] Chitra Mehta ultimately joined a crowd of political disciples who gathered outside Gandhi's prison at the Aga Khan's Palace and described being unable to sleep in fear of Gandhi's death while he fasted.

Many onlookers noted the youthfulness of the urban rebels. Teenagers and young people stood in the forefront of the rebellions, a new generation who had been only children or not yet born when Gandhi started his mass campaigns of non-co-operation. India's young population had been increasing in size and political significance and now the number of school closures, the refusals to attend examinations and the presence of youth in the crowd were marked. There was a generational gap with their elders in spirit, in language and in commitment to Gandhian idealism. Growing up with the cinema, the radio and with a new internationalist consciousness, these were young men and women aware that they had to carve out a life in a new post-war, post-imperial world. They respected Gandhi and invoked nationalist symbols but they stood for a new form of radicalism which was less tolerant of non-violence and impatient of the old order. Trilochan Senapati, a young underground organiser who was still evading the police a year on in 1943, wrote to his beloved, melding his belief in their future despite the forbidden love-match with his political vision: 'You know what we the educated of our age are going to do . . . we will show the world a new way. All shall support us in the long-run in this progressive age . . .' 'I think I can be a man', he promised her, if he could only build up his revolutionary life in the 'right way'. Tellingly, he quoted Nehru at the end of his letter: 'Don't think about the past because the past is past. We must think about the present to make our future sublime.' This was a generation seeking a radical rupture with the political standards of their parents.[16]

Aruna, meanwhile, was dodging the police, who had now issued a warrant for her arrest. Shielded by friends and sympathisers, she decided to go underground and to help organise the movement. The plan was for a number of leading politicians, wives and middle-class activists who had not been jailed to work as saboteurs and agents provocateurs. First Aruna went to Delhi, her home city, although she could not go back to her house. Police had already stripped the place of her furniture and possessions, and so she kept moving, at first living in the home of a civil surgeon and his family. The government offered a 5,000-rupee reward for her capture. Those uncaptured by the police started to organise, to hold fiery meetings and to make perilous strategies. 'We had to travel all over the country. I went to Calcutta, UP [United Provinces], Madras, Bombay, Pachim, Maharashtra. And then the others were travelling all over. It was a very hectic time and we worked under great difficulties because the CID and police were everywhere.'[17] Sucheta Kripalani recalled the early meetings, the frantic travelling between flats, offices and hideouts, rapid changes of colourful saris on trains, the attempts to merge into other families when travelling, the way that, as a young woman, she could also pass for a student and evade detection. The network gradually flowered, channelling money to protesters and saboteurs who had started attacking the railways and targeting government property including ammunition factories and army depots, as well as printing and distributing radical pamphlets and running an illegal radio station.

The rebellion was a conglomeration of different uprisings with their own logics and leaderships; it had its own regional dynamics. In towns and cities it was championed by prosperous students who led strikes, *hartals* and demonstrations. In the countryside, it was far more nebulous but also far more violent from the start. Pre-existing peasant activism and grievances fused with the movement, and at times undefined general crime and disorder segued into more organised political protest. The name of Gandhi, as in earlier decades, provided the millenarian inspiration for acts that could be carried out in his name, even if they fell outside his own sanction. The rebels dipped into the ideological resources of the Congress, invoking language and ideas distorted or derived from the nationalists. As the ruminations of Asaf Ali and Nehru in prison reflected, the Congress leadership was far from content with the course of events and was concerned by the way that the movement had spun away from their own direction or grip. There was an uneasy tension between acts being attributed to Congress, by both government and rebels, and the actual position of the leadership.

Secret radio broadcasts, made by anonymous Congress supporters from clandestine transmitters that were shifted around from apartment to apartment, instructed the public on what to do if the Japanese did reach Bengal: 'Let it be clear that in the event of Japanese invasion, the British administration will be completely demoralised as was seen before. You should capture the administrative machinery, declare the free state of India and hoist the national flag.'[18] Pamphlets and radio broadcasts blasted the government in a tone that was sensationalist, hysterical and revolutionary. The call of the hour was to self-sacrifice, even oblivion, akin to the call made to soldiers fighting in the war: '"Live Dangerously" ought to be the motto of every young man of India. Live life to the fullest and best effect. The Congress has sent its clarion call. Mahatmaji is in jail rotting in a British dungeon. It is up to you, young sons of India, to take up arms and march abreast!'[19]

Aruna and Sucheta, like other leading members of the underground movement, were cushioned by their elite status and their many friends in high places. Along with other 'absconders' Aruna surfed on a wave of goodwill from friends, sympathisers, high and humble officials, including the station director of All India Radio, Z. A. Bukhari, and distinguished civil servants. As one police officer reported, 'against nine of us who are searching for her, there are nine *lakhs* in Delhi alone to offer her protection and quarter. It is an uneven game and you cannot blame us if we cannot succeed.'[20] Networks of hospitality kept the rebels alive; they did not need to buy food or railway tickets or even carry money. Strangers ferried them from safe-house to safe-house, wanting for nothing. They even pretended, on one occasion, to be patients in the beds of a Bombay clinic. The flow of money towards the rebels was steady and generous. The government rightly suspected the larger industrialists of siphoning cash towards the move- ment, but to Linlithgow's frustration could find no traces. The big bosses of industry, among them Walchand Hirachand, G. D. Birla and Gaganvihari Mehta, the president of the Federation of Indian Chambers of Commerce, continued to secretly bankroll the under- ground rebels, anonymously channelling tens of thousands of rupees.[21]

Playing chase with the authorities, Aruna's evasion of the police was becoming a running drama in the press by September, and held par- ticular appeal for young students. S. M. Y. Sastri, a young journalist working on radio news programmes, was 'thrilled by the way Aruna Asaf Ali and the CSP [Congress Socialist Party] members were now fighting' and felt inspired to give up his job and return to his home district to join the struggle.[22] Some military men followed the story too, albeit clandestinely. When sailors from the Royal Indian Navy ship HMS *Talwar* went on strike after the end of the war, it was Aruna whom they thought to approach: 'She had endeared herself to the country and to many of us by her militant role in the Quit India movement in 1942. To some she resembled the legendary Laxmibai of Jhansi who personally led her soldiers against the British during the Sepoy Mutiny of 1857.'[23]

Over the weeks, Aruna and Sucheta were astonished by something which they had not expected, however. Congress was not in control at all. The underground activists were merely tapping into the fero- cious surge of anger that was ricocheting around the country. The leaders were themselves being carried away on a tide of protest, which went far beyond their own blueprint. 'The sabotage, destruction, whatever had happened, was spontaneous. If I say we had organised it, it would be wrong', recalled Sucheta Kripalani many years later. 'What the AICC [All India Congress Committee] did was to collect information, help the people who were hiding, send them money, send them assistance, and whenever they were in trouble we'd go and try and see in what way we could resolve their difficulties.'[24]

Peasants who came out of their fields and cotton-mill workers who left their factories were the real rebels behind the struggle. Their complex grievances, deeply rooted in long-standing inequalities but compounded by the changes of the war, now erupted with unrestrained fury, much of it far outside the bounds of centralised political control. In Midnapore, Ballia and Satara parallel administrations ran unimpeded for a number of weeks. In Ahmedabad two-thirds of the mill workers left the city, unhampered by ambivalent mill owners. Gandhi's order to 'Do or Die' was a mantra vague enough to attach to any kind of rowdiness. But this was not anarchy. This was a clear attempt to destabilise the war effort and the pamphlets in circulation unambiguously targeted the war. They voiced anger at requisitioning and wartime change:

The British, who have ruined our villages and converted our golden country into a cremation ground, will then come along with hirelings and loot all the ripe paddy that you have cultivated with such labour and care. Just think it over, whether it is better to let this happen or drive off the devil and try to live as a free man with the right to enjoy the fruit of one's labour.[25]

Some of the worst fears of the British, which had unwisely been articulated in public by Amery, now became realities. Railway engines ran covered with Congress flags, an aerodrome was burned to the ground in United Provinces, and at ammunition factories workers were being suborned and encouraged to sabotage production. Munitions workers broke equipment or manufactured faulty supplies. Railway officials leaked information to rebels. Everywhere there were degrees of complicity between some officials and policemen whose sympathies lay with the rebellion rather than the state. Determined sabotage, insurrection and disruption blazed – albeit only for a quick and brazen flash in some places – through districts in Bombay, Gujarat, United Provinces, Bihar, Central Provinces, Madras, Delhi, Bengal, Orissa and beyond. In some districts the ICS lost control completely for weeks at a time. Rebels burned post offices and government property, smashed railway signals and tore up track. Telegraph poles were uprooted and bomb explosions occurred in Poona and Bombay. Large bands of villagers with crude weapons made strikes on targeted government-owned bungalows or tax offices and then melted back into the countryside.

Some well-known leaders vocally opposed the uprising. The *dalit* leader Ambedkar called it 'irresponsible and insane'; the leftist M. N. Roy continued to champion supporting the war and called for a kind of cosmopolitan humanitarianism which did not foreground nationality. Some flysheets produced by rebels used extreme imagery, playing on terrors of interracial sex and the protection of Indian women from bestial foreign soldiers. There was a Manichaean edge to some of the Quit India speeches and pamphlets, playing on the fear of Muslims and driving a wedge between Hindus and Muslims, who were becoming increasingly politically estranged. Historians differ on the extent of the movement (if it can be called a movement at all), how radical it really was and to what ends it would have brought India. Among the revolutionaries themselves factions differed on the role of violence and on the war against fascism. Arguments raged into the small hours of the night: was tearing up telegraph wires an act of violence or passive resistance that could be squared with Gandhianism?

As ever, there was the problem of reliable news. Over the years people had become accustomed to the idea of censorship, to the sense that they were not being told the full truth. Now the newspapermen struck back at the censorship imposed on them, refusing to print at all. The printing presses for seventeen English newspapers and sixty-seven newspapers in Indian languages went cold. Word spread that the Indian Army might side with the people. In Vizagapatam, near Walchand Hirachand's moribund shipyard, a cyclostyled sheet was circulating, claiming that Indian troops had mutinied and were being shot by British troops. People rallied to the power of rumours and vague news items.

The movement shone a light on both the power and the serious weakness of the British in India; it was quickly reined in and brought under control by determined repression, but at the cost of exhausted and demoralised personnel and irreversible damage to the reputation of the empire.

*   *   *

In the Middle East, at the same time, the struggle for supremacy continued with reverses for the Allies and losses of some of their earlier advances to Rommel. The sepoys' chief response to the movement back home was to curse it and to worry. What did this mean for family back home? What did it mean for their security of employment? Who was right and who was wrong? In North Africa, now facing defeat and already concerned about the rapidly rising prices back home, sepoys fretted about risks to the stability of their country, anxious that their relatives or villages might be rebel targets. And the relatives back in India took fright at the sight of the *sarkar*'s institutions and property now coming under attack, fearing the consequences for their own modest prosperity. 'Dear Brother your deposits in the post office will be of no use to us', wrote one worried kinsman from central India to a sepoy in the Middle East. 'These post offices are being set on fire and that will be the fate of the one where you have kept your money. All the post offices at Nagpur and other places were burnt recently.'[26] With nothing but these sparse communications it was difficult to make sense of what was happening in India for sepoys stationed in other theatres.

Concern for children was paramount, especially when there were riots taking place in India, and a pained letter to Bhopal suggested the agonies and frustrations of being so far from home at a time of such dangerous instability in India. The soldier instructed his wife to keep the children 'like [a] hen keeps chicks under her wings'. She should on no account let their boy, Mian Qayum, go out of the house, even to go to school, if the danger increased; he continued:

Take greatest care in anything concerning [the] children. Oh! If only I knew it before I would never [have] come this way. I hope you will respect my feelings and take care of the children. Give me news of Bhopal, are there any riots?[27]

Axis propaganda lost no time in seizing on this chink in the psychological armour, trying to drive a wedge between the government and its army. Over the skies of North Africa fluttered leaflets depicting Gandhi's image or his iconic spinning wheel. Another showed an image of Indians chained to a map of England, with slogans printed in Hindi and Urdu. 'Long live Independent India', stated another Axis flysheet, calling itself a 'Liberty Pass'. 'Whoever shows this surrender pass will be accepted as a friend of the Axis forces. His personal freedom and liberty to follow his own religious practices are fully guaranteed. Just bring this surrender pass with you.'[28] Soldiers may have been broadly sympathetic to Indian freedom but they were irritated by the timing of a movement that could derail their efforts against the Axis at a delicate moment in the war.

For centuries the Indian Army had cultivated traditions of loyalty to king and country, and regimental pride, aspiring to political neutrality. Regimental and regional loyalties grounded on a sense of honour or *izzat* demanded steadfastness. Military steadiness was also founded on additional things by 1942: professional pride and intense training, the camaraderie and terror of shared battle at close quarters, and honouring the dead and the living. The ideological desire to defeat the Axis was strong especially amongst those who had seen action. For those who did waver, there was also sheer peer pressure, the risk of court martial and the difficulties of finding a practical way to desert once the oath of allegiance had been sworn. Above all, thoughts returned to families waiting on the next instalment of remittances. *Izzat* could have a wider meaning beyond pride in a regiment or military status: a regular army job brought *izzat* to the breadwinner who had the prestige of a steady state income and with it an elevated status among his kin.

Despite attempts to suppress the press, knowledge about the Quit India movement was widespread and it is clear that soldiers sometimes felt ambivalent, wanting to know more, encouraged by the progress of Indian freedom, at least sympathetic to the cause of Indian nationalism even if not pleased with the actual timing of events. A guarded letter from a field ambulance reveals this tension: 'I shall be interested to hear a little of the political situation in India. Recent news has been interesting and sad. I have a great respect for Gandhi because he is consistent in his policy and opinion. But it is a pity that such a time should have been chosen to press for a political advantage.' An Indian in the air force in the Middle East wrote with exasperation:

Oh the tragedy of it all! There is tremendous good will among the people [on] both sides. Life in India can't be very easy or very pleasant caught between the devil and the deep sea, an army occupation and an army of invasion! In spite of everything I still maintain that there is more at stake in this war than mere self interest.[29]

In another case, a *havildar*, who was reprimanded by officers for his letter, wrote straight from the heart about the terrors of war: 'Please inform Congress to persuade people not to join Government Service and if they do then they will all be victims of this war.'[30] A military cadet at a military college at the time remembered his teacher describing how he would like to tie Gandhi to the blades of the ceiling fan in the room and turn the speed up high, at which some of the boys laughed and some stayed conspicuously silent.[31]

Among Britons too, many now questioned their role in India. A censored letter from a military wife in the hill station of Simla, where the remnants of the Burmese government had assembled alongside numerous senior officers and officials, suggested her own hunger for truth:

You know Geoff, we have taken this jolly old war too bally casually here at Simla, picnics, dances and poodle-faking and now comes this Indian trouble. Because Simla has seen little of it does any one of us give a hoot? Do any of us women know who has been locked up or why? We know somebody was trying to sell India to Japan and if any one of us was consulted the reply would be 'Good job too, get on with it and let us get out of it and fight Germany . . .' Anyway I, for one, am going to begin asking questions even if I am described as Nuisance no. 1 until I really understand something of the whys and wherefores of this Indian trouble.[32]

Among the soldiers who had come from Britain, there was a cluster of men who felt deeply aggrieved about the old forces of empire. Clive Branson, as ever, threw a piercing light on social iniquities in his letters home:

Today things have gone so far that pacifism is impossible . . . One cannot foretell what will happen. The movement is so far confined to the towns, mainly angry demonstrations against police stations with a little shop breaking, telephone wire cutting, shop closing etc. . . . Even

though one does not agree with what the people are doing, one under-
stands why they do it.[33]

Although Branson was the most prominent of this group of men to
express such feelings in print, a number of others felt deeply uncertain
aiding the civil power to put down internal unrest in the empire, when
they wanted to be fighting in Europe. Concerned young officers shared
a sense of uneasiness about the imperial mission and their role in it.

There was not a sealed wall between troops and civilians and ideas
and information flowed between them. Nilubhai Limaye, an underground activist from Poona, closely connected to the Quit India leadership, circulated around the country meeting Indian army officers
and soldiers, trying to find out if they could be swayed and how they
felt about the movement. 'I must have gone round half the military
stations in India and, this way and that, I contacted the officers, *jawans*
and all. But I am very sorry to say that somehow the Army was very
cold about the movement. It is not that they were loyal to the Britishers
at heart but somehow they were working for them.' He was unable
to persuade the men he met: 'when some academic discussions used to
take place, they did not like the *satyagraha* business or sabotage
business . . . Even when I visited a few army officers they were afraid
to talk to me also. They would hardly give me two minutes or three
minutes.'[34] Limaye's disappointing tours around cantonments and
camps are testament both to the permeable wall between soldiers and
citizens – it was possible for them to meet and to discuss politics – and
also to the nervous distance between them. Soldiers risked punishment
by talking to men like Limaye. Even when they were broadly sympathetic to the aims of Independence, the specific timing and techniques
of Quit India were unwelcome. Looking back, Limaye could hardly
recall a time when a supportive conversation had taken place, although
there had been the occasional lengthy debate. 'Otherwise I did not
get much response from the army boys.'[35]

Soldiers did, of course, have cousins and family members who rose
up as rebels, and family connections linked some soldiers to imprisoned
protesters. The wide net of military recruitment – from Bengal to
Madras – and the nature of South Asian extended families meant that
many different opinions and views could be found within one village
or family. One *naik* in the Middle East was implored by his nephew

to help intercede on behalf of his rebellious father, Zahid Ali Mian Sahib, in August 1942, 'arrested last Friday 14th August for defiance of the Govt. of India. No bail is allowed in such cases.'[36] Service to the Crown and participation in anti-British movements could coexist, albeit uneasily within the same family. In the uncertain climate, and within a context in which the future of the British presence in South Asia seemed increasingly tenuous, it often seemed necessary for families to balance interests, to align oneself with the rising tide of power and to keep onside with municipal and local officials who had access to resources, especially if they oversaw the distribution of grain. This could dictate the pattern of so-called loyalism and rebellion in 1942, as in the heat of the moment new alliances and decisions about future political allegiances were forged.

The sheer ruthlessness with which the imperial state hit back is not in doubt. It was the most violent crackdown since the repression of the 1857 uprising. 'I am engaged here in meeting by far the most serious rebellion since that of 1857', the beleaguered Viceroy infamously told Churchill in a telegram. 'The gravity and extent of which we have so far concealed from the world for reasons of military security.' The ghosts of mutiny floated everywhere in the air.[37] And as in the previous century, local officials could take matters into their own hands. Blanket protection and promises of amnesties from the top shielded individual policemen and officials. The backlash in troubled districts drew on the use of collective fines, widespread detention without trial for vaguely named 'political prisoners' and use of corporal punishment. L. W. Russell was an extreme example and recalled in his own memoir the 'strong action' he took against twenty-eight men, part of a 'threatening' mob that had collected around a local police station in his district of Kodaram. Each man was lashed ten times with a dog-whip on the spot, to his mind a necessary deterrent to the angry crowd. As he wrote: 'Illegal without a doubt. Cruel? Perhaps. But there was no further trouble throughout the district.'[38]

Officials, trying desperately to cling on to their authority, particularly in United Provinces and Bihar, acted far beyond the limits of legality or state-sanctioned power. These provincial governments acknowledged in letters to London how police had seized rebel hostages, destroyed property if it belonged to rebels or their supporters, called in arms or radio sets without normal procedures, forced labourers to repair damaged government property and imposed collective fines beyond the allowable limits.[39]

Collective fines drew particular ire as a peculiarly pernicious type of action in India. These had long been imperial practice, and would later be applied during the Partition riots of 1947. Whole villages or communities had to pay up if members of their own village or *mohalla* had been implicated in violence. The fines aggravated anti-state feeling and drove a wedge between those fined and those not fined; in Bihar and in Central Provinces, in a blatant display of the government's desire to prevent India's religious communities from uniting in 1942, the police exempted Muslims from collective fines after lobbying by the Muslim League, unless there was a direct reason to suspect particular individuals.[40] By mid-September 1942, within weeks of the start of the uprising, people in Central Provinces and Berar had been collectively fined over 300,000 rupees. After a rebellion in the Nilgiri Hills a fortnight later, the local government suggested that any more disturbances would result in 'the forcible realisation of collective fines . . . as the rice crop ripens, this becomes a very real threat'.[41] The collection of fines could be used to subdue and intimidate, as well as to realise cash.

Officials also sought and won the possibility of exoneration from any illegal acts carried out in 'good faith', from the burning-down of villages to, in one instance, the shooting dead of one Dewoo Ganpat, a vegetable hawker, killed at short range by two policemen for shouting a nationalist slogan.[42] Other more trivial but humiliating punishments, like the stripping naked of protesters and rough house searches, also took place, while in more remote districts like Midnapore zealous Indian and British policemen razed houses and burned property to the ground.[43] Rebels used alarming rhetoric to instil the fear of rape by rampaging police and soldiers and in Bengal a number of sexual attacks on women were recorded in detail with corroborating evidence.[44] In Chimur, an isolated village in Central Provinces surrounded by dense jungle, three senior local policemen were murdered. All the men of the village took flight, leaving local women vulnerable as the authorities swooped, and there were strong insinuations of sexual attack. 'Meet any woman of Chimur and you will find her with tears in her eyes', reported women Congress workers who visited the village some weeks later, 'imploring you to try to release her husband, brother or son.'[45] The courts, manned by both Indian and British judges, attempted to uphold the rule of law and to rein in some provincial policemen and administrators by refusing to ratify some actions. But with the extraordinary powers of the Defence of India Act under their belt, many provincial governments found they could simply declare new ordinances or dodge judicial interference. Military and civil parts of the state had fused together further; newly recruited civil servants now spent five or six weeks with units of the army to familiarise themselves with the armed forces and with a view to mutual co-operation in the case of civil unrest.

For some army officers it was a chance to see action at last, even if not against the Axis. As one wrote home to Britain:

> At one time the police were completely demoralised and we were given a free hand, pretty well, to use force where necessary without the usual rigmarole of getting a magistrate's sanction written or otherwise. We had some grand fun including a number of firing incidents. But I'm sorry to say we lost one officer and four ORs at one place just overwhelmed and beaten to death by a frenzied mob . . . I myself had some excitement with my pln [platoon]. And two or three times had to open fire but that always did the trick.[46]

Churchill admitted 500 protesters had been killed, the official British statistics noted 1,060, *The Statesman* newspaper recorded 2,500.[47] Many of the nationalists pegged the figure much higher. During the autumn and winter months of 1942 there were between 60,000 and 90,000 detentions, leaving the prisons packed and insanitary. Despite fears about political 'infection' it was difficult to keep political prisoners segregated from other prisoners, including thieves and murderers, alongside errant sepoys.

Military reserves stretched to breaking point as the army balanced the defence of the border with the internal unrest. William Slim feared the Japanese might seize the moment and start an airborne invasion or lend air support to the protesters; he suffered at least a couple of intensely anxious weeks, as large chunks of the Indian countryside, particularly in Bihar, passed out of civil control altogether. Slim, with oversight of Orissa and Bengal, was reduced to forming his 'final and only reserve' from the venereal patients in the Calcutta and Barrackpore hospitals.[48] The government had considered ever since the beginning of the war the passing of a domestic martial law, or a Revolutionary Movement Ordinance, should rebellion on a major scale erupt in India, but ultimately in 1942 settled on the repurposing of the Defence of India Act as a way of keeping unrest under control. But some choice morsels from the draft of the Emergency Ordinance supplemented the Defence of India Act from 1942, included as amendments to existing laws, including the aim of waging 'economic warfare' against Congress. The military and civil functions of the state became very blurry. What was necessary for the defence of the country and what was necessary for internal stability? On 14 August the first of several attacks by military aircraft were made on protesters who were dismantling bridges and railway tracks in Kajra, Bihar, and they were strafed by machine-gun fire from above.[49] Ultimately, the wartime conditions and the unbridled possibilities offered by the blanket Defence of India rules enabled the Raj to bring down the full force of the state on the heads of the rebels without needing to justify or legislate for its own actions.

* * *

In Britain itself, the fight for civil liberties was a concern for a small segment of society, and campaigns were waged by the usual sympathetic suspects: Quakers, churchmen, union workers and communists, members of the International Women's League and the Peace Pledge Union. Whipping as a public punishment for anti-British activity during the Quit India movement hit a particular nerve with the anti-imperialists, making headline news in the UK in 1942. Members of the British public from provincial towns like Hove and Leicester wrote letters to the India Office. George Bernard Shaw commented on 'this unpardonable flogging business' and the publisher Victor Gollancz wrote a letter that was published in the *New Statesman and Nation*. The pro-Indian MP Reginald Sorensen asked in the House of Commons about the 'deplorable and medieval practice', to which Amery uncomfortably explained that whipping in India was 'administered by a light rattan cane and not by the "cat"'. The issue reached cabinet level, with ministers worrying about the idea of corporal punishment in India and Amery reporting that feeling was 'tremendously strong' against it.[50]

Nonetheless, much of the political reaction, and Amery's attempts to minimise news of floggings in India, were driven first and foremost by concerns about the propaganda issue. The Viceroy duly passed on instructions to provincial governors to keep publicity of floggings to a minimum. 'It is very difficult to know what to advise,' Amery wrote to the Viceroy, 'except that in so far as it is inflicted as a punishment – and it may have to be so increasingly if things get really critical – care should be taken to avoid publicity. There is no doubt that the Left here and our opponents in America are making the most out of it.' The Governor of Bombay demurred that whipping was only carried out on 'the tough, sturdy, bullying type of offender' in any case.[51]

Not so easily deterred, Indian voices in Britain continued to be raised against inhumane punishments and the infringement of liberties. A young Bengali student living in Oxford, D. M. Sen, wrote several letters to the *New Statesman and Nation* attacking the treatment of prisoners in Indian jails, the use of fetters and shackles, beating up by policemen and bodily punishments. Sen went on to have an extended correspondence with the Secretary of State and even managed to meet him in person. Although Amery admitted that some stories might have had truth to them, the Secretary of State brushed off Sen as an agitator who was raking up stories. When a Chief Justice of Bombay who was coming through London, and happened to be passing through the office as this matter was discussed, 'expressed a view that it was undoubtedly a fact that beatings up occurred in Police Stations' and said that he had personally seen the marks of such manhandling on the bodies of fresh inmates in jails, this was a step too far for the India Office.[52] Penderel Moon, the brilliant and maverick British civil servant who was increasingly aligning himself with the Indian nationalists, resigned his position in protest about the treatment of political prisoners, but this minor embarrassment to the government was quietly hushed up.[53] The management of news regarding the disciplinary practices in India was far more important in London than the actual practices themselves.

The priority in London was, understandably, defeating the Nazi state. This left little sympathy in Blitzed London for Indian activists. Indian nationalism was becoming increasingly divisive in British society. Krishna Menon was still touring, speaking and scribbling pamphlets, working long days and into the hours of the night. But he felt increasingly demoralised, and at one point admitted that he felt like 'packing up the whole show' and returning to India. Even a published version of Nehru's statement about the Cripps Mission didn't sell in Britain, he complained.[54] The death-knell of the Cripps Mission resounded long after Cripps had returned to London and would continue to echo throughout the war. It opened up a gulf between commentators, with many Britons suggesting that the Indians had turned away from an opportunity to settle the constitutional issue to the benefit of all, while the Indian leadership reiterated their own sense of bewilderment at the weakness of Cripps's hand. Propaganda and newspaper censorship further obfuscated the news that was reaching Britain, meaning that once again the sense of distance and separation between Delhi and London was enhanced. Yet again, the differing vantage points of Britons and Indians could not converge in the face of the wartime changes. The failure to find a legitimate channel for Indian expressions of political will would have long-lasting repercussions.

*   *   *

Asaf Ali was settling into his detention in Ahmednagar Fort. Like the other Congress leaders, Aruna's husband heard about the eruption of the Quit India movement and the events sweeping the country remotely, from inside his jail cell in Ahmednagar. He also saw in the newspapers that a warrant had been issued for Aruna's arrest and that she was absconding. Knowing her, and the recent radicalisation of her opinions, he feared that she was directly involved in violence, anathema to Gandhi's ideals. He was right: Aruna was working hand-in-glove with men who had set off bombs or sabotaged railway lines; Nilubhai Limaye was a guest at a place she was staying at in Calcutta, and said of her years later: 'I had not seen an organiser like her.'[55] From his prison Asaf Ali sensed she was close to the front line, a sympathetic comrade to the insurgents, if not directly organising the hacking of rail tracks.

Along with the other imprisoned Congressmen Asaf Ali agonised about what was taking place. In jail, he experienced a deep turmoil as snippets of news about his wife's underground activities reached him. Occasionally he would get an Urdu letter from her written under a pseudonym. 'Seeing Rene's [Aruna's] handwriting was almost like travelling home after a long absence and seeing her at the railway station', he wrote on 14 December. 'How I used to crane my neck out to catch a glimpse of her, waiting to wave to me.'[56] A month later his prison diary was becoming more anguished and angry: 'For three days I have wanted to write to Rene but each time I started to write I tore it up. I do not know how to contact Rene and not the over zealous political stranger who has dominated her mind and activities during these five months.'[57] When the government declared a new ordinance sanctioning capital punishment for stealing military goods, he feared for her future. 'I know, and feel perfectly certain, that Rene will never go near violence, but how can I be certain that the persecutors will not try to implicate her in some dire offence?'[58]

Asaf Ali's pride was also damaged. The balance of their relationship had been founded on a condescending paternalism: he had been forty when they married, she was just nineteen. At first she had appeared a clever but innocent ingénue who relied on him and looked up to him. He had been the leader featured in newspapers, the politician and the public figure, while she had been his charming but supportive companion, more noted for her saris than for her political views. Now the tables were turned as his wife's fame and popularity eclipsed his own within the Congress movement; his wife was becoming someone new, born into a new identity through her activism, as he noted in his diary 'an over zealous political stranger', bobbing her hair short and using unknown pseudonyms.

Running through Ali's diary one can detect the frustrations of the intellectual liberal questioning his own lack of passion, his own lack of willingness to use the same political methods as Aruna: 'I can't help admiring even her extravagances', he wrote, wondering if she was better fitted for the challenges of life than him. Asaf Ali profoundly disagreed with her on many of her actions, but this tipped him into pangs of despair and self-doubt. His obsession with Aruna's activities and her whereabouts was magnified by the loneliness and boredom of incarceration; her underground activity preoccupied him, until he fell into a three-day mental collapse during which he projected many of his own fears about death, ageing and colonial subjugation onto his wife's dangerous but bold escapades. '[E]verything has become stale in this place where we have been rotting as in a graveyard.'[59] He feared, rightly, both his own overshadowing and the damage that this time of separation would do to the fine balance of their relationship.

Asaf Ali's premonitions were filled with accuracy: he sensed the burgeoning influence of Jinnah, the Muslim League, the Hindu Mahasabha and the way that the political ground was being opened up to the right-wing and fascistic movements in the country. He judged, again probably rightly, that the Congress was in such disarray and indecision about the right course of action that the Working Committee members would rather remain in jail than be forced to take a position in the open political field. He was particularly prescient about the situation developing between religious political activists in the country, regarding the collapse of the Jinnah–Gandhi talks, which tried to bring the two leaders together to find a solution to the political gridlock later in the war, as a total calamity. After he heard about the failure to reconcile the two leaders, his thoughts returned to his wife and 'I prayed for her deep down in my soul'.[60]

Aruna's appeal among many students and young people in the cities and towns was burgeoning. She was celebrated as a modern woman. She had made a decision not to have children and had cut her hair short. She was a byword for bravery and emancipation, a modern-day Rani of Jhansi. She was a mirror-image of the many women working independently in war industries and as Women Auxiliaries or WAC (I). Aruna Asaf Ali's evasion of the British authorities became like a real-life detective story, echoing the popularity of detective pulp fiction in India in the 1940s. Her cat-and-mouse game with the British made a mockery of the police and surveillance powers of the state and showed up the holes in the state apparatus. Aruna was also a pin-up, modern, beautiful, pictured slightly dishevelled in her homespun saris, and the paradox of her vulnerability and her toughness caught the public mood and made her an icon of the 1942 revolution. The name Aruna became fashionable for new babies born in wartime India. Rumours (probably grounded in truth) circulated that she was moving across the country by aeroplane, even on planes requisitioned for military service. A schoolboy of fifteen at the time, later a Supreme Court advocate, who played truant from school for months in 1942 and acted as a messenger boy for the rebels, remembered her as 'the most beautiful, romantic, revolutionary inspiration'.[61] Police attempted to suborn other protesters by telling them that Aruna had been arrested and had confessed while she remained underground.

After nearly a year of incarceration, on the morning of his fifty-fifth birthday, Asaf Ali saw an article about a trial *in absentia* for his wife: 'As my eye caught her name in the chronicle yesterday, my heart stood still for the moment.'[62] From prison he read about the sale of their car and the possible auctioning of their house, although he wrote, 'I don't care what they do to the property as long as they leave her alone.'[63] So time went by, and the months dragged past; there were annoyances and disagreements in their letters. She found his pity and dismay irritating. He found her dogged determination to stay underground immature. When a parcel arrived from his wife containing a shawl, cigarettes and cologne, their growing estrangement was made palpably real. He didn't like the scent and the cigarettes were too strong. Nehru was worried about his old friend, wondering how he would feel if his wife or daughter had gone underground to take up arms for the nationalist cause.

In 1942 Nehru gave his entry to the American edition of *Who's Who*. It noted that he was now serving his eighth prison sentence, as well as the usual list of educational and biographical data. Under 'miscellaneous' his entry read: 'Dislike of politics but forced by circumstances into them.' Under the category for 'achievement' he wrote: 'That I have so far kept more or less sane in a mad world.'[64]

15

Scorched Earth

Ironically, 1943 was a year that saw little fighting for Indian and Allied soldiers in South Asia. Divisions fought in Sicily and in Naples but in India the army was undergoing a concerted phase of training, re-organisation and preparation for the looming engagements with the Japanese. Yet, if we include civilians, it was the year with the most wartime casualties for India. There is a strong case for integrating the dead of the Bengal famine into calculations of the global war dead, much as the casualties of Stalingrad and Hiroshima have become part of global war histories.

On the afternoon of 12 July 1943, a crowd of forty to fifty men, women and children gathered at the railway crossing at Sitarampur on the borders of Bihar. They had brought bags and woven baskets with them along with sticks and farming implements. Freight carriages carrying grain would be passing though on the East India Railway line and this hungry band of villagers was determined to find something to eat. When the first train passed through, the guards onboard drove back the crowd, but when a second train approached the people became desperate. The guards fired on the crowd, killing an unknown woman.[1]

This frantic attempt was one of many on the East India Railway line in 1943. In Bihar and Bengal, the line was often under attack from hungry villagers who came to meet the passing trains. In response the railways increased the numbers of guards. 'People come from as far as 15 miles to attempt to obtain small quantities of grain from railway cars', stated one report. 'The guards are often stoned and occasionally arrows are shot at them . . . railway officials are of the opinion that this is only the beginning of these troubles.'[2] Although the great hunger of 1943 was most devastating in Bengal, where it resulted in mass starvation and death, there is ample evidence that across many parts of India people were going hungry, forsaking meals and cutting back on their meagre portions of essentials by the second and third years of the war and deaths caused by starvation occurred in other provinces, including Assam and Orissa. Famine is an exceptional event but it is also the extreme end of a continuum with other forms of food deprivation and malnutrition; hunger and shortages had become endemic early on in the war. Famine was the nadir of a much wider food problem, which afflicted India and many parts of the world from 1939 until the early 1950s, amplified by precarious supply, worsened by lack of trust in government price controls, limited rationing and provincial protectionism.

Government attitudes towards food shortages consistently took metropolitan ideas of sacrifice and making-do as their reference point, ideas transferred from the British home front. The government severely overestimated the Indian peasant's ability to cut back, living as he or she often did on the margins of viable existence in the first place. As the Bhore Committee Report on public health in India had already established, most Indians had a diet 'defective in quality' at the start of the war. A peon in full-time government service was simply unable to afford to support the calorific and nutritional needs of a family of four. Almost a third of people regularly consumed fewer calories than they actually needed for their basic energy requirements. When food shortages hit Assam, the government communiqué told people that 'military requirements are bound to take precedence over others' and that this was just one more 'aspect of our sacrifice in the case of the war effort'.[3] People were advised to grow more soybeans and onions, rice and lentils. This attitude may have been applicable to those in Britain who had previously enjoyed a surplus, but was hardly relevant to subsistence share-croppers already on the edge of life.

Food quality and range was poor; even the most privileged soldiers complained of scrawny chickens, small and damaged vegetables, dirty grains mixed with stones; and good-quality milk, eggs and meat were luxuries. The military presence had also undermined the availability of foodstuffs across India and was adding to the pressures on supply around the region. Initially, American quartermasters in India dealt direct with food suppliers, negotiating prices and buying directly, with dire consequences for some local markets. It was only after a year that the forces were prohibited from procuring fresh food supplies from any source other than military depots.

Military demands for meat were outstripping supply by late 1942. Despite attempts to import South American or Australian beef, there had been little progress on this idea, and the majority of beef consumed was from local Indian cattle, sold by cultivators to the army. Cattle from Orissa and Bihar usually used for milk and ploughing were slaughtered to meet military demands. The Indian government, in response to local reactions, rapidly passed laws banning the slaughter of milch and young working cattle. The army had by its own admission 'exhausted' local supply by 1943.[4] 'The food here is not good. The meat is poor because it cannot be hung and there is little variety of vegetables', Kenneth Hulbert of the Royal Army Medical Corps wrote in his private diary. 'But when I see the local people looking like walking skeletons it makes me feel grateful.'[5] Clive Branson noticed this too: 'In the United Provinces there is a dearth of bullocks. Due to indiscriminate slaughter of cattle by military contractors and their agents *kisans* are not able to get bullocks.'[6]

Soldiers bought vegetables, eggs and other goods for themselves at some markets. In Assam, mine managers noticed that undernourished colliery workers were underperforming and affecting coal supply. 'The vitality of the labourers was being affected by the scarcity of fresh food-stuffs, such as milk, eggs, meat and vegetables in the local bazaars', the managers complained to the local military. 'All such supplies are purchased by troops, particularly the Chinese, to the detriment of the working population. Apparently the shortage of fresh foodstuffs is not so acute where the local bazaars are out of bounds to troops, and it is suggested that bazaars in all affected areas should be placed out of bounds.'[7] The broader picture of food supply was one of shortage and competition for sources, even beyond the famine-struck regions of Bengal.

Widespread famine, as was to strike in 1943, is, however, of a different order altogether. It leaves lasting imprints on the demography of a region by affecting marriages, births and deaths. It brutalises people, forcing stark choices about who will live and die, and pushes people into leaving their homes. It is often accompanied by disease, by crime and by banal evil.

Paradoxically, soldiers posted thousands of miles away were among the first to raise the alarm about the approach of the famine, or at least among the first to be believed regarding the gravity of the scenario unfolding in the distant villages. Sepoys received letters from their families stressing the rising prices, the terrible local conditions and the difficulties of getting hold of essentials, and censorship officers saw the contents of the letters. By 1943 the volume of letters reaching the Middle East had increased and many of these included a note of desperation and dire anxiety. As a Bengali from Ranaghat wrote, 'Many people can hardly get one meal a day and are almost half clad. If the war goes on for another few months many will die of starvation . . . You can never imagine the plight of the people here and it is impossible for me to describe it adequately.'[8] The military censor explained such letters as 'exaggeration' and often fell back on the old line that families were trying to get a greater remittance from their serving sons by writing about high prices. Yet as 1943 went on and many letters all repeated the same complaints while letters from Britons living in Bengal also described the horror and the shame of famine, it became readily apparent to Indian soldiers as far away as Egypt and Cyprus that India was facing an emergency. According to another censor's report, the letters ranged 'from the angry and frustrated to the hopelessly heartsick'. 'Here in the cities it is hell', wrote one correspondent to a serving soldier.[9] The tables were turned and fears about the death of sons in battle were equalled by the soldiers' own fears about their families facing high prices, malaria and even starvation back home. Enlistment in India was becoming one route of escape from the food crisis.

On 16 May 1943 an unnamed sepoy, somewhere in the Middle East, wrote to his brother back at home in Urdu. He described how, when newcomers and new recruits arrived from India, they told of the conditions back in the home country. They repeatedly reported the staggering increases in the price of food. 'Whenever it happens, we are grieved so much that it cannot be described', he wrote. News of the bleak economic picture in India 'brings sadness to my heart', wrote another sepoy from a transit camp the following day.[10] An avalanche of letters was by now flowing to theatres across the Middle East reporting unimaginable prices, relatives struggling to make ends meet, and shortages of essentials like kerosene for cooking and lighting, oil, cloth and grain. 'People are dying of hunger and if this goes on for another two or three months then you won't find a single soul alive in our village. God knows when this wretched war will end', reported a Marathi villager in September.[11] A Bengali fitter's wife from the devastated district of Midnapore in Bengal wrote to her husband, 'People have no food to live on and no cloth to cover themselves with. It is beyond imagination and unique in the history of mankind . . . I am in a fix and don't know what to do now. I don't want to write to you in detail so as not to increase your agony.'[12] Soldiers faced the pressure to return home where they could purchase grain at subsidised prices from control shops while their families were often unable to do so. Senior officers saw the agonies of their men and felt the discontent brewing among them.

Over the following weeks soldiers reported feelings of madness, helplessness, deep frustration, pain and exasperation. There was little comfort for men from poor rural districts, knowing that their families might be facing hunger or destitution, while they enjoyed army rations. 'Don't forget that here I eat 8 chapattis in one meal while you probably cook 8 chapattis for the whole family.' Even the longing for home leave began to lose its appeal: 'What is the use of coming on leave to starve', wrote one soldier candidly.[13] Long postal delays and unreliable news added to the soldiers' angst. Military censors had become inured to the pleas in letters, believing that families exaggerated their circumstances in order to extract a greater slice of the 'allotment' – the remittance sent by soldiers back to their relatives. But as the year progressed it became clear that this was different to the usual pleas. Despite soldiers sending back more of their wages, the letters had a more desperate tone to them, and there were more of them. The officer censoring the letters initially removed anything too inflammatory, 'deletions made wherever an alarmist tendency was noticed', but as the crisis went on, the censor's report admitted a large number of letters from all over India were 'painfully urgent in tone'. An increase in pay was recommended (despite an increase less than a year earlier) for soldiers who were now sending back generous sums.[14]

This time was hardest for those men from landless families: water-carriers, washermen, sweepers and cooks. They knew that their families were vulnerable to the smallest price fluctuations. Non-combatants were also less likely to get leave and could not afford to make a visit home. In one unit, at least sixty non-combatants had not been back to India or seen their families for four years. The wife of a water-carrier from Montgomery district, a popular recruitment ground in Punjab, wrote to her husband in September: 'The family allotment has not been received for the last four months. Children are in great trouble. I have not a single *pie* to purchase foodstuffs. There is acute famine over here. The children are crying with hunger and I am bewildered with trying to feed them.'[15] For these wives the absence of a letter or the failure to send a remittance was felt deeply. They wrote about the condition of their children and pitiable stories about the hardships of the youngest which touched a nerve with the men. For all ranks, news of children and instructions about how to best look after the children recurred as a subject of their letters. A *subedar*-major, writing in Gurmukhi script, told his wife, 'It simply tortures me to learn that my children undergo such hardships', when he learned that they were queuing for food.[16]

The steps towards famine occurred slowly but steadily. On 16 October 1942 a cyclone swept through districts of Bengal and Orissa, wiping out standing crops, livestock and paddy stores and causing loss of life. Shortages had already set in and now hit the price of rice – the lifeline of Bengal – so that the grain soared in cost. Shops and markets held paltry stocks of grain and there was no rationing system in place. People started to skip meals, to take inflated offers from money-lenders, to drink the water that their rice had boiled in as a substitute for a meal and to beg from their neighbours. They trekked long distances at the news of rumoured food only to find bare markets or to buy a small bag of poor-quality grains at sky-high prices. People started to wonder what they would feed their children, now that there was nothing at home. Children cried incessantly. Desperation set in.

Labourers without land or surplus began to arrive in Calcutta and other towns, in need of food. By January 1943 people in Calcutta were calling for rationing and by March, journalists from *The Statesman* newspaper were describing seeing 'something akin to starvation' in the rural districts of Bengal. An ill-advised and invasive 'food drive' by the provincial government, to try to ascertain quantities of stocks in the districts, drove more supplies underground and off the open market. By mid-May, the price of rice had nearly quadrupled in Calcutta. Yet, it was only in the summer, as the monsoon rains approached, when semi-naked, starving people were already falling to their knees on the pavements of Calcutta, that the government fully took stock of the tragedy that was unfolding. 'I am sorry to have to trouble you with so dismal a picture', wrote the obsequious Governor of Bengal, John Herbert, to Linlithgow on 2 July; 'Bengal is rapidly approaching starvation.'[17]

The sight of the victims could no longer be avoided: hollow eyes in sockets, skin like paper and showing protruding bones, the dead and dying were now sometimes indistinguishable. Without health-care, pure sources of water or basic sanitation, deaths from cholera, malaria and typhoid were rising. Families also fractured under the strain of impending death, with the sick, the aged and the weak abandoned or separated. Many starving orphans, mothers with babies and single women could be seen on the streets of Calcutta, as women tended to survive famine marginally better than men. At every turn both the elected government stumbled and central authority from Delhi and London failed to apprehend the situation or to act before it was too late. When the rains came in August, flooding exacerbated the difficulties of the peasants, and high waters down the Damodar River flooded a large area of Burdwan district. By October one and a half million people relied on famine relief and the government started forcibly relocating the destitute in Calcutta to relief camps.

The wealthy came into closest proximity with the famine when they saw corpses outside their homes and workplaces or dodged stepping on the bodies of the dead and dying in the street. As the historian Janam Mukherjee has recently analysed, the disposal of corpses was becoming a pressing problem for the municipal author-ities in Calcutta by this point, with councils resorting to mass burial pits or the throwing of bodies into rivers and canals, and the forma-tion of the grisly-named Corpse Disposal Squad.[18] Fuel shortages inhibited cremation, and so bloated bodies could be seen in waterways, while corpses rotted like carrion on the streets. Aruna Asaf Ali had her most terrible experience of underground life in Calcutta: moving around at night under the cover of the blackout, she stumbled over something in the road and found it was the dead body of a famine victim. This memory stayed with her all her life.[19] The names or identities of the victims were difficult to ascertain; ultimately the authorities settled on identifying corpses simply by whether they were Hindu or Muslim, and relied on the assistance of religious organisations for disposing of the dead by cursory religious rites. This was an arbitrary practice and also an ominous harbinger of the way that society was becoming increasingly classified along religious lines in Calcutta.

Some wealthy Bengalis hardened their hearts in the face of such overwhelming calamity, turning away from the death around them. One of the most disturbing photographs of the famine shows a prosperous thoroughfare: a well-fed man in crisp white clothes turns his back while a skeletal woman, almost naked, her hands clenched to her face, dies on the pavement at his feet. One trader made an application, in the midst of the famine, for an import licence for 'cigarettes, dried fruits, olives, olive oil and tinned foods etc' from Turkey, just a glimpse of the alternative epicurean delights available in Calcutta for those with purchasing power.[20] Flourishing hotels revealed the stark differences of income in 1943. Just beyond the grand staircases and entrance halls of the hotels, an emaciated famine victim might lie on the street, facing death. The social gulf became inescapable, as guests enjoyed sumptuous meals, dancing or chatting to the accompanying tinkle of a jazz piano. Expensive hotels thrived, kept afloat by military spending. 'In some of the big European hotels, seventeen-course dinners are being served to-day while lean, emaciated faces can be seen staring wistfully through the windows', reported Jyoti Bose.[21] The profiteering of the wealthy was censured: 'They were the ones who could buy at any price anything from a pin-up to a prostitute, create an artificial scarcity, let the market soar and then sell out or lease out in a rising market.'[22]

Then and now, the horrors of the famine elude full understanding. The pain of the sufferers is simply beyond our comprehension. And many contemporary onlookers were frozen by their own sense of ineptitude, lack of power and the sheer scale of the suffering. The individual man, woman or child at the heart of each story slinks into the margins and melts away from view. The voices of the famine are still muted in the historical record. Compared to the bloody recollections of the Partition four years later, the famine victims have often remained undifferentiated, pitied but lacking distinctive faces, personalities and desires. Certain voices always sound loudest in the archives and memoirs: journalists, bureaucrats and businessmen. But these people were less directly afflicted by famine. The experiences of the famine victims could not be easily hitched to national narratives, nor their case taken up by agonistic political leaders.

Nonetheless, many witnesses reeled with shock and outrage, and their words are often a powerful testament: 'The impression it made even on me will persist throughout my life. I said "even on me" because I thought I was a sophisticated hard-boiled egg and could take a detached view of things', wrote Satyen Basu, who had returned to India after taking part in the campaigns in North Africa and after captivity as a prisoner of war. 'But witness a baby barely two years old lying in the lap of his brother of about six, both so devitalised that they are not able even to move from the street corner and biding their time to be shifted by somebody, sometime, alive or dead.'[23] He went on to describe travelling to Chittagong by river: 'Human corpses were floating past us, entangled in water hyacinth and preyed on by vultures.'[24]

People were stunned into silence or bewilderment by what they saw, and this silence continues to haunt the historical record. Politicians, either in prison, or reluctant to become involved by association, stayed strangely mute about the famine. While some Bengali and English language newspapers bravely endeavoured to tell the world about the tragedy unfolding, the Governor of the province continued to downplay the famine and to cast aspersions and blame. Propaganda and global image remained the priority: 'I hope we can get out some effective propaganda to counteract the present unhelpful tales of horror in the Press which manifests itself largely in photographs which might have been taken in Calcutta at any time during the last 10 years', he wrote in response to the disturbing photographs of men, women and children in their final hours of life.[25]

The one question that lingered, however, was 'why?' Why had

this tragedy taken place? Were human errors culpable for death on this scale? Could it have been prevented?

* * *

Histories of the famine have always acknowledged the war as the backdrop to 1943. For contemporaries, the war and the famine were completely entwined, two interlinked horrors which had destabilised life and broken down the moral economy of the Bengali peasant. The first time that the Governor of Bengal mentioned the word 'starvation' to the Viceroy was in the context of wartime security, complaining that 'masses of beggars are boarding trains without tickets in the search for places where food may be available. They are a particular nuisance in areas where troops are concentrated . . . apart from being insanitary, [they] constitute a danger to security.'[26] At every turn, for the Raj, the preservation and prosecution of the war was the most important consideration. The trains that carried grain out of Bengal and up to the soldiers stationed in the north-east were therefore protected by security guards. For the famine victims themselves, the war was often cited as the cause of their plight; there was even a rumour doing the rounds at the time that the famine had been sent to punish Bengalis for lack of support for the war effort.

There can be little doubt, in a general sense, that the war had distorted local markets and that, whatever the direct causation of famine, which has been the subject of complex debates, the fears of bombing, rations for factory workers, the severance of rice supply from Burma, military demands and the general war economy were inextricably linked to Bengal's trauma in 1943. Yet, at the time, India was not regarded as an official war zone, and the United Nations Relief and Rehabilitation Administration (UNRRA) established in 1943 to help civilian victims of war did not consider Bengal within its remit. Bengal was caught at the administrative interstices of war; between civilian and military control, between a troubled provincial government and a national government that was too slow to recognise the crisis.

Controversies continue about the actual available food in Bengal in 1943, the role of hoarders and traders who sold the rice on at avaricious prices, and the speculators and agents who drove food upwards in price. Historians have debated the role of the provincial government, the shortages of shipping and the callousness of a government in London far more concerned with keeping people fed at home and with winning the war than with the death of Bengalis.

Some decades since Amartya Sen published his classic work on food availability decline, scholarly controversies about the famine's causes still rage on.[27] He argued that the hoarding of food by black marketeers and more affluent traders and the inequitable distribution of food in Bengal were to blame, rather than a sheer absence of food. The nub of this debate turns on whether there was enough food in Bengal in 1943 or not, on whether those with more stocks had held them back and hoarded rather than delivering them to market. Others have fiercely defended the idea that there simply was not enough food available, and that attempts to dig out the secret hidden hoards came to nothing because there was just not enough food obtainable in Bengal in 1943, hidden or not. The government itself suspected the role of hoarders and arranged inspections in order to root out the hidden mountains of grains, suspected to be locked away in *godowns*, shops and private homes. In fact, this campaign found far less hidden stock than expected. The figure of the unnamed 'hoarder' became a bogeyman of the colonial state, and was also cited by provincial ministers as a culprit, but in reality this idea was heavily contested even at the time. 'Statements that people have concealed foodstuffs in jungles or removed them by boats are utterly incredible', declared the *Amrita Bazaar Patrika* newspaper. 'Bengal is faced with famine.'[28]

A range of other causes has to be factored in, beyond these crucial, but somewhat narrow, debates over supply: cover-ups and tardy responses by the British, poor leadership, press censorship and propaganda which consistently masked the scale of the problem unfolding, and a breakdown in communications and in the ability to distribute food by rail, road or boat. Some officials doggedly pursued ideas which would prove fateful. Some officers simply could not cope. One ICS man, Lionel Pinnell, who had played a leading role in the denial scheme and in managing civil supplies, had a nervous breakdown and resigned after realising that his anti-hoarding campaign was not yielding results.[29] The Governor of Bengal, John Herbert, resigned and three months later died. The lack of international relief or rapid assistance from Britain and the intersection with wartime shipping priorities and delays created a black hole. Scarce resources were still being diverted to essential factory workers and to the troops. In Bengal poor diet and mono-crop culture (almost complete reliance on rice, comparable with the Irish reliance on the potato a century earlier), the lack of medicines and hospitals and the spread of disease all compounded people's vulnerability.

Some agriculturalists had, in their enthusiasm for the new wartime profits, also turned to the growing of cash crops instead of using the land for grains and pulses. The Americans received complaints that promised orders for jute had been overestimated and that this had had a detrimental effect on cultivators. The question was debated in the Bengal Legislative Assembly. But ultimately, it was rice that was needed. In the aftermath of the famine a 'grow more food' campaign addressed the problem of self-sufficiency and yields directly. It also made more attempts to get accurate statistics of crop yields, for instance, by random sampling. But this all came too late for the victims of 1943.

Administrative bungling and inadvertent stockpiling compounded the horrors. G. S. Khosla, who was managing the railway traffic at Dacca in late 1943, found that so many bags of food grains had piled up in Dacca Station that he was forced to request Calcutta to stop sending more, as the movement of the stocks onward had not been arranged. He remembered it as a 'dismal failure'. Many years later when interviewed he was still moved by the memory of 'stacks of gunny bags of wheat mounting up in various parts of the station' and the place being 'choked' with food which had not yet reached the starving.[30] The stresses on communications, administrative blockages and problems of railway freight (especially the prioritisation for military stocks) added to the difficulties of distributing food even when it was publicly and visibly available. The shortages of boats and vehicles, and the legacies of the 'denial scheme', also contributed to the problem of getting food out to remoter areas. The food secretary told Wavell in early 1944 that the 'crux' of alleviating the famine was now to 'get stocks of food into districts in time'.[31] Even getting civil telephone and telegraph messages through in Bengal was proving more difficult and slower than in the preceding years.

The debates about why the famine happened may never be fully resolved. The statistical data may be too unreliable and incomplete ever to be fully conclusive. But more significant than the practicalities was the importance of mentalities. Some people's lives were not seen as worthy of preserving. The state was geared in every way to the war and prioritised this at all costs. Human negligence and failure to prioritise other human lives as equal was the root cause. Certain lives were not seen as worthy of mourning, or as fully valid as others, and the lives of the people of Bengal had been sacrificed towards the greater global aim of winning the war. The lives of the famine victims were a cost of the Second World War but these casualties were not counted as such. A safety net protected the general population of Britain from starvation although everywhere people suffered shortages; in Bengal these shortages were fatal and that safety net was never put in place.

Meanwhile, the War Cabinet in London blocked and delayed imports that could have prevented further deaths in late 1943 and into 1944. Linlithgow handed over power to the new Viceroy, Wavell, on 20 October 1943 and when the retiring Viceroy met his successor on his arrival in India he told him that he had never been so glad to welcome anybody in his life. On arriving back into port in England, the former Viceroy was picketed by Indian students holding placards, protesting against the famine. Returning to Britain, where he 'referred little to Indian affairs after his return', Linlithgow died prematurely several years later.[32] The no-nonsense and taciturn Wavell injected some new vigour into the administration. He brought the famine situation in Bengal under clearer control, visiting the province imme-diately after he arrived and co-ordinating military assistance. But soon, the new Viceroy was raging at the desultory way in which his messages to London were being handled. Each agreement to release more British food stocks for export to India was a hard-won conces-sion for which Wavell had to wait many weeks and fight in the strongest language. A number of requests for imports were repeat-edly turned down or renegotiated. By March 1944, Wavell had requested a million tons of food grains and the government had agreed to one-quarter of the amount. Clearly shaken by what he had personally witnessed, even as a battle-hardened general, he told London that the famine was 'one of the greatest disasters that has befallen any people under British rule and damage to our reputation both among Indians and foreigners in India is incalculable'.[33] He was frequently writing in his diary of the 'unfavourable view of my request for grain imports'. By March 1944 he was thinking he 'might have to resign to bring the situation home' to the Cabinet. In June 1944, he waited five or six weeks for a reply about a request for greater shipping tonnage to India. This was turned down too. Towards the end of 1944, after a year-long struggle, Wavell was still battling against the callous attitude of Churchill towards India. 'I feel that the vital problems of India are being treated by His Majesty's Government with neglect, even sometimes with hostility and contempt', he told the Prime Minister directly. 'In spite of the lesson of the Bengal famine, I had during the last nine months literally to fight with all the words I could command, sometimes almost intemperate, to secure food imports.'[34] Even after this letter, and well into 1945, he was still locked in a struggle with London over imports, which consistently fell below not only the amounts requested, but also the amounts agreed, and continued to be contested right up until the end of the war.[35]

*   *   *

In Bengal, soldiers waiting for action in Burma now found themselves on the front line of a very different kind of calamity. They witnessed deaths more shocking than the violence of war itself. Clive Branson was apoplectic with frustration and rage at the famine.

> The ordinary, decent people in England *must* do something – this is *their* Empire. I have no doubts about our beating the Japanese in spite of the state of India; but what fills me with horror is the post-war payment we shall have to make. It is all very well to parade members of the 4th Indian Division around England – but the sincerity of that praise wears a bit thin if those men's relatives are dying of hunger in the villages of Bengal and elsewhere.[36]

Soldiers of all nationalities felt disturbed by what they saw in Bengal in 1943 and many, deeply moved by their inability to alleviate suffering, did what they could, offering up their own rations and helping children to welfare centres. Kenneth Hulbert, of the Royal Army Medical Corps, wrote of the sound of death in his private diary:

> After sunset a dull low moaning sound started up and seemed to go on all night. I asked one of the Indians what this was and he said that it was coming from the Indian village around us. He said it was the sound of people dying of hunger. What a dreadful place this is. The distressing thing is that there is nothing we can do to help them.[37]

In Calcutta men and women in the military encountered famine victims on a daily basis. 'I remember speaking to the Staff Sergeant about the body of a young girl lying at the entrance to the cantonment', Peggy Tench, a nurse with the Queen Alexandra's Nursing Corps, recalled.[38] Some GIs in Assam donated money to send a boy who had lost both his parents in the famine to school. He was called Moniruddin, 'a bright young lad who served for many months as office boy in the civilian personnel office at this base'.[39]

For the soldiers, the sights were distressing and disorienting. How could they justify their presence as colonial overlords if this was the result of British rule? How could they help alleviate such a tragedy? And what was the war all about if the empire was unable to protect its own inhabitants? 'People feel', one intelligence official expressed it, that 'economic conditions are so bad [in parts of Bengal] that they could not be worse under the Japanese.'[40] Some soldiers – both Indian and British – were praised for sharing their rations with the starving on the street.

The sight of the generic, nameless 'homeless man' became so much a part of the ordinary GIs' experience that it featured in an official guidebook for the US Army in India, alongside other Indian 'castes' like the Brahmin and the avaricious merchant:

> The Homeless Man. At some time or other while you are here you will witness the sight of a crowd of men, women, and children who seem to move together like a herd of sheep. They huddle together, or they rush across the street in a mob, or they gather in a group shouting and jabbering – they are new arrivals in the city. Driven here by the famine, by flood, drought, or other causes, they come from Bengal itself, from

Bihar, Orissa, or Assam. Homeless, helpless, hopeless when they reach
Calcutta, they fare as men have always fared, in that the able-bodied
and the strong among them as usual survive and soon find their way
into the immense labor corps around the city – the rest, they soon
vanish – some die in the epidemics, others just disappear.[41]

Soldiers also came into close quarters with famine victims through
the distribution of medical and food aid. Public appreciation for their
work was pronounced; 'their work has been uniformly good and
efficient in whatever type of relief job they have been engaged', wrote
T. G. Narayan, who wrote an eyewitness account of the famine.[42]
People did not blame individual soldiers for the consequences of the
famine even though they blamed the war overall. Soldiers started
transporting food, maintaining free kitchens and bringing medical
relief with mobile dispensaries. Those trained in jungle warfare even
taught people how to find food from local grasses and leaves. Military
units also circulated a pamphlet to clinics and doctors with the frank
title *Treatment and Management of Starving Sick Destitutes*. The distribution of quinine and inoculations against typhus was one of the most
significant contributions of the Indian Army, although this work did
not commence until late in 1943. The military medical units provided
17 hospitals with 2,150 beds and 61 mobile centres and treated 1,135,589
cases in these centres until the end of April 1944.[43]

*   *   *

When Gandhi was released from prison in 1944, the Bengal famine
had not yet faded from memory. It was still haunting people well
beyond Bengal's provincial borders. 'I have no shadow of doubt in
my mind', Gandhi declared, 'that the Bengal famine, as also famines
in other parts of India, were man-made and not God-made.'[44] The
famine added to his steely determination to ensure that *swaraj* (self-
rule) arrived at the end of the war. It also undermined further the
remnants of imperial credibility, both among South Asians and Britons.
'I had never seen such distress in all my life and the utter callousness
with which the government behaved and did not give them relief was
perhaps one of the reasons that really drove the iron into our souls',
recalled the Congresswoman Sucheta Kripalani many years later.[45] In

Europe, however, the famine blended into other wartime horrors and
knowledge of it remained strangely blunted. But in Bengal anger about
the famine simmered, adding piquancy to later nationalist campaigns
and cementing nationalist convictions, which would resurface with
explosive force in 1945.

*   *   *

In April 1943 Subhas Chandra Bose arrived in Japan, carried by submarine for many weeks through the oceans from Germany to Sumatra,
and then finally flown from Singapore to Tokyo. After his public arrival
back in Singapore on 2 July 1943, the Indian National Army and the
Indian Independence League became his personal vehicles. These
organisations, which had been formed in early 1942, struggled under
factional strain in South-East Asia, with many becoming sceptical
about the ability of the INA to work as an equal partner with the
Japanese, who simply liked the propaganda significance of the Indian
renegade soldiers. Bose gave his followers the slogan 'Chalo Delhi!'
(Advance on Delhi) and like an alchemist was able to turn the volatile
situation among Indians in South-East Asia into political gold, by
welding together men and women of different religious and linguistic
backgrounds and inspiring them to fight under one banner and one
leadership. In bold and uncompromising language Bose spoke single-
mindedly of victory against the British and of the triumph of Indian
nationalism. His speeches relentlessly referred to India's subjugation
by Perfidious Albion and the machinations of a ruthless alien empire.
Certainly, many of the INA men who joined him in the newly christened 'Azad Hind Fauj' shared this belief and were born again into
the movement with a fervour that compelled them to risk everything.

Shah Nawaz Khan was a tall, gentlemanly officer from a long line of
military professionals, and was bitterly disappointed by the surrender
of 1942 and by his status as a prisoner of war in Singapore. He was
already a member of the INA but held many reservations about it,
and remembered his own conversion from scepticism to becoming a
fully fledged leader of the Indian National Army:

When Netaji [as Bose was known] arrived in Singapore, I watched
him very keenly. I had never seen or met him before, and did not know

very much about his activities in India. I heard a number of his public speeches, which had a profound effect on me. It will not be wrong to say that I was hypnotized by his personality and his speeches. He placed the true picture of India before us, and for the first time in my life I saw India, through the eyes of an Indian.[46]

Shah Nawaz Khan was tried during the Red Fort trial of 1946 and became one of the national heroes of the INA. Women, too, found Bose quite irresistible. In South-East Asia, many women who had been fearful about the future prospects of their community now turned to Bose. The INA's recruitment of women into the famed Rani of Jhansi Regiment was consistent with the transformative changes that were taking place for women across South Asia. Among the local population in South-East Asia, the support of women was vocal and one fervent, anonymous supporter of Bose recorded in her diary:

The women's section of the IIL [Indian Independence League] convened a mass meeting of Indian women. It was addressed by Netaji. The audience hung on each syllable as it dropped from the powerful jaws of our beloved leader. Women had walked ten and twelve miles to the meeting place . . . A Gujarati lady gave away all her jewellery: bangles, rings, necklace that she was wearing, as gift to Netaji for work by women.[47]

At a distance and from across the Indian Ocean, the subcontinent could be simplified and idealised as Mother India, and Bose was able to bring co-ordination and security to the shattered South-East Asian community of Indians. 'What is most note-worthy is the way all petty intrigues have been abandoned, all quarrels forgotten', wrote the same woman in her diary. 'Netaji has certainly transformed all of us. We feel different.'[48] She went on to join the Rani of Jhansi Regiment. This was a bracing modern form of nationalism with potentially fascist overtones. But unlike German fascism, it also played heavily on an inclusive vision of Indian identity, wiping aside differences of caste, class, religion and even gender. It inspired visions of revolutionary transformation, though one which Bose grounded on ideas about the will of the people. His rallies, funding drives and public orations during whirlwind tours to Rangoon, Shanghai, Bangkok, Nanking and the Andamans brought out crowds of thousands.

In reality, though, in South-East Asia there were far more complex undercurrents and complicated negotiations needed to sustain the INA movement on a daily basis. Doubts over Japanese intentions persisted and could not be easily ignored. There was also the need to co-ordinate with the Japanese and to organise everything from food and medical supplies to military tactics, military discipline and regulations. Bose persisted in trying to make his movement a genuinely inde-pendent and serious fighting machine – despite the fact that many of his recruits had no experience of military life – and to imbue the provisional government with autonomy, but ultimately relied on Japanese authority. For instance, in the Andaman Islands, where Bose hoped to formally acquire some control of Indian soil for his provi-sional government, he was able to rename the islands Shahid and Swaraj Islands and acquired nominal control, but failed to get the Japanese to relinquish any real sovereignty or military power.[49] Despite Bose's lobbying to have his troops integrated into the military assault on India, ultimately only 8,000 of the INA would see action when the Subhas Brigade took part in the Imphal campaign of 1944, leading to death, desertion, capture and appalling struggles for survival for these men and women. Within South-East Asia, many workers from the rubber estates continued to be caught in these cross-currents of im-perialism and nationalism, with little choice but to join the INA or be used as forced labourers.

But for those on the other side of the Indian Ocean, within India's actual borders, listening to Bose and simply the knowledge of the existence of the Indian National Army (and the establishment of the Provisional Government of Azad Hind (Free India) from October 1943) gave a focal point for nationalism. From the time of his arrival in South-East Asia, Bose's broadcasts intensified in frequency and popularity back in India and were heard by many. The Japanese radio stations in Singapore and Burma directed propaganda towards India from 11 p.m. until 3.30 a.m. and used Hindi, English, Bengali, Marathi, Urdu, Tamil and Punjabi. At least two hours a day were allotted to Bose and his programme and Rash Behari Bose also broadcast directly from Tokyo. People huddled around clandestinely to listen to these addresses, although their ability to sway opinion – rather than simply to bolster those already committed to nationalism – remains unknown. Broadcasts were well informed by conditions in India and dwelt on themes such as the futility of the Cripps Mission, the impact of air raids on South Asia and, from 1943, the famine.[50] Significantly, Bose continued to refer to the Mahatma and to pay deference to Congress symbols and history, despite his differences with Gandhi, melding the Indian National Congress with the aims of the INA in the minds of some. Ultimately, the INA lost their military battles but they won the propaganda war, and the myth of Netaji became indefatigable. This would become even more important at the cessation of war when the celebration of the INA heroes would become a national cause célèbre and propel forward the collapse of the Raj.

16

The Cogs in a Watch

At the end of 1943 the King-Emperor examined the design of a new recruiting medal and approved it, 'as an award for Zeal and Success in recruiting on the part of India'. The medal was a star surrounded by a scroll, suspended by an emerald-green ribbon. The Raj awarded the medal to Recruiting Officers and ex-servicemen but also to women. Mothers who had a husband and two or more children in the services or any parent with three children serving could now be the recipients of a special imperial medal. It was recognition of the heavy reliance on certain families by the state in the 1940s and of the part that all family members played in encouraging their youth to serve. But it was also another act of desperation by the Raj as officers needed to find novel ways to harness the morale and support of Indian families.[1]

In 1944, there was also another increase in pay for combatant soldiers. The fighting sepoy was now drawing 37 rupees and 8 annas a month when his basic pay before the war was 16 rupees. This new pay was also being topped up with proficiency pay, deferred pay and a special overseas allowance.[2] This was above the rate of inflation, suggesting the determination of the state to keep the Indian soldier fighting on the side of the British irrespective of cost. As the army continued to suck up more recruits, and more Indian manpower was deployed around the Mediterranean, securing the loyalty of the sepoy and ensuring his morale stayed steady continued to be a pressing problem which occupied civil and military officers from Delhi to London.

How to continue to champion victories in the war while the appetite for conflict in India was waning? To add to their woes, the Raj's most pivotal ally in Punjab, the Unionist government, was fracturing and losing its grip, precipitated by the untimely death of Sikander Hyat Khan from a heart attack and ever-increasing challenges to the Unionist authority from the Muslim League. The urban youth of Lahore now daily challenged the old, privileged allies of the Raj on the streets. Others railed against the cost of living and the decadence of the old feudals, and championed new political firebrands. Women as well as men staged mass demonstrations in support of a Muslim homeland, although exactly what form that state might take, if it ever came into existence, remained unclear.

In May 1943, as famine loomed and prices rose, with grim determination the government handed out money to every provincial government to celebrate victory in North Africa. Tunis had finally been captured in the first week of May. In large cities like Calcutta, Bombay and Madras, it was suggested that 'meetings on the Hitler model might be organised with as much theatrical effect as possible'.[3] The provincial governments laid on parades, bands, displays of tanks, guns and arms, sporting contests, processions and illuminations and handed out sweets. Delhi suggested that government servants should be assembled for 'talks', and religious meetings with prayers for the success of the Allies should be encouraged. Every small step forward in the global war was presented as a sign of the ultimate invincibility of the Allies. Morale needed boosting and the Indian Army still needed new recruits.

The war was a painful but culturally prolific era for numerous writers and artists in India, who turned to painting, cinema and novels to evoke the darkness of the world around them, to find a voice for the everyman which went beyond the simplifications of political rhetoric. Stagy military efforts were no match for the grass-roots effloresence of travelling public theatre. This caught the attention of villagers and spoke to them directly. The Indian People's Theatre Association (IPTA), formed in 1942 and linked to the Communist Party of India, was able to reach people in a way that centralised propaganda could not. On basic stages and under trees, with minimal props, these touring theatre groups performed five or six times a day to thousands. Highly celebrated among the plays performed by IPTA was *Nabanna*, or New Harvest, which toured the villages of Bengal and enacted the suffering of a family afflicted by the famine. Cathartically, people saw their own pain acted out in front of their very eyes. IPTA also staged plays about the wider global issues of the war, from depictions of Hitler and Mussolini and Japanese aggression (one play was called *The Downfall of Hitler*), to dramas on debt, peasant exploitation and impoverishment.

Saadat Hasan Manto was writing Urdu short stories for All India Radio, writing for Bombay cinema and producing some of his own best literature. There was a flow between theatres and cinemas, actors and directors like Ritwik Ghatak working in both worlds of film and theatre. Amateur film clubs started to thrive, sometimes organised and patronised by army personnel too; Ferenc Berko, a Hungarian photographer employed to make images by the Indian Army, organised art house screenings in Bombay above the Eros Cinema. The government propaganda machine had little hope of formally competing with more vernacular and localised expressions of theatre, cinema and music that used local languages and artists. Indian theatre troupes and new forms of cinema captured the inner meaning of people's lives in a complex and ever more violent world.

For the troops, theatrical offerings were more limited. Singers and performers did not tour in the East to the same extent as some of the other theatres, and the military was criticised for failing to boost morale. As one letter to the *Spectator* complained, 'ENSA has at last put in an appearance in India. I saw a show by one of their parties this week. It was worse than any third-rate show in England, and such people would be booed out of anywhere but low-class hovels at home.'[4] Complaints reached the highest quarters that ENSA in Asia was operating on a shoestring, and that malaria and travel restrictions undermined attempts to entertain the troops. Tickets remained limited and morale suffered as a result. In response, entertainers such as John Gielgud and Vera Lynn were sent to India and Burma. Noël Coward arrived for a tour in early 1944, invited personally by Mountbatten, and toured Calcutta, Assam, Delhi, Bombay, Madras and Ceylon. His convoy drove through mud and rain close to the north-eastern front, navigating hillside roads with a piano strapped precariously to a lorry. He saw a number of the dead and dying on his tour, and was repelled by the stench of battlegrounds and hospitals. One of the songs he penned during this time, 'I Wonder What Happened to Him', poked fun directly at the old regimental traditions of the Indian Army and at the wider structures of the Raj, which had been crumbling under the duress of war:

> The India that one read about
> And may have been misled about
> In one respect has kept itself intact.
> Though Pukka Sahib traditions may have cracked
> And thinned
> The good old Indian army's still a fact.

But not all of his entertainment struck the right note with the men, and his reception was mixed. His presence in many ways seemed outmoded and out of step with the modernised, international army which now manned the borderlands of India and on one occasion he was jeered off stage by 2,000 black troops.[5] Many other entertainments for the troops remained ad hoc improvisations and relied on the ingenuity of the men themselves. Indian troops liked wrestling, cinema and improvising music and shows, and a number of circus troupes, local entertainers and dancers, many of them Russians and Poles, became popular with the men.

For the civilian population, the formal channels of propaganda often looked stodgy and simplistically jingoistic. The short films produced for *Indian Movietone News* and later *Indian News Parade* – which had to be played before any feature film by law – tended to dwell on battles, pageantry and pomp and rarely captured the hearts of cinema-goers, who often whistled and chatted through them, or arrived late. Over time the government's own Information Films of India became more sophisticated and subtle, using more Indian cameramen and producers. They developed films which reflected less overtly militaristic themes, for instance, showing the daily lives of village labourers or taking a more anthropological angle, recording the music and singing of 'loyal' hill-tribes in the north-east. Nonetheless, the ultimate aim of winning round hearts and minds to the war was never far from the surface of these films.[6]

Within the army itself, Commanding Officers had honed morale-boosting techniques and approached their men with new levels of honesty, sensitivity and openness. In the mess, men discussed politics and wartime strategy. They could listen to the radio. Propaganda

papers aimed at soldiers, like *Fauji Akbar, Jang ki Kabren and Duniya,*
Indian Information and the *War in Pictures,* used professional journalists
and intrepid photographers. Officers advocated a light touch when
censoring letters home.[7] Men felt far more committed to their work
if they had reliable news from home and knew the truth about their
families and their circumstances. But alongside this new strategy of
openness the men were also subject to manipulation by propaganda
that played up the fear and loathing of the Japanese and targeted the
particular soft spots and sensitivities of the Indian troops. Soldiers
heard stories of heinous crimes by the Japanese, the rape and sexual
exploitation of Indian women in South-East Asia, and lurid accounts
of crimes against places of worship and religious customs, such as
Sikhs forced to cut their beards and hair and Muslims and Hindus
forced to eat pork and beef.[8]

*   *   *

Many soldiers had been promised modern goods like radios and electricity installed in their villages, as a way of encouraging them to
come into the army. As the war dragged on, more money and effort
were being spent on trying to improve the morale of men, particularly those overseas, but these efforts were often insufficient. Frank
Lugard Brayne, an energetic and resourceful stalwart of the Indian
Civil Service, was disapproving of most of what he saw when he
reached the Middle East and began inspecting the local scene. 'The
troops particularly Indians like wandering in the bazaars but the prices
of everything are prohibitive, the towns are extremely squalid and un-
attractive, the villages look like *chamar busties* [slums], VD is extremely
prevalent and altogether, the less the troops visit the bazaars the
better.'[9] He found the men bored, inactive, uncertain about when they
might see action, merely waiting around for future orders with little
to distract them. They were cold at night and had little to take their
minds off homesickness by day. Brayne was an evangelical Christian
and a reformer, and he believed that the imperialists had a mission to
improve and develop India and to spread better living standards among
villagers and peasants.

As a veteran of the Indian Army's First World War, Brayne was
attached to his charges, knew Punjabi (and he did not hide his

British tanks during riots in the North-West Frontier Province, 1935. At the outbreak of war the focus was on India's north-western border and the fear of war with Russia rather than the Japanese.

British soldiers at Chitral on the Afghan border with khassadars, or locally raised militias in 1940. One third of the Indian Army was stationed on the North-West Frontier at the start of the war.

A propaganda poster used in Britain to reassure people of the unity of the British Empire and Commonwealth. Canada, Australia, Britain, South Africa, New Zealand, India, and Africa are represented.

THE BRITISH COMMONWEALTH OF NATIONS

TOGETHER

Three stokers on board the Royal Indian Navy sloop, HMS Sutlej, 1944. In addition to navy seafarers, Lascars or Indian merchant seamen were critical to the war and over 6,600 lost their lives.

Recently enlisted recruits at an Indian Army Training Centre. By late 1940, 20,000 a month were joining up and by the end of the war the Indian Army was over 2 million men strong.

A Recruiting Officer inspects a potential recruit in Northern India. There was no conscription in India but men joined up for many reasons often seeking the chance for a regular income and more plentiful food.

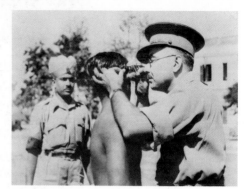

Men of the 4th Indian Division with a captured German flag at Sidi Omar, close to the Egyptian-Libyan border, part of the North African campaign of 1941.

An Indian fighter pilot of the Royal Indian Air Force. South Asian pilots also joined the RAF in Britain.

Subhas Chandra Bose arrived in Germany in early 1941, after he escaped house arrest in Calcutta, and held meetings with the senior Nazi leadership including Heinrich Himmler.

Indians living in Burma evacuate Rangoon in fear of the advancing Japanese army in 1942. At least 600,000 Indians are believed to have fled Burma after the Japanese invasion.

Subhas Chandra Bose delivering a speech in Japanese occupied Asia as part of the Indian National Army programme, c. 1943.

YOUR HELP WILL BRING
VICTORY

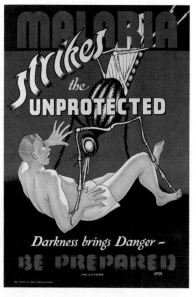

A propaganda poster showing South
Asians rubber tapping. Ceylon, Malaya
and Burma were all important producers
of wartime rubber. Posters such as this
one circulated in many local languages.

Malaria was a major threat to the Fourteenth
Army in the Burma campaign and invalided
many more soldiers than combat. This
poster, printed in Bombay in 1940, was
circulated by the British Army in India.

An aerial view of the Ledo Road linking India, Burma and China.
Much of the road was cut by hand by Asian labourers.

A nurse adjusts a doctor's mask at a hospital in Calcutta. Shortages of trained nurses was a major problem during the Burma campaign and civilian hospitals lost trained staff to the war effort.

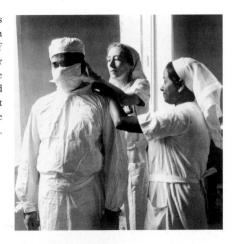

Parsi women training on an air raid precaution course in 1942 in Bombay. As fears of a Japanese invasion of India intensified, recruitment of ARP wardens was widespread.

Sir Stafford Cripps meets Gandhi in Delhi during his mission to reconcile the British government and Indian National Congress in March 1942. Despite the smiling faces the diplomatic mission failed and Gandhi was imprisoned later in the year.

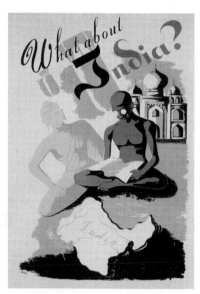

Aruna Asaf Ali, a charismatic leader of the underground movement during the Quit India campaign of 1942 and later a prominent politician after Independence.

This poster suggests the dilemma of how to resolve India's constitutional gridlock at a time of war, with so many uncertainties about when Independence would arrive and the future of the constitution.

Four unknown women, likely to be students, demonstrating against the government during the Quit India movement, August 1942.

An aircraft plotter of the WAC (I), a force which was rapidly raised in 1942 and placed elite Indian and Anglo-Indian women on equal terms with memsahibs.

Policewomen from the Women's Auxiliary Air Force purchasing fruit from a stall in Bombay.

Clearing land to make way for airfields. Over 200 new airfields were built during the war in South Asia and much of the land was requisitioned from peasant farmers.

Construction workers at an American airfield in India. Millions of men and women laboured for the Allies on roads, airfields, at docks and in mines.

Hungry children try to pierce sacks of grain along a railway line in the midst of the Bengal famine of 1943.

A family arrives from rural Bengal to Calcutta during the devastating famine.

A free kitchen run by the Rotary Club distributing food in Calcutta in 1943. The recently appointed Viceroy, Archibald Wavell, who was greatly disturbed by events in Bengal, stands on the centre-right, accompanied by his wife and senior members of the Indian Civil Service.

partiality for the Punjabi troops) and wanted to return to India, which he clearly considered home. Paternalistic towards young soldiers, he urged British officers to take an interest in the family lives and homes of the sepoys: 'A week spent by an officer in a recruiting area is worth a year in a unit for learning about his men, their way of living and their troubles.'[10] Suspicious of urban literate Indians, he saw villagers as the true heart and soul of the country. But as a leading Welfare Officer he also wanted conditions for these soldiers to be as palatable and comfortable as possible, to bring them up to standard and in the process to extract as much cash and as many concessions as possible from the British and Indian governments and charities like the Red Cross.

Brayne was in charge of enabling the smooth delivery of parcels, the acquisition of musical instruments like harmoniums and *tablas* and ensuring the right kinds of newspapers and periodicals arrived in the right numbers. Sepoys read novels and newspapers (if they could read – and many did become literate and learn new languages during army employment), played games, listened to the radio if they could, smoked, talked, sang and played musical instruments. Some took up knitting, making scarves, fingerless gloves and balaclavas as a way to while away the time but also as a practical necessity once cold weather set in. 'Remember it is the small things that irritate most', Brayne wrote back to India. On his first visit, he was dismayed by the barren landscape of Iraq, the widely dispersed Indian troops and the short-ages of small comforts. 'The walls of barracks, recreation huts etc. are painfully bare', he wrote in his diary, and he made arrangements for railway officials to send coloured posters of Indian scenes to cheer up the barrack walls.[11]

Brayne also courted newspaper editors and publishers, asking them to produce lively papers and books for soldiers in languages they could read. He railed against radio sets arriving with parts missing or broken in transit. He was well attuned to the soldiers' preferences and they did not hesitate to tell him what they wanted: they liked Lifebuoy and Lux soap and Sunlight bars for washing their clothes, they did not necessarily want *bidis* and were developing more of a taste for pouch tobacco and cigarettes, for cooking they needed a better supply of spices and condiments from cloves and cumin to chillies and ghee, Sikhs wanted hair-oil and combs, and the oversupply of Bengali gramophone records wasn't to their liking: 'Don't let any more Bengallee gramophone records come out but heaps and heaps more of the "martial languages".'[12] Crucially, the living standard of the average sepoy on active service remained much higher than that of the average peasant back home. Soldiers on leave carried back goods from the NAAFI shops of the Middle East in their kitbags because these had trebled in price in Indian towns. Many soldiers owned small personal possessions – razor blades, pen and paper and soap – which they could never have afforded in India.

*   *   *

By this point in the war, many officers allowed that Independence was inevitable and liked to stress that the future modernisation, prosperity and development of India, from electricity to paved roads, women's education to aviation, were inextricably linked to victory in the war. In *josh* talks, common rooms and on the screen, this message was underscored. But the promise of 'development' was an elusive one and the Indian Army encouraged men to serve the empire 'today' in order to work towards a better future for their own country 'tomorrow'. As it became clearer that Independence would soon come to India, the army promoted its ability to bring modernisation, technical skills and development – from irrigation to literacy – as one of its main assets. 'Development' had become the new ideological benchmark. As one British Ordnance Corps officer put it in a letter home, every country was already thinking about the future of its soldiers. In Britain the 'Bevin plans' gained traction, 'but what are the plans for Indian soldiers? Is anyone thinking of it?'[13] Back in Britain, Ernest Bevin, the powerful Minister of Labour, was drawing up ambitious plans for keeping British workers in full employment after the cessation of war. Many of the more enlightened officers, often strongly influenced by socialism and by wartime changes back in Britain, wanted to use the army as a way of spreading material progress. They had idealised versions of sanitised, model communities in mind, with modern agricultural techniques, well-staffed clinics and schools.

By 1944 the Indian government and army were both laying the

groundwork for demobilisation and post-war reconstruction. But this was planned as segmented reconstruction, not aimed at the population as a whole, still based on the old grid of loyal and disloyal communities, which would be used as a guide for the distribution of state largesse after the war. It was also intended to be apolitical and technocratic, carried through from the top without reference to politicians or people. For a society reeling from famine and politically radicalised, and for the 2 million men who would have to be demobilised at the end of the war, these plans would go neither far nor fast enough.

* * *

By 1944, even in the traditional recruiting regions, recruitment was not straightforward. Families made strategic decisions about whether to send their sons into the forces, trying to avoid sending more than one or two sons into the army and so spreading their risk. In regions with long histories of recruitment, it had always been traditional for one son to stay behind, to till the land and to care for ageing parents. Rajinder Singh Dhatt, from the district of Hoshiapur in Punjab, remembered how in a family of three boys, his mother had put her foot down when the third son wanted to join up. 'Our mother told [us] that "You two are in the army and you are taking this third one also, no, we can't send him" so he didn't join army.'[14] South Asia in the 1940s may have outwardly looked like a patriarchal society but at home women often knew exactly how to apply moral pressure and played the decisive part in determining whether their sons left home for the war or not.

In the villages of India, the young, hardy and keen were in shorter supply in the latter years of the war. John Ffrench, who had led men at Keren and Monte Cassino before a serious injury, was back in Rajputana drumming up recruits in 1944, touring by horseback and camel, but soon discovered 'there were literally no recruits available'. Recruiting in Rajputana was organised by a network of retired *subedar*-majors.

These honourable old gentlemen knew of every young man available and had them signed on and off for training as soon as they reached enlistment age. But at that stage in the war the only men left were the eldest sons of families who were responsible for working the land and were often approaching middle age anyway. Gone were the days of pre-war recruiting when there were twenty applicants to fill every vacancy.[15]

In Bihar, the picture was more promising and Ffrench was more successful, pushing up the numbers of recruits from 40 sepoys to 200 per month, but he soon realised that recruiting was providing ample opportunity for kickbacks. When swearing in new recruits he was taken aback when they placed rupees on his office table. 'When I asked what on earth that was for they replied that it was *dastur* [the custom] for each man to give one rupee to the recruiting officer and eight annas each to the doctor and the clerk.' Like many other types of secure state employment, acquiring the job was worth a small initial sweetener. The doctor denied all knowledge of the 'custom', although he was soon after dismissed for putting in false travel claims for tours in Bihari villages when he was actually, the officer suspected, taking time out in the less salubrious parts of Calcutta. At the same recruiting office, the *havildar* also had a scam running. He had connived with a team of 'professional recruits' who would enlist at one village, collect their signing-on pay and army-issue blanket, pullover and plimsolls. Before long, the new soldier would rapidly desert, sell his kit, and turn up at another village again in order to repeat the trick.[16]

In Nepal, the effect on youth was also striking. Nepal's population was sharply affected during the 1940s. 'The heavy recruiting programme for the last four years has drained the manpower of the country to such an extent that I am afraid the quality of the recruits that can be made available now will be poorer.' Nepal's ruler explained this unambiguously to the British government. 'Please direct the Recruiting Officer for the Gurkhas to instruct the Gurkha Recruiters to explore the remotest corners of the hills where intensive recruiting has so far not been carried out.'[17] Even ten years after the end of the war one close observer of a heavily combed region of Nepal commented, 'The handful of young men who live in Mohiriya is almost exclusively composed of those suffering from tuberculosis, the lame, those with rickets and other abnormalities. Certainly it is a limited case, but it shows to what extent mercenary soldiering can weaken a Gurung

village.'[18] Nepal was disproportionately affected by the wartime recruitment because of pre-existing traditions of recruitment of Gurkhas
and because of the ruler's wholesale backing for the war and acqui-
escence to British demands for men. The British government policy
towards the Rana ruling dynasty was, as one senior official frankly
put it, 'keeping them sweet', and so there was little organised opposition. The fledgling Nepali Congress was an organisation in exile,
building up opposition to the Rana regime from northern towns in
India. And the Nepalis had very poor sources of information. There
was no independent newspaper or magazine being published in the
whole country, and it was very difficult to find out what was happening
in the war. All radio sets (mainly imported from India by a handful
of privileged individuals in any case) had been confiscated to avoid
the circulation of German propaganda.[19]

Younger boys easily found a way into the army. Across South Asia,
the age constraints remained only loosely adhered to and younger
boys often found a way to join. Recruiting forms for non-combatants
asked only for an 'assumed age' to be written down in any case.
Anecdotal evidence abounds about the recruitment of teenagers.

> I was 17 or 17 and a half or maybe 16. I'm not sure. I haven't got a
> birth certificate, when I went to the office of the military. At that time
> I say may be 17 years. They say you can't go. I say alright. They say,
> you write 18 years and you be alright. So I said alright. So he wrote 18
> years and enrolled me,

remembered one sepoy.[20] One officer described how among the men
he commanded in a Pathan regiment, 'most were no more than boys.
A few in fact were very young, not yet shaving in some cases.'[21] When
a rifleman called Abir died from a bullet wound in Italy, the *subedar*
in his company of the 7th Gurkha Rifles started to sob:

> The Gurkha officer [Chaturman] told me that Abir was his nephew
> – they had lived in the same village in East Nepal; Abir had been killed
> before his seventeenth birthday and to make Chaturman's guilt worse,
> he had persuaded the recruiting authorities to enrol the lad under age
> or, more accurately, had told Abir to falsify his age on enlistment.[22]

The elderly could also slip through the net. On one extraordinary occasion a very elderly man was found working as a camp follower. In Geneifa in Egypt, one of the officers, Rupert Lyons, heard that one of the camp followers was ill and was 'astonished to see how old he was'. Lacking medical services and stretchers, he placed the elderly man on a sheet of corrugated iron and hitched a lift with a colleague to the hospital. 'When we arrived at the Indian Military Hospital the fellow was pronounced dead. The doctor said that he was about eighty years old and that his death was due to senile decay . . . he was recorded on the roll of camp followers as being aged eighteen.'[23] The Indian Army had exploded in size and scope and needed an eclectic and miscellaneous cast of characters which had resulted in much unorthodoxy by the middle of the war.

In India, the recruitment of non-combatants or camp followers was also still in full swing, drawing in more skilled labourers from poorer and lower castes and from increasingly far-flung regions. These non-combatants had a lower priority for leave, which they could scarcely afford even if it was granted. A Parsi captain in the Indian Army Medical Corps (IAMC) remarked in a letter home that 'about 60 of our followers – cooks, *bhisties*, sweepers – came out with this unit in 1939 and are nearly 4 years without leave'.[24] By 1944 these long separations were telling on family relationships and on the men themselves. Relatives continued to ask in letters when their men would be coming home. A Punjabi barber, who had been away for over three years, wrote a poignant note to his family: 'I always replied I am coming on leave shortly. But actually that was because I did not want to disappoint you. I tried so many times but was not lucky enough to get leave.'[25] Once discharged from the army, these men received little or no pension and they suffered if they were no longer able to work in their trades. In a small village called Chetru near Dharamsala in the Himalayas the writer Compton Mackenzie was introduced to a cook. The man had been wounded in the back by a shell in Libya and was unable to work due to his damaged lungs.[26]

These jobs, though, however lowly, also came with a considerable amount of pride attached and even the most menial could be made to feel that they were contributing in essential ways to the war. Nila Kantan, who ferried water during the battle of Keren, remembered

how 'we were very, very crucial to the action'.[27] The men assiduously
noted and cultivated subtle differences in rank, status and pay, whether
troops or non-combatants. When a 'British Cook', a Muslim from
Lucknow, who had been trained to make anglicised custards, gravies
and puddings for officers, was requested to cook Indian food for the
mixed officers of his regiment instead he protested vigorously to the
senior officer in charge, Kartar Singh:

> When I told him he said 'I'm a BT [British troops] cook not an IT
> [Indian troops] cook.' I had to coax him and tell him he was an Indian
> and surely he knew how to make chapattis and things like that . . . and
> after a lot of pep talk I was able to persuade him to make Indian food
> . . . Slowly he started making nice Indian food and the British officers
> started enjoying that.[28]

The cook's obstinacy was based on the marginally higher status of the
'British cook'. Status and hierarchy were passionately defended. Field
Marshal Slim was emphatic about making all the parts of the Indian
Army feel like the cogs in a watch, insisting that non-combatant clerks
and secretaries took part in physical drills. The condition and training
of the men varied considerably depending on their unit and regiment,
where they had been recruited and posted and the tasks that they were
charged to do. Men who had been recruited as troops found themselves
working as hospital porters and orderlies in some regiments.

For the units left back home, often not deployed to the battle
fronts, and in regiments that had been milked of inspiring officers
and frustrated by long and boring routine work, standards easily
slipped. Satyen Basu was posted near Madras in 1944, commanding
a unit which had already mutinied, 'A unit in rags, with forty
deserters and a recent mutiny to its credit'. As the men worked
long days loading and unloading hospital cars and trains, 'to a
casual observer they looked more like prisoners than free sepoys'.
Basu was immensely irritated at the lack of loyalty and discipline
among the men, 'pilfering and insubordination were common
crimes and summary disposal of cases by convictions of one to
four weeks imprisonment was a daily occurrence'. But he also
commented that there was one water tap for 280 men, they were
in ragged clothes and spent hours without breaks loading and

unloading coal. 'The average sepoy in this unit is just a mercenary soldier who is fighting for money', he wrote in an irate report to his superiors, 'the lofty ideal of fighting for king and country is foreign to them. The standard of education and common sense is so low that it is difficult to drive any point home, and they can little realise the gravity of the calamity in case of an enemy event.'[29] This scene was a far cry from the dashing action of finely honed sepoys depicted in imperial propaganda, yet these labourers were also unsung heroes, keeping the supply lines of the eastern war functioning, if only for a meal and a monthly wage. This unevenness in the Indian Army was inevitable given the size and rapidity with which the army grew.

17

Longing and Loss

Above the hills of the battlefields of Europe, North Africa and Burma, leaflets on thin paper floated down from the sky, dropped by circling planes. Although they had been trained to ignore Axis propaganda, some of the propaganda reaching the Indian troops was extremely unnerving, just as its German and Italian creators intended. It was directed at the weakest spots in the psychological armoury of the sepoys. It played on their homesickness, on their anxieties about hunger at home and on their desire for the war to end. In monochrome cartoons, smirking white officers chatted up alluring Indian girls against an oriental skyline or hid behind brave sepoys on the battlefield who charged forward obliviously. Officers use men as cannon fodder, so the storyline went; why would Indians fight for an imperial master? As well as targeting the sepoys' darkest fears, propaganda was aimed at their desires and fantasies. One bizarre German leaflet promised the Indian soldier troupes of dancing girls and a holiday in London after victory. Thousands of 'safe conduct passes' fluttered from the sky, luring deserters, and promising decent care in prisoner-of-war camps. The war for the mind of the sepoy was cheap and could be bitterly fought.

The longer the war went on, the more subtle the propaganda became and it was based on ever better information. 'Do you ever wonder why India is so poor?' the Grim Reaper asked, holding the Union Jack and standing amidst the cadavers and wasted figures of famine victims. 'If you think about answering this question with all your new experiences and ideas you can figure out what can you do for betterment of India once the war is over.' The propaganda emphasised the ability of the individual soldier to be master of his own destiny.[1]

Some of these cartoons remained crudely obvious. Churchill, cigar-smoking and rotund, was portrayed as a particularly nasty and avaricious character, wheeling off cartloads of Indian money. And Axis illustrators never quite failed to make the Indian sepoy himself look like a malevolent Aladdin, with pointed beard, goggly eyes and ludicrously oversized turban. But others hit a more poignant note. At Monte Cassino in 1944, Gandhi's unmistakable image floated down to soldiers on hundreds of leaflets: 'Your children should not have to join the army to fulfil their hunger and earn a living, and they shouldn't have to give up their life for free for another country and race. Like you! And if you lose your life for this army all of the sacrifices of the Mahatma will go to waste.'

Omnipresent throughout, the sepoy's lonely wife and his children appeared time and again on Axis propaganda. A barefoot woman, looking out into the distance, with a chubby child in her arms while another one clings to her sari. 'After bidding farewell to you, we kept on looking for you on the horizon', one pamphlet titled 'Milap' or 'Reunion' reminded the soldiers in Urdu calligraphy and roman letters; it was Urdu *ghazal* poetry in the midst of industrial warfare. Like soldiers everywhere, the separation from family was punishing and the defeat of the enemy was longed for because it would mean the chance to go home.

Like all soldiers, the sepoys missed their homes and their women. In memoirs, letters and interviews, the need for female company and the longing for home recur repeatedly. When sepoys saw Indian films they remembered the women of their villages and home towns: 'These Indian pictures are very much appreciated by all', a *havildar* of the 8th Division wrote home, 'because it reminds us of India when we see our own ladies in saris etc.' Another found watching the films almost unbearably poignant: 'Indian films come very seldom and make me recollect past days when you and I both used to go to cinemas in our own beloved country.'[2] When they wrote home, talked among themselves and when they went to sleep at night, the memories of home and the familiar comforts of extended families floated back to the men. Remembering the difficulties of war as older men, the separation from domestic life was one of the hardest and most painful adjustments for many. As everywhere in the world, it was a time of fractured relationships, longing for marriage and consummation, worry about fidelity and uncertainty about reunion. A captain of the IAMC in Egypt told a potential recruit who had not joined that it was 'Quite a good thing that you did not join otherwise you would have been trapped and cut off for six years from your wife and children which of course will certainly be painful to you [sic]'.[3]

Angela Bolton, the nurse working in the Combined Military Hospital in West Bengal, used to speak to Indian patients through an orderly, Abdul Bahadur from Allahabad, who acted as a translator. 'He would stand among a group of patients as they sat outside in the cool of the evening smoking *biris* and say expansively, "Sister Sahib, what you wish to know?"' The patients she treated had parasitic infestations, TB, typhoid or dysentery, as well as several suffering from psychological disturbances. But Bolton found they were also concerned about the health of their families back in their home villages.

> I would ask him what the patients liked to eat, what they thought of the army and – the question they liked best – how many children they had. Thus I discovered how fraught with uncertainty was their life in the agricultural villages; how their debts, passing from father to son, weighed them down; and how few of their children survived infancy.[4]

Above all, the men longed for leave. But for many, this did not come for four or five years. And, again as elsewhere in the world, it was inevitable that men away for many years at a time would find alternative comforts, and meet women in the places where they were stationed. Relationships developed, erratically, surreptitiously and outside the usual conventions. An Indian officer in Burma was struck by the fact that local Burmese women in an oil town spoke excellent Punjabi.

> They had married Indians, Sikhs from Doab area and all that. In fact, it used to be a regular thing for these families. They knew that this soldier, this individual, has a wife in India, and the wife in India knows that he has a wife in Burma and so he looks after these two families, separately, then when the Japanese came they [the men] had all gone away and these Burmese girls were left without anybody. They could speak Punjabi and they were quite pro Indian.[5]

Relationships between local women and sepoys were particularly common in Italy and Greece. Men held as prisoners of war in Italy struck up relationships with Italian women where and when they could. Satyen Basu, captive behind a barbed-wire fence in Italy, watched 'an old dame trying to convey her sincere sympathy to us by her gestures and her grandchild corroborating her sentiments' and how local girls would come up and make flirtatious gestures to the men.[6]

Officers and sepoys did not have the same advantages in this matter. Status and higher pay gave officers a better chance of finding a girl-friend. Unmarried officers occasionally took new wives home with them. One Sikh officer from Patiala married a woman he met in Greece and she has lived in India ever since. Another man 'with some seniority in rank' guarding airfield, wireless and radar stations on Cyprus wanted to marry one of the local women in the town but the colonel 'put a stop to it'.[7] These were happy matches on the whole but if the men were already married, these affairs could create compli-cated and unhappy circumstances.

Usually soldiers sent back the greater part of their wage to India. But there was no *compulsion* to send this and the precise percentage sent back to India was up to the individual sepoy. Most men sent back everything they could spare. Fifteen rupees from an eighteen-rupee wage was quite typical. A soldier had most of his basic needs looked after by the military and could live a modest existence without much cash while in service. Families placed considerable pressure on soldiers to send back the maximum that they could afford. As we have already seen, the soldier was often not perceived as an individual, making decisions about his own salary, but as the elected breadwinner for his whole extended family network and was expected to send back money accordingly.

On occasion, however, where marriages had been arranged *in absentia*, or where relationships had broken down due to feuds or fights, the soldier might turn his back on his wife, causing hardship and heartache back home. Nazir Begum, the wife of a sepoy from Jhelum, who was posted overseas with the Rajputana Rifles, pleaded with his Commanding Officer to intercede on her behalf with her husband, who had been away from home for four years serving in the Middle East, North Africa and Italy. She claimed he had not sent

a penny in her direction and employed a letter-writer to write a
letter:

> Sir, I most humbly and respectfully beg to state that my husband, No
> 13312 Naik Boota Khan, has been serving the Crown on Overseas service.
> Since his departure from India or from home no maintenance or family
> allotment is being paid or remitted to me. I am living at my parents'
> house who owing to indigent circumstances can hardly provide to
> maintain me. Owing to this trouble my father has run into debt as all
> the necessaries of life are too dear that can better be imagined than
> described. I venture to submit this my humble petition in the earnest
> hope that some measures may kindly be adopted to order my said
> husband to send me money from the date i.e. four years I am living
> at my parents' house. In the absence of any monetary help I will be
> sunk into a deplorable posture.[8]

Women would often move back in with their own parents while
their husband was away from the home, particularly if they still had
young children. Nazir Begum was becoming a burden and her family
was no longer in a position to support her. Her final plea was that
she might be released from the marriage altogether by her husband
and be granted a divorce if the soldier continued to refuse a remittance: 'At the end I will also request if he is not willing to provide
for my maintenance he can by all means extricate me from his
clutches by a divorce deed.' For a woman in such a position, this
fate was worse than that of a war widow as she was unable to access
any kind of pension or hardship fund and did not see the benefits
of her husband's pay packet. The British were reluctant to intervene
in such cases: the soldier was signed up to serve as an individual,
and although harmonious family life was the military ideal, there
was a limit to the extent that the *sarkar* could, or would, dispense
family justice.

Women could initiate separations too, although at the risk of family
censure and personal immiseration. The district soldiers' boards
reported that appeals connected to broken marriage contracts were
'very numerous and difficult to deal with' and complained of 'exaggerated claims' of cash paid or jewellery gifted as dowry.[9] Women
had often been married young to absent soldiers, had not yet conceived

and faced troublesome relationships with in-laws. Stories circulated about 'miserable and desperate' women who, when their husbands were home on leave, threatened to end the marriage if he returned to his unit.[10] Among the Kumaonis in the Himalayan foothills, a prospective bride could be dressed for marriage – with a nose ring, black glass bangles, a necklace of black beads, and a ceremonial skirt tied at the waist – and publicly taken to the groom's house, perhaps with accompanying trumpets, while the absent groom was already away serving overseas. Further ceremonies would be performed when the groom came back, sometimes after many years. Occasionally a marriage to an absent soldier would be conducted without any ceremony at all; the price was simply paid and the bride taken to the husband's home. Other families would wait until the man was on leave or had just returned from the army – both seen as opportune moments to seal marriages.

Some wives in Punjab barely knew their husband's name and would be presented with silver spoons engraved with a name or army enlistment number as a marker of marriage, and a useful aide-memoire. While men were away from home for so long, women also found new lovers and struggled with the consequences. 'An illegitimate baby always brings problems', said one female doctor working as a Welfare Officer in an Indian princely state:

> Sometimes the mother has the courage to keep and care for her infant and face the music when her husband returns. This has happened in two cases. Sometimes she gives the baby to the hospital authorities in the hope that it will die. One cold November morning a newborn baby was found abandoned on the veranda of the hospital. The mother was found to be a soldier's wife, and the WO [Welfare Officer] was able to bring her and the baby together again. There were many difficulties but eventually husband and wife were reconciled. Fear is often stronger than maternal instinct.[11]

As in Europe and America, during the long absences of war, both women and men suffered in loneliness and in love.

One of the most popular Bollywood films of the 1940s, a veritable wartime blockbuster called *Kismet*, was released in 1943. Unusually, it depicted an illegitimate pregnancy. Distinctively, the hero, played by Ashok Kumar, was an anti-hero, in and out of jail, a rebel and petty criminal. The film captured the spirit of the war in India and angry youth in the towns and cities flocked to see it. It skirted censorship because nobody could accuse the film directly of disloyalty. But the animating spirit of the film was youthful rebellion. It was a story of an underdog finding courage but also highlighted the problems of fidelity and illicit love. It caught the mood of many young Indians.

The close proximity of troops and local societies in India naturally created plenty of chances for sex, and soldiers of all backgrounds and nationalities took the opportunity. By 1944, the rates of venereal disease had soared in India, in both the civilian and military populations.[12] Prostitution became endemic wherever soldiers were stationed; women sold sex illegally from notorious streets and brothels, or from more discreet and expensive establishments. Many parts of cities such as Calcutta, Delhi, Karachi and Bombay had been declared off-limits to soldiers and Military Police patrolled these areas to ensure that servicemen did not enter them. They also raided brothels on numerous occasions.

The Americans, particularly concerned at the impact on the well-being of their own men, took matters into their own hands. There was deep-seated unease among the American military leadership about the widespread existence of brothels close to army bases in India. Around the Chakulia air base in Bihar, for instance, American military officials took 'prostitutes and operators of illegal liquor houses in surrounding villages' into custody and turned them over to the local police with requests for prosecutions.[13]

The Americans and the British in India differed in their attitude towards servicemen visiting brothels in India, and the British attitude was less strict. Up until 1943, if American men in India failed to declare that they had sex with a prostitute without the use of prophylaxis they could be court-martialled. This order was eventually rescinded but men could still be court-martialled for concealment of venereal disease and medics were entitled to carry out random bodily inspections. Among the British the policy was slightly different: there were penalties for the concealment of disease but no courts martial, and the approach was generally more lenient. Among the British military command tacit acceptance of the inevitability of prostitution was combined with education and warnings, determined provision of condoms ('Defeat the Axis, Use Prophylaxis' was one catchy slogan) combined with much discretion and turning of the proverbial blind eye.[14]

Still, high levels of sexually transmitted diseases posed a concern for all armies. A fervent, almost evangelical, strain of thought stressed how wholesome amusements and worthy occupations such as team sports could distract men from the more unsuitable and destructive habits of drink, drugs and sex. Sepoys recruited from towns and cities, not from the traditional 'martial races', came under particular suspicion as being 'more sophisticated than the recruits from rural areas and also more accustomed to consorting with prostitutes', noted one army medical report.[15] But increasing levels of sexually transmitted diseases could also be put down to more mundane reasons: the long stretches of time away from home – even while stationed in India, Indian Army troops could be many hundreds of miles from their own district – and the steadily increasing wages of the Indian soldier as well as the ever-present fear of death which haunted serving soldiers. Anti-prostitution propaganda films with alluring titles like *Mitha Zahar* (Sweet Poison) failed to frighten Indian soldiers away from the brothels. Frank public information advertisements appeared in respectable national newspapers, warning the general public that abstinence was the only protection against disease and that 'syphilis affects most of the professional, clandestine and amateur prostitutes'.[16]

For the majority of enlisted men their only opportunity for sex was as paying customers and as a result Calcutta recorded some of the highest levels of sexually transmitted diseases among troops anywhere in the world in the Second World War. In a 1944 survey of two American bases in India approximately 60 per cent of the men surveyed said that they had had sex in the China–Burma–India theatre and had paid for it and a majority said that it was likely that they would consider doing so in the future.[17] 'V.D. seems to be the prevalent disease here, due probably to the large garrison', a British soldier wrote home. 'The fault is entirely the Army's, as a normal man cannot stay out here at the most impressionable period of his life, without some outlet for his passion. The authorities who understand are all in agreeance [*sic*] about re-opening regimental brothels, but stupid parliamentarians in England veto the idea.'[18]

The Governor of Bengal described the levels of venereal disease in Bengal as 'appallingly high' and in Calcutta the visibility of prostitution was generating political protest and deepening anti-war feeling.[19] Two hundred extra Military Police were recruited in Calcutta at a time of extreme manpower shortage to patrol brothels and unusually the military invested in civilian clinics. Field Marshal Slim hinted at the problem of 'less reputable relaxations' in Calcutta, which offered 'the whole scale of vice from doubtful dancehalls to disease-ridden dens of perversity'. Clive Branson also commented on a visit by men to a brothel near Poona 'under official patronage' and on the 'well known fact that white sahibs go into cheap brothels with native women'.[20]

People in Britain and in India continued to believe that some brothels were maintained for the use of troops, although this was never official policy. The Secretary of State for India had to deny any such thing to a member of the British public who wrote to him, 'Do the Government run brothels for the troops in India? A number of soldiers etc. have stated that brothels are run for the troops in that country.'[21] There may have been confusion among troops themselves about the legality of the matter. Commanding Officers reluctantly accepted that troops did sleep with 'coolie' women, presumably low-caste Indian women workers, either agriculturalists or manual labourers, many of whom were employed by the Allies in the construction of aerodromes and roads and in military supply centres. It was suggested that the men themselves turned to poor coolie women only when their own 'morale was low'.[22] Naive white soldiers, it was argued, became confused and subject to the predatory advances of Indian 'pimps and prostitutes', especially when under the influence of alcohol.

As so often in history, the women who sold sex were blamed. The military correspondence depicted 'Eastern' and 'Anglo-Indian' women as sensuous, immoral and lascivious. Other Indian women who had sex with soldiers were described as disease-ridden, filthy and easy.[23] The reality was that poverty had driven many women into selling sex by the later years of the war. The historian Paul Greenough, who personally conducted interviews in the 1970s with some sex-workers as part of his research into the famine, recalled how families in Bengal sold their daughters for small sums and how reports of boatloads of women and girls circulated.

Two of the women he interviewed told their own stories: widowed by the cyclone in Midnapore and driven to destitution by the famine, exploited and raped by other men, they had eventually survived and carved out a new life in Calcutta as sex-workers; one even bought a small piece of land and procured other women.[24]

Rumours spread about trafficked women, families selling their own daughters, and the rising numbers of single women on the streets. This question even reached the House of Commons in 1944 after an article was published in the *Birmingham Mail* about the purchase of an Indian girl by a British officer in Bengal for less than two rupees, although the Secretary of State denied any knowledge of the purchase of destitute children.[25] A wartime survey carried out by Santosh Mukherji claimed that while interviewing women joining the brothels in Calcutta, he found 62 out of 100 gave 'starvation' as their motive for prostitution.[26]

For Indian politicians of all hues the noticeable increase in urban military prostitution was inflammatory and politically sensitive. Politicians angrily raised the issue in the Legislative Assemblies and in vernacular newspapers. Fazlul Haq, the former premier of Bengal, gave a speech about the exploitation of starving Muslim women by American and African soldiers, reportedly saying that 30,000 Muslim women had been sent to American and African troops in Bengal and that when he had tried to raise the issue in the Legislative Assembly he had been stopped by his rival, Nizamuddin.[27] An Urdu paper, the *Ansari*, published in Delhi and owned by a municipal commissioner of the capital, printed an article stating that Calcutta's population had increased markedly because of the large numbers of soldiers stationed there:

Most of them are young and have not brought their families with them. They have money and get a large number of currency notes from the Government treasury. How do they spend these currency notes? They use them to buy those starving Bengali women who lost their brothers, fathers and husbands in the Bengal famine. These unfortunate women can be counted in millions and they are to be found in every street, lane and side-road of Calcutta. Prostitution goes on openly.

This neatly crafted a form of anti-colonialism which linked the famine, ideas of moral purity, communal identity and a nasty evocation of racial miscegenation: 'What will this generation be like? Matters will not end here. In the veins of some American blood will flow, in others English, while in others again the blood of Indian soldiers of different communities will flow. An entire generation of bastards will thus come amongst us.'[28] This raised the spectre of familiar nationalist tropes about the protection of 'our' women, the threat of racial 'impurity', and championed the symbolic threat to women in service to a broader political cause.[29]

Many local men profited during the war from their ability to provide services, directly or indirectly, to the military bases stationed in Calcutta, Karachi, Bombay and beyond. Taxi or *gharry* workers would help soldiers locate brothels and men employed at military bases could earn extra income by acting as intermediaries. Around the bases and encampments a service culture grew of local men who would procure women, alcohol and other services. Smuggling, sex-trafficking and petty crime were often closely linked. The Anglo-American shop in Karachi was a first stop for some troops who wanted to find women for sex. Afterwards, they became 'friendly' with the shop owner and struck a deal to supply him with stolen goods like stocks of paracetamol taken from army stores. One investigation uncovered the regular delivery of US goods in an army vehicle to an Assamese village twice a week. Undercover Indian personnel discovered that army rations were being delivered under cover of darkness in exchange for 'coolie' girls from local tea estates. The rations, sold onwards by a local trader, then appeared on the black market.[30]

Civil and military leaders decried the sanitary and political implications of this increase in prostitution. India was full of journalists from around the world. Keenly aware of international political opinion and the risk of negative Axis or nationalist propaganda, British civil servants, politicians and Allied military leaders had to be responsive to critical voices from Indian nationalists and international campaigners. The military priorities of sustaining the war effort and keeping up the morale of fighting men had to be balanced against local domestic concerns. There could no longer be any straightforward endorsement of military prostitution in the colonial setting by the 1940s (as there had been in the nineteenth century), but the increase in interracial sex was undeniable. This all added to the sense in India of a world gone awry, and was fodder for those propagandists who wanted to demonise the imperialists.

18

Catalyst of Change

I came on duty tonight to find the wards in a very disturbed state. There was nobody to hand over the day report to me and sisters were hurrying about from *basha* to *basha* with dressing trays in their hands. 'What is happening?' I called to Isobel Mckenzie, who was preparing a drug at the medication trolley. 'Haven't you heard? Wounded from Kohima,' she answered. 'There's an officer for theatre right away.' I followed her into the ward, where she administered the pre-operative injection to an Indian in the bed at the far end of the room. 'Who is he?' I asked. 'Captain Magid [Majeed]. Both his legs have been blown off and he is being taken to theatre to see if they can save his right arm.' 'Oh God!' I said. 'How terrible' . . . Captain Magid died on the operating table under anaesthetic.[1]

The Japanese did make an ambitious incursion into Indian territory but by 1944 the Allies were fully prepared for it. In March 1944, the Japanese pushed into the north-east, and advanced along the Imphal–Dimapur Road, in an attempt to cut Imphal's supply lines and to capture the strategically pivotal Kohima. The 14th Army – an eclectic collection of nearly half a million troops including British infantrymen, Canadian and American pilots, the Assam Rifles, the King's African Rifles and troops from the Gold Coast – had been trained, equipped and honed into a modern fighting force by now. Among the infantry morale was high, there was an effective organisational *esprit de corps*, and powerful air support gave the Allies a distinct advantage. Nonetheless, the Japanese made a massive thrust, sending in 85,000 men, far more than had been expected, and for a time it looked as if they might cut off and occupy north-east India at Kohima. But in stark contrast to 1942 the Japanese quickly became overstretched as

their supply lines were bogged down over hundreds of miles of difficult terrain, winding back into South-East Asia.

The fighting was bitter and often intensely personal with men
enclosed in claustrophobic spaces and foxholes, exhausted by prolonged
siege and locked in hand-to-hand combat. Vicious and bloody experiences of the bloodshed during the Arakan campaigns of 1944 as well
as at Kohima and at Imphal left a deep imprint on the soldiers of all
nationalities who fought there and many Indian infantry soldiers
recalled later their single-minded focus and determination to defeat
the Japanese. This was fuelled by the intimate experiences of brutal
battles. 'Firstly, they shelled our mules in their line and killed dozens
– this made us mad', recalled Gian Singh, who was in the 7th Indian
Division and fought in the Battle of the Admin Box.

> Secondly on the night of about 8th or 9th of February, the Japanese
> broke into our defences. They chose to break in where we had our
> field hospital. About 500 of them killed the wounded and even doctors
> who were operating. They took a few prisoners who we found the
> next day when we sent out patrols. They found Indian surgeons and
> orderlies bayoneted . . . We saw our men who, when captured, had
> been tied to trees by their turbans and used for bayonet practice. Also,
> on that night I learnt how easy it is to push a bayonet into someone's
> body. I was surprised that it made me feel somehow good. After all
> we were fighting those who did not behave as people should.[2]

For many men on the front line, winning the war became the only
focal point and temporarily obliterated all other considerations.
Ultimately the Japanese 15th Army lost 53,000 dead and missing, while
the British (including the Indian Army) sustained 12,500 casualties at
Imphal and another 4,000 casualties at Kohima. Stinking and bloated
corpses literally littered the ground.[3]

The local people in the hills and valleys of present-day Manipur
and Nagaland, in the region around Imphal and Kohima, lived through
these epic battles, caught in the crossfire between the Allies and the
Japanese. Their lands became battlegrounds and their lifestyles were
changed irrevocably by the new contact with armies from around the
world and by the massive influx of money, hardware and manpower
necessary to defeat the aggressors. Many had already been affected,

as we have seen, by the presence of refugees and troops, by requisitioning and by price rises. By the autumn of 1943, 20,000 homes had
been requisitioned by the British in the Imphal region and many
villagers now lived with friends and family. But far worse was to come.

The rapid approach of the Japanese along the Tiddim Road in early
1944 took everyone in that area by surprise; although the Allies were
braced for a Japanese move, this route was chosen to try and cut off
supply lines further to the north. On the retreat, the British quickly
evicted villages, burned paddy and requisitioned livestock as part of
the continued denial policy and many villagers fled. Further north in
Ukhrul, villagers ran into the forest and waited expectantly for the
Allies to recapture the region.[4] Others who remained, especially in
villages that happened to lie along roads and supply lines, encountered
Japanese soldiers passing through, many of whom were ravenous for
food, and especially meat. Neipezu-u Chirhah of Chizami village in
Nagaland shared her childhood memories of fleeing from the
advancing army with Kazimuddin Ahmed:

> I lived with my grandmother and my maternal uncle. The Japanese
> took my uncle to act as a porter for them. Grandmother and I fled the
> village carrying whatever we could with us. We were very scared when
> we heard that the Japanese killed our chicken. Even in the forest we
> had to move around as the Japanese were everywhere. They killed
> many of our livestock. Sometimes some of the brave ones would visit
> the village from our places of hiding and returned with the leftovers
> of those kills, which we would eat. There was so much fear.[5]

Hungry cultivators watched on while soldiers seized their goods
and fed their harvest to their mules. The subsistence farmers in the
region of the Manipur plains were completely cut off from the rest
of the country from late March until late June 1944 and people deserted
their villages, foraged or lived on rations. Barely a single chicken or
pig could be found in the whole region and the fields stood empty
and untended. Further north, destruction was even more severe, with
numerous villages completely ruined by shelling and Kohima itself
was burned to the ground by fire before the inhabitants could save
their paddy or household goods.[6]

Local people's allegiances were uncertain. Much has been written about the determined efforts of British officials and hill chiefs to mobilise local support, to organise the Chin and Kachin levies and to resist Japanese incursions. In the complex, hilly terrain the knowledge, support and guerrilla actions by local indigenous hill tribes, especially the Nagas – recruited to assist the regular troops and known as V-Force – were pivotal to the Allied victories. But among the different ethnic groups of the north-east, including Meiteis, Tangkhuls and Kukis, responses were sometimes ambiguous and although there were incredible instances of loyalty to the British, there was also a smaller core of people who favoured the Japanese. The Japanese carried pictures of Bose inspecting Indian troops and wore armbands in Congress colours and greeted people with 'Victory to India!'

Although still a matter of controversy among scholars of the region, a number of people sided with the aggressors, especially among the Kukis of the hills, and provided information or supplies to the invaders.[7] One man was believed to be a deserter from the Assam Regiment and was identified by many people for his pro-Japanese propaganda. A small but influential pro-INA group worked in the Kabow valley and claimed that the Japanese were coming to bring *swaraj*. Local people were crucial in this situation as with deteriorating access to food and struck by ill-health, the Japanese desperately needed help with supplies, labour and intelligence in order to survive. Some Kukis resorted to foraging for wild roots, not only for themselves but also to support starving Japanese soldiers.[8]

By mid-1944, when the Japanese had been pushed back from Kohima and Imphal, local people from the hills and valleys could start to return to their homes. There had been no harvest, while rice barrels stood looted and empty. The British Raj in conjunction with the Allied forces made significant efforts to rehabilitate the region and to protect local people who had been caught up in the battles from famine or destitution. As people gradually returned to their empty villages, ration depots were opened, new varieties of seed supplied to villagers, sums of cash distributed for those who had been looted by the Japanese, agricultural tools and ploughs supplied in their thousands and pigs and chickens sent for restocking. Cash reliefs and compensation were handed out for loss of livestock. Doctors were sent to all the dispensaries of the state and corrugated tin and bamboo sent to

Manipur and Nagaland for the building of new homes. This relief and rehabilitation effort meant that the region could recover from the ravages of war, but made a striking contrast to the relief efforts after the Bengal famine, where spending per capita was significantly less.[9]

★ ★ ★

Soldiering was a mental and a physical challenge. The battles that sepoys fought with ill-health, depression and debilitating diseases, particularly malaria and dysentery, were often as extreme as any fought with combatants. As Lieutenant-Colonel B. L. Raina recalled, 'In the Eastern Theatre of war the diseases threatened the troops more than the enemy'.[10] On the Burmese front, health was *the* determinant of military success. In the 14th Army, as Field Marshal Slim was at pains in his memoir to point out, the ability to treat soldiers and to restore them quickly to service was an ongoing struggle, although one that the Indian Army was winning by the midpoint of the war, and which the Japanese with their tattered supply lines were unable to match in Burma. In Assam and Burma, among some sepoys, 'loss of weight was so great in a large number of cases that they were reduced to a bag of bones' and many needed four months or more in hospital in order to recover their strength.[11]

Along the Burmese front, Allied soldiers pitted themselves not only against the Japanese but against the swampy sickness of the jungle, spending protracted weeks bogged down in ditches in the wet and cold. The stench of dead bodies in the humid battle zone, amidst burned-out trees and scorched foliage and the nervous anticipation of unexpected attacks in the shadows, made this a particularly harrowing campaign, with the nagging feeling for many soldiers that they had been forgotten or given secondary Cinderella status compared to the troops back in Europe.

Across India, military medical services expanded in response. Nehru would later remember as Prime Minister of India that this was 'the best aspect of war' for the subcontinent as it acted as 'a catalyst of change'.[12] As in Beveridge's Britain, public health modernisation escalated in the 1940s, although it would be far-fetched to call it a revolution. This shift had older roots in the internationalism of the 1930s but was encouraged by the sheer military necessity of confronting the medical problems that beset the Indian and Allied armies.

Many recruits were physically depleted on joining up, long before they even saw a battlefield. In fact, the physical health of many recruits in the Indian Army tended to improve rather than deteriorate, especially during training. Sepoys could take advantage of healthcare they would otherwise be unable to dream of back home (and this was noted in a number of letters home) and also benefited from inoculations, malaria control and a regular and regulated diet, often supplemented with multivitamins. Numerous military doctors agreed that the bodies of sepoy recruits were not always in a good state to begin with. Malnutrition and anaemia were not just problems caused by time on the front line; they could be evident in raw recruits. As the official historian of the Indian wartime medical services commented, 'it was impossible to depend on the old sources of supply of men with characteristically fine physique' and multiple vitamin deficiencies were due to the recruitment of men with 'low nutritional status'.[13]

Some doctors continued to believe in pseudo-science, and that the martial races were more innately suited to military life. There was concern that vegetarian soldiers from South India lacked vital protein. But it was also the case that as the army cast the net ever wider, relaxed its requirements, and recruited boys in their teens, poorly fed peasants and those who paid backhanders in order to circumvent normal rules, the fitness of some sepoys was called into question. Men with lower body weight were particularly susceptible to disease.

British nurses struggled to care for their charges and experienced the effects of jungle warfare at the rockface. They also acted as whistle-blowers, making humane and persistent demands on the authorities, horrified by the conditions of their patients. Lilian Pert, in her mid-forties, slender with boyish hair and a direct manner, was volunteering as a nurse in Indian General Hospitals throughout the war, in Karachi and later in South India, doing, as she believed, 'the most exhausting work physically and mentally that an educated English woman can undertake in this country'.[14] Her husband, Claude, a brigadier in the Indian Army and a polo-player of some repute, had been stationed in the north-east. Lilian Pert asked some tough and persistent questions of her superiors, pointing out the blatant differences between hospitals for Indian troops and hospitals for foreign soldiers.

The numbers of properly trained nurses in the Indian hospitals was negligible. Pert estimated that the ratio of properly trained nurses to beds in the Indian General and military hospitals was 1:100–200 compared to 1:20–30 in the British military hospitals. She was worried by the lack of doctors as well as nurses. On many wards a part-time civilian doctor would show up for a few hours in the morning before going back to his own private practice:

> When the Burma show was on trains came in daily packed with wounded and the hospitals didn't know which way to turn . . . What will be the conditions in overseas hospitals staffed like this when heavy casualties start coming in from a future Burma campaign? Shall we not get more hospital scandals? . . . Something *must* be done before we are swamped with heavy casualties from the far east. I should hate to have it on my conscience that I condemned, by inaction, these future casualties to the same neglect as was suffered by seriously wounded men of the 4th Indian Division at the IGH Karachi and elsewhere in India. This is the only reason I go on struggling with this highly unpopular problem.[15]

Wounded soldiers lacked good food and company and often found it difficult to communicate with hospital staff or fellow patients because of linguistic differences. Hospitals were chaotic with members of the public wandering in and out, and sometimes lacked even basic bathrooms. When her ideas for encouraging more British women volunteers into Indian hospitals were rebuffed by a non-committal letter from senior military officers, Lilian Pert retorted, 'By the tone of their remarks [I] might almost have made an improper suggestion by saying that English women should nurse Indian soldiers!!' The soldiers suffered from the lack of care and Pert carefully recorded particular cases that had occurred in 1942. An Indian soldier with a fractured femur was transferred on a train for a seven-hour journey: 'head and neck unsupported by stretcher, no pillow, no blanket, no urinal, food or drinks. Given pillow by first class passenger on train also drinks. No orderly or doctor visited cases during journey.'[16] Pert's damning criticisms of her superiors and of the organisation of health provision for Indian soldiers were being echoed by other nurses, arriving from Canada, New Zealand and Britain, who saw the visible discrepancy between the healthcare on offer for Indian and British soldiers.

Mrs G. E. Portal, another nurse who had seen the fallout from the Burma retreat at close hand, when working in the hospital at Ranchi, was equally scathing about the conditions:

> The hospital is heart-breaking . . . It is a shocking crime and may God forever damn the Eastern Command staff, in fact the whole of GHQ . . . patients touching each other, people moaning for water and sicking up and so on everywhere. 150 of my surgicals are now on the floor . . . The nursing sepoys and the menials are thoroughly overworked and very Bolshy, but one has to drive them like galley slaves, and this I find the worst of all my jobs . . . But I hate worst of all having to refuse help to patients in great pain because we haven't even got aspirin.[17]

This compassion and readiness by women to tend the bodies of soldiers and to alleviate suffering, irrespective of race, was new and not always altogether welcomed. Again, war was reordering imperial society. As the war went on, Indian and British soldiers were increasingly treated side by side and newer, mixed hospitals emerged. A great push to improve medical facilities accompanied a greater sense of the need to ensure racial equality between soldiers.

In the eastern campaign there was a steady improvement in medical services close to the front line. Field ambulances, field hospitals and casualty clearing stations all radically improved morale and survival rates, and blood transfusions and mobile surgical units saved lives. Base hospitals were threaded throughout the subcontinent with a large number in the United Provinces, others in Ranchi, Poona, Bangalore and Karachi. By 1944 there were even flights out from the battlefield for emergency care in stark contrast to the disorganised rout of 1942. By the last months of the war a patient in Burma with a gunshot wound to the head might reach a specialist neurosurgical unit within a few hours. Penicillin, the wonder drug that was rapidly transforming wartime medicine and could avert amputations, was available in the last two years of the war, although still in short supply even in the best-equipped General Hospitals and 'therefore as precious as gold'.[18]

★ ★ ★

How much did civilians benefit from these changes? There were some areas in which medical modernisation had a direct effect: in research, in scientific innovation and in the new familiarity with surgical procedures and certain medicines. In the long run, there *was* a direct effect on civilian healthcare, although much of this would become evident only in the 1950s. Many benefits were transferred to India after demobilisation, when the advances made in the war gradually started their slow osmosis into civilian treatments; for instance, artificial limbs manufactured for maimed soldiers could easily be used for civilians and by August 1944 the artificial limb centre in Poona was fitting 100 a month. Modern dentistry, reconstructive surgery, nutritional therapies and ophthalmic care also received a professional boost because of doctors active in the military. For the rest of the population, military priorities skewed areas of research in some directions while other areas such as maternal and paediatric health remained under-resourced. The Bhore Committee Report pointed out, for instance, how the Indian TB association had been 'crippled' by the outbreak of war, how laboratory work had stalled in a number of research institutions as young scientists moved into military employment and existing civilian facilities could not get hold of adequate stocks of equipment, chemicals or other supplies.[19]

Although charitable acts by the Friends Ambulance Unit, the Indian Tea Association and the Indian Red Cross Society did not necessarily distinguish between men in uniform and needy civilians, there was often still a stark division between the state's provision for ordinary people and soldiers. In reality, it was a three-tiered system with the best care for the British and other Allied armies, the second-best care for the Indian Army and with civilians left far behind at the bottom of the pyramid. There were about 172,000 hospital beds available for the Indian Army at the end of the war, while less than half this amount, just 75,000, in Indian civilian hospitals for the entire remainder of the population.[20] In some areas, the creaming-off of doctors, nurses and resources for the war effort was denuding the scanty local medical provision even further and actually damaging the limited resources available to the Indian peasant or worker. The Bhore Committee Report did not gloss over the widening gulf between the best medicine on offer, the aspirations of the state and the reality of hopelessly ineffective and paltry provision for the majority of Indians. The military's need for doctors was still insatiable and training was not keeping up with the demand, so that even the army was actively advertising for licentiates, partly trained local healers with a rudimentary knowledge of first aid and drugs.[21]

The yawning gulf between the best and the worst hospitals widened. Urban hospitals came under duress because of rapidly growing populations, and industrialisation and other schemes faced setbacks. In Madras, a ten-year plan for the rural water supply agreed in the late 1930s faltered because of the priorities and conditions of war. In the civilian population as a whole, health often deteriorated because of poor nourishment. With the proliferation of sexually transmitted diseases soldiers received cutting-edge care but there was little additional treatment for others, except in Calcutta where the government set up seven clinics in 1944 for civilian men and women because of the seriousness of the epidemic. Over 200,000 people, men and women, made use of these clinics in less than a year.[22] Beyond Calcutta, those with sexually transmitted diseases had to make do with clinics of 'indescribable squalor', in the words of an untiring consultant venereologist, Eric Prebble, where further infection was more probable than cure, and where there was an embarrassing lack of privacy. Prebble watched on incredulously as over fifty men with suspected cases of syphilis and other diseases, crammed in one room, used old cigarette tins to soak their sores.[23]

This litany of horrors was not new, and was not eradicated in post-Independence India, but once again the clash between the modern and the antiquated, the well-resourced and the underfunded, was glaring. Compared to the rural poor, the soldiers were materially better-off. The slow improvements and investment in medical treatment in the later part of the war created strains elsewhere which rebounded on civil hospitals; as Slim put it, the army 'milked the hospitals of India to danger point to help us'.[24] The modern colonial state was capable of engineering almost miraculous solutions to some human problems in the midst of the war, while leaving much of the population almost untouched by medical advances.

⋆   ⋆   ⋆

There was another new weapon in the armoury of the military: psychiatry. As in Britain, the sciences of the mind were reaching new audiences and shaping the way that people understood mental health. The British Army had begun to recognise the utility of psychiatric treatment to rehabilitate soldiers and to restore them to active duty, to maintain unit discipline and to help men to withstand the stressful conditions of combat. One soldier involved in the Arakan campaign, Gian Singh, recalled, 'In those days there was no such thing as counselling. A cup of tea and a cigarette was sometimes the best therapy you were offered – if you were lucky.'[25] Nevertheless, there was an increased sensitivity to the complex interplay between poor morale, mental health and the conditions of war, and also wider recognition that minor interventions, like rest and recognition of exhaustion, might alleviate symptoms. Wartime neuroses were no longer simply viewed as permanent aberrations. From 1942, within the British Army there was a level of screening for mental health, potential recruits could be referred for psychiatric assessment and men could be assessed on admission to the army for their mental fitness for combat roles. Psychotics would be ejected from the military. Doctors used hypnotic drugs to control aggression, sometimes straitjackets and physical restraint to the bed too. But the majority of mental-health cases were much milder and more readily treatable forms of neuroses and there was a concerted effort to rehabilitate them as quickly as possible in order to return them to active duty.

Throughout the 1930s, psychiatry and psychoanalysis had been gaining wider acceptance among medical professionals in India, and Jung had made an extensive tour of India in 1937–8. In October 1942, Edward Bennett, a highly respected Jungian analyst, arrived in Delhi to advise the military from the progressive environment of London's Tavistock Clinic. The number of qualified psychiatrists serving the Indian Army increased from four to eighty-six during the war, including some Jewish refugee doctors, and a number of junior medical officers also received training in psychiatric care. Specialist wards were developed in General Hospitals like Ranchi, Moradabad, Poona and Comilla. Nurses were reading the latest works on psychoanalysis, pavement bookstalls sold the works of Jung and Freud, and the role of domestic, emotional and child-hood neuroses and their contribution to an individual's ability to with-stand the tensions of battle all became more thoroughly understood.

Needless to say, Indian soldiers did not benefit from these medical innovations in psychiatric care to the same extent as their British comrades, despite psychiatric cases accounting for 10 to 15 per cent of all casualties in the Indian Army. In the forward areas of North Africa and the Western Desert, neuroses ranged from exhaustion and home-sickness to fear of battle. The Indian Army's approach was less nuanced and responsive than the British Army's. The 'trick-cyclists' of the psychiatric profession still tended to believe people had predilections towards certain mental illnesses; this might be because of an indi-vidual's background or childhood but might also be predetermined by ethnicity or by race. The idea persisted that Indians were peculiarly predisposed to certain types of mental ill-health, particularly hysteria. This idea had gained currency in the First World War and continued to inform the treatment of Indian soldiers, even among the more liberal and progressive psychiatrists.[26]

Wilfred Abse, an eminent psychiatrist from Cardiff, worked with patients suffering from mental health issues in the Indian Military Hospital in Delhi. He wrote emphatically about the differences in hysteria between Indians and westerners, convinced that it was a peculiarly Indian phenomenon, and something to which Bengalis were particularly prone; indeed, he argued, it was the illness 'second only to malaria in Bengal'.[27] There had been a long suspicion that Indian soldiers had a particular susceptibility to hysteria and among the nervous disorders Abse saw in Delhi, he detected hundreds of cases of hysteria – convulsions, paralysis and sensory disturbances – among Indian soldiers who had been hospitalised. Psychiatrists from Europe rarely knew Indian vernaculars and they had to interview patients using a translator, often failing to grasp the subtleties of the social and economic strains on the Indian soldier.

Wilfred Abse included photographs in his case-notes of patients manifesting physical symptoms because of their mental distress. One patient's limbs had been studded with thorns ('Hysterical anaesthesia of legs. Thorns plunged into the skin were ignored by patient'), other sepoys were pictured with bloated stomachs or bent perpendicular with bad backs. He saw convulsive attacks as 'frequent manifestations of hysteria in Indian soldiers' in addition to amnesia and abdominal pains. In one case, a soldier had not been able to sleep for two months and his insomnia was so severe that he had been hospitalised. Abse's notes give a slender glimpse into the multifarious tensions weighing on some Indian soldiers and in particular their strong sense of responsibility towards their kin and the burden of responsibilities back home. In the case of the insomniac soldier, 'Questioning revealed that two months earlier his mother had died. Owing to his absence from home in the Army, he had been unable to carry out the appropriate religious ceremonies. He felt that he had insulted his mother and that in consequence the divine power had rendered him incapable of sleep.'[28] In this instance the patient responded well to sympathetic discussion of his concerns and to the use of hypnosis but also, not remarkably, to some home leave.

In another case a sepoy, identified only as a twenty-five-year-old Muslim soldier, was under observation in hospital for muteness. He did not utter a sound for two months but the doctors could find no physical explanation. The patient scribbled in notes that the cause was the intervention of a malignant spirit and that he could only be cured by returning home and seeing the local *hakim*, 'though he thought even this would take a long time'.[29] When he was told firmly that he would have to stay in hospital until he spoke, the patient continued to beseech for release in his handwritten notes, before he finally began speaking. While the doctor found a convoluted explanation for the muteness as 'a fear of the homosexual instinct', the modern reader is tempted to wonder if the sepoy was using desperate measures to try to acquire home leave. Dr Abse stayed alert to the fact that his patients often felt homesick, missed their wives and grieved over lost parents whom they had not been able to see. However, he was unable to fully articulate the difference of the Indian sepoy's experience of war, or to fully navigate his way to understanding the complex social pressures on the shoulders of many sepoys.

Nonetheless, treatment was more successful than during the First World War and about a quarter of psychiatric casualties in the Indian Army returned to active duty. There was far more recognition of how physical and mental symptoms might be interwoven and how soldiers with malaria or dysentery might fall into a depressed state. There was greater understanding of the mental impact on soldiers in Burma who saw their comrades killed or injured or who endured long weeks of uncertainty, waiting for the apparently indefatigable Japanese, struggling with the heat, mosquitoes, monotony and alienation of the war. Sepoys on the Burmese front were anxious about injury and apprehensive of the peculiar cruelties and persistence attributed to the enemy. On one three-day boat-trip from Gauhauti to Dacca on a medical steamer of 172 Indian casualties, half of the passengers were classified as *pagals* – or mentally ill sepoys.[30] 'Most were sad quiet men suffering from depression', recorded the nurse Angela Bolton, who was charged with accompanying the hospital ship as it slowly navigated the river. 'Those who were a danger to themselves or others occupied the large wire-mesh cage at one end of the deck which was otherwise used for prisoners of war.'[31]

19

The Man-a-Mile Road

'Ledo, in December 1943, seemed rather like the end of the world', remembered Field Marshal Slim.[1] The immense strategic problems caused by the complex geography of the terrain in north-east India had dominated the response of the Allies to the war in India. The questions were, how to get goods to China, how to build roads in order to enable a reconquest of Burma that could be supplied from the towns in Assam? The efficient unloading of vast supplies at docks in Calcutta, well-co-ordinated internal supply chains and the provisioning of men had now become more slick, but the 14th Army was supplied along a 700-mile front from the Chinese frontier to the Bay of Bengal.

Up in Assam, bordering Burma, the world of the hills, the tea plantations and lives of local people, both in the Patkai hills and the Brahmaputra valley, had been thrown into turmoil by the war since 1942. The massive influx of jeeps, bulldozers, aeroplanes and men, widespread seizure of land, the upheaval of labourers and the sudden hacking of giant roads out of pristine forest and through quiet paddy fields and backwaters, had all been taking place. The Allied war machine steamed onwards. But much of this created transformations for those caught in the middle.

At the end of December 1942 the British had agreed to support a project initiated by the Americans and the Chinese to build an immense road which would connect India and China via Myitkyina and provide an overland supply line to China. This would be an alternative route to 'the Hump' while China was being precariously supported by airlifts over the Himalayas. The road would be over 465 miles long and reach up into previously untrammelled mountains. The terrain was forbidding and the plan divided military planners in the China–Burma–India

(CBI) theatre, who doubted if building the road was possible, even if it was desirable. The Government of Assam looked on with scepticism, regarding the plan as potentially impossible to implement.[2] The sheer chutzpah of even contemplating building a road that would cut through from India to China via North Burma, through some of the highest passes, jungle and Japanese-occupied terrain, left many doubting that the results would reward the effort. The road, imagined as the solution to China's supply problems and a way of rewarding Chiang Kai-shek, was also a trophy project for Stilwell. He was determined to avenge his routing in Burma, march his men back in along his road (it eventually took his name) and recapture the country.

The most ominous nickname for the Ledo Road was the man-a-mile road. The road's construction rested on a bedrock of Asian labour and meant a never-ending supply of work, but also extreme risks. Particularly in the early days of the road, when accommodation and supplies had been barely assembled, the risk of death for taking on the work was high. From early 1943, barefooted, men and women heaved baskets of rocks and building materials on their heads and broke rocks with pickaxes. Slim remembered them at work, 'pick, shovel and basket roads, made by human labour with an almost laughable lack of machinery'.[3] Male labourers thrashed through the jungle with hoes called *khodalies* and long knives called *dahs*.

Wages and the promise of rations magnetically pulled in labour from around India. Marathas, Madrasis, Bengalis, Punjabis, Oriyas, Biharis, Nepalis, low castes, *dalits* and *adivasis* all worked side by side on the road: 'An anthropologist's dream but a mess sergeant's nightmare.' In the 14th Army there were thirty different ration scales, based on religious dietary requirements but also conditions of contract.[4] American troops gathered strength in Ledo and black American GIs shovelled grit on the road alongside the Indians. An American supply surgeon, John Tamraz, hiked through the jungle from Hellgate to the Tagung River in late February 1943. He was shocked by what he found. If the labourers stay up here building the road through the monsoon, he warned, the sickness rate could reach over 75 per cent.[5]

By 1944, the work on the road was becoming more orderly; for instance, labourers might be given inoculations by military medics. But for the Indian workers the main tools remained the humble pickaxe and shovel. The Indian government was insisting that workers should be allowed home during the rainy months. Men were brought in by the Tea Association but also through other gang-masters, word of mouth and labour contractors. So many labourers moved into the hills from the brick-kilns and coal mines on the plains of Bihar and central India, attracted by the prospect of these rumoured wages, that work in coal mines in eastern India was threatened. (The solution to labour shortages in the mines was to permit women to work underground again. The Government of India had banned this in 1943 but lifted the ban again as the war progressed.) Initially, the Americans fixed pay rates but soon returned to paying for days worked when sickness rates shot up. In return the labourers gambled with their own lives. Different contractors tussled to get hold of the best men.

At the Indo-Burmese border, weeks on end of waterlogged, back-breaking work confronted officers and labourers alike. 'The mud that forms on the main road between Hellgate and Pangsau pass is a heavy yellow "soup" that does not drain well and must be removed by hand.'[6] Red ants, leeches and lice clung to the skin and hair, and clothes stank of mildew. Tigers, disturbed in their habitat, mauled and killed a number of soldiers and labourers, and landslides roared down the mountainsides, 'without warning anything up to 100 tons of rock would crash down on the ground', enough to flatten a jeep.[7]

The construction workers on the Ledo Road were plagued by flash floods and rockfalls. Jeeps could easily go tumbling into deep ravines below, tired drivers could make small but fatal errors of judgement on hairpin bends or be washed away by flash-flooding, and great chunks of sodden hillside could spontaneously crumble into the valleys. Over time the American organisation of the Ledo Road became more ordered, although it was always a grim and forbidding task. Bulldozers were brought in to carry out the design of the engineers, supply lines became more efficiently managed and workers rotated and were housed in bamboo and tarpaulin *bashas*. Alongside the labourers, GIs, predominantly black conscripts, made up the military manpower on the road, driving and handling heavy machinery but also working with spades and hoes. These drafted men often intensely resented the work. One black GI, Herman Perry, became a notorious murderer and deserter, hunted through the jungle by his officers and eventually court-martialled and hanged. Many GIs lived to tell the tale of building the Ledo Road, although the labourers who worked along-side them have barely featured in historical accounts. 'Many of these workers were dumped in anonymous roadside graves, their impover-ished families never notified', writes the journalist Brendan Koerner in one of the few books which depicts the building of the Ledo Road.[8] Indian labour provided 7,800,000 man days for building the road, the US Army engineers provided 6,618,000 and Chinese labourers another 735,000. A British engineer could point to an area on the road where '600 of his own coolies had died'.[9]

Labourers from the South Indian coast, 1,000 miles from the work site, had been contracted for one-year terms into the Travancore State Labour Unit. One-quarter of the workers were usually unable to work because of sickness. Those who were well enough quarried gravel, thrashed through the forest and dug embankments. Indian Pioneer Companies of 400 men worked with similar casualty and sickness rates too and included Bengalis, Sikhs, Punjabis, Madrasis, Mahrattas and Chamars from central India and small detachments of armed sepoys. The Assam Civil Porter Corps enrolled 1,000 men at a time for earthwork, jungle clearance, construction of temporary bridges and huts while the Garo and Nepali porters carried their loads over water-logged trails, working for six-month terms without a break, recruited by provincial governments. Provincial governments also recruited 1,400 men at a time into Civil Pioneer teams who carried out skilled duties more akin to police work, acting as guards, handling ammunition, supply-handling and checking stocks. Contract labourers were also signed up for skilled and semi-skilled work, taking up positions as mechanics and carpenters contracted to specific jobs or as day labourers. Frank Moraes, who spent some days on the Ledo Road as a war correspondent, later recalled the 'mosaic of races' and described how 'a sort of contrived Esperanto seemed to be the main medium of communication between the myriad races working on the road'. Tamil labourers had picked up fragments of American patois, declaring in English, 'All right, let's go.'[10]

As time dragged on the Ledo Road, the military newcomers and the hill tribes found new ways to interact and learn from each other. As a new world was thrashed out of the old jungle, new consumer goods became visible and available to locals for the first time, from chewing gum to cans of beer. Food and drink were traded with locals or siphoned off from PX stores. In return, the local people knew how to protect themselves from insects and snakes, how to foretell the weather and how to eat local berries and plants. 'Nearly everyday we find some new use for bamboo,' one GI wrote home to his family, 'some of it is original and the rest is from observance of how the natives or other soldiers down the line use it. You can use it for making almost every needed type of household article, including some kitchen utensils. Some parts and types are even used for food. What an item.'[11] By the final months of the war, troops offered people cigarettes, locals hitched rides in jeeps, children ran after vehicles and posed for photographs. When Herman Perry escaped after murdering an officer, he was sheltered by a Naga family and married one of the daughters of the village before finally being captured a year later. The harsh and challenging environment of the Ledo Road could conjure surprises and unexpected kindnesses.

Punishing completion targets for sections of the road looked impossible to meet. Perhaps it is unsurprising that in the first year, the Ledo Road had only progressed forty-two miles.[12] Orders from the military top brass exerted pressure on the workers: 'It was a case of catch-as-catch-can. Any organization lucky and quick enough to "acquire" laborers got its work done.'[13] The labourers appear fleetingly in the historical record, slipping wordlessly into margins and footnotes. *Life* magazine printed a photograph showing faceless huddled lumps, unrecognisable as human beings, 'like a row of strange tropical plants . . . natives crouched beneath rain-capes'.[14]

How many labourers died building the Ledo Road? This is completely unknown, and no figure has ever been calculated. We know that 1,133 Americans lost their lives, a significant if small number in the context of global wartime tragedies, and Indian workers faced much higher risks: more exposure to the weather, poorer diets, lower body mass and less access to medicine. 'Coolies' did not have the chance of airlifting to a military hospital. Indian labourers did the bulk of the manual work and often completed the initial work clearing the jungle in advance of the arrival of machinery and equipped troops. They provided nearly 8 million man days, although they shared this with many black American GIs and Chinese soldiers. Once the road was finally nearing completion, in December 1944, to relieve the pressure on the military, Indian civilian drivers joined servicemen in driving the long dusty road to China.

* * *

In 1944 Irwin Reiss was an American officer working as a young labour contractor on the Ledo Road. He spent his time criss-crossing the land between Assam and Burma. He suffered incessant ill-health and became dangerously thin, was repeatedly hospitalised and pined terribly for his wife and a newborn son that he had never seen. He would have much rather been back on his farm in Illinois. 'The rainy weather is becoming almost unbearable. Everything that I have is moldy.' He complained of the mildew that was embedded in his clothes and even clogged up his camera lens. 'My clothes feel like a wet dish rag when I put them on in the morning. In the past 3 months I have seen one continuous day of sunshine.'[15] Reiss's antipathy for India and Indians burned strongly throughout the war and his bitter complaints about persistent beggars and unscrupulous merchants were only matched by his distaste for the British colonials that he encountered.

Irwin Reiss's job was to find, allocate and pay Indian and Burmese labour. This brought its own tribulations and he had to travel thousands of miles by road and air to find the 'coolies' he needed and to meet the demand of 'dozens of units screaming for labour'. Using local middlemen and interpreters, he was responsible for employing, feeding and paying thousands of workers and would often awake to find crowds outside his bamboo *basha* clamouring for food or for pay. Reiss's linguistic skills (he had trained in Chinese at Yale) were wasted in north-east India and he was thrown into a mystifying new cultural cocktail, bargaining with labour middlemen over pay, working 100-hour weeks, often carrying long ledger rolls and heavy sacks of cash containing 15,000 rupees at a time to hand out to his labourers. Those who did not yet know a cash economy took payment in other ways. The Nagas treasured bottle tops and cowrie shells from which they made jewellery. Others were rumoured to be receiving payment in opium. Even wage-workers looked sceptically at rupee notes and wanted the rupee coins that were in such short supply. In one photograph the labourers look on inquisitively, perhaps cynically, arms folded across their chests as the labour contractor sits in front of great piles of coins. Their headman is taking receipt of the payment, signing with an inked thumbprint, counting the coins against days worked which he had measured by tying knots in a piece of string.

As workers became scarce, Reiss travelled further and deeper into the jungle to find suitable men and women. As an army newspaper put it, the coolies were 'clearing right of way for communications and pipelines, packing rations and gasoline through hip-deep mud for bulldozer crews . . . ditching and shelving the road overhang, loading supply convoys, unloading railroad freight cars . . . carving sub-depots from the jungle, assisting with air dropping, and performing a thousand other tasks unknown to the outside world'.[16] In return the Indian and Burmese contractors made their own demands for food and better conditions clear. 'To Washington one coolie is like another coolie, but actually the picture is very different', recorded Reiss, as he grappled with vocal demands and complaints about unsuitable rations, and as he struggled to find the necessary quantities of grains and rice.[17]

Inflation was driving up salaries but not matching prices, and the locals drove the best deal that they could manage with the Americans. 'I pay these jokers more in a week than they used to earn in a month in peacetime', Reiss commented. Daily rates of pay had tripled in the past two years for the average labourer and the 'coolies' also found inventive ways to evade the tough contracts which they had entered, or swapping the metal identification tags that they had been given and working under different names, leaving in the night to return to their village fields at harvest time.[18]

Chinese civilians also found employment on the Ledo Road, particularly skilled craftsmen, but could also fall foul of the complex borders, citizenship rules and uncertainties over national belonging as the theatre of war expanded over the borders of China, Burma and India. Two Chinese carpenters, for instance, Cheng Chee-Ching and Hsu Kee Pao, were hired for specialist work on the Ledo Road but were arrested by local Assamese police. Cheng Chee-Ching was locked up for being a foreign national in Assam without a permit. He was taken away and imprisoned in Dibrugarh Jail for nearly two months without trial, unable to return and to collect his pay. 'Mr Hsu tried to go to his rescue but was advised that the police were then also contemplating to arrest him too.' Mr Hsu lobbied the Consulate and eventually managed to get his friend released and his overdue wages restored to him.[19]

The Ledo Road was finally opened for military traffic in January 1945 with great fanfare, hailed as a triumph of persistence, engineering ingenuity and sheer sweat and blood. Fifteen Labour Corps officers had managed teams of labourers each numbering around 50,000. They did not know their workers' names and only dimly heard of the ways in which some of them had run away to join the Labour Corps, hoping for a quick profit or encouraged by their families to take up seasonal work while it was available. Few knew who had died or when. Slowly the workers were demobilised and began to make their way back to villages in South India, to Burma, Orissa and Nepal with the money that they had saved sewn into saris and pockets. Their tag-line in one American GI newspaper was not the forgotten army but the 'unknown army'.[20]

20

Insults and Discriminations

By 1944 in the cities and towns of India it was not unusual to see a black man in uniform. Of the 150,000 American servicemen who came to India in the 1940s, some 22,000 were black GIs. This was, the Commanding Officers feared, potentially unsettling to many in South Asia. Caste hierarchies and distasteful comparisons of skin colour had a long domestic history. In the nineteenth century some Indians had indulged in phrenology and had taken up Social Darwinism with gusto, celebrating their own 'Aryan' origins and denigrating Africans as inferior. The officers of the Raj fervently believed that the presence of too many black troops in India was politically inflammatory and that local people would become incensed simply by the sight of black soldiers.

At the same time, the barefaced discrimination and maltreatment of black GIs was not welcomed either. The segregation of the American South permeated the American Army, and while stationed in India black and white GIs faced blatant and enforced separation. Black soldiers worked in segregated platoons, had different and fewer canteens, poorer sources of entertainment, less tolerable living conditions and had to take on harder menial labour, from building the Ledo Road to unloading at ports and docks under the unrelenting sun. In Calcutta, there were segregated Red Cross canteens with black Red Cross women shipped in especially to staff them. One anonymous black staff sergeant relived the indignity of being turned away from a CBI canteen:

> When we first came to this Theater a friend and myself dropped into the Red Cross for a sandwich and [were] very rudely told that they didn't serve colored soldiers. It so hurted that until [now] I haven't had

the feeling of attending anything that is given by them – don't feel like
I can ever live down that being a soldier of the US Army didn't mean
anything. Even [though] there is a colored Red Cross now, would rather
stay away.[1]

The one service swimming pool in Calcutta had white days and
black days. Black troops were given second-class medical treatment,
were more likely to catch malaria, had less chance of leave, received
harsher treatment from officers and drew the ire of Military Police.
The officials of the Raj (like some of their counterparts back in
Britain) barely knew what to think or how to react to these unprecedented new troops: Allied and imperial troops coming to help
save the empire? Or racial and national threat? Did the treatment
of black soldiers suggest American hypocrisy about democracy and
freedom? Was the Raj any better or worse in its treatment of
Indians?

Black troops and Indians found common cause contrary to imperial expectations. Local people chatted and traded with the troops,
striking up friendships even in the marketplace and the streets. Banned
from using some of the facilities allocated for white soldiers and
housed initially in the densely populated area of Howrah in Calcutta,
black GIs spent more time in local markets and backstreets. They
used local barbers, tea shops and rickshaws and came into conversation with local people. As a consequence black soldiers made new
friends, received invitations to local parties and dances and were more
likely to have an Indian or Anglo-Indian lover. Black troops in the
trucking units in the north-east interacted with Chinese, Burmese
and Indian workers.[2]

There was recognition between people in Asia and America, albeit
complex and shot through with ambiguities, that Indians and black
people shared racial subjugation and were on the wrong side of the
imperial worlds that they still served. As with so many aspects of the war,
the daily interaction of people in the imperial context was entangled
deeply with much broader political considerations. At the heart of
Washington DC and London, race was a weighty issue of wartime
diplomacy. Many colonised peoples had started to argue with increasing
stridency that America should resolve the glaring anomalies in its own
backyard. Gandhi himself stressed the problem of America's internal

racial problems. A number of American voices spoke up for a 'global double victory', stressing how America could win a double advantage by remedying its own racial inequalities and thus winning hearts and minds in the British Empire.[3]

One *Times of India* journalist who watched at the port of Chittagong as gangs of sweating Indian dockworkers struggled to load heavy crates onto a naval vessel noted how a white sergeant shouted at them. '"Coom on yer black bastards git goin"' was among the mildest of his abuses . . .'[4] Men who championed black civil rights could find common cause with Indian nationalists, from the American singer Paul Robeson who had an enduring friendship with Nehru to the GI and the man on the street. A number of prominent Indians had spent time in the USA, and had forged sympathetic bonds with black leaders by the 1940s. Some eighty black intellectuals in the USA wrote to President Roosevelt in the midst of the Quit India movement to urge action on behalf of Indians.[5] Those Americans who supported a people's war, and intended not only to defeat fascism, but to construct a new world order, looked to Gandhi and the Indian nationalists with admiration and sympathy.

A black staff sergeant based on the Ledo Road, who had been in India for nineteen months, expressed his fury with his own second-class status and also articulated his sympathy for the Indian nationalists when completing a questionnaire for the military:

I am a Negro soldier. Whether the Army wants to believe this or not, morale among Negro soldiers is deplorably low and it will continue to be so as long as negroes are delegated a second class position in the army . . . The effect has been to make America lose her number one position among ideologically respected nations. The writer has made numerous contacts with intelligent, educated Chinese and Indians and he is convinced that a deep mistrust and even an actual dislike of America now exists among these peoples. The Indians of course, are powerless since they are an economically and politically enslaved people; these voices are not heeded today . . .

The list of insults and discriminations to which we have been subjected because of race since donning the khaki is too long for detailed discussion here, but it is pertinent to state that it has been long and disgusting enough to make the writer indifferent and apathetic

with regards to this war and to tempt him on more than one occasion
to request imprisonment rather than continue to accept the indignities
to which the Army insists on subjecting him. There are barber shops
and hospitals at this base which will serve Chinese and Indians, but
refuse to serve us. My own Army tells me in no uncertain terms that
it prefers to cater to alien peoples than to me – and I am expected to
be proud of my unit and Army.[6]

At times, Indian labourers and Americans worked side by side
performing exactly the same tasks. Along the Ledo Road, military
truckers and Indian drivers made the same difficult runs along
hundreds of miles of muddy tracks, sharing the same tiredness and
danger. Down at the Calcutta docks, American and West African
soldiers could be seen working alongside a stevedore battalion made
up of 1,800 specially trained Indian 'coolies'. As the historian Nico
Slate has commented, 'American racism fundamentally structured the
experience of black soldiers in India'.[7] This created another layer of
complexity in the social world of the Raj. Hierarchies and pecking
orders along racial lines became confusing and contradictory. Who
was the real protector of development, democracy and freedom in
India?

Over 100,000 African troops were also disembarking, readying for
the fight back in Burma. The first East African units from Kenya and
Tanganyika arrived in Ceylon in 1942, followed by West African divisions from Nigeria and the Gold Coast in 1943 and 1944. Military
commanders fretted about sending African troops to India in the
build-up to the campaign and the men were rushed through Indian
towns, quarantined from local contact as far as possible, kept in remote
encampments far from civilians and watched with nervousness by
their officers.[8]

Adding to the military melting pot in India, Chinese troops also
became more visible in North and East India from the midpoint of
the war. In Ramgarh in present-day Jharkhand, a camp of Chinese
soldiers had been set up in the barracks of an old POW camp, on
large chunks of land requisitioned using Defence of India rules. 'Soon
Chinese troops began to arrive', remembered Gian Singh, who was
stationed nearby in Ranchi. 'We had never seen Chinese troops before
and they aroused our curiosity. We saw NCOs hitting men for various

reasons. This never occurred in the Indian Army and it was never forgotten. It drew many comments . . . In a short time they became smart soldiers but they had strange customs.'⁹ This camp for Chinese soldiers was initially a contingency plan and part of the response to the initial crisis in Burma as Chinese soldiers who had become detached from their units started to reach India. These men needed feeding, housing and rehabilitating; many were very sick and so malnourished on arrival that some gained twenty pounds in weight during the first weeks of their stay.¹⁰

Soon, encouraged enthusiastically by Chiang Kai-shek, it became part of the official policy to train up Chinese troops in India, and men were flown over from China to Ramgarh. Part diplomatic softener, part serious military strategy, the Chinese base grew and buildings and facilities became established, roads and power developed. The soldiers were equipped by the Americans and given state-of-the-art training. Officers from West Point taught them tactics and graduates from Ivy League universities were engaged to teach them English. But conditions could also be tough and rural Bihar was a strange and spartan environment to the newcomers. Miss Elsie Chin, a Chinese American nurse working at the camp, wrote, 'Life during the past four months in India has hardened me quite a bit.'¹¹

Stilwell was a strong believer in using India as a base and a training ground for strengthening the Chinese Army; at one point he asked the Raj to allow the camp to grow to 100,000 men at which Amery baulked: half that number was 'the limit which we can accommodate in India without serious inconvenience'.¹² The Viceroy worried about the British losing their sovereign grip and also about the local effects of more foreign soldiers in central India, and the Government of Bihar objected to the presence of the camp because of the risk of conflict with villagers. The camp was close to a colliery run by Bird & Co. and the managers complained about the presence of Chinese miners frightening away seasonal labourers and of the local women 'selling their bodies for a few annas'.¹³ The Government of India tried to block the camp's expansion, but by December 1943, 5,368 officers and 48,124 enlisted men from the Chinese Army had trained in India. Many of these troops would join the Allies on the road to Assam, and take part in the reconquest of Burma. Ultimately, Amery's protests came to nothing and over 100,000 Chinese soldiers were in India at the end of 1944.[14]

*   *   *

In 1944 for one week the Stars and Stripes and the Chinese flag hung alongside the Union Jack on central New Delhi's great ceremonial roads, and fluttered from all central government buildings in Delhi and Simla. The Viceroy had ordered this to mark American Independence Day and the anniversary of the start of China's war of resistance. The sight of international servicemen had now become commonplace in Indian cities. Women too, Anglo-Indian, Indian, British, Canadian and Australian, could be seen taking on all kinds of new responsibilities and living in all kinds of ways that challenged the usual gendered conventions of the Raj, walking and cycling about freely, buying and selling from market traders, smoking, wearing trousers and working in canteens, hospitals and blood banks. Unmarried women travelled and lived together. Wives of white civilian officers were now joined increasingly by well-educated professionals from the Queen Alexandra's Nursing Service, American Women's Auxiliary Corps and women recruited especially into the Women's Auxiliary Corps (India).[15]

Women even when working long hours in strenuous jobs regarded cheering up the men and boosting their morale as duty. And many of them also wanted to find boyfriends and husbands. Single white women in the WAC (I), nursing corps or Red Cross were encouraged to court officers and often had a large contingent of suitors. Margaret G. Schmertz, an American in the Army Nursing Corps, remembered that 'Green's Hotel [in Bombay] was the first place I had ever seen men dancing with men. But the Russians would come in, and they danced together, or some of the British.'[16] Heavily outnumbered, European, Canadian and American nurses and Red Cross women dated officers and officials, who received access to better food and supplies and whirled women around the dance floor, took them up in planes and whisked them off to Kashmir or Simla for holidays.

American and European women in the WAC (I), Red Cross and Queen Alexandra's Nursing Corps were in demand for attendance at every kind of social event and outing in India, and had to negotiate a sexual minefield of demands and expectations. Joan Boss, a British nurse who arrived in 1942 in her early twenties, was fully alive to the opportunities, difficulties and dangers for nurses in India during the war: 'Usually when they looked at a girl they thought how pretty she was or what a lovely figure she had. They looked at me and thought "I bet she can sew".' Joan had already been asked to mend and stitch for a colonel on her journey to India. She worked in an army hospital in Secunderabad where the nurses were barred from attending the local club in uniform and had to wear evening dresses 'which frequently cost nearly a month's salary'.[17]

The majority of the 11,500 women who joined the WAC (I) were Anglo-Indian or Anglo-Burmese and others belonged to the Indian Christian community. Some of the women came from princely families with old ties to the Raj, others found the work appealed because of an opportunity to circumvent domestic constraints, to travel and to enjoy the adventure of war. This was bringing a change in attitudes that would leave a post-war imprint in India, although one, as elsewhere in the world, shot through with ambiguities and challenges. As one Auxiliary Nursing Service advert put it, 'Society no longer requires a girl to be a stay at home idler'.[18] In Bose's Indian National Army, a women's regiment, the Rani of Jhansi Regiment, was being raised and in political parties all over India middle-class women were becoming involved in political and social work. Just as Aruna Asaf Ali was enrapturing an audience of nationalist men and women across India, women working in war employment found new opportunities to develop their own ideas, to travel and to form new friendships. Some of them relished the emancipation from the confines of their homes and the chance to adventure into hazardous and unfamiliar landscapes, and to take pride in their work.

But behind each one of them stood another 1,000 Indian women, working long back-breaking days employed as labourers on war contracts. The women in the coal mines of central and eastern India often worked up until shortly before childbirth, a matter that was raised in the House of Commons back in London. Women were employed thrashing through scrubland with hoes to make way for aerodromes, carrying bricks on their heads and constructing new barracks and buildings and carrying away rubble and cement from roadsides, often with children tied to their backs or playing in the building sites around them.

★   ★   ★

The curiously named Anglo-Indian Eglind Roze – he sometimes appears as Egland Rose – was a sixteen-year-old boy by the time the war was drawing to a close. All his years as a teenager had been spent in wartime and, as his parents' home was on the Lower Circular Road in Calcutta, he was living in the thick of things; he would have been accustomed to seeing troops in the city, military vehicles going down the thoroughfares, and uniformed troops walking about in the town. Eglind's parents were in their early fifties; his father had a job on the railways but was worried that he had no pension for his imminent retirement, their eldest son was unemployed and their two daughters made little money. Eglind, one of the youngest in the family, was 'irregularly employed' and turned over all his earnings to his mother. His parents were used to him being out and about in the streets at odd hours, taking bits of work when he could.[19]

The shock of the arrival of a British policeman at their door at ten o'clock one night must have been tremendous. Mr and Mrs Roze had to go to the hospital urgently, Eglind had been shot. He was bleeding terribly and the doctors needed to operate, but would not do so without his parents' permission; somehow the police had managed to find the right address and Mr Roze left in a hurry in the vehicle of the policeman. Along the way he learned what had happened.

That night Eglind had noticed a US army jeep stationed outside the Great Eastern Hotel. It was tempting. Unmanned and easy to steal. Eglind had been involved in vehicle thefts in the past and he was still waiting for a court date relating to an earlier incident. He did not know that this time it was a trap set by the US Army to capture the thieves who had been plaguing them with jeep theft in Calcutta, taking out the batteries and removing parts and selling them on. As soon as Eglind started the engine, a group of soldiers immediately gave chase, some on foot, some in another jeep, swerving and careering at high speed. Eglind managed to drive for some distance until he was eventually run into the kerb, crashing into a large metal dustbin on Central Avenue. He jumped down from the jeep, ran between some buildings to get away, but, like a scene in a film, found he was in a yard with no exit. As he ducked and dived and tried to flee between the soldiers, one of them shot into the air and then, suddenly, at Eglind. The .45 calibre automatics left pistol shots in his leg and abdomen.

The next day the policeman who had accompanied the family to the hospital wrote solemnly, 'At the time of writing of this report, the accused was still alive but not expected to live longer than another day. He had not regained consciousness since he was operated on.'[20] Eglind never recovered from his operation and died the next day. The coroner's report recording 'culpable homicide amounting to murder' was signed by the Commissioner of Police, Calcutta, R. E. A. Ray, who was patently furious in his reports, describing the killing as 'quite unjustified by law' and 'an unwarranted and totally illegal killing'.[21]

The US Army offered 1,000 rupees compensation to Eglind's family but the Government of India persisted in asking for this to be tripled, arguing that the circumstances in which the boy met his death were 'most deplorable and contrary to ideas of British justice' and that the money being offered as an ex-gratia payment by the US government was 'wholly inadequate'.[22] This was argued on technical grounds, but the political context was the need to secure local goodwill. A cheque was finally despatched to Eglind's father on 16 January 1946 for 3,000 rupees.

★   ★   ★

Petty conflict between soldiers, local townsmen and villagers featured routinely in newspapers by 1944, and was particularly noted as a problem in Bengal and Assam. There was a low-level but persistent potential for conflict. The effect on local communities of even one sensational murder could be damaging, undoing months of liaison work and providing plenty of ammunition for national outcry. For many people living with the changes of the past few years, such cases only confirmed their negative feelings about the war.

Rickshaw and taxi drivers had daily encounters with troops, and sometimes fights over fares erupted. Around three o'clock in the morning one November night in 1944, at the crossing of Circular Garden Reach Road and Ram Kamal Street in Calcutta, a group of labourers and rickshaw drivers, sleeping out under the night sky in their rickshaws, were awakened by a loud bang and cries of 'Help me!' Some of them later claimed to have seen a black soldier rushing away in the darkness on foot. Confused, and aroused from sleep, they saw their co-worker, Dila Mia, lying on the pavement and bleeding from the neck. He had been shot. 'During Investigation,' the police later recorded, 'one spent cartridge case was found lying on the pavement and one bullet was found in the hollow of the rickshaw underneath the seat. One penetrating bullet mark was found on the wooden frame of the seat and stains of blood were found on the side screen and cushion of the rickshaw.'[23] The driver, Dila Mia, bleeding profusely, was carried by his mates to the local *thana* or police post, from where he was rushed to hospital. A month's stay on the ward followed. The pistol shot to his neck did not kill him, but it did leave him disabled on his left side and unable to work.

He recounted to the police how he had been jerked awake in the middle of his sleep by a soldier in uniform. He had wanted a ride somewhere and Dila Mia refused. This could have been racism (it would not be the first time Indian rickshaw *wallahs* refused black passengers) or merely tiredness and exhaustion. Frustrated and angry, the soldier, Captain Felix Arbolaiz, grabbed him by the neck and shot him. The soldier was drunk and acting wildly, and later also fired shots at a Sikh taxi driver down by the King George's docks. He was caught wandering drunk and disorientated in Calcutta, locked up and an immediate court martial was held. Felix Arbolaiz was sentenced to seven years' rigorous imprisonment on 1 December 1944. Dila Mia, paralysed and unable to work, received a compensation payment of 4,300 rupees – an extraordinary sum.[24]

Earlier the same year, in another case, an American soldier, new to the country, who had driven from the Grand Hotel to Howrah Station, had a dispute with his Sikh taxi driver over the fare, which ended with him stabbing the taxi driver in the chest. The taxi driver later died and his body was taken in procession from the Howrah General Hospital to the Shyamnagar burning ghat in Calcutta, where it was cremated. The Sikh protesters at first proposed to take their procession past the

American Headquarters and to carry a banner inscribed 'Work of Americans: Murder' but police managed to steer the procession in another direction. The taxi drivers of Calcutta then went on strike for three days against the 'behaviour of American soldiers'. On other occasions soldiers were court-martialled, punished or fined for smashing up shops, stabbing civilians, being drunk and disorderly in public spaces and stealing items, such as a group of soldiers who stole an idol from a temple in Calcutta the same year.[25]

Legally troops were under the jurisdiction of military law but there were numerous grey areas around policing and the Allies swiftly learned that in reality if they wanted to achieve their aims on the ground then they needed to acquire leverage with local Indian power-brokers and work closely with local police and District Magistrates. A claims commission was established by the Government of India which made recommendations on all compensation cases involving military and civilians, whether the force involved was Indian, British or from the dominions. Military Police stationed in major towns worked closely with their counterparts and the CID.

The military and civil authorities acted stringently. If a case was likely to cause a political reaction it would be handled punitively: Indian witnesses were invited into court martial hearings; compensation payments to Indians injured or who had a relative killed by military action were made publicly and with ceremony. To some extent, these cases may have been handled with more rigour (and certainly awarded higher compensation payments) than the British Indian courts would have allowed. Black soldiers who committed crimes against local Indian people should be 'taught a lesson', in the words of one officer, and these cases were given hard sentences. In one instance a manslaughter charge was upgraded to murder, on the grounds that the Provost Marshal recorded:

I feel him to be guilty. There have been numerous reports of colored soldiers causing trouble in the Assam area . . . to try him on the lesser charge may make it appear to the local people that we view the case lightly merely because it was an Indian who was killed. This may lead to unfavourable criticism of American Forces by the Congress Party who grab at every opportunity to discredit British and American forces.[26]

An obvious driving force was the need to avoid involvement in Britain's internal political struggle with Indian nationalists and the fear of Indian public opinion and political leadership turning against Americans as co-sponsors of the war.

Outside the cities, incidents in poorer villages received less political attention, especially when they involved women. In villages and rural areas, where prostitution tended to be less formalised, there were even more ambiguities around trafficking and exploitation. In 1944 soldiers of all nationalities became involved in clashes with villagers on a weekly basis, usually while 'looking for' women, particularly in Bengal and Assam but also in areas of Bihar. The typical pattern was for a lone man or a few military men to be found in a village at night and then to be rounded upon and attacked by a group of villagers and possibly to lash out in return. On one occasion four soldiers attempted to enter a woman's house in Bankura district, failed, and set fire to the house before departing. The accusation that a 'prostitute' was involved was often cited as a cause or to provide immunity from prosecution, the assumption being that prostitutes themselves could not be legitimate victims of rape or violence.[27]

*　*　*

There was a nexus between pimps, brothels and drug peddlers; raids and undercover detection of drug rings tended inevitably to start in the brothels of Calcutta and Karachi. Bad characters who hung around the bases and camps were identified, such as one M. D. Jaffer. 'He is a procurer for all the prostitutes around the Surendranath Banerji area', wrote the undercover Military Policeman who trailed him. 'I asked him if he knew where I could buy a lot of opium and he said he knew of a place.'[28] Local authorities also alerted officials in America when Lascars and Chinese seamen were suspected of smuggling opium from India into North America. The Blue Funnel Line was suspected of running a racket between New York and Calcutta, masterminded and financed by Chinese residents in the USA. Newspapers featured stories of conspiracies to import and export opium and *charas* (cannabis) both from overseas and from the Indian provinces.[29]

Servicemen could easily acquire narcotics as licensed shops could sell drugs. Karachi, for instance, was estimated to have about fifty shops selling opium, and about the same number supplying *bhang* (cannabis) and *ganja*. Shopkeepers could legally sell people small, medicinal quantities of opium (although soldiers faced stiff penalties if caught purchasing it) but it was easy enough to find locals to purchase from or to make a deal for larger quantities with obliging shopkeepers. The military feared addiction in the ranks, and sting operations, initiated from Washington DC but also taken up on the ground by officers, reported on Indian shops selling excessive quantities of drugs to servicemen. Indian police reluctantly co-operated, with some foot-dragging and grumbling.

Alcohol was by far the more popular intoxicant with troops. Even though drugs were cheap and easily available, the moral panic about this proved unnecessary and sensationalist. Servicemen had imbibed a deep-seated fear of the dangers of opium (a fear inculcated in nineteenth-century Dickensian portrayals of the oriental opium eater) and preferred the devil that they knew, which was alcohol. Some soldiers did puff on marijuana, and in the eastern jungles some took to opium, but this never became a serious cause for concern in the Indian cities. Among Indian soldiers the use of *ganja* and opium was also occasional, usually on leave or during times of sickness. When the kindly and sensible nurse Angela Bolton found a sticky black lump under the pillow of one of her patients his fellow patients told her it was opium and that he would 'die happy'. She rapidly replaced it where she had found it.

By the latter years of the war, the nationalist press in India often complained about the relations between the military and local society, adding to the wider array of wartime frustrations. Criticisms came from all sides of the political spectrum. The *Hitavada* of Nagpur suggested that 'Those who live in Calcutta will testify that the soldier coming to India for a good time has become a menace'. The communist paper *The People's War* took up the story in 1945 with a leader headed 'STOP SOLDIERS' MISDEEDS AGAINST THE PEOPLE'. While acknowledging that only a small minority of troops behaved poorly, the paper argued that the incidents were far from stray or solitary, that the military authorities and provincial governments had not gone far enough in responding to them and that the political parties had been complicit in silencing issues, especially around crimes against women. The Raj could not sustain this kind of new challenge to its authority and prestige or maintain the pretence of racial or moral superiority in the changed circumstances of war.

21

Empires, Lost and Found

All this time, inside Ahmednagar Fort, the weeks dragged on for Nehru, Asaf Ali and their colleagues. The men stayed up talking late into the night. Nehru mumbled and talked in his sleep. They read books and wrote; Nehru was writing a tome about history and politics, *The Discovery of India*, on reams of thin brown paper, which he would later dedicate to his jail-mates. They knew about the famine, but only in sketchy outline, and would only find out the full horrors long afterwards. The Congressmen debated political ideas, talking over their previous political manoeuvres, their past mistakes and their relationship with Gandhi. They thought about the failure to negotiate out of the political deadlock with the British and pondered if they had made the right decisions in 1942. The Muslim League and its sudden advancement as a serious force in Indian politics was a constant concern.

The men longed for release yet also felt apprehensive about the world they would have to face when they finally emerged. In the meantime Asaf Ali and Nehru shared a passion for gardening and dug and laid out beds and created planters and boxes. 'We had the privilege of witnessing the first appearance of the seedlings yesterday', wrote Asaf Ali. 'Patel noticed it first and then Jawaharlal shouted the glad tidings to me and I felt like a child on securing his first toy.'[1] Cornflowers, nasturtiums, petunias and sweet peas flowered in the prison gardens. But even the pleasures and distractions of gardening wore thin as more months went by. The men started to snipe at each other and there were times of illness and depression. Asaf Ali still worried constantly about Aruna's location and whether she was alive or not. Every time they caught sight of a news article about her he was relieved to hear that she was still living and had not been captured.[2]

*   *   *

On 6 May 1944 Gandhi was released from prison because of his fragile health, to great excitement and expectation around India. The other Congress leaders in their separate jail site in Ahmednagar would stay confined for another year. Gandhi's release was also a symptom of the new-found confidence of the Government of India in a summer of successive victories for the Allies around the world. Continental Europe was being pounded by bombs in preparation for the D-Day landings which would begin on the beaches of Normandy in June 1944, with three-quarters of a million Allied troops preparing to take back France. Encircling the Axis, the Red Army was pushing towards the eastern Crimea and Sebastopol and in Italy the final push past Monte Cassino meant that the Allies could roll up to Rome in June. The signs of victory mounted. The Japanese were retreating from Imphal with very heavy losses, although in India the news from the Burmese jungle was often confused and uncertain and many anxious rumours continued to circulate. By mid-July the radio was broadcasting news of the Imphal victory and by 3 August Myitkyina was in Allied hands.

In response to Gandhi's release, the film producer and writer K. A. Abbas published a book entitled *A Report to Gandhiji: A Survey of Indian and World Events during the 21 Months of Gandhi's Incarceration.* Drawing on newspaper clippings, acerbic cartoons and his own experiences, the 'report' was also a testament to Abbas's own conflicted feelings and confusion about the war. A vocal opponent of fascism, he wanted to make Gandhi 'an ally of the Allies'. He strongly supported the ideological basis for the war and believed in the need to defeat the Japanese, but he was also bitterly exhausted and fed up with the imperial power. He tried to summarise the general feeling in the country:

> The Government of India have created a desert in India and call it peace. In her new Avatar, Pax Britannica is known as the Defence of India rules! Politically we are supposed to be in cold storage; mentally we live in a furnace![3]

Abbas also evoked the changes that had taken place in the months since the Congress leaders had been jailed and the rapid transformation of the Raj:

> The Yankees have been with us these two years. A Chinese force has been training in India. Recently even West Africans have been brought over to fight for us. The entire civil administration is subordinated to the military needs. The Indian Army – a voluntary army, it is rubbed in again and again! – has passed the two million mark . . . A Field-Marshal has been installed in the Gadi [throne] of the Grand Moghul in New Delhi.[4]

Abbas struggled to articulate a way in which anti-imperialism and pro-war feelings could be maintained, and how these two positions might coexist in the changed climate. Massive social and economic changes were evident to those who lived through them, and not simply confined to the front line of war or to the provinces of Bengal and Assam. Transformation had occurred all over India. The world that you are being released into, Abbas was telling Gandhi, is not the same one that you left when you entered jail.

*   *   *

'What every official in Orissa really needs is some leave – hardly anyone has had any for four years which probably explains the general dopiness which seems to surround high official quarters.'[5] Since Ian Macdonald wrote this, the situation had only become more strenuous for the British ICS. Many men complained of nervous strain and anxiety. Many officials felt run into the ground; they had been moved around repeatedly from post to post to fill gaps in the state functions as the state overreached itself and expanded its hold on food committees and distribution, and controlled rationing (which commenced in 1944), censorship, policing and surveillance. There had been few British or Indian recruits into the ICS since the start of the war and the existing officials had been forced to work extremely long hours without rest.

There was also the persistent feeling of being left out of the war, a sort of mild survivor's guilt, as contemporaries took part in the historic battles in Europe.[6] The sense of distance from the metropolis was heightened by the long postal delays and the shortage of shipping. When memsahibs met new nurses coming out from Britain they longed to know about the latest fashions in Britain, examining even the most modest dresses to see if they could get the local tailor to copy them, and 'they cross-questioned us closely about all the happenings in war-time, anxious to hear any items of news, no matter how trivial, even though we protested that the information was already three months out of date'.[7] Criticism voiced in the House of Lords in early 1945 of British memsahibs, implying shirking of their responsibilities during wartime, stung deeply and compounded this sense of neglect for British administrators who had struggled under testing circumstances, and had often achieved more than was recognised. As the military prepared to recapture Burma, the Allies gradually learned to co-ordinate their complex organisations. But despite the misgivings of the ICS officials, there was no longer any doubt that India was a war zone: a garrison, gargantuan supply depot, training ground and labour exchange.

The Indian state had expanded beyond recognition. All the offices of the state, high and humble, now employed many more people and had extended their coverage, from post offices to police stations, revenue offices to information ministries. This had created vast opportunities for employment but also for privileging certain applications, giving advantages to people who were well connected to municipal or provincial councils. This more extensive and interventionist state appeared more bureaucratic and labyrinthine than ever before. For many people who had lived through the repercussions of the war and the way that it had rebounded in India, price rises, famine and a general deterioration in the everyday working of life had become commonplace. Privileged access to goods was a very valuable asset. Corruption, which is so often cited as part of the democratic post-war order, was well embedded by the rapid expansion of the wartime state.[8]

Indians fully recognised this. In July 1944, emulating the Mass Observation Survey in Britain, which detailed the mundane but critical aspects of people's everyday lives, a survey was circulated in Calcutta. Members of the public answered questions about their daily lives and their encounters with the state, for example, 'Is it your personal experience that you have to offer bribes to public servants, Government, railway or municipal?' The results were conclusive: of 1,564 people questioned, 1,169 said yes and the remainder said that they knew it occurred even if they had not personally paid a bribe. 'It was universally agreed that corruption is rampant in virtually every dept. of Government with the possible exception of Education and Post Office. Very few people, however, appear to condemn it but content themselves with saying that it is inevitable on account of the low salaries earned by the average public servant.'[9]

The picture that this survey painted of the wartime state was not appealing. People paid bribes for gun licences, for marriage licences, to get contracts with government departments and the military, to get cases through the courts or to shake off criminal charges, to secure driving licences, to ensure packages reached their destination, to collect goods from the post offices and to acquire ration cards. Taxi and *tonga wallahs* (cart drivers) complained about police harassment for petty fines; passengers complained about ticket inspectors on trains taking their share. Even air raid wardens took a cut, a businessman from Barra Bazaar commenting: 'The other day two ARP wardens demanded from me threatening me that they would report against me for violating the Lighting Restriction order and I had to give them Rs. 10.'[10] Even people with middling jobs, such as clerks or policemen, had to supplement their income at a time of great scarcity. Many people agreed that things had got worse during the war, that corruption was becoming more demanding and that the imperial state, overstretched and underfunded, was rotten.

Wearied by war, barely cheered by the news that the tide was turning now in the Allies' favour, the Indian peasant and urban worker looked to their own needs. But as K. A. Abbas argued, this was not a sign of political apathy. Cynical and suspicious of the state, those young people who lived through the war were also becoming drawn into alternative forms of politics and finding other outlets, dreaming of radical political transformation while the Congress leaders languished in jail. The onward march of the Muslim League and the success of Jinnah's Pakistan demand, which was by now drawing in millions of passionate supporters, can be understood only in this context. Similarly, there was a rash of small private armies, routine drilling and armed militias that were attracting enthusiasts around the country, both on the left and the right, from the Khaksars and RSS to the Communist Party. They offered a refreshing and liberating vision and the promise of radical social transformation, transcending the bitter disappointments and stifled political life of the country over the past five years.

*　*　*

In Bombay, on the afternoon of Friday, 14 April 1944, the heat was receding. Muezzins started their call for Friday prayers and workers began to return home. Inspector A. B. Dongre was off duty. He was at home reading his newspaper when he was hurled off his chair by an explosion. He immediately presumed, like everyone else who heard it, that it must be a bomb. 'The whole building shook with violence. Some of the windows came out of the hinges and the tiles of my kitchen roof fell down.'[11] The inspector reached for his uniform and hurried down to the police station, where he rounded up all the men he could find, and they headed out towards the harbour. As they went down Frere Road, towards Prince's Dock, Inspector Dongre could see people carrying out the wounded, many bloodied and missing limbs, and he stopped an empty goods lorry and put the injured men in the back. As he was doing this, a second explosion ripped through the sea-front area of Bombay and Inspector Dongre and his men cowered in a building. 'We had to save our lives', he recalled. The policemen's thoughts turned to their wives and children – many of them lived in the Wadi Bunder lines where fire was breaking out – and they rushed back towards them.

Nearby, M. D. Murdeshwar, assistant manager of the docks, who had been trying to reach the scene, was forced back: 'I laid myself flat down on the ground and crawled underneath one of the military trucks parked there unattended. I remained there until all the splinters had come off; they were coming like a hailstorm.'[12]

Sir Benegal Rama Rau, chairman of the Port Authority, had been looking out towards the docks from the roof of his office and saw the explosion. 'Immediately I sent for my car. The chief engineer Mr Terry and myself got into my car and we proceeded to Victoria dock. We stood there for some time. We could not go further as the fire was blazing and we could not see the way.' The thick smoke was blocking any path through the Victoria Dock. As they stood there, dazed and helpless, some 'seriously injured' firemen were carried out of the smoke. Benegal Rama Rau put five of them into his own car but did not have room for the others. A military lorry turned up but the driver did not know the way to a hospital. Despite the confusion, somehow they ferried the burned and bleeding men to hospital, where chaotic scenes unfolded, with most of the injured and dead being laid out on the verandas as the wards overflowed.

But this was not a bomb, after all. A large ship stationed in Bombay Harbour, laden with TNT, had exploded. The SS *Fort Stikine* had been carrying a part-cargo of cotton on top of explosives. The vessel completely disintegrated, 'only odd pieces of ship to be seen', reported the salvage officer days later.[13] The decks of the SS *Empire Indus* nearby 'buckled' in the blast and the fires instantly jumped to other nearby ships, some of which were, lethally, storing cotton bundles and bamboo, and gutted eleven other ships. Country craft loaded with grain or cotton broke their moorings and drifted down the harbour and men jumped ship. Crew were killed by falling debris while others scrambled ashore. Glass and shards of metal rained down on dock-workers and servicemen, causing ugly injuries. Before long the fire was spreading to the surrounding *bustees*, bazaars and *godowns* directly abutting the waterside. A strong west wind fanned the flames. As labourers fled for their lives, other men tried to enter the dock area to help with moving the stocks of ammunition which would be fodder for the fire. But chaos was reigning. Padden Rowe, a Special Branch detective, fearing foul-play and sabotage, was stopping men in uniform and rescue workers from getting to the scene unless they showed security passes. It could have been sabotage, and 'It is possible to have a uniform made at a tailor's shop', he later told a committee of inquiry.[14]

The fire was out of control. It raged on for the whole night and much of the next day, and could be seen from great distances. By the next day, 2,000 or more had been admitted to hospital and more than 300 had died, among them 23 policemen. The whole residential and commercial area of flats and *bustees* in downtown Bombay along the harbour stood blackened and charred. Official figures estimated 60,000–80,000 homeless. One unknown man, presumed to be a dock-worker, remarkably survived the whole night in the waters of Bombay

Harbour, by wearing a life jacket and clinging to pieces of debris while the fires flickered on around him. 'It took my men 2½ hours to bale him out and arrange for an ambulance and doctor', reported an Indian officer who had been at the scene at nine o'clock the next morning. 'He was crying "Hai Allah!" and somebody heard him and they all tried to help him out.'[15] Religious charities, as in the aftermath of the Burmese refugee debacle, plugged the gaps in social service provision and doled out meals to the homeless. The poorest and those who had lost their ships were taken to relief camps: Lascars, *khalasis*, cranemen, labourers and their families.

Later on the Sunday, when the fire was finally extinguished, and the water was thick with floating cotton, the recriminations began. This was the kind of news that the government seriously wanted to avoid. A news blackout on the story enraged the Indian media: the *Bombay Sentinel* published a blank column on its front page with the words, 'This space should have been occupied by a report of disastrous explosions which occurred in the city docks yesterday', and the paper was suspended as a result. Wild rumours about culpability and compensation circulated. Fifty thousand tons of grain had been lost in addition to cotton and other goods. The Indian government squeezed Lloyd's of London for insurance claims, but the company was reluctant to take any liability. The Bombay government handed out five *lakhs* for distress relief and the Government of India awarded a scheme of compensation for death or disablement. Wavell personally asked the Red Cross to supply artificial limbs.[16]

The main battle, though, was the propaganda story and in particular combating the idea that British negligence and lack of preparedness had caused the explosion and the failure to contain it. Controversially, the proceedings of the inquiry were partly held *in camera* and the first report made trenchant criticisms of the government. The fire had started sometime before the first explosion. The stowing of cotton near explosives, which had been carried out in Karachi, where the ship was loaded, was of course criticised, but also the lack of warning signals to other ships once the fire began, and the sorry state of fire-fighting and water supply – trailer pumps in private possession had not been used on the fire. It all led to a damning picture of careless, poorly co-ordinated responses. The government then assigned a second committee of inquiry to try to engineer a more even-handed response, as it would not accept the strength of condemnation in the first. This was a public relations disaster and the news travelled around the globe; as far away as Midwestern America, wives of GIs wrote to their husbands in India asking about the Bombay Docks explosion.[17]

* * *

The war was placing so many strains on the state by this point that the CID could freely admit that it no longer knew who was in the country, in what numbers or where they had come from. Police chiefs faced entirely new questions about stowaways, smuggled and black-market goods, escaped POWs and incoming refugees. As the war drew closer to its end, the military crisis was passing but the domestic fallout of war was just getting into full swing and the start of demobilisation would only bring new crises and questions. Military deserters, runaway prisoners of war, white women selling sex, refugees from Burma and from across South-East Asia could all be found in India. Although small in number, the presence of these different individuals was widely commented on during wartime in Indian cities. Any old pretence about clear racial differentiation, of clear blue water between rulers and ruled, had been exposed as a sham by the war.

Many Polish refugees had by now been in India for three years or more and over this time they had met local people and had often become more closely intertwined with the war effort. Gradually they overcame language difficulties; a tall and softly spoken Tamil, Benjamin Appadurai, who had escaped Japanese capture in Singapore, was employed to teach English to the refugees at the Valivade camp. Some of the young Polish men joined the British Army and some single women courted British soldiers from a nearby military camp two miles away, relationships blossoming despite attempts to block these liaisons. Mothers learned to shop in the local markets, adapting their recipes for pancakes and stews to unfamiliar ingredients, and local shopkeepers learned smatterings of Polish vocabulary. At the camp post office, as people waited for news from Russia and Germany, 'the Indian postmaster, Mr Salokhi read out the names of the addressees in faultless Polish . . . He was pleased if there was a large post and worried if there were only a few letters.'[18] Local Indian women offering to wash clothes walked along the verandas of the refugee camp, calling out in pidgin Polish, and door-to-door vendors sold ice-cream, calling out 'Warsaw ice cream, Krakow ice-cream!' A local surrounded by flies sold pork surreptitiously outside the camp gates.[19]

Raj society stayed mostly aloof from the refugees, distanced by language and by the spectre of these fair-skinned but impoverished Europeans, but the refugees remembered small kindnesses from *chow-kidars* (guards), *ayahs* (nannies), teachers, shopkeepers and drivers. There was a handful of marriages between Polish girls and Indian boys and some Polish women stayed on as married women after Independence, in cities like Karachi and Poona. Some Poles found creative inspiration from their new homeland. A young Polish dancer, Hanker Dytrych, left the camp and joined a famed Indian dance troupe, the Ram Gopal Ensemble, mastering classical Kathak dance and touring cities from Madras to Lahore. 'We . . . carried a great theatrical wardrobe – trunks of costumes, among which were the famous "crowns" set with semi precious stones designed by Ram', she later remembered. 'The work was very exhausting . . . We often travelled by night and had to practise in the morning for several hours under the watchful eye of our Guru.'[20] Although the Poles were largely unconcerned with the details of Indian politics, the general aspiration towards Independence resonated with them as they awaited the liberation of their own nation.

Sometimes it was no longer possible to ascertain *who* people were at all. As the density of servicemen increased in India, so, too, did the number of runaways and deserters who cropped up in Indian cities. One such case was Stafford Wilkie Palmer, a seventeen-year-old who said he was born in Houston and had been living in hotels, at military camps and then among the poor on the streets of Bombay until he turned up at the American Consulate asking for a passage back to America in 1945. He was wearing an outfit assembled from bits of military uniform marked with a variety of serial numbers and was suspected of going AWOL from the army. He denied having joined up. Was he a stowaway, boy soldier, identity fraudster or deserter? He claimed he had smuggled himself aboard a ship to India from New York. He had been living on the streets of Bombay in 1945, carrying his few possessions in a gas mask. In his statement, he told police how he had reached India and also gave insights into his life on the run:

At the port of embarkation in New York I cleverly managed to git on boat with colored GIs. Because I was very anxious to git Overseas as I thought the whole world was just like the United States with colored people too living in them . . . We were two colored boys that came over from the States the same way. And I sure Bernard Shaw, the other guy is killed by the Indians as he was trying to fok with them gals at Karachi. It is hunger, suffering and fear that forced me to come to report to US consul at Bombay the last two days I stayin in Bombay was without dam food and I was sleepin in the street.[21]

Police questioned the man he described as his father, Lacy Palmer, in Houston. On oath, Lacy Palmer said he'd met the man in the photograph once, when he was based in India, but he had no idea if he was an African, an American, a soldier or a civilian. He swore on his life that the young man was most definitely not his son. The home address that Stafford Palmer provided did not exist. Stafford Wilkie Palmer was kept in the stockade for the remainder of the war.

Among sepoys, too, deserters could be found roaming in India in the later years of the war. Desertion was a desperate act, often only a fantasy if a soldier was based miles from home in North Africa or Italy. Getting back home from the theatres of Burma, or from training in India, was more tempting. The self-mutilations of the First World War to secure home leave were rare and sepoys tended to find more imaginative ways to strike off, failing to return from leave on the grounds of sickness or absenting themselves because of a family crisis, never to be seen again.[22] The highest numbers of desertions tallied neatly with peak moments of food shortage and political crunch points. In Bengal in 1944 every fortnight there were fifty to a hundred deserters, about half of them caught and the rest left to dissolve into the countryside.[23] Nobody wanted to draw too much public attention to the issue and so often deserters were not pursued ruthlessly. The army did not have the time or the resources to track down individuals and provincial governors did not want military deserters adding to their crammed civilian jail populations. Occasionally these desertions were in order to join the INA: a platoon from the 1/15 Punjab Regiment vanished while on patrol one day and turned up many weeks later as part of the INA near Kalewa on the Chindwin River. Weekly disappearances, often by men carrying arms, continued to irritate the army chiefs: '[R]ecent desertions with arms include two parties of Mazbhi Sikhs, three from 10 Mule Company Bareilly and two from Indian Engineer Battalion Poona.'[24] Yet the ability to keep restocking and remanning the gargantuan army from India, and the care taken to cultivate the well-being of officers and their infantry units, provided a buffer against any real erosion of the Indian Army's effectiveness.

Some deserters found they could roam India undetected for months. Numerous people crafted new autobiographies for themselves in wartime, or fell through the gaps in the new nation-states that would soon be emerging. In Europe too, a number of Indians found themselves stranded or caught up between the warring powers. One unidentified Indian, for instance, found at Ilag Kreuzberg Camp in Germany towards the end of the war, was mystifying the authorities: he claimed to be a circus performer born in the Himalayas. The man, who said his name was Joseph Kandou, had been imprisoned as a civilian internee. He spoke a little French, German and English, could read Marathi and was requesting rice, 'Indian smokes' and some Marathi books. 'Poor chap,' the Red Cross worker trying to solve his case wrote in a letter to the India Office, 'he has no one to send him anything privately.'[25] Such stories reflect the porous nature of borders and nationalities in the tumultuous years as the end of the war approached and decolonisation loomed.

The state had the ability to crush dissent, but was also mortally weak in areas such as everyday surveillance, policing and border control. Around the country, the interned and prisoners of war seized their chances, kept close watch on indolent or distracted guards and fingered the meshed grilles around their camps. Among European prisoners of war several audacious escapes took place from Indian camps in the 1940s.[26] The police were under strain and could not apprehend the majority of escapers. Local villagers, sympathetic or at least hospitable, gave freely of directions, water and goodwill to strangers on the run.

Italian and German prisoners of war in India fantasised about escape and some of them made it. Elios Toschi, an Italian submariner, shipped to India as a prisoner of war, claimed to have made three different escapes. Before his first attempt he applied himself to plotting his flight. Along with his friends, Camillo and Faggioni, he studied Hindi and the intricacies of Indian society for months while interned. In the manner of a self-appointed orientalist he questioned sweepers at the camp and watched the mannerisms, gestures and deportment of all the Indians that he encountered. 'I spent my days drawing, calculating scales and dimensions, constructing networks of meridians and parallels, writing out, rewriting, thousands of times, the names of cities or villages', he later recalled. 'India gradually became familiar to me, more familiar even than Italy.'[27] When he and his friends did manage to escape from the camp in Kangra in the Himalayan foothills, he lived for some time in a mountain hut, with the help of a local shepherd called Kalah and his family. Passing themselves off as locals in turbans, with long beards and woollen smocks, Toschi was under no illusions about their disguise, and admitted that it was clear that 'down below on the plain, in the villages and isolated houses everyone knew of our presence up here'.[28] As Toschi made his way up into the higher Himalayas his presence was an open secret and villagers offered extravagantly generous meals that they could ill afford, opened their homes and ran errands for the runaway POWs, even producing a prized railway timetable. Twice, Toschi was captured and reinterned but on his third and final escape, again with the connivance of locals, he made it to the tip of the Gujarati peninsula, to the Portuguese protectorate of Diu, where he remained a free man.

Among Indian POWs there were also problems with information, record-keeping and poor knowledge about who was captured and where. Indian prisoners of war in Europe and in South-East Asia could have been anywhere across a wide arc of territory. They may not have been captured at all, might have joined the INA, begun trekking back to India after melting into the jungle border regions, died or been held captive in POW camps. Even the basic names, or details of who had been captured, when and where, remained elusive. Everywhere in the world, loved ones cherished information about those declared 'missing'. The 'delay in receiving news caused many thousands of anxious relatives and friends to wonder if everything possible was being done'.[29]

Poor documentation exacerbated the problem but also the haste with which recruitment had often been carried out. 'About half the men who fought in Malaya and Burma were not on any Indian recording system; so that no authority in this country had any idea as to who was missing or from what unit.'[30] Local corps, hurriedly formed during the Japanese invasion, had been swept up in the Japanese mopping-up operations. From Malaya, the majority of reports about POWs concerned Europeans; 'in spite of efforts by the Indian war organisation to ascertain conditions of the Indian POWs', the information received was 'very scanty', leaving many families in suspended anxiety for years on end.[31] The Japanese did release some names of Indian prisoners in Hong Kong, Shanghai and Bangkok but only a small proportion of the 70,000 or so that it was believed had been seized in the Japanese occupation.

Ultimately liberating forces recovered 24,935 Indian POWs and internees in the Far East, but the stories of their experiences remain obscure and often barely known.[32] Some, like Captain Mateen Ansari, did not live to tell the tale: kept captive and tortured in the infamous Stanley Road Jail in Hong Kong, he was executed in 1943. Indian prisoners of war in the Far East sometimes experienced the same kinds of terrible treatment as white captives. Summary executions, floggings, beatings, cruel punishments and forced labour, according to one of the few historians of the Indian POWs, 'equivalent or worse' to those punishments meted out to Europeans. John Baptist Crasta, a Catholic, born near Mangalore, who was imprisoned on New Guinea, wrote of a prolonged ordeal at the hands of a sadistic camp commander. He describes fellow prisoners being tied with battery wires, urinated on, beaten, made to do harsh manual work for twenty hours or more, Sikhs being forced to shave their beards off and prisoners made to stand out in the sun with their arms outstretched until faint; 'my physical condition at this stage was extremely bad. My body had become very thin. When I walked a few yards, I felt giddy and close to fainting. My weight then could not have been more than 100 pounds.'[33] During his three and a half years in confinement, Crasta received one letter. His wife heard no information about him, and for the duration of the war would not attend any party or celebration. Major Chint Singh recalled, 'We were declared "missing" by the British Government and our kith and kin were missing to us. We were living in absolute darkness. Our hearts had become as hard as stones, our feelings were crushed.'[34]

The Thai-Burma Railroad and the South Pacific Islands became hellish worlds for some. Men on New Britain and New Guinea (if they survived the gruelling journey, held in the hold of packed, insanitary ships with contaminated drinking water) faced a prolonged physical and mental ordeal that stretched over a number of years. Evidence is still patchy and contested, but it is likely that the 6,000–8,000 Indians sent there had been among those most resistant to the Japanese. Thousands of men lived without medicine, clothes, sheets or basic amenities and with little or no contact from the Red Cross. A small number were killed or injured by Allied raids on Wewak. Extreme shortages of food in 1944, when the Japanese were cut off from their own ships, left the men foraging to survive and there were strong accusations made by these prisoners against some of the Japanese guards in the later war crimes trials. When they were left wandering in the jungles and on the beaches of isolated islands, their full experiences and tactics for survival remain hazy to this day, and the Allied soldiers were often surprised to discover the Indian soldiers as they occupied the region from 1944. Disturbing photographs of Indian men, liberated in the Pacific by Australian troops, show the weak and emaciated condition of their bodies. The men had often dropped down to half their previous body weight, and their skin had become papery and dried out. The images evoke startling parallels with the famine.

There had always been people in India from other countries, and those who did not fit into the neat categories of the Raj. Similarly, there had been a wide and heterodox Indian diaspora living, trading and travelling beyond the subcontinent for generations. However, the numbers of strangers, the 'missing' and the unidentified multiplied in India in the 1940s, symbolic of the uncertainty and unprecedented change that was taking place. Similarly, the failure of the state to trace or pass on information about Indian prisoners of war deeply unsettled their families and kin. Widespread corruption and the impression of a state which was less accountable and more rapacious continued to erode faith in the offices of government, and disasters such as the Bombay Docks explosion compounded the problem. By the end of 1944, the victory in Burma looked more assured but the fallout from the war on civilian life was becoming clearer. The Raj's finely honed veneer of order and control had been ground down and the legitimacy of the colonial state had been ever more undermined.

22

Celebrations and Recriminations

As the war drew to a close, rationing had finally started in India, but there was little respite from the shortages which still affected millions.[1] Government shops had already acquired a reputation for poor and inedible grains, corruption and unreliable stock. By January 1945 another subsistence crisis was hitting the country, this time not just food but also cloth shortages. Many of the poor, owning only one or two saris or *dhotis*, usually replaced them when necessary. Now they could not even acquire cloth to dress themselves, while the better-off complained they could not find cloth for mosquito nets, towels or curtains. Even if they had the money, people just could not find cloth to buy. Lurid stories circulated with some basis in fact of dead bodies awaiting shrouds and grave-robbers taking the cloth from the recently buried. In villages, some people hid inside their homes, unable to cover their naked bodies.

It is difficult for the modern reader to understand what this cloth shortage really meant for people and their daily lives. A member of the Friends Ambulance Unit in Bengal wrote:

> One of the major problems of the more destitute is the difficulty of replacing their worn out garments. Those who can't, remain indoors rather than exposing themselves unclad. This means, among other things, they are unable to go about their work and the situation goes from bad to worse. Cases of suicide for want of clothing are frequently reported in the newspapers.[2]

In Moradabad, some bales of cloth had to be sold by magistrates to prevent corruption and rioting. At government-controlled cloth shops police pickets were established on occasion, as crowds fought and clamoured for cloth.

There was a plague outbreak in South India and coal shortages were so bad that cotton mills sometimes could not function in early 1945. A shortage of yarn also meant that handloom weavers and spinners could not work. 'A number of letters from this part of India refer to shortage of yarn, and the condition of the weavers is growing worse daily. Even at the black market rate of 40 Rs per bundle it is almost unobtainable', described one report:

> Cattle disease is prevalent in most areas . . . Labourers continue to ask for very high wages and thefts and dacoities [crimes] are increasing. In most places the price of paddy and rice is still rising . . . Nowadays nothing is available in the market, one cannot purchase things even by offering extraordinary prices for them . . . the position with regard to foodstuffs is equally bad. Half the quantity of rice being supplied from the government ration shops is stones.[3]

In Lucknow, cloth shops were besieged on appointed days by people fighting and struggling with each other, and were guarded by police with *lathis*.

The processes of war went into reverse gear. Demobilisation of labourers on mammoth building projects like the Ledo Road was beginning. Many workers were back on the roads and trains, heading back to their villages, often with savings which would help them in the short term but with poor prospects of future work. Underemployment and unemployment would now start to afflict workers who had flocked to the slums of India and had become accustomed to finding day wages during the boom. Even those who had engaged in prostitution were now 'demobilising', with reports of widespread impoverishment and unemployment for women who had earned their living for the past few years as camp-followers.

District Magistrates, charged with solving yet another grave crisis which was not of their own making and was beyond their control, were at their wit's end and, ultimately, desperate for leave. Morale was hitting a new low and stories circulated of ship's captains bribed for passages away from Bombay. British officials waited for news of leave or passages out of India. 'No one seems to worry very much about the poor hardworking civilians . . . nearly every civilian has done 6 years or even 8 without leave and most of us have worked at top pressure nearly the whole of that time . . . six years away from one's family is a big slice of one's life', complained one administrator. 'Work inside is just as plentiful as ever,' wrote another, 'the strain is beginning to tell, not only on the staff but on the men as well. Six years is no joke.'[4]

All of this made the news of peace in Europe rather distant and academic. For people in India who had suffered the devastation of famine, it was bitter-sweet; their own war in the East was not over yet. 'We were aware that the war had finished in Europe, but it wasn't yet finished for us', remembered a schoolgirl at the time, Nandita Sen.[5] The end of the war was welcome but it was barely something to be celebrated. Many people in India could not share the same elation as their European contemporaries.

The ghosts of the famine were never far from mind. In a cynical attempt to bury the story, the government published the long-awaited Bengal Famine Inquiry Report the very same week that VE Day was announced. The report was therefore eclipsed in the international radar, and in India had to jostle for column inches with stories about the fall of Berlin, the death of Hitler, the liberation of concentration camps in Europe, the Allied landings at Rangoon and the victory celebrations in London. Nonetheless, *The Statesman* steadfastly covered the inquiry report in full. The publication of the first photographs of the starved concentration-camp inmates from Buchenwald made, perhaps unintentionally, an eerie juxtaposition with the contents of the famine report.[6] A woman from Bombay wrote to friends in England, 'You have conveyed much of the terrible havoc that this . . . war has wrought amongst the peoples of Europe . . . The sufferings of the people have touched our hearts deeply. None the less so because of the agony of starving to death that has been the lot of enormous masses of our own people.'[7] A British lady from Calcutta, reflecting on the pictures of concentration camps emerging in the press, made a comparison that sounds shocking to twenty-first-century readers: 'The newspapers have a lot to write about . . . The German atrocities apparently do not compare with the Bengal famine so the pictures didn't shock the folk out here.'[8] People looked back at years of hardship and the changes that had taken place in India in five years of war and started to think about how history would record events that they had lived through.

The famine victims tended to be remembered in dry statistics, rather than as individuals. Compared to other global tragedies in the 1940s, there was no deliberate strategy behind the deaths of so many Bengalis, and nobody could be targeted as a culprit. Remembering the victims became more amorphous as a result. Blame was apportioned to Bengali people who stockpiled and made profits at the time, to the Government of India and the Government of Bengal, the British and Churchill, as well as the more general fortunes of cyclone, poverty and war. There was a litany of mistakes and oversights, which had resulted in famine, but there was little time for contemplation or recriminations before the next wave of relocations and deaths caused by the Partition of 1947.

For many, the celebrations about the end of the war were overshadowed by another question mark: what would be the future constitutional settlement of India, when would the British leave, and what would the future look like if and when they did? An Indian lady writing to a relative in England pointed out the poignancy of the moment in India:

> You have won the war at last. Please let us know how you celebrated Victory day there. We couldn't enjoy the victory celebrations fully here. It is all the same to us whether you win the war or not. We are in the same darkness we were in before. One must be fortunate to live in a free country.[9]

The fears about how power would be distributed in a free India had intensified greatly over the past months and were beginning to show in increasing incidents of violence between Muslims and Hindus in the towns: outbreaks of petty violence at the time of religious festivals, fights over music played near mosques at the time of prayer, or riots because of news that a cow had been killed for meat. But increasingly, there were more pernicious and prolonged acts of economic boycott and exclusion, and a more hysterical note in some of the right-wing Urdu and Hindi press. The shortages undoubtedly played a role in this. The running of food committees and ration shops at the local level, for instance, was providing the perfect opportunity for some Congress and Muslim League supporters to ostracise and penalise their enemies.

The Simla conference, the first step taken by the British Cabinet to show that negotiations with the Indian political parties would commence again, and that a constitutional deal was in the offing, was opened on 25 June 1945 while the war was still ongoing. This was the week that the Viceroy met Gandhi for the very first time, although Wavell had been Viceroy since 1943. The message was: war is nearly over, national politics can resume again. But too much had taken place to pick up the pieces as if the war had been a simple interlude.

The dropping of the bombs on Hiroshima and Nagasaki on 6 and 9 August added to the continuing sense of a marred victory, of a war that had done much damage as well as good. For Gandhi, it was final confirmation of the innate violence of the world. Despite Japanese atrocities, the dropping of the bombs on Hiroshima and Nagasaki was shocking, especially for people closer to the East. The Viceroy, Wavell, who had fought so long against the Japanese and whose own son had a hand amputated on the Burma front, was also evidently caught unawares. He noted in his private diary that 'matches' weren't safe in the hands of most humans; what would they do, therefore, with atomic bombs? 'It is not a weapon that any thinking man would willingly put in the hands of the present-day world', wrote Wavell.[10] Gandhi described it as 'an empty victory to the Allied arms', which 'resulted in destroying the soul of Japan . . . The moral to be legitimately drawn from the supreme tragedy of the bomb is that it will not be destroyed by counter bombs.'[11] Nehru had a stronger streak of realpolitik about India's place in the new world order and would ultimately favour India's becoming a nuclear nation. He had already spoken before Independence of India needing to defend herself using all means at her disposal. The civil nuclear energy programme in India was a product of wartime scientific investment, and had begun in 1944.[12] But Nehru also warned against the horrors of a bomb that represented a completely new world order, the end of the old world which was dying and being replaced by something as yet unknown.

Nonetheless, the end of the war had come at last. Soldiers, especially those still in Burma, felt the ecstasy of relief and exultation:

While all of us were sleeping in our tents, one British officer – a non technical man, he was in the officers' mess and – the middle of the night – he heard on the radio the Japanese have surrendered. He got quite wild about it and went straight to the tent of the CO and brought him out of bed in his night suit. And when they heard that news they sent the *subedar* and ordered all officers to come to the mess as they were. And so the whole mess was quite informal . . . some were dressed in their *lungis*, some in their pyjamas, and they kept on celebrating and drinking for a long time feeling that we have survived . . . but as luck would have it, the Japanese were fighting in a place called Pegu Yamas in the hills and they had not heard this news and they kept fighting in spite of our repeated messages to them through loudspeakers that your government has surrendered, they refused to believe it and therefore they kept fighting and we kept on getting the casualties from that area.[13]

Many, particularly those who had seen action, shared in the universal feelings of joy and relief that they had survived, and anticipated with relish the promise of homecoming. 'On 14 August, the day Japan surrendered, I was the only member in the Mess which was not much fun. So I explored Kandy town', recalled General Gul Hassan Khan, who was in Ceylon at the time, 'and discovered a most agreeable club. There were hundreds of officers celebrating the end of the war and I joined in. I knew no one but it was an occasion when such formality was unnecessary. The party finally broke up after breakfast the next day!'[14] 'I was euphoric and there were massive celebrations in Burma. We partied into the night', recalled Brigadier Parampal Gill.[15] When asked in old age their best memories of the war, former sepoys seemed unanimous that it was the news of peace: 'Only that we won the war that's the happiness'; 'Victory! When Japan surrendered that's when we were victorious and we were also happy when we got two months holidays that was the best day for us. Victory.' 'When the war finished and the way we celebrated it that is the best memory, all the soldiers came together and we had a big feast, food and all the banter that usually goes on, that's how we celebrated it all together.'[16] Some marked it in other memorable ways: crowds flocked to the Taj Mahal; in New Delhi there were dances and route marches, parties and a Victory Parade.

But the tone of triumphalism hit an off-key note with some listeners, as Frank Moraes recalled:

I was in Bombay when Allied Victory came at last in May 1945 and I heard Churchill's victory speech relayed over the BBC through amplifiers in the streets. His tone was understandably triumphant: 'Advance Britannia!' he perorated. 'Long Live the cause of freedom! God save the king!' It sounded incongruous to Indian ears . . . How could the cause of freedom live with the simultaneous advance of Rule Britannia?[17]

Nor was it entirely clear that fighting was really over. The victory over Japan fused into other missions: to suppress the communist guerrillas appearing in South-East Asia and to restore order to the region and reoccupy the Japanese-conquered territories. The continued deployment of Indian troops, first to reoccupy South-East Asia and then to put down communist insurgency in Malaya, tasks in which Indian and Gurkha soldiers were immediately redeployed, meant that it was not always clear when war ended and peace began. This phase of political upheaval and wartime change was also deeply intertwined with the struggle over Partition and the creation of the new states of India and Pakistan, as soldiers also became involved with internal policing, the control of riots and ultimately were divided into the new armies of the two free states.

★   ★   ★

Nehru and the other Congress leaders who had emerged from their prison gates in June 1945 needed to quickly catch up with the pace of change in India and to link themselves to the momentous events that had been taking place while they were behind bars. They immediately invoked the image of the 'heroine of '42', Aruna Asaf Ali. She was still on the run, heading her letters 'somewhere in India', living with amenable friends, shielded by sympathetic civil servants and police officials. 'If my voice can reach her I want to send her my love and esteem', Nehru declared in his very first speech after release from jail. 'I want to tell her that whatever she has done shall not be wasted and will bear fruit. It will leave its impress on her countrymen.'[18] Abul Kalam Azad pleaded with the Viceroy to lift her arrest warrant. A chorus of Congress voices rang out for Aruna, who was more than a little irritated by all the paternalistic concern and had already strongly disagreed in print and in letters with Gandhi and other Congressmen, who she felt were trying to disassociate themselves from the underground's more extreme actions or to tame them.

INA men were captured, interrogated and kept in jail but gradually thousands were released in the winter of 1945–6, as the government realised both the technical and practical difficulties of understanding who had done what during the war and also the political costs of continuing to prosecute INA men. The released followers of Bose found themselves (sometimes to their own astonishment) garlanded on release from jail, celebrated in pamphlets, books and photographs, embraced by politicians and paraded down the streets. The INA became the real heroes of the war in India. Nehru admitted at the end of the year that the INA trial was arousing passions even in remote villages. As they adjusted to life after incarceration, Nehru and many of the other Congress leaders – who had all along been cautious about celebrating violence and had differed with Bose – became loud champions of the INA. The reason why is simple. Deprived of their liberties during the war, newly freed from prison, Congressmen could not resist capitalising on the mass groundswell of support for the INA. Now that the real threat of Japanese invasion had been averted, it was safe to shout from the rooftops about the bravery and heroism of Bose's men. This was opportunistic but also part of the ferment of the moment and part of the great sweep of enthusiasm, expectation and millenarianism that was running through the country. The Congress was also flexing its military muscle-power, showing that it had the backing of army men and that it was prepared to use violence in the cause of Indian nationalism.[19]

By attaching themselves to the legacy of the INA, the Congress leaders hoped some of the glory and vitality of the movement would be transferred to them. Asaf Ali, who had been so cautious about the rebellions while he was in jail, now acted as a barrister in New Delhi defending the INA rebels. The INA also looked like the only organisation capable of championing the major Indian religious communities simultaneously, as Bose had rigorously insisted that the INA was built on inter-religious co-operation and had Hindu, Sikh and Muslim leaders. This added greatly to the appeal for Asaf Ali and Nehru, who wanted to emphasise secularism in the future life of the country and counteract the Muslim League. 'Though Shah Nawaz, Sehgal and Dhillon are no longer officers of the Indian Army, they have the whole of their lives before them to serve the country and the cause of India's freedom for which they risked their lives', Asaf Ali pronounced. 'They fought outside for the attainment of Independence and, I may add, for communal harmony. I sincerely trust . . . they will become ambassadors of the unity of India.'[20] The men were freed and the story of the INA was soon calcifying into a national myth, albeit one which celebrated officers rather than more junior ranks. Some of the sepoys who had joined the INA became more disgruntled in later years about their lack of pensions and their neglect by the Indian state where they had not been reaccepted back into the army.[21]

Asaf Ali was also visited by prisoners of war. Everyone was clamouring to tell their side of the story and to have a stake in the memory of India's war. Prisoners of war were freed and returned to life in India. For John Baptist Crasta,

> that was the happiest day of my life. A second birth, a resurrection from death, I thought. Now I would be returning to India, the India whose shores I had left four and a half years ago and to which I never hoped to return. I was free again after nearly three and a half years of captivity. I thanked God that he gave me that day. Everyone's face was now lit up with a bright smile.

As Crasta recalled:

> Most of us were in torn and tattered clothes, some with only a *langoti*, barefoot and bare headed, with long beards, thin and emaciated bodies grown dark on account of three and a half years hard toil, wrinkled foreheads, and drooping eyes. With the majority of us the hair had turned grey or fallen off due to increasing worry and care. This spectacle presented a striking contrast to that in which we first landed in Malaya: full of vigour and fine specimens of manhood.[22]

*   *   *

Eventually Aruna did come out of hiding but only when the state cancelled her arrest warrant on 26 January 1946, four years after she had first disappeared. It was another concrete admission of British imperial defeat. Many years later she would recall the depressing realisation that her dreams of a more sustained revolution had failed and express her bitterness towards some of the jailed Congress leaders:

> Inexperienced, lacking dynamic leadership, their fine spirit of reckless-ness ridiculed by those who played for safety, the 'Augusters' of 1942 grew dejected and gradually drifted away either to different groups or complete inaction . . . It is one of the ironies of our situation that those who participated in the '42 struggle had to submit to the leader-ship of men and women who had only heard of it from behind prison bars.[23]

Her marriage had not survived the strains of the war. Asaf Ali was destined for Washington DC as India's first ambassador to the USA, an appointment that was made before actual Independence and signalled the dawning of India's new status in the world. Nehru decided to send his old prison cell-mate, with whom he had shared so much, to be a figurehead for the composite identity of India that he wanted to project and protect at a time when Partition loomed. Asaf Ali recorded in his diary how Delhi, his home town, 'was almost convulsed with elation at the news of my appointment as Ambassador to Washington'.[24] Gandhi sent Aruna a note, trying to patch up the differences between the Alis, recognising both the personal and diplomatic utility of the couple working as a team, and writing that 'I think it is your duty to accompany Asaf'.[25] The couple was very much in the public eye. 'Why am I not going to Washington with my husband?' Aruna said to a public crowd in Karachi on the day of his departure. 'This is the question which confronts me wherever I go. In return I ask, is it possible for a mother to leave her ailing child? India is sick and is passing through critical times.'[26]

Aruna went with Asaf Ali to the airport. Shortly before sunrise, while the stars were still in the morning sky, his plane took off while she looked on.[27] Aruna stayed behind to forge her political career in India, where she later became one of the leading Members of Parliament in independent India. The two had drifted too far apart, both politically and personally, and as she later wrote, 'The thread of happy domestic life which was snapped by the gravest of national crises, nearly five years ago, could not be picked up again'.[28] But they wrote letters and she visited him in Washington. Aruna was always respectful of her husband's erudition and humanism, but while he worked for the economic relationship with America and promoted India's foreign policy agenda, she kept determinedly to leftist causes. They had both experienced such different events during the turmoil of war, and their political ideologies had shifted so far out of alignment, that even Gandhi could not reconcile them.

*　　*　　*

The Americans weighed up their future in South Asia in 1945. They made attempts to secure a permanent foothold and suggested keeping air bases in Karachi and Calcutta, requests which the British hurriedly rebuffed.[29] The seeds had been laid for the cold war in the region, though, and bases established all over Asia as a result of the war would not be so easily relinquished and would form the platform for a global conflict with the USSR over the decades ahead.

Dumps of ammunition and war goods lay awaiting decommissioning at the end of 1945. The scale of seepage onto the black market, the sale of arms and the ways in which the Allies disposed of their hardware have tended to be overlooked by historians. At Belur Salvage Yard in Calcutta vast quantities of scrap metal scarred the landscape. Some was sold onwards, some stolen and passed on to the black market. Near Digboi, Compton Mackenzie noticed 'two big American dumps where such vehicles as had not been stolen were being sold off gradually'.[30] The Afghan government bought jeeps but was not allowed to buy the guns it requested. Some opportunities for acquiring decommissioned goods would pay lucrative dividends. Military Police in Calcutta spent many weeks tracking down both US Army personnel and Indian civilians 'engaged in widespread thefts and black market disposals of large quantities of US army property'.[31] Soldiers pocketed whatever they could get their hands on, 'losing' pieces of uniform and kit on their journeys back home or during the long waits for demobilisation.

Decommissioning was also an opportunity for industrialists. They could buy up army stocks and machinery and turn military production to civilian causes. Walchand – now branching out into civil aviation

– bought ten Dakotas and two smaller planes from the US Foreign Liquidation Commission. The foundations for Air India and PIA were being laid on the basis of wartime aviation. In the regions that would soon become Pakistan, many of the great industrial families of Karachi and Lahore, who would dominate Pakistani economy and politics for generations, had solidified their wealth through wartime contracts. The Muslim League was backed by many industrial and commercial interests who had developed their own power in the 1940s and now preferred a federal or decentralised future for India where they could escape state regulation. Memons, Khojas, Bohras, and Muslim businessmen like the Ispahanis, Habibs and Adamjees supported the league. Muslim shipping and banking interests, in a shrinking economy, started to look to securing their own capital.

Mecca was also accessible now that the war had ended and the haj could resume again. The centre of the Muslim world had started its shift westward, and the growth of air transport would transform links between Asia and the Middle East over the coming decade. A Saudi Arabian minister in London suggested that the British government 'should encourage Indian soldiers now serving in Egypt or elsewhere to make the pilgrimage to Mecca', which would be both 'good British propaganda' and also useful for Saudi revenues.[32] In Britain, the London Central Mosque (which had been initiated in 1940 and authorised by Churchill's War Cabinet) served the burgeoning communities of South Asians and was also a gift of the state to thank Muslims for their notable contributions to fighting the war.

Indian Independence, although certain to take place, still looked likely to face potential delays. 'In many people's minds there is a vague assumption' – particularly if the different Indian parties did not come to a consensus about the constitution – 'that there will be a continuance in some form of British control,' wrote Penderel Moon in 1945, 'unless English people clearly grasp that the time has come for them to divest themselves once and for all of political power in India.'[33]

In the uncertain, transformed world after the war in India, the political future had started to cleave along religious lines and the growth of the Muslim League had been badly underestimated by the Congress leadership. At the provincial and local level, nationalist parties were now drawing heavily on the power of religious iconography in anticipation of a general election. This election was announced in 1946 as a quasi-referendum, as a way of testing the relative support of the various parties in the country. The severing of the ties between soldiers of different religious backgrounds would take place in 1947 when the Indian Army was split into the two national armies of India and Pakistan, but already at the end of war, tensions and problems had irrevocably altered the political possibilities for a future settlement.

23

The Sepoy's Return

By 1945, there had been 89,000 Indian casualties in the war. Frequently, news had not reached home to confirm who had survived. For prisoners of war and families of members of the INA, the end of the war was also a time of angst. Mothers and wives waited nervously for news. Ramesh Benegal was reunited with his mother in Poona after four years: 'What a reunion it was! . . . After a dinner that I don't remember eating, I passed into a deep sleep. I heard that my mother sat beside me all night, and touched me now and then to make sure that she wasn't dreaming, and that this was really her son, come back to life.'[1] Fate afflicted families randomly. Benegal's friend, Gandhi Das, had survived with him through ordeals in the jungles of Burma and Thailand and had been one of only a small number of survivors when his ship was torpedoed in the South China Sea. He then contracted an illness soon after the end of the war, when safely back in India, but before he could see his parents again. 'After all this he died in obscurity in a village in Madurai district, not from enemy action or world calamity, but typhoid', wrote his closest friend, who had been alongside him every step of the way, 'I could not understand it.'[2] In Rajinder Dhatt's family two brothers came back from war safely but the third, whom their mother had not permitted to leave home for fear of his death in battle, stayed behind and died of typhoid.

Officers felt the responsibility of trying to explain to families – in letters or in person – what had happened to their sons. H. M. Close toured the small villages on the frontier, from where his company had been recruited, and met the father of a man he had seen shot by a German gun in Greece.

Mian Dad and I went together to Nasrullah's village and met his father. I gathered that Nasrullah, though not the only son, had been the favourite and the hope of the family. I told how well he had died. "On the whole I'm alright," his father said to me – a kindly, charming old man – "but sometimes at night when I'm on my bed I think of Nasrullah and then it troubles me."[3]

The overwhelming pattern was one of private, quiet grief and contemplation. 'The philosophical question of the innocent casualties of war troubled him all his life', wrote the daughter of Victoria Cross winner Premindra Singh Bhagat. 'Like all soldiers, he would spend his life preparing for war but always think of it as damaging and evil.'[4] Others kept captured weapons and souvenirs as trophies. Japanese swords and Gurkha *kukris* were popular with both Indian and British soldiers. Gian Singh took a silver ring from a Japanese soldier in the jungle who had nearly killed him: 'As soon as I saw it, I knew I was going to have it, even if I had to cut off his finger . . . I took it off and put it on my finger.'[5] Trophies and war souvenirs were ways of remembering the war for those who found it too difficult to recall in words the battles that they had experienced.

British officers felt the deaths of men in their companies acutely. J. H. Voice's memories of the battle at Keren are punctuated by the grief for a dead friend:

> At about 10:00 I heard that our mortars had received a shell and that Subedar Sharin Khan had been killed. Sharin Khan, a Khattak, was a very nice man indeed, an officer and a gentleman (I don't know how else to put it) and his death coupled with that of Stanley Wilson about ten days earlier was quite a blow to me.[6]

The British officers felt responsible for their men and guilty if they were separated from them, particularly at the time of their death. John Ffrench of the Rajputana Rifles had pangs of regret later in life about the men who died at Monte Cassino. On the death of Jemadar Ghulam Hussein he wrote many years later, 'He had only just returned from leave in India and was said to have had a premonition that he would not see India again. It was a real blow to the whole company.' In the midst of battle, when the company needed every man, he released a *subedar*, Mohammad Yusuf, to perform the necessary Islamic rituals and to give Hussein a prompt and proper burial, 'such was his esteem to the men'.[7]

Later, Ffrench was wounded in the leg at Monte Cassino during a battle on Hangman's Hill. Evacuated to hospital in Sorrento, he fretted about the fate of his Indian soldiers while he looked out over the Bay of Naples. He was reunited with them later when they all boarded a ship at Suez heading for India. 'I was devastated to find what had happened to A company,' he wrote on learning of the deaths of eight of the men, 'I really felt that I had let them down by not staying with them and tried to tell them so. Being mostly fatalistic, they replied that there was nothing I could have done about it, as it was all *kismet* anyway.'[8]

There could be a chasm between officers and men of any nationality, the untranslatable distance between elite wealth and the everyman. In the case of the Indian Army this was even wider, as the men came from villages and places that were, after a point, literally and figuratively unreachable for the British officer. The reliance on caste and tribe stereotypes and clichés about the fatalism and loyalism of the Indian soldier recur in stock images. Yet also shining through the surface are stories of real mutual affection. By the end of the war, after all that they had shared and experienced together, like men all over the world, the company, unit and regiment had become a surrogate family, bonded through new ties of adversity and experience. Written from Waziristan in November 1946, a letter from Subedar Kartar Singh, to his former British officer, expressed the nostalgia of men now separated by nation and distance.

I am very glad to receive your kind letter. It gave me much pleasure . . . I cannot express in words how happy your D coy [company] is when I tell them your Ram Ram [greetings]. I am just doing roll call, everybody from D coy is present here on R call ground. They all remember you very much. The old fellow, Jem. Hari Singh has gone for release. I am applying for short-term commission . . . All sepoy, cook remember you very much. Would you like to come to India again, if so write me? I am very anxious to show you the villages in my district . . . I know that you have got true love for India and it is bad luck that she lost experienced officers like you . . . Good bye sir for now, kindly let me know your news. I long to hear your programme. All VCOs, NCOs and

Jawans of this Bn [battalion] and especially from your Coy send their
Ram Ram to you and hope you will not forget them.[9]

Many sepoys slotted back into their old lives, apparently seamlessly,
picking up the plough, returning to the fields. They certainly had more
money in their pockets than most of their fellow villagers and were
greeted with joy. The songs of marriage parties and the aroma of feasts
filled the village air. Unmarried men found themselves much in demand,
mothers had already lined up suitable brides and many families fused
together welcoming parties with wedding festivities. 'These were
pleasant hours that we spent in the shade of his lemon trees', said H.
M. Close, who accompanied a soldier named Umar back to his village.

> Giving the wheel a turn he would draw water from the well and gather
> fruit and bring sugar from the house and so make sherbet. Then perhaps
> we would stretch ourselves on the string beds and doze for a time. I
> met his brother and some of his friends and, mixing with them, he
> seemed still what he had been before he enlisted, a simple country lad.[10]

He recalled his time there with more than a touch of romanticism.

Gurkhas hiked back to their villages, often a long walk of many
days. They carried with them gifts of Kashmiri shawls and Indian
fabrics, hurricane lamps and packets of tea. They also brought with
them books: on combat techniques, maths and science primers, Hindi
alphabets and Hindu mythology. Often, after a brief time of celebration, rest and rejoicing, men were absorbed back into the rhythms of
village life. All that they had seen and heard seemed so far away. Wives
and friends began hinting that they needed extra help in the fields, and
it was not long before soldiers became peasants again. Some men
became noticeably prosperous, particularly officers and those who had
accrued savings and could now make investments in land.

The evangelical social reformer and Welfare Officer Frank Brayne
was anxious that the soldiers should not just slip back into their bad
old ways. He wanted the state to make the most of this opportunity
for 'development' and for the soldiers to act as vectors for modernity
and progress. 'Don't start quarrelling and litigation and don't throw
expensive parties and weddings', he warned men as they were demobilised.[11] He hoped that they would no longer tolerate unhygienic

toilets or smoky, unventilated kitchens and that they would tutor their families in the lessons that they had learned while in military service. The Punjab provincial ministry published enlightening tracts on improving agricultural methods with titles such as 'A chart of vegetables', 'One hundred Agricultural proverbs' and 'Family budgets of cultivators' for soldiers to take home with them. All manner of schemes, from soap-making and livestock-breeding to crafting wooden toys and cricket balls and bats, were established, especially in Punjab, to ensure that the men had something useful to apply their energies to. The soldier would be, Brayne hoped, a cipher for development.[12]

Underneath this return to an apparently bucolic idyll there was often an undercurrent of unease and far more violence accompanied demobilisation and the post-war transitions than idealised accounts by officers suggest. Protest was burning with a new fervour, and the unrest that was sweeping through the country caught up many demo-bilising men, who became caught up in the Punjabi whirlwind, often taking part in Partition riots, training and leading self-defence cadres and private militias. The danger of war was over, the British were clearly going and the country was in freefall. News was emerging about the actions of the INA and some of the truths about wartime repression and the Bengal famine started to circulate. While waiting for demobilisation many sepoys became caught up in the political cauldron. Even if they had stayed straightforwardly focused on the job in hand during the war, now they re-evaluated their own political allegiances. They wanted the uncertainty about India's Independence to be settled and for their own conditions to be secure. A naval mutiny among young sailors in Bombay in 1946 was the most notorious example but there were outbreaks of resistance and anger showing all over the country. As B. C. Dutt, one of the Royal Indian Navy sailors who mutinied in 1946, put it:

I was 22. I had come through a war unscathed – a war fought to end Nazi domination. I began to ask myself questions. What right had the British to rule over our country? Nationalist India had asked the British to leave Indian affairs in Indian hands. The British always proved intran-sigent. To nationalist India we were mere mercenaries. It was up to us, I felt, to prove this was not so. Without quite realising it, I had become a conspirator.[13]

In Nepal, too, the return of so many young men was worrisome for the Rana regime. Nepal's *ancien régime* looked unguarded and vulnerable now that its British allies were retreating from South Asia. Nepali political prisoners released from Indian jails picked their way back home and there was disaffection in the undernourished Nepal State Army, billeted around Kathmandu. Would the return of 200,000 young men – most without pensions, but well trained and many newly literate – be enough to destabilise the rulers altogether? Jhuddha Shumsher Rana, presciently, as if seeing the writing on the wall for his creaking autocracy, resigned in order to become a *sanyasin* (a Hindu holy man) in November 1945. He handed over power and retreated to live out the rest of his life meditating in the Himalayas. Nepal's isolation from India's political currents could no longer be preserved and Nepalis began to witness strikes and marches in the Kathmandu valley for the first time in their lives.[14]

For injured and disabled sepoys in India the adjustment was also taxing. Disabled soldiers posed a special challenge in villages poorly geared towards their needs and where old prejudices about disability persisted. St Dunstan's in Dehra Dun was a care home and rehabilitation centre for permanently blinded soldiers, some of whom also had other disabilities: it provided expert care for 328 men, including 4 African soldiers and a number of Gurkhas. The majority had lost their eyes in action involving hand grenades and mortar shells. The home attempted to rehabilitate them and to help them to adjust to a life with disability, to introduce them to Braille, fit them with artificial limbs, help build morale and restore mental order. In particular, the men were taught skills like weaving that might give them a chance of earning an income in the post-war world.

Many of the men arrived deeply depressed about their injuries. Havildar Kuttan Pillai was 'typical'. He arrived at St Dunstan's blinded, his hearing in his left ear destroyed, and his left arm amputated. 'He was so depressed that it was with difficulty he could be persuaded to speak or eat.'[15] A fellow Malayalam speaker, also blinded, extended his friendship, and eventually Kuttan Pillai started typing with one hand and learned how to use a spinning wheel. He went on to set up a shop in Trivandrum. But alongside these successful stories of rehabilitation, many of the men had experienced 'long periods of loneliness on wards of sighted men', or had been completely cut off from others in hospital, isolated from anyone who could speak their own language. In addition, they suffered from concerns about supporting families in the future or being rejected by fellow villagers, and anxieties about adjustment to the world after the war.[16] If the medics diagnosed that the blindness or disability was not due to wartime injury, but a consequence of disease, they might lose the right to a military pension, which tipped some men into extreme worry. Everywhere pensions were a major concern, and vastly different depending on rank and length of service.

Many other sepoys looked immediately for further employment, in the Indian or British armies. Men who had fulfilled fifteen years of service qualified for a pension and could return to their village and live relatively peacefully, and some did so – but many sepoys went back to Indian cities before long to look for work, as *chowkidars*, guards on the railways and policemen. This may not have always been an economic choice. It was difficult for some to shake off the routines (and comforts) of army life, to take to hard manual labour again, to find their place once more in the intimate confinement of an extended family. In one village, a retired *subedar* took a job on the Indian railways even though his family was relatively well-off and his wife remained behind in their village. Men found themselves torn between missing their families and missing the army. Over the years they had changed imperceptibly and now had to turn time back and find their old place in village hierarchies and relationships. For some, it was easier to keep moving, to leave the village behind altogether.

*   *   *

On 15 August 1947, far away from the Punjab and the gruesome massacres and refugee upheavals that were unfolding there, another group of Indians and Pakistanis celebrated Independence. In central London it was a warm summer morning. On Aldwych, cars stopped as loudspeakers broadcast from the interior of India House, celebrating Indians spilled out onto the pavements, some in white suits and bright saris, many others soldiers and sailors in uniform. Curious passers-by stopped to watch the crowds of merrymakers. Inside, Krishna Menon, the new High Commissioner, was the centre of attention as he stood under the domed roof of the library, in front of a full-length portrait of Gandhi, and welcomed people into the building. The happy crowds went out into the courtyard outside, to hoist the national flag amid cheers and anthems. Pakistanis joined them, before moving on to their own celebrations at Lancaster House – the building was loaned for the occasion by the British government as the Pakistanis did not have a building in London yet to call their own. 'The friendliness pervading both ceremonies was widely felt to be the happiest of auguries', commented one *Times* journalist.[17] The Indian leaders passed through a guard of honour formed by Indian soldiers and airmen, among them the pilots who had flown aeroplanes alongside the RAF in the battles over Europe. The High Commission was Menon's new home; the bedsits of Camden were no more.

Krishna Menon had, in the way of postcolonial leaders, apparently been transformed from *persona non grata* to establishment figure almost overnight. Privately, his appointment as the new High Commissioner for India was opposed by Stafford Cripps and by the new Prime Minister Clement Attlee.[18] Tracked by MI5 for years as a suspected, dangerous pseudo-communist, Menon was emerging as one of the leading diplomats of his age. Once he had dreamed of being a British Member of Parliament, but Menon's rapprochement with his beloved Labour Party had come too late for that: in May 1945 the Labour Party had come knocking at his door again and he had been welcomed back into the party with open arms, and encouraged to stand as a candidate for Parliament once more. Menon, however, and India, had moved on. Now he was destined for diplomacy, a post at the United Nations, the front cover of many magazines, and in his old age would become a controversial Indian Defence Minister. It is difficult not to regard the war as a time of frustration and dashed hopes for Menon, and a period when he felt cut off from old friends and alienated because of Indian affairs that he felt about so deeply and cared about with such a strong sense of righteousness. It is also perhaps not too far-fetched to imagine that the more strident form of Indian nationalism that Menon promoted later in life, like so many of his fellow Congressmen, was a product of his experiences and frustrations during the war.

Other Indians in Britain had also been transformed by wartime. Menon would eventually settle back in South Asia, but many of his compatriots would not. Lascars and soldiers who had been brought to Britain for wartime service comprised the vanguard of the new settlers in the post-war world, serving the demands of post-war British industry. They laboured in the foundries of the Midlands, the warehouses around Heathrow Airport and the new NHS hospitals being raised in the 1950s. Entrepreneurial Lascars invested in turning their basic canteens into the restaurants serving masalas around the land. Some Punjabis – Sikh, Muslim and Hindu – found their villages had been lost or sundered by the Partition and decided to try their luck in Britain. The ability to speak English that many had learned in the Indian Army was an asset. British officers often became the link in the chain, giving a hand to former soldiers that they had commanded, offering a foothold in a firm or sponsoring an application. The war was a portal for global settlement and travel, the upheaval that it caused generating new patterns of migration, new ideas about what life might be like. On occasion, just proving that one had been in uniform for the Allies was enough to change attitudes. Respect for the Indian Army's role in the war persisted among those who had served with the sepoys. In the 1960s, Rajinder Singh Dhatt, newly arrived in England, found that talking about his war service with factory managers was a way to get an interview. At a foundry in Birmingham, he was told by a manager to mention his war service at every opportunity. 'He asked me, "which army you joined?" I told [him the] Indian Army when British were ruling at that time. "In which year?" I told [him] in 1940. "Oh! You were in the Second World War." Because he was also, he also fought in the Second World War.'[19] This worked and he finally found work at an engineering company in Feltham weeks later, after a manager thoroughly checked his wartime credentials; 'He said, "We haven't got a job but we will take you."'

Many men found their way to Britain. In the first ten years after Independence, thousands of South Asians migrated to Britain in the shadow of war, often building on networks established during wartime. By 1946 there were around twenty Indian restaurants in London, mainly Sylheti-owned, many serving a double function as a meeting place, and exchange for news on work and accommodation. Two brothers from Sylhet opened Oxford's first Indian restaurant on Turl Street in 1945, along with a string of other restaurants staffed by former Lascars.[20] Many settled communities of several generations were already established in cities such as Cardiff and Coventry. As the demand for wartime and post-war labour grew, unskilled work could be found in the docks, factories and aerodromes. The community in Liverpool included men like Miralam, Baijneth Randev and Bahadur Singh Chand, who had arrived in the

UK in 1939 and served with the British Army during the Second World War. The Indian community in Birmingham had grown from a hundred to over a thousand people during the Second World War. By early June 1945, approximately 9,460 Indian POWs had arrived in the UK on their way back to India. Many had been held in Italy earlier in the war, then moved on to Germany and now passed through Britain after liberation from camps.

As the dust settled on Independence and Partition in 1947, Field Marshal Claude Auchinleck sat at his desk at his home in London. The former Commander-in-Chief of India was thinking about the past. Now he penned a letter by hand to the Prime Minister, Clement Attlee. Auchinleck pressed for a monument or a memorial in central London to mark the role of the Indian Army in the Second World War. The general suggested it would be 'a mark of gratitude from the British people to those soldiers who served Britain and the Empire for 200 years', for men who, 'putting their trust in us, fought and fell in our wars all over the Old World'.[21] A statue of a sepoy was proposed, or, potentially, a series of orientalised figures, modelled on the 'chief classes enlisted in the old Indian army'.[22] The space that Auchinleck suggested was Green Park, but the Minister of Works suggested the South Bank in London. The site then under construction was part of Britain's post-war reinvention, and the place where the Festival of Britain would be launched in 1951. The Cabinet cast an eye over the proposal, and the governments of India and Pakistan were agreeable, as long as they were consulted on the design. But the British government decided not to formally back the plan and as no committee was formed, no funds were raised. The site for the memorial remained undecided and without more sustained backing, the general's idea fizzled out and the file was closed in 1949.

In Britain, post-war reconstruction and regeneration quietly erased the Indian contribution which was at odds with the story of plucky small-island British heroism and outdated in the heady days of post-war British modernism and architectural innovation. In post-war Britain, certain war stories became amplified and mythologised, became part of the curriculum, and made into films, while others slipped away from view. Everyone remembered the Blitz, but fewer remembered the Asian merchant sailors who had kept the British ports going.

Everyone remembered the major battles – Imphal, Kohima, Monte Cassino – but fewer knew about those who had fought there from African and Asian colonies.

The Imperial War Graves Commission had further intentions to memorialise the war. In 1949, both the Indian and the Pakistani governments agreed to centralised memorials in their capital cities. In time, monuments were erected in Delhi and Karachi and also in Chittagong and Bombay to commemorate the Royal Indian Navy and seafarers. As these designs came to fruition, the officers of the Imperial War Graves Commission who were involved in planning and erecting these monuments debated whether the memorial books listing the names of the dead, which would accompany the monuments, should be accessible to the people. It did not really matter, it was argued, the books should not be handled by the public as they might be damaged, and who would care to see them in any case? By this time, India's war was passing from South Asian memory, replaced by new national myths and stories in India and Pakistan centred around Independence and Partition. As a member of the commission wrote candidly in 1955, 'It is anticipated that the numbers of visitors who will wish to see the names will be infinitesimal. The relatives of the greater number of those commemorated will be too poor to afford the trip to either cemetery, and, in fact, will know nothing about the Memorial.'[23]

In South Asia, 1947 became a byword for the pain of Partition but also for the joy of Independence. In her old age, Aruna Asaf Ali, whose own life was changed irrevocably by the war, reflected on those momentous years of her youth: 'Wars, ancient and modern are curious phenomena, while they bring death and desolation to many they also unshackle millions.'[24] The war was certainly the catalyst for the unshackling of south Asians from imperial rule, and made the granting of immediate Independence unavoidable. Nationalist historians in India and Pakistan recast the events of the 1940s as stepping stones, leading towards liberation. The new monuments and museums of the post-colonial states placed the patriarchs and freedom fighters of the early twentieth century at their core. They lionised the great sweep of political struggle and long years of persistence through the 1920s and 1930s, which finally resulted in the downfall of the Raj.

Midnight's children wanted to build up a new world and looked to the future development of the state, the construction of power plants, dams and military hardware. The story of the war did not sit easily with this new era. It belonged to the old colonial world: archaic, illegitimate and even irrelevant. A British author, Compton Mackenzie, who had been commissioned to write a work on the Indian experience of the war, was taken aback when meeting a Congress minister in Madras, Raghavan Menon, in 1946. 'He said at once that he was not interested in the book because he and his party had not considered it their war.'[25] The minister was right: it was not India's war, it was the British Empire's. The war grievously lacked legitimacy with colonial subjects in South Asia. But this does not foreclose the possibility of greater historical enquiry or the writing of new books on the subject.

Sepoy or prince, magistrate or mother, rebel or British soldier: the 1940s in India left a deep imprint on millions of lives. The war forced terrible decisions, produced strange juxtapositions and unforeseen consequences. Our own understanding of this global war, and appreciation of its severity, is enhanced by realising its fullest extent. There is still much more to be said about the ways in which the inhabitants of the British Empire served and suffered through the 1940s, and still much more to be understood about the demands of war on many different kinds of people.

Chronology of Major Events

1939

1 September	Government of India Act centralises executive authority
3 September	War declared
3 September	Recruiting stations in India opening; internment of Italians and Germans starts
3 November	United Provinces and Bombay Congress ministries resign, followed by ministries in Orissa, Central Provinces and NWFP

1940

13 March	Udham Singh assassinates Michael O'Dwyer in London
22–4 March	All India Muslim League meeting declares Lahore Resolution
10 May	Churchill becomes Prime Minister in Britain
3 July	Subhas Chandra Bose imprisoned (until 5 December 1940)
8 August	'The August Offer' presented in a White Paper (rejected by Muslim League and Congress)
18 September	Sinking of the SS *City of Benares*
17 October	Gandhi authorises individual *satyagraha* followed by 20,000 arrests
25 October	Eastern Supply Group meets in Delhi to discuss war supplies

1941

January	Indian language broadcast service started for Indian troops in Middle East
January	Subhas Chandra Bose escapes India overland for Germany
February–April	East African campaigns, e.g. battle of Keren
April	India celebrates Allied North and East African victories
22 June	Operation Barbarossa begins; Hitler invades Russia

7 August	Rabindranath Tagore dies
November	First Victoria Crosses awarded to Indians during the war
7 December	Japanese attack Pearl Harbor, American entry into war

1942

15 February	Singapore falls to the Japanese, first INA being formed
	American troops arriving in Calcutta
19 February	Subhas Chandra Bose makes first open broadcast to India
27 February	Japanese aircraft raid Port Blair in Andaman and Nicobar
6 April	Vizagapatam and Cocanada bombed
14 April	False alarm in Madras, city evacuated
7–8 March	Rangoon falls; flow of refugees from Burma increasing
23 March	Cripps arrives in India
29 March	Burma Road cut by Japanese
5–6 April	Bombing raids on Ceylon
April	Formation of Women's Auxiliary Corps (India)
10, 16 May	Bombing raids on Imphal
May	Allies withdraw from Burma
June	Grady technical mission in India from USA
July	First battle of El Alamein
14 July	Congress Working Committee meets at Wardha
July	Communist Party of India legalised
8 August	All India Congress Committee adopts Quit India resolution
9 August	Gandhi and Congress leaders arrested
August	Quit India movement breaks out across the country: at least 2,500 deaths and 60,000–90,000 arrests
October	Second battle of El Alamein
	Cyclone hits Midnapore
13 December	Chittagong bombed
17 December	British forces occupy parts of Arakan region in Burma
20–8 December	Air raids on Calcutta
December	Building of the Ledo Road initiated

1943

10 February	Gandhi fasts for ten days and risks death
	African troops start to arrive in India
7 March	Japanese counter-offensive at Arakan
	Scale of famine in Bengal becomes apparent
9 May	Evacuation of Maugdaw in Arakan region of Burma
21 May	Public holiday to celebrate victory in North Africa

19 June	Announcement of Wavell's appointment as Viceroy and Auchinleck's as Commander-in-Chief, India
21 June	Bose's first speech from Tokyo broadcast
2 July	Bose lands in Singapore in a Japanese aircraft
25 August	Announcement of Mountbatten's appointment as Supreme Allied Commander, South-East Asia
December	43,600 US troops arrive in India
5 December	Renewed bombing of docks in Calcutta

1944

March	Battle of Imphal, Burma
4 April	Japanese attack Kohima, Burma; battle lasts until June
14 April	Major ammunition dock explosion in Bombay
6 May	Gandhi released from detention
6 June	Allied invasion of Normandy begins
24 June	Appointment of Indian Famine Inquiry announced
3 August	Myitkyina in Burma in Allied hands
23 August	Paris liberated
August	VD levels in Calcutta peak 376/1,000

1945

9 May	End of war with Germany
	Bengal Famine Inquiry Report published
15 June	Nehru and Congress Working Committee released
25 June	Simla Conference opens in Simla, India
6 August	First atomic bomb dropped on Hiroshima
14 August	War ends with Japan
September	Liberation of Japanese prisoners of war
7 October	Allied British force reoccupies Andaman and Nicobar
5 November	First trials of members of the Indian National Army, Delhi

1946

3 January	Sentences passed on three Indian National Army officers
18 February	Royal Indian Naval Mutiny in Bombay

1947

14–15 August	Partition and Independence: Indian and Pakistani Independence from British colonial rule

List of Illustrations

British tanks in the North-West Frontier Province, courtesy of Mary Evans Picture Library/Sueddeutsche Zeitung Photo

British soldiers at Chitral, courtesy of Mary Evans Picture Library/Grenville Collins Postcard Collection

'The British Commonwealth of Nations Together' poster, courtesy of Mary Evans Picture Library/Onslow Auctions Limited

Three stokers on board the Royal Indian Navy sloop © Imperial War Museums

Indian Army Training Centre © Imperial War Museums

Inspecting potential recruits © Imperial War Museums

Men of the 4th Indian Division © Imperial War Museums

Indian fighter pilot © Imperial War Museums

Subhas Chandra Bose and Heinrich Himmler, courtesy of Mary Evans Picture Library/Sueddeutsche Zeitung Photo

Indians evacuating from Rangoon © George Rodger/Magnum Photo

Subhas Chandra Bose delivering speech, courtesy of GandhiServe Foundation

'Your Help Will Bring Victory' poster, courtesy of Musée d'Histoire Contemporaine, Paris, France/De Agostini Picture Library/G. Dagli Orti/Bridgeman Images

'Malaria Strikes the Unprotected' poster © The National Army Museum/Mary Evans Picture Library

The Ledo Road © Alamy

Nurses at a hospital in Calcutta © Imperial War Museums

Parsi women on an air raid precaution course © Imperial War Museums

Sir Stafford Cripps with Gandhi in Delhi © Imperial War Museums

Aruna Asaf Ali © RIA Novosti/Alamy

'What About India?' poster © Alamy

The Quit India movement, August 1942, courtesy of GandhiServe Foundation

Policewomen from the Women's Auxiliary Air Force © Imperial War Museums

An aircraft plotter of the WAC (I), courtesy of National Archives and Records Administration

Clearing land for airfields, courtesy of NARA

An American airfield in India, courtesy of NARA

The Bengal famine of 1943 © William Vandivert/The LIFE Picture Collection/Getty Images

A family during the Bengal famine © Keystone/Getty Images

A free kitchen in Calcutta, 1943 © Keystone/Hulton Archive/Getty Images

List of Abbreviations

AIML	All India Muslim League
ARP	Air raid precautions
ATS	Auxiliary Territorial Service
CBI	China–Burma–India
CID	Criminal Investigation Department
CSAS	Cambridge Centre for South Asian Studies Oral History Collection
CWGC	Commonwealth War Graves Commission
CWMG	*Collected Works of Mahatma Gandhi*
ENSA	Entertainment National Service Association
FNR	Fortnightly Reports
GHQ	General Headquarters
IAMC	Indian Army Medical Corps
ICS	Indian Civil Service
IGH	Indian General Hospital
INA	Indian National Army
IOR	India Office Records / Indian Other Ranks
IPTA	Indian People's Theatre Association
IWM	Imperial War Museum
NAAFI	Navy, Army and Air Force Institutes
NAI	National Archives of India
NARA	National Archives and Records Administration
NCO	Non-commissioned officer
NWFP	North-West Frontier Province
POW	Prisoner of war
RAF	Royal Air Force
RIAF	Royal Indian Air Force
RSS	Rashtriya Swayamsevak Sangh
SOAS	School of Oriental and African Studies
SWJN	*Selected Works of Jawaharlal Nehru*

TOP	*Transfer of Power Series*
VCO	Viceroy's Commissioned Officer
WAC (I)	Women's Auxiliary Corps (India)

Glossary

adivasi	member of 'tribal' or 'indigenous' community of India
ahimsa	non-violence
anna	small unit of Indian money
ayah	nanny
azad, azadi	free, freedom
basha	Assamese hut made of bamboo
bhang	cannabis
bhisties	someone who carries water
bidi	Indian hand-rolled cigarette
bigha	a measurement of land
bustee	slum or shanty town
charas	cannabis
charpoy	low bed
Chettiar	a merchant caste
chowkidar	nightwatchman, guard
coolie	labourer, manual worker
crore	ten million
dal	lentils
dalit	literally: oppressed, members of the lowest caste, 'untouchables'
dastur	custom
dhobi	washerman
dhoti	male clothing, wrapped round waist
dukha	sadness
durbar	ceremonial gathering of princes
ganja	cannabis
gharry	horse-drawn carriage
godown	warehouse
gurdwara	Sikh place of worship
haj	Islamic pilgrimage to Mecca and Medina

hakim	local doctor
hartal	strike or protest, specifically shutting shops in protest
haveli	old house around a courtyard
havildar	non-commissioned officer in the Indian Army (equivalent to sergeant)
hilsa	fish
izzat	honour or pride
jawan	literally: youth, used to describe soldiers
jemadar	an officer rank in the Indian Army
josh	cheering; morale-boosting
kala pani	literally: black water; oceans
khadi	homespun cloth
khalasi	dock-worker or seaman
kisan	peasant
kismet	fate
kukri	Gurkha knife
laddu	celebratory sweets
lakh	100,000
langoti	loin-cloth
Lascar	seaman
lathi(s)	long cane(s)
lungi	male clothing, worn around waist
maidan	park or open field
Marwari	a trader or merchant caste; businessmen
maund	unit of mass, equivalent to 37.3 kg
mela	religious fair or festival
memsahib	a white woman, usually associated with the Raj
mohalla	quarter of a town; ward
munshis	Islamic religious leader
naik	non-commissioned officer in the Indian Army (equivalent to corporal)
pagal	mad or crazy
pandit	Hindu priest
patwari	local land registrar
pie	small unit of Indian money
pir	descendant and trustee of a Sufi shrine
pukka	solid, built of fired bricks
sadhu	Hindu holy man
sarkar	government; the state
satyagraha	'truth force', key Gandhian term often translated as 'passive resistance'

satyagrahi	truth force activist, passive resister
sepoy	soldier in the Indian Army (equivalent to private)
subedar	officer in the Indian Army (equivalent to captain)
subedar-major	officer in the Indian Army (equivalent to major)
swadeshi	locally made
swaraj	literally: self-rule; Independence
tabla	drum
tehsil	basic administrative unit, subdistrict
thakur	honorific, used for headmen, landlords and leaders
thana	police station
tonga	horse-drawn cart
topi	hat
zamindar	landholder

Note on Sources

'India' and 'Indians' are used throughout the book as shorthand terms for the inhabitants of the subcontinent before 1947. This includes people in the post-1947 countries of Pakistan and Bangladesh as well as India. The book also refers to Nepal, Ceylon (later called Sri Lanka) and Burma, countries that were administered as separate parts of the British empire. I have used contemporary place names; many of these have changed since Independence.

Recapturing quotidian South Asian voices from the 1940s poses particular source challenges and the generation who lived through the war are now very elderly. In the 1940s many sepoys were illiterate. In addition to my own interviews I have made extensive use of the Indian Army censorship reports found in the India Office Records of the British Library. These include invaluable snippets of letters from sepoys and their families, but these are often extracts that have been taken from letters, made anonymous, translated, collated and filtered by the colonial state and have to be handled with some caution. A number of writers including David Omissi, Santanu Das and Gajendra Singh have written about the utility of these documents but also the necessary circumspection that should be applied given the conditions of their creation in the First and Second World Wars. I have also used earlier interviews accessible on the internet, in films and documentaries and others made available through community and oral history projects.

Most of the documents I have consulted are freely accessible in the national archives, museums and libraries of capital cities, in London, Delhi, Washington DC and beyond. These archives include war diaries, intelligence reports, personal memoirs, letters and diaries, party political literature and newspapers. The National Archives in

Delhi and London and the British Library's Oriental and India Office Collection both contain military records documenting many details of the Indian Army and the records generated by the central and provincial Indian Civil Service. Film and visual sources are also magnificent, although usually products of the well-oiled propaganda machines they can still tell us much beyond the written word. By reading against the grain, South Asians are far more visible in the historical record than many later accounts might have us believe.

Acknowledgements

An army of librarians and archivists offered suggestions and retrieved files and simply made work on the book possible; staff particularly at the National Archives in Delhi and Washington and the British Library in London; I can't acknowledge everyone by name but your work is so crucial and appreciated. A number of scholars have meticulously edited and published collections of archival material, making them much more accessible for all; their edited editions are in the bibliography. Funding from the Leverhulme Trust and the Arts and Humanities Research Council was vital as it enabled me to research in India, Nepal, the USA and the UK and also meant I could meet with academic colleagues who helped to enrich the work. A number of people who served in the war or lived through the time gave interviews to myself or to Iqroop Sandhiawalla for which I am immensely grateful.

For sharing their insights, asking good questions, giving hospitality or helping me at particularly tricky or important moments (and sometimes all of those things) thank you to Dick Alford, Sarah Ansari, Seema Ansari and family, Liz Buettner, Antara Datta, Lawrence Goldman, Alpa Shah, Sandra Halperin, Ben Hopkins, Steffi Ortmann, Sayeed Hasan Khan, Ashwani Sharma, Heather McCallum, Bill Schwarz, Adam Tooze, Andrew Whitehead, Deepak Thapa and colleagues at Social Science Baha, Tarak Barkawi, Joya Chatterji, Judith Brown, Shuddhabrata Sengupta, Ian Talbot, Benjamin Zachariah, Talat Ahmed, Rebecca Loncraine, Faisal Devji, Christopher Bayly, Indivar Kamtekar, Pillarisetti Sudhir and Sulochana Simhadri, Francis Robinson, Gajendra Singh, Crispin Bates, the staff at Blackburn Museum. Kazu Ahmed generously shared his images and interviews from Manipur and Nagaland. Dr Gajendra Singh of Delhi University who helped with an interview of Captain Yadav, INA, in New Delhi. James Holland gave permission to use the story of Mangal Singh whose full interview is available on his website.

Chiki Sarkar and Will Sulkin who helped develop my initial ideas and Stuart Williams, Kay Peddle, Meru Gokhale, Fazal Rashid, Katherine Ailes and Emmie Francis and all at Penguin Random House who have steered and crafted the book at different stages, at times making a silk purse out of a sow's ear. Emmie was particularly forgiving and patient at the final stages. Jim Gill remained brilliantly positive and encouraging throughout. Iqroop Sandhiawalla was a fantastic help at the beginning of the project by carrying out interviews in Delhi and Punjab and enthusing about the subject more generally.

Aashique Ahmed, Gajendra Singh, Alpa Shah and Timothy S. J. Phillips kindly took the time to read drafts and made helpful comments while busy with their own writing and saved me from a number of errors and Aashique checked some last minute details for me as things were drawing to a close and Amira was about to make her appearance. Ashley Jackson has been collegiate and helpful from the start and has shared his extensive knowledge of the empire and the war, and has pioneered the broader subject. Andrew Stewart helpfully read the chapter on the East Africa campaign. Everyone who attended the conference 'An Imperial World at War' in September 2013 at Kellogg College: I look forward to the volume from that conference. The editors of History Workshop Journal, to former colleagues at Royal Holloway, University of London, and more recently the President and Fellows of Kellogg College, Oxford, and the Department for Continuing Education at the University of Oxford.

My family is the perfect antidote to dwelling in the past and, among many other gifts, they remind me to stay in the present. Adam, Leo and little Amira, thank you for your tolerance and good humour. Markus has been understanding in every sense of the word and has helped in innumerable ways. My mother, Finola Khan, passed away unexpectedly before this book was finished. She was a great reader and a great travelling companion and is very much missed.

Notes

Prologue

1 N. Mansergh and E. W. R. Lumby (eds), *Constitutional Relations Between Britain and India: The Transfer of Power, 1942–7* (London: Her Majesty's Stationery Office, 1970–1983) [hereafter *TOP*], vol. 6, pp. 554–6. Wavell to Pethick-Lawrence, 27 Nov. 1945.

2 Gurbaksh Singh Dhillon, *From My Bones: Memoirs of Col. Gurbaksh Singh Dhillon of the Indian National Army, including 1945 Red Fort Trial* (New Delhi: Aryan Books International, 1998), p. 509.

3 Malcolm Darling, *At Freedom's Door* (London: Oxford University Press, 1949), p. 17.

4 *The Times*, 25 Aug. 1939.

5 Jawaharlal Nehru, 15 May 1961, quoted in G. N. S. Raghavan (ed.), *M. Asaf Ali's Memoirs: the Emergence of Modern India* (Delhi: Ajanta, 1994), p. 246.

6 See in particular Christopher Bayly and Tim Harper, *Forgotten Armies: Britain's Asian Empire and the War with Japan* (London: Penguin, 2005); Indivar Kamtekar, 'A Different War Dance: State and Class in India 1939–1945', *Past and Present* no. 176 (2002): 187–221; Kaushik Roy (ed.), *War and Society in Colonial India, 1807–1945* (New York: Oxford University Press, 2006); Gajendra Singh, *The Testimonies of Indian Soldiers and the Two World Wars: Between Self and Sepoy* (London and New York: Bloomsbury Academic, 2014); Ashley Jackson, *The British Empire and the Second World War* (London and New York: Hambledon Continuum, 2006); Daniel Marston, *The Indian Army and the End of the Raj: Decolonising the Subcontinent* (Cambridge: Cambridge University Press, 2014); Benjamin Zachariah, 'The Creativity of Destruction: Wartime Imaginings of Development and Social Policy, c. 1942–1946', in Heike Liebau *et al.* (eds), *The World in the World Wars* (Leiden: Brill, 2010), pp. 547–78.

1 An Empire Committed

1   IOR MSS F309/1 Ralli Diary, 8 Sept., 12 Sept. and 19 Sept. 1939.

2   Desmond Young, *Try Anything Twice* (London: Hamish Hamilton, 1963), p. 265.

3   IOR MSS Eur C808 Memoir of Margaret Stavridi.

4   IOR MSS F309/1 Ralli Diary, 19 Sept. 1939.

5   IOR MSS E360/14 I. H. Macdonald, letter to parents, 14 May 1941.

6   Ibid., 19 May 1941.

7   Santha Rama Rau, *Home to India* (London: Victor Gollancz, 1946), p. 56.

8   In the ICS there had been a deliberate policy of 'Indianisation' – increasing the ratio of Indians holding posts – since the early 1920s and by 1939 of 1,299 posts in the ICS, 540 were held by Indians. Maintaining a European presence in the ICS became a struggle for the Indian Government during the war and ICS recruitment in Britain ceased in 1943. In the Indian Army, positions for Indian officers had been opening up since the 1920s, with ten reserved places at Sandhurst for Indian officers in the 1920s and the Indian Military Academy for officer training opened in 1932. By Jan. 1941 the ratio of Indian to British officers was 12:1.

9   These changes and differences within the ICS are discussed in more depth in Chapter Five.

10 J. Nehru, *The Discovery of India* (New Delhi: Penguin Books, 1960), p. 446.

11 John Glendevon, *The Viceroy at Bay: Lord Linlithgow in India, 1936–1943* (London: Collins, 1971), p. 161. This account is by Linlithgow's son.

12 IOR MSS Eur D609/18 Letters from Linlithgow to the Secretary of State for India, July–Dec. 1939.

13 IOR MSS Eur D609/18 Linlithgow to the Secretary of State for India, 14 Sept. 1939.

14 Ibid.

15 IOR MSS Eur D609/18 Linlithgow to the Secretary of State for India, 4 Sept. 1939.

16 Francis Tuker, *Gorkha: the Story of the Gurkhas of Nepal* (London: Constable & Company, 1957), p. 215.

17 A. K. Azad, *India Wins Freedom* (New Delhi: Orient Longman, 1959; new edn, 1988), p. 29.

18 B. R. Nanda (ed.), *Selected Works of Govind Ballabh Pant* (Delhi and Oxford: Oxford University Press, 1997), vol. 8, p. 466. Nehru to G. B.

Pant, 8 Dec. 1938. Indian nationalists and the Indian nationalist press vocally denounced anti-Semitism from early in the war, but the Indian public at large was far more divided about Jewish refugee settlement and later about Zionism and the creation of Israel. For further discussion see Yulia Egorova, *Jews and India: Perceptions and Image* (Abingdon, Oxon: Routledge, 2006), pp. 31–60.

19 S. Gopal (ed.), *Selected Works of Jawaharlal Nehru* (New Delhi: Orient Longman, 1972–1982) [hereafter *SWJN*], vol. 11, p. 31. To Rajendra Prasad, 16 May 1940.

20 P. R. Lele, *War and India's Freedom* (Bombay: Popular Book Depot, 1940), p. 32. Gandhi's statement at Simla, 5 Sept. 1939.

21 IOR MSS Eur D609/18 Linlithgow–Zetland Correspondence, 4 Sept. 1939.

22 Quoted in Sugata Bose, *His Majesty's Opponent: Subhas Chandra Bose and India's Struggle Against Empire* (Cambridge, MA: Harvard University Press, 2011), p. 169.

23 Young, *Try Anything Twice*, p. 265.

24 IOR MSS E360/14 I. H. Macdonald, letter to parents, 17 Jan. 1941.

25 *SWJN*, vol. 11, p. 31 and pp. 22–3. To Krishna Menon, 27 April 1940, and to Rajendra Prasad, 6 May 1940.

26 IOR MSS E360/14 I. H. Macdonald, letter to parents, 8 Sept. 1942.

27 *India. Legislation and Orders Relating to the War* (Delhi: Manager of Publications, 1942).

28 Young, *Try Anything Twice*, p. 250.

29 IOR MSS F309/1 Ralli Diary. Anglo-Indians – people of Eurasian or mixed heritage – were the descendants of mixed marriages dating back to the age of British conquest in the eighteenth century, when many early pioneers of empire had taken local wives. Their white descendants often quietly erased these mixed births from their family tree but small communities of Anglo-Indians lived on, often finding a niche in Raj employment, particularly on the railways. Enumerated in the 1941 census at only 140,422 people, Anglo-Indians were a small but critically important group in wartime, as many gravitated to the war services, regarded as much-needed 'loyalists' by the British.

30 Heinrich Harrer, *Seven Years in Tibet* (London: HarperCollins Perennial, 2005), pp. 1–2.

31 Muhammad Asad, *This Law of Ours and Other Essays* (Gibraltar: Dar al-Andalus, 1987), p. 1.

32 National Archives and Records Administration, Washington DC [hereafter NARA], NARA Calcutta Consulate General Records 1944: File 820.08, Box 143. Letter from A. Joschkowitz to the American Consulate in India, 11 Jan. 1944.

33 IOR L/PJ/7/4794 Letter addressed to Churchill, Sept. 1941.
34 Interview at SOAS with Christoph von Fürer-Haimendorf in 1996, https://www.soas.ac.uk/furer-haimendorf/biography/interview-with-christoph-von-furerhaimendorf.html.
35 IOR MSS Eur 272 Philip Finney papers, memoir dated 1979.
36 Ibid.
37 IOR L/PJ/5/238 Fortnightly Report [hereafter FNR], Punjab, Sept. and Aug., 1940. These are just some examples of action taken under the Defence of India Act; for instance, there were some forty-four cases in the first two weeks of Sept. 1940 in Punjab.
38 Ibid.

2 Peasants into Soldiers

1   Mulk Raj Anand, *Across the Black Waters* (Delhi: Orient Paperbacks, 2000 [1939]), p. 1.
2   IOR L/PO/5/32 memorandum by the Viceroy on frontier policy, Oct. 1939.
3   IOR L/PO/5/32 Cunningham to Viceroy. Frustration with the frontier and the uncertainty of events on the border was a perennial worry for viceroys. At the start of the century Lord Curzon had said, 'I do not prophesy about the future. No man who has read a page of Indian history will ever prophesy about the Frontier.' See also L/WS/1/298 and L/WS/1/1007 on the North-West Frontier.
4   National Archives, Kew, WO/106/3643, messages between the Commander-in-Chief of the Indian Army and the War Office, 1939–40.
5   Lionel Carter (ed.), *Punjab Politics 1936–1939: The Start of Provincial Autonomy; Governor's Fortnightly Reports and Other Key Documents* (Delhi: Manohar, 2004), p. 67. Craik to Linlithgow, 25 Nov. 1938.
6   Shah Nawaz Khan, later of the INA, recalled in his autobiography that 'every able-bodied member of my family joined the army' and that sixty-two members of his family were serving as officers in the Indian Army by 1945. *The INA Heroes: Autobiographies* (Lahore: Hero Publications, 1946), p. 13.
7   *SWJN*, vol. 11, p. 245, 17 Oct. 1940.
8   IOR R/2/593/50 Recruitment of Rajputs, 1940.
9   Ibid.
10 Ibid.
11 B. L. Cole, *The Recruiting Handbook for the Rajputana Classes* (Simla: Government of India, 1922). For further discussion of these handbooks

see the work of Gajendra Singh, *The Testimonies of Indian Soldiers: Between Self and Sepoy* (London and New York: Bloomsbury Academic, 2014), Kaushik Roy (ed.), *War and Society in Colonial India, 1807–1945* (Oxford and New York: Oxford University Press, 2006) and Tarak Barkawi, 'Culture and Combat in the Colonies: the Indian Army in the Second World War', *Journal of Contemporary History* 41, no. 2 (1 April 2006): 325–55.

12   J. Evatt, *Garhwalis Handbook* (Calcutta: Government of India, 1924).

13   Cole, *The Recruiting Handbook for the Rajputana Classes.*

14   'Memoirs of an old Koi Hai' (John Ffrench, unpubd manuscript, National Army Museum), Ref. 9507–79. Written in 1989.

15   Interview conducted with Sardar Ali by Youth Action, Blackburn and Darwen, 2012.

16   Mohammed Khan, b. 1922. North West Sound Archive. Interviewed 7 June 2004. Ref. 2005. 0194A.

17   Quoted in Christopher Somerville, *Our War: How the British Commonwealth Fought the Second World War* (London: Phoenix, 2005), p. 57. See also the transcripts of these interviews conducted by Christopher Somerville now held at the IWM.

18   National Archives, Kew, FO 766/18. Colonel G. Betham (British minister in Nepal) to the Maharaja of Nepal, 2 Dec. 1940.

19   Mary Des Chene, *Relics of Empire: A Cultural History of the Gurkhas* (PhD thesis, Stanford University, 1991), pp. 287–8.

20   Bernard Pignede, *The Gurungs* (Kathmandu: Ratna Pustak Bhandar, 1993), p. 253.

21   Des Chene, *Relics of Empire*, p. 248.

22   Gurkha Army Ex-Servicemen's Organization *et al.*, *The Gurkhas: The Forgotten Veterans* (Kathmandu: Gurkha Army Ex-Servicemen's Organization, 2005), p. 50.

23   For a general history of the Gurkhas, see Tony Gould, *Imperial Warriors: Britain and the Gurkhas* (London: Granta Books, 1999) and Chris Bellamy, *The Gurkhas: Special Force* (London: John Murray, 2011). For related aspects of Nepal's twentieth-century history, see Pratyoush Onta, *The Politics of Bravery: A History of Nepali Nationalism* (PhD thesis, University of Pennsylvania, 1996), and for an assessment of how Gurkhas have been depicted in the west, Lionel Caplan, *Warrior Gentlemen: 'Gurkhas' in the Western Imagination* (Providence: Berghahn Books, 1995).

24   This translation is from the Gurkha Museum, Pokhara, Nepal.

3 Into the Middle East and North Africa

1 Nila Kantan quoted in Christopher Somerville, *Our War* (London: Phoenix, 2005), p. 57.

2 Krishna Kumar Tewari, *A Soldier's Voyage of Self-Discovery* (Auroville: Tewari, 1995), p. 12.

3 John Saville, *Memoirs from the Left* (Talgarth: Merlin, 2003), p. 56.

4 'Memoirs of an old Koi Hai' (John Ffrench, unpubd manuscript, National Army Museum) Ref. 9507–79. Written in 1989.

5 Ashali Varma, *The Victoria Cross: A Love Story* (Delhi: Pearson, 2013), letter from Sudan, 16 Nov. 1940. This account is by his daughter and includes copies of the letters Premindra Singh Bhagat sent back to India.

6 *Indian Army Post Offices in the Second World War* (New Delhi: Army Postal Service Association, 1982), p. 321.

7 Varma, *The Victoria Cross* (The War in North Africa 1940–41).

8 IOR L/Mil/17/5/2333 Matters of interest to Indian Soldiers and their families.

9 IOR L/PJ/12/654 Censorship Reports, 5 Nov.–19 Nov. 1942.

10 Ibid.

11 Ibid.

12 Author's interview with Mr Simar Narayan Singh, son of Harnarain Singh, Oct. 2011. He was a major during the war but later served as military secretary to the prime minister of India and was also military attaché in London.

13 Bernard Pignede, *The Gurungs* (Kathmandu: Ratna Pustak Bhandar, 1993), pp. 260–1.

14 IOR L/PJ/5/188 FNR Twynam to Linlithgow, 12 Jan. 1940.

15 Partha Sarathi Gupta, *Radio and the Raj 1921–47* (Calcutta: K. P. Bagchi Centre for Studies in Social Sciences, 1995), pp. 33–5.

16 Author's communication with Sayeed Hasan Khan. See also Sayeed Hasan Khan, *Across the Seas: Incorrigible Drift* (Karachi: Ushba, 2013).

17 IOR MSS E360/14 I. H. Macdonald, letter to parents, 28 March 1940.

18 M. A. Quraishi, *Indian Administration, Pre and Post Independence: Memoirs of an I.C.S.* (Delhi: BR Publishing, 1985), pp. 86–7.

19 IOR FNR, L/PJ/5/238 Punjab, first half of Jan. 1940.

20 *SWJN*, vol. 11, p. 378. Nehru to Michael Carritt, 23 March 1940.

21 IOR, FNR, L/PJ/5/238 Punjab, 1 Dec. 1939.

22 Clive Branson, *British Soldier in India: The Letters of Clive Branson* (London: International Publishers, 1945), p. 24. Sept. 1942.

23 Varma, *The Victoria Cross*, letter dated 10 Feb. 1941.

4 Free and Willing Human Beings

1   IOR L/PJ/12/500; IOR L/PJ/7/1715; MSS Eur C826 (1940) Udham Singh
    Papers. A number of hagiographies exist such as B. S. Maighowalia Sardar,
    Udham Singh: A Prince amongst Patriots of India (Hoshiarpur: Chhabra
    Printing Press, 1969). Trial transcripts are reproduced in Navtej Singh and
    Avtar Singh Jouhl (eds), *Emergence of the Image: Redact Documents of Udham
    Singh* (New Delhi: National Book Organisation, 2002).

2   IOR/L/PJ/12/500 Udham Singh: activities outside India; assassination
    of Sir Michael O'Dwyer; trial, appeal and execution in London.

3   Indians took part in the Battle of Britain as fighter pilots in the RAF.
    An Indian contingent of the Royal Indian Army Service Corps, including
    a unit of the Bikaner State forces, served in France during the campaign
    on the Western Front, and some were evacuated from Dunkirk.

4   Savitri Chowdhary, *I Made My Home in England* (Laindon: Grant-West,
    undated), pp. 50–2.

5   Rozina Visram , *Lascars and Princes: Indians in Britain, 1700–1947* (London:
    Pluto Press, 1986), p. 253.

6   National Archives, Kew, MT 9/3423 SS *Prome*.

7   Conditions of the Lascars are discussed in a number of books, including
    Gopalan Balachandran, *Globalizing Labour? Indian Seafarers and World
    Shipping, c. 1870–1945* (New Delhi: Oxford University Press, 2012), and
    Ravi Ahuja, 'Networks of Subordination – Networks of the
    Subordinated: The Ordered Spaces of South Asian Maritime Labour
    in an Age of Imperialism (c. 1890–1947)', in Ashwini Tambe and Harold
    Fischer-Tiné (eds), *The Limits of British Colonial Control in South Asia*
    (Abingdon and New York: Routledge, 2009).

8   National Archives, Kew, MT 9/3423.

9   Ibid.

10 Ibid.

11 I am grateful to Nick Hewitt of the IWM for this information.

12 Quoted in Georgie Wemyss, 'Litoral Struggles, Liminal Lives: Indian
    Merchant Seafarers' Resistances', in Rehana Ahmed and Sumita
    Mukherjee (eds), *South Asian Resistances in Britain, 1858–1947* (London
    and New York: Continuum, 2012), p. 48.

5 Not a Paisa, Not a Man

1   Amery described Churchill's reaction in his personal diary, quoted
    in Wm Roger Louis, *In the Name of God Go! Leo Amery and the*

British Empire in the Age of Churchill (New York and London: Norton, 1992), p. 133.

2 B. R. Tomlinson, *The Economy of Modern India, 1860–1970* (Cambridge: Cambridge University Press, 1996), pp. 160–61. By the end of the war Britain owed India £1.3 billion.

3 *SWJN*, vol. 11, pp. 275–7. Letter to Gandhi, 19 Aug. 1940.

4 M. A. Quraishi, *Indian Administration*, p. 21, p. 33.

5 Tan Tai Yong, *The Garrison State: Military, Government and Society in Colonial Punjab, 1849–1947* (New Delhi: Sage Publications, 2005), p. 284.

6 William Gould, *Bureaucracy, Community and Influence in India* (London: Routledge, 2010), p. 37.

7 IOR L/PJ/7/3970.

8 IOR L/PJ/12/655 Censorship reports dated 14–27 July 1943.

9 IOR L/PJ/7/3970 Linlithgow to Provincial Governors, 9 Oct. 1940.

10 Ibid., Linlithgow correspondence with Provincial Governors, 9 Oct. 1940; 24 Sept. 1940.

11 This vacancy in the Public Works in Punjab attracted only four British applicants, of whom only three appeared for interview. 'The only one who has accepted and has arrived in India is the son of a retail grocer in Liverpool', Craik complained, 'and the impression of the Chief Engineer who has seen him is that he is entirely unsuitable.' Craik to Linlithgow, 22 Nov. 1938 in Lionel Carter (ed.), *Punjab Politics 1940–1943: Strains of War: Governors' Fortnightly Reports and Other Key Documents* (New Delhi: Manohar, 2005), p. 264.

12 For discussions about the changing nature of the ICS see among others the work of Judith Brown, *Modern India: The Origins of an Asian Democracy* (Oxford: Oxford University Press, 1994), Benjamin Zachariah, *Developing India: An Intellectual and Social History, c. 1930–1950* (New Delhi: Oxford University Press, 2005), Clive Dewey, *Anglo-Indian Attitudes: The Mind of the Indian Civil Service* (London: Hambledon, 1993), David C. Potter, *India's Political Administrators, 1919–1983* (Oxford: Clarendon, 1986), and William Gould, *Bureaucracy, Community and Influence in India* (London: Routledge, 2010).

13 *Collected Works of Mahatma Gandhi* [hereafter *CWMG*], vol. 68, pp. 332–3, 28 March 1936.

14 'Should India help the Commonwealth's war effort?': extracts from a speech by the Hon'ble Sir Muhammad Zafrullah Khan, law member in the Central Legislative Assembly, on 18 Nov. 1940 (Accra, 1940).

15 *The Health Survey and Development Committee Report* [hereafter the *Bhore Report*] (New Delhi: Government of India, 1946), p. 9.

16 Aruna Asaf Ali, *Fragments from the Past: Selected Writings and Speeches*

of Aruna Asaf Ali (New Delhi: Patriot Publishers, 1989); Asaf Ali papers in the Nehru Memorial Museum and Library, New Delhi; IOR files on Asaf Ali IOR/L/I/1/1269.

17 CSAS, Sucheta Kripalani, interviewed by Uma Shanker in 1974.

6 Bombed to Hell

1 *The Tiger Strikes: India's Fight in the Middle East* (Calcutta: Government of India, 1943), p. 57.

2 National Archives, Kew, WO 169/2838, War Diaries British Troops, Sudan and Eritrea: Infantry, 4/6 Rajputana Rifles, 1 Feb. 1941.

3 Ibid., 7 Feb. 1941.

4 IOR MSS F274/15 Diaries, intelligence summaries and eighteen photographs concerning the capture of Keren (Italian East Africa); and the capture of Asmara in the Sudan, Feb.–March 1941. More generally on Keren, for military accounts see Compton Mackenzie, *Eastern Epic* (London: Chatto & Windus, 1951), and A. Brett-James, *Ball of Fire: The Fifth Indian Division in the Second World War* (London: Gale & Polden, 1951). A good personal account is Peter Cochrane, *Charlie Company: In Service with C Company 2nd Queen's Own Cameron Highlanders, 1940–44* (Stroud: Spellmount, 2007).

5 National Archives, Kew, WO 169/2838, War Diaries British Troops, Sudan and Eritrea: Infantry, 4/6 Rajputana Rifles, 7 Feb. 1941; 8–9 Feb. 1941.

6 Cochrane, *Charlie Company*, p. 66.

7 National Archives, Kew, WO 169/2838, War Diaries British Troops, Sudan and Eritrea: Infantry, 4/6 Rajputana Rifles, 12–13 Feb. 1941.

8 Ibid.

9 Ibid.

10 Ibid.

11 National Archives, Kew, WO 373/28/69, Recommendation for Victoria Cross for Richpal Ram, 4/6 Rajputana Rifles.

12 Details of these graves can be found at the CWGC website, http://www.cwgc.org/

13 There are discrepancies between published casualty figures for Keren. The official British history of events published in 1954 describes 3,765 casualties in the entire six-week battle and this figure has been repeated elsewhere in later accounts. But the Official British Ministry of Information book on the East Africa Campaign published the year after the battle gave the figure 4,000–5,000. A more contemporary

manuscript, lecture notes for senior military staff written in the imme-diate aftermath of events by Thomas Wynford Rees, a colonel in the Indian Army in command of a brigade of the 5th Indian Division, and held today in the India Office Library in London, cites potentially higher figures. He estimated in the second battle in early–mid-March that the 4th Division alone took 1,800 casualties and the 5th Division took another 1,800 including the wounded. See IOR MSS F274/15.

14   Mackenzie, *Eastern Epic*, p. 60.

15   Winston Churchill, *The Grand Alliance*, vol. 3 (London: Mariner Books, 1986), pp. 79–80.

16   *The Tiger Strikes*, p. 57.

17   National Archives, Kew, WO 373/28/69, Recommendation for Victoria Cross for Richpal Ram, 4/6 Rajputana Rifles. Medal citation, 4 July 1941.

18   Quoted in Varma, *The Victoria Cross*.

19   IOR MSS E360/14 I. H. Macdonald, letter to parents, 24 Jan. 1942.

20   *The Times*, London, 11 Nov. 1941. See also Indian newspapers including *The Statesman*.

21   *The Tiger Strikes*, p. xi.

22   Ibid., p. 13.

23   Interview conducted by Iqroop Sandhawalia with Major General Kartar Singh, 2011.

24   IOR L/PJ/12/654.

25   For an excellent and detailed analysis of this debate about courts martial and many other aspects of officer relationships see Marston, *The Indian Army*, p. 91.

26   Typescript copy of a report, 2 March 1943, from an anonymous officer of the 2nd Bn Cheshire Regiment, National Army Museum, enclosed in the papers of Lt-Col. J. A. C. Greenwood, Ref: 1992–08–36–57.

27   Cited in Tarak Barkawi, 'Army, Ethnicity and Society', in Kaushik Roy (ed.), *War and Society in Colonial India* (New York: Oxford University Press, 2006), p. 439. See also Tariq Rahman, 'The British Learning of Hindustani', *Contemporary Perspectives* 2.1 (2008), pp. 46–73.

28   This idea about the reliance on intermediaries is also developed in some of the interviews with Indian Army officers by Barkawi, 'Army, Ethnicity and Society', in Kaushik Roy (ed.), *War and Society in Colonial India*, pp. 439–41.

29   Transcript of interview conducted with Rajinder Singh Dhatt by Dr Kanwaljit in Hounslow, 2008. See also, National Army Museum, Ref: 2008–05–26, oral history of Rajinder Singh Dhatt, interview conducted by Justin Saddington in Hounslow, London, April 2008.

30 IOR W/S/1/1358 DCGS India, to India Office, 26 Jan. 1943.

31 IOR L/WS/1/1433.

32 There was also another brothel set up for more senior military officers, as noted in IOR MSS F274/15.

33 Satyen Basu, *A Doctor in the Army* (Calcutta: Sri Bajendranath Bose, 1960), pp. 96–100.

34 IOR L/WS/1/1363 Subversive activities against the Indian Army by Germany and Italy.

35 By November 1941 at least 46,000 Italian POWs had arrived in India.

36 Elios Toschi, *Ninth Time Lucky* (London: William Kimber, 1955), p. 90.

7 *Money Coming, Money Coming*

1   IOR MSS F309/1 Ralli Diary.

2   For a discussion of this see Taylor Sherman, 'From Hell to Paradise? Voluntary Transfer of Convicts to the Andaman Islands, 1921–1940', *Modern Asian Studies* 43, no. 2 (2009). Strategically, the Andamans were believed to be barely significant, shielded by the might of British power vested in South-East Asia's arc and the fortress of Singapore.

3   IOR L/PJ/8/485 Waterfall to Linlithgow, 5 July 1941.

4   *Foundation stone laying ceremony of the Scindia Co.'s shipyard at 'Gandhigram', Vizagapatam, by Babu Rajendra Prasad on Saturday the 21st June 1941* (Bombay: Scindia Company, 1941). See also G. D. Khanolkar, *Walchand Hirachand* (Bombay: Walchand, 1969), pp. 392–7.

5   Walchand was a shipowner and entrepreneur. Born into a Gujarati trading family in 1882 he had started building his fortune as a railway contractor and had soon diversified into sugar refining, insurance and newspapers but his real interest was in shipping and transport companies. See G. D. Khanolkar, *Walchand Hirachand*.

6   CWMG, vol. 79, p. 51. Gandhi to Linlithgow, 26 July 1940.

7   See Ashley Jackson, *The British Empire and the Second World War* (London and New York: Hambledon Continuum, 2006), p. 358.

8   Medha Kudaisya, *The Life and Times of G. D. Birla* (Delhi: Oxford University Press, 2003), p. 214.

9   *India at War, Rising Flood of Vast Resources* (London: Ministry of Information, 1941).

10 Quoted in Georgie Wemyss, 'Litoral Struggles, Liminal Lives: Indian Merchant Seafarers' Resistances', in Rehana Ahmed and Sumita Mukherjee (eds), *South Asian Resistances in Britain, 1858–1947* (London and New York: Continuum, 2012), p. 46.

11 For discussion of wartime labour and industrial conditions see in particular, Rajnarayan Chandavarkar, *Imperial Power and Popular Politics: Class, Resistance and the State in India c.1850–1950* (Cambridge: Cambridge University Press, 1998).

12 *Bhore Report*, p. 68.

13 Daniel Thorner, 'Problems of Economic Development in India', *Annals of the American Academy of Political and Social Science* 268 (March 1950), pp. 96–7.

14 IOR L/PJ/7/4704 Air Raid Precautions in India, Mar. 1939–Dec. 1943.

15 The India Office Records contain many files about propaganda and information efforts during the war, for instance IOR/L/I/1/847, MSS Eur E360/23, IOR L/I/1/1084. For a detailed account of propaganda and information efforts, see Sanjoy Bhattacharya, *Propaganda and Information in Eastern India 1939–45: A Necessary Weapon of War* (Kolkata: Routledge, 2000).

16 NAI Home F. 161/41 Police (1941).

17 IOR MSS E360/14 I. H. Macdonald, letter to parents, 19 May 1941.

18 For details of inflation and money supply see J. M. Brown, 'India', in I. C. D. Dear and M. R. D. Foot (eds), *The Oxford Companion to World War II* (Oxford: Oxford University Press, 2001), p. 557.

19 Hitler was making direct comparisons in 1941 between Britain's control of India and Germany's future control of Russia, reportedly saying, 'What India was for England, the territories of Russia will be for us.' See Romain Hayes, *Bose in Nazi Germany* (London: Hurst, 2011), n. 5.

20 This letter is reproduced in full in Krishna Dutta and Andrew Robinson, *Rabindranath Tagore: The Myriad-minded Man* (London: Bloomsbury, 1995), p. 371. Letter to Leonard Woolf, 9 March 1941.

21 For a longer discussion see Sumit Sarkar, *Modern India, 1885–1947* (Basingstoke, Hants: Macmillan, 1989), pp. 384–5.

22 CSAS, B. P. Jain, interviewed by Uma Shanker in 1987. On the career of M. N. Roy, Kris Manjapra, *M. N. Roy: Marxism and Colonial Cosmopolitanism* (Delhi: Routledge 2010).

8 An Empire Exposed

1 George Orwell, *Orwell: The Observer Years* (London: Atlantic Books, 2003), pp. 2–3. Article in *The Observer*, 22 Feb. 1942.

2 National Archives, Kew, WO 106/3684, Plan for the Defence of North East India 12 Feb. 1942; Famine Inquiry Commission, *Report on Bengal* (Delhi: Government of India, 1945), p. 27.

3 National Archives, Kew, War Office 106/3684.

4 It is perhaps not incidental that Indian industrialists lobbied hard against the scorched earth policy being used against their own factories. See, for example, NARA, New Delhi General Mission records, 1942: 832–851.5, Box 14.

5 *CWMG*, vol. 82, p. 240. *Harijan*, 3 May 1942.

6 Quoted in Francis Hutchins, *India's Revolution: Gandhi and the Quit India Movement* (Cambridge, MA: Harvard University Press, 1973), p. 191.

7 IOR L/PJ/5/149 Herbert to Linlithgow, 19 June 1943.

8 Famine Inquiry Commission, *Report on Bengal*, p. 27.

9 Ibid., p. 27. Asok Mitra, *Towards Independence: Memoirs of an Indian Civil Servant* (Bombay: Popular Prakashan, 1991), p. 105. See also Asok Mitra, 'Famine of 1943 in Vikrampur Dacca', *Economic and Political Weekly* 24, no. 5 (4 Feb. 1989), pp. 253–64.

10 Ashley Jackson, 'Defend Lanka Your Home', *War in History* 16, no. 2 (2009), p. 217.

11 W. J. Slim, *Defeat into Victory* (London: Pan, 2009), p. 150.

12 A. K. Azad, *India Wins Freedom* (New Delhi: Longman, 1988), p. 40.

13 IOR FNR 19/01/42.

14 Philip Mason, *A Matter of Honour: An Account of the Indian Army, Its Officers and Men* (London: Jonathan Cape, 1974), p. 493.

15 Slim, *Defeat into Victory*, p. 125.

16 Ramesh Benegal, *Burma to Japan with Azad Hind* (Olympia Fields, IL: Lancer, 2009), p. 7.

17 Benegal Dinker Rao, 'Barefoot from Burma to India, 1942', http://www.dadinani.com, accessed June 2013.

18 IOR MSS Eur C394 Veronica Downing memoir.

19 IOR MSS Eur F174/1309 Indian Tea Association report on the evacuation of troops and civilians from Burma by the Pangsau route, May to July 1942.

20 Benegal, *Burma to Japan with Azad Hind*, p. 6.

21 Angela Bolton, *The Maturing Sun: An Army Nurse in India, 1942–45* (London: Imperial War Museum, 1986), p. 77.

22 Ibid., pp. 77–8. Diary entry, May 1942.

23 Dr Krishnan Gurumurthy, 'Exodus from Burma, 1941: A Personal Account', http://amitavghosh.com/blog, accessed 2011.

24 IOR MSS Eur F174/1309, Indian Tea Association report on the evacuation of troops and civilians from Burma by the Pangsau route, May to July 1942.

25 Dr Krishnan Gurumurthy, 'Exodus from Burma, 1941: A Personal Account', http://amitavghosh.com/blog, accessed 2011.

26 M. M. Kudaisya, *The Life and Times of G. D. Birla* (Delhi: Oxford University Press, 2003), p. 221.

27 IOR FNR L/PJ/5/204 second half June 1942; IOR FNR L/PJ/5/205, second half of May 1942.

28 NARA US Consulate Calcutta, Classified General Records 1943: 030–1943: 711.5 Box 8, Report on Civil Evacuation from Burma by Martin Hillenbrand, 6 Feb. 1943.

29 *The Statesman*, 3 March 1942.

30 Quoted in Rana Mitter, *China's War with Japan, 1937–1945: The Struggle for Survival* (London: Allen Lane, 2013), p. 248.

31 *CWMG*, vol. 82, p. 377. *Harijan*, 14 June 1942.

9 Urban Panic

1 Richard Symonds, *In the Margins of Independence: A Relief Worker in India and Pakistan, 1942–1949* (Karachi: Oxford University Press, 2001), pp. 12–13.

2 IOR L/PJ/7/4704 ARP Bombay, Governor's Report, 23 Feb. 1942.

3 Ibid. Press statement by Gandhi at Bardoli, 19 Dec. 1941.

4 G. Allana (ed.), *Pakistan Movement: Historic Documents* (Lahore: Islamic Book Service, 1988), p. 301, 21 March 1942, Jinnah speech.

5 Author's communication with Sulochana Simhadri Pillarisetti, 2011.

6 IOR L/PJ/7/4704 Amery in House of Commons, 18 Dec. 1941.

7 Ibid. For a detailed assessment of air raid protection and the distribution of gas masks in Indian cities see the forthcoming work of Susan Grayzel.

8 IOR L/PJ/7/4704 Air Raid Precautions in India, Mar. 1939–Dec. 1943.

9 Ibid., ARP Problems of Recruitment, Dec. 1941.

10 IOR L/PJ/4/4731 *Shelter Discipline*, published *c.* Jan. 1942.

11 *Harijan*, 8 Feb. 1942.

12 C. A. Bayly and T. N. Harper, *Forgotten Armies* (London: Penguin, 2005) pp. 337–8. Purana Qila would also be used as a refugee camp during Partition in 1947.

13 G. D. Khanolkar, *Walchand Hirachand*, p. 427.

14 S. K. Bose and S. Bose (eds), *Azad Hind: Subhas Chandra Bose Writings and Speeches 1941–3* (London: Anthem Press, 2004), pp. 63–4. This first radio broadcast speech on 19 Feb. 1942 also referred to 'Anglo-American Imperialism'.

15 Ibid., p. 74. Speech broadcast over Berlin Radio, 19 March 1942. Bose was wrong about this of course and privately had begun to doubt

the intentions and policies of the Japanese and Germans. But he did not criticise the internal politics of the Third Reich or Japan, and regarded these policies as their own domestic issues. For details of this, see Leonard Gordon, *Brothers against the Raj* (New York: Columbia University Press, 1990), p. 462.

16 IOR L/PJ/4/4731 *Shelter Discipline.*

17 IOR L/PJ/4/4704 29 Dec. 1942.

18 IOR MSS E360/14 I. H. Macdonald, letter to parents, 9 June 1943.

19 IOR, FNR, L/PJ/5/204, Feb. 1942.

20 IOR, FNR, L/PJ/ 5/204. Hope to Linlithgow, 18 April 1942.

21 *TOP*, vol. 2, p. 4. Congress Working Committee Resolution, 28 April 1942; A. Srivasthan, 'When 5 lakh fled the city in 2 weeks', *The Hindu*, 3 Oct. 2012,and other articles by Srivasthan on related subjects in *The Hindu*.

22 W. J. Slim, *Defeat into Victory*, p. 181.

23 Sunil Amrith, *Crossing the Bay of Bengal: the Furies of Nature and the Fortunes of Migrants* (Cambridge, MA: Harvard University Press, 2013), p. 103.

24 Ibid. Also Sunil Amrith, 'Reconstructing the "Plural Society": Asian Migration Between Empire and Nation, 1940–1948,' *Past and Present* 210, no. suppl. 6 (2011): p. 237.

25 T. R. Sareen (ed.), *Select Documents on the Indian National Army* (Delhi: Agam Prakashan, n.d.), p. 173. 3 May 1943.

26 Kevin Blackburn, 'Recalling War Trauma of the Pacific War and the Japanese Occupation in the Oral History of Malaysia and Singapore', *Oral History Review* 36.2 (2009), p. 246.

27 *The INA Heroes: Autobiographies* (Lahore: Hero Publications, 1946), p. 74. This story is recalled by Shah Nawaz Khan in his autobiography.

28 Interview conducted by Iqroop Sandhawalia with Major General Kartar Singh, 2011.

29 G. Allana, (ed.), *Pakistan Movement: Historic Documents*, p. 304. Resolution of AIML, 6 April 1942.

30 Dr Krishnan Gurumurthy, 'Exodus from Burma, 1941: A Personal Account', http:/amitavghosh.com/blog, accessed 2011.

31 NARA US Consulate Calcutta, Classified General Records 1943: 030–1943: 711.5 Box 8, Report on Civil Evacuation from Burma by Martin Hillenbrand, 6 Feb. 1943. See also Hillenbrand's memoir, *Fragments of Our Time: Memoirs of a Diplomat* (Athens, GA: University of Georgia Press, 1998). He later became an important cold war ambassador to Germany.

32 Hugh Tinker, 'A Forgotten Long March: The Indian Exodus from

Burma, 1942', *Journal of Southeast Asian Studies* (1975): 1–15. Tinker, later an academic, was present at the time as an eyewitness in Burma.

33 Indivar Kamtekar, 'The Shiver of 1942', *Studies in History* 18, no. 1 (2002).

10 *The World at the Door*

1   *The Telegraph*, India, 28 Dec. 1942.

2   G. Allana (ed.), *Pakistan Movement: Historic Documents*, p. 299. Muslim League Council Resolution, 23 Feb. 1942.

3   Documents reproduced in Association of Poles in India, *Poles in India, 1942–1948* (London: Amolibros, 2013), p. 74. See also IOR/L/PJ/8/412.

4   This was partly because of an old friendship between his own father and a Polish pianist which dated back to the First World War.

5   *Times of India* cited in Association of Poles in India, *Poles in India 1942–1948* (London: Amolibros, 2013), p. 91.

6   IOR L/PJ/8/412 Linlithgow to Amery, June 1942.

7   NAI, f. 93/41 – Jails (Home, 1941). Secret telegram, Home Department to Chief Commissioner, Andamans, 21 Dec. 1941.

8   Ibid.

9   NAI, f. 93/41 – Jails (Home, 1941). Secret letter from Port Blair – C. F. Waterfall in Andamans to E. Conran-Smith in Delhi, 23–24 Dec. 1941.

10 Ibid.

11 NAI f. 93/41 – Jails (Home, 1941). Evacuation of ex-military prisoners and other dangerous convicts from the Andamans and convicted and detained fifth columnists from Burma.

12 *The Statesman*, 12 April 1942. Waterfall was later awarded a knighthood for his services in the Andamans and lived until 1952.

13 NAI f. 93/41 – Jails (Home, 1941). Mercy petition of ex-military prisoner Bhajan Singh, forwarded by the Government of Central Provinces and Berar, 14 May 1942.

14 Ibid.

15 Ibid.

16 NAI, Home Dept 46/2/39 – Jails. Letter from Bombay's Home Department to Home Dept Government of India, 18 Dec. 1942.

17 NAI, Home Dept 46/2/39 – Jails. Secretary Home Dept. Bombay to Home Dept. Government of India, 12 Jan. 1943.

18 NAI, Home Dept 46/2/39 – Jails. Letter from Government of India to all provincial governments, 14 May 1943.

19 Jayant Dasgupta, *Japanese in Andaman and Nicobar Islands: Red Sun over Black Water* (New Delhi: Manas, 2002), p. 45.

11 Thirty Months Too Late

1   *The Statesman*, 16 March 1942.

2   George Orwell, *Orwell and Politics* (London: Penguin, 2001), Orwell Diary, 14 March 1942; Nicholas Owen, 'The Cripps Mission of 1942: A Reinterpretation', *Journal of Imperial and Commonwealth History* 30, no. 1 (2002), p. 79. See also R. J. Moore on the Cripps Mission in *Churchill, Cripps and India, 1939–1945* (Oxford: Oxford University Press, 1979).

3   Derision of the Cripps mission on the Azad Fauj radio service may also have been influential. See Jane Robbins, 'The Radio Battle for India', *Japan Forum* 7, no. 2 (1995), p. 218.

4   *Statesman*, 31 March 1942.

5   *Statesman*, 12 April 1942. My analysis is in agreement with the assessment of Nicholas Owen, who also emphasises the centrality of the defence portfolio. As he writes, 'Congress was in no position to accept the Cripps Offer unless it conceded a real and far-reaching transfer of power, sufficient to negotiate peace terms with the Japanese if it proved necessary'.

6   Quoted in Wm Roger Louis, *In the Name of God Go!* (New York: W. W. Norton, 1992), p. 151.

7   Ibid., p. 133. This article unpicks the subtle and complex relationship between Amery and Churchill but also draws attention to some of Churchill's more extreme views about India. See also Madhusree Mukerjee, *Churchill's Secret War* (New York: Basic Books, 2011).

8   J. Ahmad (ed.), *Speeches and Writings of Mr Jinnah*, vol. 2 (Lahore: Shaikh Muhammad Ashraf, 1964), p. 245.

9   Ibid., p. 230. Presidential address of Jinnah, March 1940.

10 M. A. Quraishi, *Indian Administration* (Delhi: B. R. Publishing, 1985), p. 71.

11 See, for example, Ian Talbot, 'The Role of the Crowd in the Muslim League Struggle for Pakistan', *Journal of Imperial and Commonwealth History* 21, no. 2 (1993): 307–33. Also the work of Ayesha Jalal and David Gilmartin on the development of the Muslim League.

12 Allana (ed.), *Pakistan Movement: Historic Documents*, p. 255. Resolution of Working Committee, 17 June 1940.

13 See for example on the Khaksars, Markus Daechsel, *The Politics of*

Self-Expression: The Urdu Middle-Class Milieu in Mid-Twentieth-Century India and Pakistan (London: Routledge, 2006), and Markus Daechsel, 'Scientism and its discontents: the Indo-Muslim Fascism of Inayatullah Khan al-Mashriqui', *Modern Intellectual History* 3, no. 3 (2006). There is an extensive literature on the development of right-wing Hindu groups including the work of Christophe Jaffrelot, Thomas Blom Hansen and William Gould. On wartime paramilitary groups and militias, there is the forthcoming work of Ali Raza and Franziska Roy.

14 CSAS, Ram Krishna, interviewed by Uma Shanker in 1987.

15 Figure quoted in Ian Copland, *The Princes of India in the Endgame of Empire, 1917–1947* (Cambridge: Cambridge University Press, 2002), p. 183.

16 *Life*, 12 May 1941. On the economic and political transformations of Indian princely states see Ian Copland's excellent account in *The Princes of India*, pp. 183–228. Also, the studies by Janaki Nair and Barbara Ramusack.

17 *TOP*, vol. 2, p. 216. Amery to Linlithgow, 16 June 1942.

18 B. L. Raina, *Official History of the Indian Armed Forces in the Second World War (1939–45): Medical Services, Administration* (New Delhi: Combined Inter-Services Historical Section, 1990 [first published 1953]), p. 418.

12 Welcome to Bombay

1 The number of British troops stationed in India rose from 43,000 in 1939 to 240,000 in 1945; while by 1943 American members of the forces in India were estimated to number 120,000.

2 *Welcome to Bombay*, 1945, p. 3.

3 John Saville, *Memoirs from the Left* (Talgarth: Merlin, 2003), p. 57.

4 Thomas Ray Foltz, 'My Life as a GI Joe in World War II', http://cbi-theater-1.home.comcast.net.

5 Clive Branson, *British Soldier in India* (London: International Publishers, 1945), p. 9. 31 May 1942.

6 Frank Moraes, *Witness to an Era* (London: Weidenfeld & Nicolson, 1973), p. 111.

7 E. E. Prebble, 'Venereal Disease in India', *Sexually Transmitted Infections* 22, no. 2 (June 1946), pp. 55–62.

8 See Wendy Webster, *Englishness and Empire 1939–1965* (Oxford: Oxford University Press, 2007).

9 IOR L/WS/1/1357 Morale of British troops in India.

10 Nonetheless, some Indian politicians made direct appeals for US intervention. J. P. Narayan made a long appeal to US servicemen mentioning his own education and time spent in the USA: 'tell folks the true state

of affairs here'. See P. N. Chopra and S. R. Bakshi (eds.), *Quit India Movement: British Secret Documents* (New Delhi: Interprint, 1986), p. 401.

11 On US–British relations over the Indian question during the Second World War and the details of the Johnson mission see Kenton Clymer, *Quest for Freedom: The United States and India's Independence* (New York: Columbia University Press, 1995).

12 Quoted in Tom Pocock, *Alan Moorehead* (London: Pimlico/Random House, 2011). The India Office noted internally: 'It is not an easy matter for the authorities in India to "handle" these American correspondents' and that policy should be to 'nurse them as much as possible'. See IOR L/I/803 American Journalists and Photographers in India, 14 Oct. 1941.

13 Douglas Devaux Collection (AFC/2001/001/89168), Veterans History Project, American Folklife Center, Library of Congress.

14 *Hellbird Herald*, 20 Feb. 1945.

15 Ibid.

16 E. E. Prebble, 'Venereal Disease in India', *Sexually Transmitted Infections* 22, no. 2 (1946), p. 56.

17 IOR L/PJ/12/654, 1942.

18 IOR FNR L/PJ/5/205 Hope to Linlithgow, 25 Jan. 1942.

19 Ibid.

20 *CWMG*, vol. 82, p. 129. Letter to Desmond Young, 21 March 1942.

21 IOR MSS E360/14 I. H. Macdonald, letter to parents, 25 Feb. 1943.

22 NARA US Consulate New Delhi, Classified General Records 1943: 800–1943: 181.33, Box 9. Memorandum, 6 Feb. 1943.

23 Nico Slate, *Colored Cosmospolitanism* (Cambridge, MA: Harvard University Press, 2012), p. 134.

24 IOR L/WS/1/1433 anonymous quote from a letter by a British officer, India Internal Intelligence Summary, 10 April 1942.

25 IOR L/WS/1/1357 Morale of British troops in India, 1943.

26 Ibid.

27 Ibid.

28 Ibid.

29 National Archives, Kew, WO 32/10664, On the formation of the WAC (I). The WAC (I) had been formed in April 1942 in the midst of the crisis surrounding the fall of Burma and the bombing of India's coastline.

30 IOR MSS F309/1 Ralli Diary. One afternoon, on her way home from cipher work in Government House, Sydney Ralli saw a crowd at the gate outside Birla House. Above the crowd, she glimpsed Nehru standing on the bumper of a car talking to the people and stopped her car: 'Dressed in spotless rough kaddar he was most impressive. He spoke with few small gestures. His eyes looked sunken and his face

with deep troughs in it. He looked older than the numerous press photographs of him show.'

31 IOR MSS Eur C394 Veronica Downing memoir.

32 W. J. Slim, *Defeat into Victory* (London: Pan, 2009), pp. 230–1.

33 *IBT Roundup*, Oct. 1942.

34 Advertisement in *The Statesman*, 11 March 1942. On the career of the jazz musician Teddy Weatherford and his wartime popularity in Calcutta, see Brendan Koerner, *Piano Demon* (New York: The Atavist, 2011).

35 IOR MSS E360/14 I. H. Macdonald, letter to parents, 19 May 1941.

36 Santha Rama Rau, *Home to India* (London: Victor Gollancz, 1946), pp. 33–4.

37 NARA, Consul New Delhi, General Records, 1942: 820.02–1942: 830, Box 13. Correspondence between the American Consul in Karachi and Howard Donovan, US Consul, 3–16 Oct. 1942.

38 NARA, 811.11–840.6, Box 33. The contemporary novel *Coolie* by Mulk Raj Anand also describes a large billboard of Marlene Dietrich in Bombay. 'Her large eyes and long lashes seductively askance, her milk-white body naked save for a pearly bodice and a pearl loincloth.' *Coolie* (Harmondsworth: Penguin, 1993), p. 157.

13 *Plantations and Paddy Fields*

1   A. H. Pilcher, *Navvies to the Fourteenth Army* (Calcutta: Private Circulation, c. 1945), p. 3.

2   Ibid., p. 14.

3   John Tamraz's contemporary report quoted in Leslie Anders, *The Ledo Road* (Oklahoma: University of Oklahoma Press, 1965), p. 44.

4   IOR MSS Eur F174/1309 Indian Tea Association report on the evacuation of troops and civilians from Burma by the Pangsau route, May to July 1942.

5   Geoffrey Tyson, *Forgotten Frontier* (Calcutta: W. H. Targett, 1945).

6   NARA, Records of Adjutant General, General Correspondence, 702–720, Box 87. Prohibition of cultivation at Chakulia, 21 June 1943.

7   IOR L/PJ/5/150 FNR Bengal, 25 Feb. 1942.

8   Vinita Damodaran, *Broken Promises: Popular Protest, Indian Nationalism and the Congress Party in Bihar, 1935–46* (Delhi and New York: Oxford University Press, 1993), p. 212.

9   IOR L/PJ/12/654.

10 Famine Inquiry Commission, *Report on Bengal* (Delhi: Government of India, 1945), p. 27. Numerous issues over the use of land for military

purposes arose in the 1940s, including the issues of ownership and rights of use, such as temples, stalls and shops encroaching on military land. See NAI, Defence Department, military indexes, 1941–5.

11 IOR FNR L/PJ/5/149 Herbert to Linlithgow, 8 May 1942. Janam Mukherjee, *Hungry Bengal: War, Famine and the End of Empire* (London: Hurst, forthcoming 2015), particularly chapter two on detail of denial policies in Bengal. See also, Famine Inquiry Commission, *Report on Bengal* (Delhi: Government of India, 1945).

12 *TOP*, vol. 2, p. 418. Compensation arrangements for requisitioning.

13 Quoted in Mukherjee, *Hungry Bengal*.

14 NARA, Calcutta Consulate, 1943: 815.4–820.08, Box 127.

15 IOR FNR, L/PJ/5/149.

16 *Facts about Indian 'National' Shipping* (Bombay: Indian Annalist, 1941).

17 NARA, Calcutta Consulate, 1943: 815.4–820.08, Box 127, Birla Brothers to Supply Department. This file contains other appeals by firms against requisitioning.

18 *CWMG*, vol. 82, p. 199. Article in *Harijan*, 19 April 1942.

19 IOR V/27/600/9 The American Technical Mission to India [Grady Report], Delhi, July 1942. For discussions about the British reaction to the report and decision to keep it confidential, IOR L/I/8/106. See also Henry Grady, *The Memoirs of Ambassador Henry F. Grady: From the Great War to the Cold War* (Columbia, MO: University of Missouri Press, 2009).

20 Syed Babar Ali, interviewed by Markus Daechsel in Lahore, 2007.

21 NARA, Calcutta Consulate General Records 1944: 814.3–822B, Box 143.

22 Reverse Lend-Lease was the granting of goods and services to US forces by the British Indian government without wartime payment, in exchange for the US military presence. While no official report has yet been received from the Government of India, our Army reports total expenditures by India for reverse lend-lease aid of approximately $56,900,000, divided as follows: Military stores and equipment $5,421,000; Transportation and communication $3,161,000; Petroleum products $13,127,000: Construction $31,413,000; Subsistence $3,778,000; Total $56,900,000. We have received aviation gasoline, motor gasoline and lubricating oil, and lesser amounts of other petroleum products from the Indian Government for use by American forces. A part of the motor fuel has been used in a number of trucks and passenger cars given our troops without payment as reverse lend-lease aid. In addition, United States Army groups have been afforded postal, telegraph, and telephone facilities, water and electric power, furnishings for buildings, and items of clothing, including mosquito- and gas-proof outfits. President Roosevelt's Report to Congress on Reverse Lend-Lease, 11 Nov. 1943.

23 *CWMG*, vol. 81, pp. 98–9. 18 Sept. 1941.

24 NARA, Calcutta Consulate General Records 1944: 814.3–822B, Box 143.

25 Personal recollections quoted in Gita Paramal, 'How M. S. Oberoi became India's Greatest Hotelier', *The Smart Manager*, 21 Oct. 2005.

26 IOR/L/E/8/1711 Establishment of an aircraft manufacturing industry in India; Pawley–Walchand Scheme, Dec. 1939–Apr. 1943. See also G. D. Khanolkar, *Walchand Hirachand*, pp. 360–74.

27 Indian pilots in the RAF flew missions across France, Germany, North Africa and the Middle East.

28 'Memories of No. 8 Squadron, IAF' by T. J. Thomas (1981), http://www.bharat-rakshak.com/IAF/History/1940s/TJThomas.html, accessed 2011.

29 'My days with the IAF (1940–48)' by V. S. C. Bonarjee (1997), http://www.bharat-rakshak.com/IAF/History/1940s/VSCBonarjee.html, accessed 2011.

30 IOR, FNR, L/PJ/5/204. Madras, 23 Dec. 1941.

31 *TOP*, vol. 2, p. 87. Amery to Linlithgow, 15 May 1942; p. 141, Amery to Linlithgow, 28 May 1942.

32 Clive Branson, *British Soldier in India* (London: International Publishers, 1945), p. 15. 20 June 1942.

33 Quoted in Charles Romanus and Riley Sunderland, *Stilwell's Mission to China* (Washington, DC: Office of the Chief of Military History, 1953), p. 207.

14 Living Dangerously

1 My account is largely based on National Archives, Kew, KV 2/2510, Security Service files on Menon. See also, Menon's wartime writings, *Why Must India Fight?* (London: The India League, *c.* 1940) and *India, Britain and Freedom*. (London: The India League, 1942). Biographies include Janaki Ram, *V. K. Krishna Menon: A Personal Memoir* (Delhi: Oxford University Press, 1997), and T. J. S. George, *Krishna Menon: A Biography* (London: Cape, 1965).

2 National Archives, Kew, KV 2/2510, Security Service files on Menon, 26 Feb. 1942.

3 National Archives, Kew, KV 2/2510, Security Service files on Menon, 2 March 1942.

4 National Archives, Kew, KV 2/2510, Security Service files on Menon, 18 May 1942.

5 Indivar Kamtekar, 'The Shiver of 1942', *Studies in History* 18, no. 1 (2002), pp. 81–102.

6 IOR, FNR, L/PJ/5/204 Hope to Linlithgow, 23 July 1942.

7 Nehru and Azad both believed that Gandhi thought the Japanese would win in 1942.

8 *CWMG*, vol. 82, p. 257. *Harijan*, 10 May 1942.

9 Aruna Asaf Ali, 'Memories of 1942', in *Aruna Asaf Ali, Fragments From the Past: Selected Writings and Speeches of Aruna Asaf Ali* (New Delhi: Patriot Publishers, 1989).

10 CSAS, Sucheta Kripalani, interviewed by Uma Shanker in 1974.

11 Azad, *India Wins Freedom*, p. 88.

12 Raghavan (ed.), *M. Asaf Ali's Memoirs*, pp. 248–9. Prison diary dated 31 Aug. 1942.

13 There is an extensive literature on the Quit India movement with many regional studies and also a great deal of published documentation. See for example, Francis Hutchins, *India's Revolution: Gandhi and the Quit India Movement* (Cambridge: Harvard University Press, 1973), Gyanendra Pandey (ed.), *The Indian Nation in 1942* (Calcutta: Centre for Studies in Social Sciences/K.P. Bagchi, 1988), Vinita Damodaran, *Broken Promises: Popular Protest, Indian Nationalism and the Congress Party in Bihar, 1935–46* (Delhi: Oxford University Press, 1993), and Bidyut Chakrabarty, *Local Politics and Indian Nationalism: Midnapur, 1919–1944* (New Delhi: Manohar, 1997).

14 Chitra P. Mehta, *I Fought for My Country's Freedom* (Bombay: Hamara Hindoostan Publications, 1946).

15 P. N. Chopra and S. R. Bakshi (eds), *Quit India Movement: British Secret Documents* (New Delhi: Interprint, 1986), p. 184. Interception of correspondence in Bengal, 24 Sept. 1942.

16 Ibid., *Quit India Movement: British Secret Documents*, pp. 321–4. Letter of Trilochan Senapati, 2 July 1943, translated from Oriya. Senapati was arrested within a month of writing this letter but went on to become a Member of the Legislative Assembly in post-Independence Orissa.

17 CSAS, Sucheta Kripalani, interviewed by Uma Shanker in 1974.

18 Syamalendu Sengupta, Gautam Chatterjee, and National Archives of India, *Secret Congress Broadcasts and Storming Railway Tracks during Quit India Movement* (New Delhi: Navrang, 1988).

19 Quoted in Paul Greenough, *Prosperity and Misery in Modern Bengal* (New York and Oxford: Oxford University Press, 1983), p. 367.

20 Aruna Asaf Ali, *A Life Sketch* (Lahore: New India Publications, 1947), p. 18.

21 Kudaisya, *The Life and Times of G. D. Birla*, p. 206; G. D. Khanolkar, *Walchand Hirachand*, p. 593.

22 CSAS, S. M. Y. Sastri, interviewed by Arun Gandhi in 1970.

23 CSAS, B. C. Dutt, interviewed by Arun Gandhi in 1970.

24 CSAS, Sucheta Kripalani, interviewed by Uma Shanker in 1974.

25 Quoted in Paul Greenough, 'Political Mobilization and the Underground

Literature of the Quit India Movement, 1942–44', *Modern Asian Studies* 17, no. 03 (1983): 353–86.

26 IOR L/PJ/12/654 Censorship Reports. Letter from a family to a Sepoy, 28 Oct. 1942.

27 IOR L/PJ/12/654 Censorship Reports. Aug.–Sept. 1942.

28 Examples of Japanese propaganda for use among Indian civilians and soldiers are included in IOR/L/PJ/12/480, activities of Indians in Japan and Japanese propaganda in India. See also illustrations, http://www. kingscollections.org, the cartoon in wartime propaganda, and http:// www.psywarrior.com.

29 IOR L/PJ/12/654 Censorship Reports. Aug. 1942.

30 Ibid.

31 Bikram Singh and Sidharth Mishra (eds), *Where Gallantry is Tradition* (New Delhi: Allied Publishers, 1997), p. 163.

32 IOR L/PJ/12/654 Censorship Reports. Sept.–Oct. 1942.

33 Clive Branson, *British Soldier in India*, p. 19. 20 Aug. 1942.

34 CSAS, Nilubhai Limaye interviewed by Uma Shanker in 1970.

35 Ibid.

36 IOR L/PJ/12/654 26 Aug.–1 Sept. 1942 inclusive.

37 Later in the war, *The Times* of London would advertise a new book about the Northern Irishman John Nicolson, *The Hero of Delhi*, who ruthlessly suppressed the 1857 uprising, as 'a tale to inspire England today'. *The Times*, 10 March 1944. And Indian nationalists also invoked the mutiny, for instance, Abdul Qayyum Khan suggesting if Gandhi died there would be disorder on the scale of 1857. See P. N. Chopra and S. R. Bakshi (eds), *Quit India Movement: British Secret Documents*, p. 288. The language of the INA was also suffused with references to 1857, such as the name of the Rani of Jhansi Regiment.

38 Quoted in Taylor Sherman, *State Violence and Punishment in India* (London: Routledge, 2012), p. x.

39 Francis Hutchins, *India's Revolution*, p. 177.

40 *TOP*, vol. 2, p. 909, Stewart to Linlithgow, 5 Sept. 1942; P. N. Chopra and S. R. Bakshi (eds), *Quit India Movement: British Secret Documents*, p. 164.

41 P. N. Chopra and S. R. Bakshi (eds), *Quit India Movement: British Secret Documents*, p. 164; p. 200.

42 Hutchins, *India's Revolution*, p. 177.

43 Rob Johnson, 'The Indian Army and Internal Security', in Kaushik Roy (ed.), *The Indian Army in the Two World Wars*, p. 302.

44 Paul Greenough, *Prosperity and Misery*, p. 374.

45 P. N. Chopra and S. R. Bakshi (eds), *Quit India Movement: British Secret Documents*, p. 243.

46 IOR L/PJ/12/655 Censorship Reports, Aug. 1942.

47 Hutchins reproduces government statistics on civil disturbances, pp. 230–2.

48 W. J. Slim, *Defeat into Victory*, p. 156.

49 Vinita Damodaran, *Broken Promises*, p. 174. Aerial attacks were also made on rebels in Bengal and Orissa. There was support for a firm line of strafing saboteurs in the House of Commons on 8 Oct. 1942.

50 IOR L/PJ/8/608 Civil disobedience: protests against use of whipping as punishment, Aug. 1942–Jul 1944; IOR/L/PJ/8/494 Punishments: legislation to allow whipping as punishment for civil disobedience offenders in Bombay, Jul. 1932–Oct. 1945. For discussion of changing methods of punishment in colonial India, see Taylor Sherman, *State Violence and Punishment in India* (London: Routledge, 2012).

51 IOR L/PJ/8/608 Civil disobedience: protests against use of whipping as punishment, Aug. 1942–Jul. 1944.

52 Ibid.

53 Benjamin Zachariah, 'Rewriting Imperial Mythologies: The Strange Case of Penderel Moon', *South Asia: Journal of South Asian Studies*, no. 12 (2001), p. 58.

54 National Archives, Kew, KV 2/2510, Security Service files on Menon, telephone checks, 25 June 1942.

55 CSAS, Nilubhai Limaye interviewed by Uma Shanker in 1970.

56 G. N. S. Raghavan (ed), *M. Asaf Ali's Memoirs*, p. 292. Prison diary dated 14 Dec. 1942.

57 Ibid., p. 293. Prison diary dated 10 Jan. 1943.

58 Ibid., pp. 293–4. Prison diary dated 22 Jan. 1943.

59 Ibid., p. 293. Prison diary dated 10 Jan. 1943.

60 Ibid., p. 285. Prison diary dated 29 Sept. 1944.

61 R. K. Garg, 'Aruna Remembered', in T. N. Kaul (ed.), *Aruna Asaf Ali: A Profile* (Delhi: Lancer Press, 1990), p. 60.

62 G. N. S. Raghavan (ed), *M. Asaf Ali's Memoirs*, p. 297. Prison diary dated 11 May 1943.

63 Ibid., p. 299. Prison diary dated 22 Jan. 1944.

64 Ibid.

15 *Scorched Earth*

1 NARA, US Consulate General Calcutta, 1943: 800–1943: 861.33, Telegram to Washington DC, 18 July 1943.

2 Ibid.

3 *Statesman*, 24 April 1942. Government of Assam Communiqué on Food Shortages.

4 Daily requirements for the US military were 12,800 lb and for the British Army 6,000 lb.

5 Kenneth Hulbert Diaries, BBC People's War, Article ID A4442564, 29 May 1943.

6 Clive Branson, *British Soldier in India*, p. 66. 23 May 1943.

7 NARA, Adjutant Gen., Gen. Correspondence, Box 84, 634–674, Major Gen. Wheeler, SEAC, 23 Dec. 1943.

8 IOR L/PJ/12/655.

9 Ibid.

10 Ibid. Censorship Reports, letters by sepoys, 16 and 17 May 1943.

11 IOR L/PJ/12/655 Censorship Reports, letters by a Marathi villager to a sepoy, 1 Sept. 1943.

12 IOR L/PJ/12/655 Censorship Reports, 25 Aug.–7 Sept. 1943 inclusive.

13 IOR L/PJ/12/655 Censorship Reports, 11 Aug. 1943–24 Aug. 1943 inclusive.

14 IOR L/PJ/12/655 Censorship Reports 1943.

15 Ibid.

16 Ibid.

17 Janam Mukherjee, *Hungry Bengal: War, Famine and the End of Empire* (London: Hurst, 2015).

18 Ibid.

19 Jyoti Bose, *The Man-Made Famine* (Cambridge: B. Rajan and D. Sen, 1943), unpaginated.

20 NAI, Dept. of Commerce, File no. 21 (10)ITC/42 Serial nos 1–7 Part C.

21 Bose, *The Man-Made Famine*.

22 Ibid.

23 Satyen Basu, *A Doctor in the Army*, p. 190.

24 Ibid., p. 192.

25 IOR L/PJ/5/150 FNR Herbert to Linlithgow, 28 Aug. 1943.

26 IOR L/PJ/5/150 FNR Herbert to Linlithgow, 21 July 1943.

27 Sen's classic work is *Poverty and Famines: an Essay on Entitlement and Deprivation* (Oxford and New York: Oxford University Press, 1982). For the social history, Paul R. Greenough, *Prosperity and Misery in Modern Bengal: The Famine of 1943–44* (Oxford: Oxford University Press, 1983). For an excellent comparative approach of famine, its causes and consequences, Cormac Ó Gráda, *Famine: A Short History* (Princeton: Princeton University Press, 2009). A new account is Janam Mukherjee, *Hungry Bengal: War, Famine and the End of Empire* (London: Hurst, 2015).

28 *Amrita Bazaar Patrika*, 9 Aug. 1943.

29 Pinnell's career is discussed in Janam Mukherjee's *Hungry Bengal*.

30 CSAS, Gurdial Singh Khosla interviewed by Uma Shanker in 1976.

31 *Wavell: The Viceroy's Journal*, p. 52. 17 Feb. 1944.

32 John Glendevon, *The Viceroy at Bay* (London: Collins, 1971), p. 269. Photographs of demonstrations against Linlithgow on his return to the UK were banned from the Indian press.

33 *Wavell: The Viceroy's Journal*, p. 54. 9 Feb. 1944.

34 Ibid., p. 95. 24 Oct. 1944.

35 Ibid., p. 122. 4 April 1945.

36 Branson, *British Soldier in India*, p. 94. 17 Sept. 1943.

37 Kenneth Hulbert Diaries, BBC People's War, Article ID A4442564, 1 June 1943.

38 Peggy Tench Memoir, BBC People's War, A5864358, contributed 22 Sept. 2005.

39 *Hump Express*, 26 April 1945.

40 IOR L/PJ/5/150 Confidential report on political situation in Bengal, second half of Aug. 1943.

41 *The Calcutta Key* (Guidebook for US Army in India, Information and Education Branch CBI, 1945).

42 T. G. Narayan, *Famine Over Bengal* (Calcutta: The Book Company, 1944), p. 155.

43 B. L. Raina, *Official History of the Indian Armed Forces in the Second World War (1939–45): Medical Services, Administration* (New Delhi: Combined Inter-Services Historical Section, 1990 [1953]), p. 410.

44 *CWMG*, vol. 84, p. 253. Interview to the press, 30 July 1944.

45 CSAS, Sucheta Kripalani, interviewed by Uma Shanker in 1974.

46 *The INA Heroes: Autobiographies* (Lahore: Hero Publications, 1946), p. 77.

47 Anon., *Jai Hind: The Diary of a Rebel Daughter of India with the Rani of Jhansi Regiment* (Bombay: Janmabhoomi Prakashan Mandir, 1945), p. 37, 28 June 1943.

48 Ibid., p. 41, 5 July 1943.

49 Bose visited the Andamans for three days from 29 Dec. 1943 and stayed in the Governor's House which had once been occupied by Charles Waterfall. See Sugata Bose, *His Majesty's Opponent* (Cambridge, MA: Harvard University Press, 2011), p. 264.

50 Jane Robbins, 'Freedom Under Britain or Freedom Under Japan: The Radio Battle for India, December 1941–September 1945', *Japan Forum* 7, no. 2 (1995): pp. 217–24. See also S. K. Bose and Sugata Bose (eds), *Azad Hind: Subhas Chandra Bose* (London: Anthem Press, 2004).

16 *The Cogs in a Watch*

1 IOR L/Mil/7/18599 Lascelles to Amery, 10 Dec. 1943.

2 IOR WS/1/707.

3 IOR R/2/767/280 Directive on Victory Celebrations for the North African Campaign, issued by the National War Front in Simla, 13 May 1943.

4 *Spectator*, 4 May 1944.

5 For a full account of Noël Coward's tour in South Asia, see Frank McLynn, *The Burma Campaign: Disaster into Triumph 1942–5* (London: Vintage, 2011), pp. 362–3.

6 For details of these films see http://www.colonialfilm.org.uk/archives. I am grateful to Francis Gooding for screening a selection of these films in Oxford in Sept. 2013.

7 Sanjoy Bhattacharya, 'British Military Information Management Techniques and the South Asian Soldier: Eastern India During the Second World War', *Modern Asian Studies* 34, no. 2 (1 May 2000).

8 Ibid.

9 IOR MSS Eur F152/59–62 Papers of Frank Lugard Brayne, 22 Dec. 1941, Notes as Inspector of Amenities for Indian troops in Iraq. Brayne's pre-war career is analysed in depth by Clive Dewey in *Anglo-Indian Attitudes: The Mind of the Indian Civil Service* (London: Hambledon Press, 1993).

10 IOR MSS Eur F152/59–62 Papers of Frank Lugard Brayne.

11 Ibid.

12 Ibid.

13 IOR L/PJ/12/655 Middle East military censorship fortnightly summaries covering Indian troops.

14 Transcript of interview conducted with Rajinder Singh Dhatt by Dr Kanwaljit in Hounslow, *c.* 2008. See also, National Army Museum, 2008–05–26, oral history of Rajinder Singh Dhatt, interview conducted by Justin Saddington in Hounslow, London, April 2008. Also, author's personal conversation with Rajinder Singh Dhatt in Aug. 2011.

15 National Army Museum, 'Memoirs of an old Koi Hai' (John Ffrench, unpublished manuscript, National Army Museum), 9507–79. Written in 1989.

16 Ibid.

17 Jhuddha Shumsher Rana to Auchinleck quoted in Mary Des Chene, *Relics of Empire* (PhD thesis, Stanford University, 1991), p. 153.

18 Bernard Pignede, *The Gurungs* (Kathmandu: Ratna Pustak Bhandar, 1993), p. 23. Pignede was an anthropologist who lived among the Gurungs in the 1950s.

19 Frank Brayne would describe the Gurkhas as the most 'newless of all' in 1941. See IOR MSS Eur F152/58–62. Papers of Frank Lugard Brayne.

20 Mohammed Khan, b. 1922. North West Sound Archive. Interviewed 7 June 2004. Ref. 2005. 0194A.

21 H. M. Close, *A Pathan Company* (Islamabad: National Book Foundation, 1994), p. 42.

22 E. D. Smith, *Even the Brave Falter* (London: Robert Hale, 1978), pp. 15–16.

23 Rupert Lyons, transcript of audio memoir, BBC People's War, Article ID A6062988, 8 Oct. 2005.

24 IOR L/PJ/12/576.

25 Ibid.

26 Compton Mackenzie, *All Over the Place* (London: Chatto & Windus, 1948), p. 32.

27 Quoted in Christopher Somerville, *Our War* (London: Phoenix, 2005), p. 65. See also the transcripts of these interviews conducted by Christopher Somerville now held at the IWM.

28 Interview conducted by Iqroop Sandhawalia with Major-General Kartar Singh, 2011.

29 Satyen Basu, *A Doctor in the Army* (Calcutta: Sri Bajendranath Bose, 1960), pp. 202–15. Basu's note on Discipline dated 6 June 1944.

17 Longing and Loss

1 For examples of this propaganda, Herbert A. Friedman, 'Axis and Allied Propaganda to Indian Troops', prepared with the assistance of Arunkumar Bhatt, http://www.psywarrior.com/AxisPropIndia.html.

2 Ibid.

3 Ibid.

4 Angela Bolton, *The Maturing Sun*, pp. 91–2.

5 Interview conducted by Iqroop Sandhawalia with Major-General Kartar Singh, 2011.

6 Satyen Basu, *A Doctor in the Army* (Calcutta: Sri Bajendranath Bose, 1960), p. 143.

7 Compton Mackenzie, *All Over the Place* (London: Chatto & Windus, 1948), p. 47.

8 Letter of appeal by Nazir Begum included in Ffrench papers, National Army Museum.

9 IOR L/Mil/17/5/2333.

10 IOR L/WS/1/707 Indian Army Morale. Intelligence report on one Jat unit, 30 Sept. 1943.

11 Francis Yeats-Brown, *Martial India* (London: Eyre & Spottiswoode, 1945), p. 144.

12 Calcutta had some of the highest rates of VD among soldiers recorded anywhere in the world during the Second World War; in the British Army in Calcutta in 1944 rates reached 376 per 1,000. See IOR V/24/3671 *Annual Report on the Health of the Army in India*, 1943, vol. 4, part 1. Among US forces in CBI the rate reached 200 per 1,000 in the same year.

13 NARA, CBI, Adjutant-General, General Corresp. 1944: 720.3–726.1, Box 88.

14 Mark Harrison, *Medicine and Victory: British Military Medicine in the Second World War* (Oxford: Oxford University Press, 2008).

15 IOR V/24/3671 *Annual Report on the Health of the Army in India*, 1942, vol. 4, part 1.

16 *Statesman*, 2 April 1945.

17 NARA, Secretary of Defense, Research Divn Box 1025. Attitude reports on overseas personnel, 1944.

18 IWM, HHS/1, Private Diary of Signalman H. Somerfield, 23 Nov. 1939.

19 IOR L/PJ/5/151 Casey to Wavell, 15 May 1944.

20 W. R. Slim, *Defeat into Victory* (London: Pan, 2009), p. 153; Clive Branson, *British Soldier in India* (London: International Publishers, 1945), p. 34. 12 Oct. 1942.

21 IOR L/MIL/7/13899 Letter to Secretary of State for India, 25 March 1946.

22 NARA, CBI, Adjutant General corresp. 720.3–726.1, Box 88. American soldiers were banned from marrying while in India, making it impossible to legitimise unplanned pregnancies even if a couple wanted to do so.

23 IOR V/24/3671 *Annual Report on the Health of the Army in India*, 1943, vol. iv, part 1, p. 57.

24 Paul R. Greenough, *Prosperity and Misery in Modern Bengal: the Famine of 1943–44* (Oxford: Oxford University Press, 1983), p. 222.

25 Bhowani Sen, *Rural Bengal in Ruins* (Bombay: People's Publishing House, 1945) quoted in Greenough, pp. 177–8; Hansard, 17 Feb. 1944.

26 Santosh Kumar Mukherji, *Indian Sex Life and Prostitution* (Burnpur, Burdwan: Anil Kumar Das Gupta, 1945). This survey is, however, of dubious authenticity as this document is informed by some of the author's own fantasies.

27 NAI, Home Dept 68/44 Political (1), 1944.

28 Ibid.

29 There were a large number of discussions on the subject. One civil servant explained that increases in prostitution 'inevitably occurs owing

to the concentration of large military forces'. NAI, Home Dept 11/27/44 Police.

30 NARA, Consulate Karachi Classified Gen. records 000–832, Box 1; CBI, Provost Marshal Activity reports (July 1945).

18 *Catalyst of Change*

1 Angela Bolton, *The Maturing Sun*, p. x.

2 Gian Singh, *Memories of Friends and Foes* (Neath: Cwmnedd Press, 1995), p. 13.

3 The literature on these battles is extensive. See in particular Fergal Keane's brilliant account, *Road of Bones: the Epic Siege of Kohima* (London: HarperPress, 2011). Also, Frank McLynn, *The Burma Campaign: Disaster into Triumph 1942–5* (London: Vintage, 2011). Rajinder Dhatt recalled how the stench of bodies was one of the worst aspects of the Burma campaign, and how the men made efforts to send back or cremate bodies if they were far enough away from the fighting in order to be able to do so.

4 N. Lokendra, *Manipur during World War II, 1941–45: Socio-Economic Change and Local Responses* (Imphal: Manipur State Archives, Directorate of Arts & Culture, Govt of Manipur, 1993). See also, John Parratt, *Wounded Land: Politics and Identity in Modern Manipur* (New Delhi: Mittal Publications, 2005).

5 Neipezu-u Chirhah interviewed by Kazimuddin Ahmed in Nagaland, 2013.

6 Lokendra, *Manipur during World War II*, p. 9.

7 A recent article estimates that 6,000 Manipuri Kukis lent assistance to the Japanese and points out that 148 Kukis from Manipur have got INA pensions and that 70 local Kukis were charged by the British with assisting the Japanese after the war. See Jangkhomang Guite, 'Representing Local Participation in INA–Japanese Imphal Campaign: The Case of the Kukis in Manipur, 1943–45', *Indian Historical Review* 37, no. 2 (2011): 291–309.

8 Ibid.

9 Lokendra, *Manipur during World War II*, pp. 23–6.

10 B. L. Raina, *Official History of the Indian Armed Forces in the Second World War (1939–45): Medical Services, Administration* (New Delhi: Combined Inter-Services Historical Section, 1990 [1953]), p. 36.

11 Ibid., p. 38.

12 Nehru in 1952 quoted in Raina, *Official History*, pp. 147–8.

13 The annual sickness rate on the Indo–Burmese front rose in 1943 to 1,196.10 per 1,000, i.e. statistically each man was hospitalised more than once. Almost half of hospital admissions were due to malaria, the most important single cause of sickness. Other causes of morbidity included malaria, dysentery and skin diseases and there was a very high ratio of sickness to battle wounds on the Indo-Burmese front mid-war: for every soldier wounded on the Indo-Burmese front in 1942, 204 were sick and in 1943 this was 142.

14 National Army Museum, Lilian Pert Papers, 1982–08–215. March 1943, Lilian Pert's note on Indian military hospitals.

15 Ibid., 8 Oct. 1943, Lilian Pert to General Rankin of the Southern Army.

16 Ibid., Report on evacuation of cases from Ranipet to Bangalore, 29 June 1943.

17 Quoted in Mark Harrison, *Medicine and Victory* (Oxford: Oxford University Press, 2004), p. 189.

18 Raina, *Official History*, p. 136.

19 *Bhore Report*, p. 94.

20 Raina, *Official History*, p. 136.

21 Ibid., p. 136; *Bhore Report*.

22 E. E. Prebble, 'Venereal Disease in India', *Sexually Transmitted Infections* 22, no. 2 (1946), 59–60.

23 Ibid.

24 W. J. Slim, *Defeat into Victory* (London: Pan, 2009), p. 203. This quote refers particularly to nursing.

25 Singh, *Memories of Friends and Foes*, p. 7.

26 Ben Shephard, *A War of Nerves* (London: Pimlico, 2002), pp. 221–2; H. R. A. Prabhu, 'Military Psychiatry in India', *Indian Journal of Psychiatry* no. 52 (Jan 2010); D. Wilfred Abse, *The Diagnosis of Hysteria, etc.* (Bristol: John Wright & Sons, 1950), B. L. Raina, *Official History of the Indian Armed Forces in the Second World War (1939–45): Medical Services, Administration* (New Delhi: Combined Inter-Services Historical Section, 1990) [first published 1953], pp. 150–220.

27 Abse, *The Diagnosis of Hysteria*, p. 2. Abse was from a distinguished Welsh family; one of his brothers became a British MP and another a well-regarded poet.

28 Ibid., pp. 13–14.

29 Ibid., p. 18.

30 Bolton, *The Maturing Sun*, p. 152.

31 Ibid.

19 *The Man-a-Mile Road*

1 W. J. Slim, *Defeat into Victory* (London: Pan, 2009), p. 284.

2 IOR L/PS/12/4622 Routes to China, 1940–1947.

3 Slim, *Defeat into Victory*, p. 196.

4 Charles Romanus and Riley Sunderland, *Time Runs Out in CBI* (Washington DC: Office of the Chief of Military History, 1959), p. 300.

5 John Tamraz contemporary report quoted in Leslie Anders, *The Ledo Road* (Oklahoma: University of Oklahoma Press, 1965), p. 45.

6 Contemporary report quoted in ibid., p. 59.

7 Ibid. See also IOR/M/4/3064 Ledo Road.

8 Brendan Koerner, *Now the Hell Will Start: One Soldier's Flight from the Greatest Manhunt of World War II* (New York: Penguin Press, 2008).

9 Romanus and Sunderland, *Stilwell's Mission to China* (Washington DC: United States Military, 1953), p. 307.

10 Frank Moraes, *Witness to an Era* (London: Weidenfeld & Nicolson, 1973), p. 118.

11 Anonymous letter quoted in Eric R. Craine, *Burma Roadsters* (Tucson, AZ: Western Research Company, 1992), p. 75.

12 Romanus and Sunderland, *Stilwell's Mission to China*, p. 308.

13 Ibid., p. 307.

14 *Life*, 14 Aug. 1944.

15 Stephen Reiss (ed.), *From Burma with Love: Fifteen Months of Daily Letters between Irwin and Mary Reiss during World War II* (Bloomington: AuthorHouse, 2011), p. 401. Letter from Burma, 20 Sept. 1944.

16 *India Burma Theater Roundup*, IV, no. 7, 25 Oct. 1945.

17 Stephen Reiss (ed.), *From Burma with Love*, p. 433. Letter from Burma, 14 Oct. 1944.

18 Ibid.

19 NARA Calcutta Consulate General Records 1944: 814.3–822B, Box 143. 16 Sept. 1944.

20 *IBT Roundup*, 5 April 1945.

20 *Insults and Discriminations*

1 NARA, Secretary of Defense, Research Divn, Box 1025. Attitude reports on overseas personnel, 1944.

2 See Brendan Koerner on Teddy Weatherford's career in Asia, and death

in Calcutta in 1945, *Piano Demon: The Globetrotting, Gin-soaked, Too-Short Life of Teddy Weatherford, the Chicago Jazzman who Conquered Asia* (New York: The Atavist, 2011).

3 On the dynamics between American issues of race and British imperialism, see in particular Gary Hess, *America Encounters India, 1941–7* (Baltimore, MD: The John Hopkins Press, 1972), Gerald Horne, *The End of Empires: African Americans and India* (Philadelphia: Temple University Press, 2008), Nico Slate, *Colored Cosmopolitanism: The Shared Struggle for Freedom in the United States and India* (Cambridge, MA.: Harvard University Press, 2012), and Gyanendra Pandey, *A History of Prejudice: Race, Caste and Difference in India and the United States* (Cambridge: Cambridge University Press, 2013).

4 Frank Moraes, *Witness to an Era*, p. 112. Moraes also noted the embarrassment of young British officers watching this spectacle with him from the deck.

5 Nico Slate, *Colored Cosmopolitanism*, p. 144.

6 NARA, Secretary of Defense, Research Divn, Box 1025. Attitude reports on overseas personnel, 1944.

7 Slate, *Colored Cosmopolitanism*, p. 152.

8 IOR L/WS/1/647 1944–1945. See also the work of David Killingray including *Fighting for Britain: African Soldiers in the Second World War* (London: James Currey, 2012).

9 Gian Singh, *Memories of Friends and Foes*, p. 8.

10 B. L. Raina, *Official History of the Indian Armed Forces in the Second World War, (1939–45): Medical Services, Administration* (New Delhi: Combined Inter-Services Historical Section, 1990 [1953]), Chapter 13, 'Reception and distribution of casualties'.

11 NARA, Calcutta Consulate, 1943: 815.4–820.08, Box 127.

12 IOR L/PS/12/2320 Training of Chinese troops in India.

13 NARA, Adjutant-General, General Correspondence, 600.9–611 Box no. 80.

14 IOR/L/PS/12/2320.

15 National Archives, Kew, WO 32/10664 On the formation of the WAC (I).

16 Margaret Schmertz, Library of Congress Veterans History Project (No. AFC/2001/001/21628), Veterans History Project, American Folklife Center, Library of Congress.

17 Joan Boss, *Love and War in India: My War Years, 1942–1945*, vol. 2 (Boss Bros, 2005), pp. 13–17.

18 *Statesman*, 2 April 1945.

19 NAI, Home – police, 7/84/44. Coroner and Jury's Report, 13 Dec. 1944.

20 NAI, Home – police, 7/84/44. CID Report, 26 Nov. 1944.

21 NAI, Home – police, 7/84/44. Coroner and Jury's Report, 13 Dec. 1944.

22 Ibid.

23 NAI, Home – police, 7/73/44.

24 Ibid.

25 See various incidents recorded in NAI, Home – police including 7/4/44 and 7/23/44. Also IOR FNR, L/PJ/5/151 Bengal.

26 NARA CBI Adjutant General, General Correspondence 250.1–251.2 Box 29. Note dated 27 Nov. 1943.

27 In Burma, this was even more common, and there were numerous rapes, or murders perpetrated by villagers in self-defence against rape.

28 NARA, Adjutant General Correspondence 250.1–251.2 Box 29.

29 See for instance, the *Sunday Statesman*, 29 March 1942.

21 *Empires, Lost and Found*

1 G. N. S. Raghavan (ed.), *M. Asaf Ali's Memoirs*, p. 254. Diary extract dated 24 Oct. 1942.

2 Ibid., p. 301. Diary extracts June–July 1944.

3 K. A. Abbas and N. G. Jog Shankar, *A Report to Gandhiji: A Survey of Indian and World Events During the 21 Months of Gandhiji's Incarceration* (Bombay: Hind Kitab, 1944), p. 45.

4 Ibid., p. 49.

5 IOR MSS E360/14 I. H. Macdonald, letter to parents, 23 May 1942.

6 Ian Hay Macdonald wrote home: 'Most of my inside knowledge of what has happened in the war comes from stray conversations with people who seem to have come from all parts of the world, and seen and done everything, while we have been buried alive in India – rather a lost generation in fact.'

7 Angela Bolton, *The Maturing Sun*, p. 75.

8 For further discussion of the changes in the wartime state, see William Gould, *Bureaucracy, Community and Influence in India*.

9 IOR L/PJ/5/151 FNR Bengal for fortnight ending 14 July 1944.

10 Ibid.

11 In an interview in 2011 with Iqroop Sandhawalia, Colonel Prithipal Singh Gill, who was in Bombay that year, recalled, 'when the ship full of ammunition exploded at the Bombay docks everyone thought that the Japanese had attacked India' and that children had been sent away from the city for their safety.

12 IOR L/I/1/1152 Bombay docks explosions, Proceedings of committee of inquiry report and related papers and testimonies, 1944–1947.

13 Ibid.

14 Ibid.

15 Ibid.

16 Ibid.

17 Another fatal wartime industrial accident took place at the Kanchapura Ammunition Depot on 25 Nov. 1945.

18 Memory of Wiesia Klepacka in The Association of Poles in India, *Poles in India 1942–1948* (London: Amolibros, 2013), p. 421.

19 Ibid., p. 424.

20 Ibid., p. 424.

21 NARA, CBI, Provost Marshal General Correspondence, 200385. 2, Box No. 773.

22 Although there were also at least occasional cases of self-mutilation in the early years of the war. See, for instance, the case of Abdul Wahad Md. Jaman, twenty-two years old, who was given seven years rigorous imprisonment, by summary court martial held in the field in Sudan on 28 Dec. 1940 for 'voluntarily causing himself hurt'. NAI, Home Dept 46/2/39 Jails.

23 Ascertaining accurate numbers of desertions is difficult and official statistics mention a rate of 5 per cent. A number of documents suggest surprisingly high figures. L/WS/1/1433 (India Internal Intelligence Summary) suggests 2,161 desertions in Dec. 1941, mainly among men with little active service. IOR L/PJ/5/238 FNR Punjab for first half of June 1943 describes '28,188 deserters at large' in Punjab alone and 'stemming desertion' is mentioned again in March 1944 as a reason for increasing soldiers' pay. Large numbers of military prisoners (including deserters but also those punished for other misdemeanours) were arriving in Assam in 1944; 'there are practically daily admissions of new arrivals into jails'. See NAI, Home Dept 46/2/39 Jails.

24 Quoted in Peter Ward Fay, *The Forgotten Army: India's Armed Struggle for Independence, 1942–45* (New Delhi: Rupa & Co., 1997), p. 412.

25 IOR/L/PJ/12/763 Indian prisoners of war in Europe.

26 This was also the case for some Quit India prisoners, most notably J. P. Narayan's escape from Hazaribagh Central Jail in Nov. 1942.

27 Elios Toschi, *Ninth Time Lucky*, p. 86.

28 Ibid., p. 133.

29 Raina, *Official History*, p. 460–3.

30 Ibid.

31 John Baptist Crasta, *Eaten by the Japanese: The Memoir of an Unknown*

Indian Prisoner of War, 3rd edn, (New York: Invisible Man Press, 2013) p. 23; B. L. Raina, *Official History*, pp. 460–3.

32 For some detailed analysis of the experience of Indian prisoners of war see G. J. Douds, 'The Men Who Never Were: Indian POWs in the Second World War', *South Asia: Journal of South Asian Studies* 27, no. 2 (2004): 183–216, and G. J. Douds, 'Indian POWs in the Pacific, 1941–1945', in Kevin Blackburn and Karl Hack eds., *Forgotten Captives in Japanese Occupied Asia* (Abingdon, New York: Routledge, 2008), pp. 73–93.

33 John Baptist Crasta, *Eaten by the Japanese*, p. 66.

34 Narinder Singh Parmar, 'The Story of Major Chint Singh, POW', *Hill Post*, 29 July 2007.

22 Celebrations and Recriminations

1 Rationing was put in place slowly in India and mainly as a result of the famine. In July 1943 only 13 cities and areas were fully rationed, but by Feb. 1944 this had increased to 103 towns and cities in response to the insistence of the Foodgrains Policy Committee of 1943. Still, by the end of the war, rationing schemes covered less than a fifth of the total population and the conditions of rationing varied greatly, and depended on local conditions, availability of foodstuffs and provincial decision-making.

2 IOR L/PJ/12/576 Censorship Control Department Fortnightly Reports on India, June–Aug. 1945.

3 Ibid.

4 Ibid.

5 'Nandita Sen's Story', Jan. 2005, http:timewitnesses.org/english/~nandita.html, accessed 2013.

6 See *The Statesman*, 3–10 May 1945. Wavell had noted in his diary on 10 Nov. 1943 that it would be 'disastrous to have any enquiry now'.

7 IOR L/PJ/12/576, Censorship Control Department Fortnightly Reports on India, June–Aug. 1945.

8 Ibid.

9 Ibid.

10 *Wavell: The Viceroy's Journal*, p. 125. 7 Aug. 1945.

11 CWMG, vol. 91, p. 221. *Harijan*, 7 July 1946. See also discussion in Faisal Devji, *The Impossible Indian: Gandhi and the Temptations of Violence* (London: Hurst, 2012), p. 147.

12 India tested its first nuclear weapon in 1974.

13 Interview conducted by Iqroop Sandhawalia with Major General Kartar Singh, 2011.

14 Gul Hassan Khan, *Memoirs of Lt. Gen. Gul Hassan Khan* (Karachi: Oxford University Press, 1993), p. 54.

15 Interview conducted by Iqroop Sandhawalia with Brigadier Parampal Gill, 2011.

16 Interviews conducted with Sardar Ali, Khadam Hussain, Haji Mohammed Sadiq and Ali Akbar Khan by Youth Action, Blackburn and Darwen, 2012.

17 Frank Moraes, *Witness to an Era*, p. 136.

18 *SWJN*, vol. 14, p. 2.

19 For a fuller discussion see the work of William Kuracina and Daniel Marston.

20 Cited in G. N. S. Raghavan (ed.), *M. Asaf Ali's Memoirs: the Emergence of Modern India* (Delhi: Ajanta, 1994), undated, *c.* Dec. 1945, p. 327.

21 INA soldiers were granted military pensions in 1972 but had been denied them before that date.

22 John Baptist Crasta, *Eaten by the Japanese*, p. 72.

23 Aruna Asaf Ali, *Fragments From the Past: Selected Writings and Speeches of Aruna Asaf Ali* (New Delhi: Patriot Publishers, 1989), p. 140.

24 G. N. S. Raghavan (ed.), *M. Asaf Ali's Memoirs*, p. 342–3. Dec. 1946.

25 *CWMG*, vol. 93, p. 159. Gandhi to Aruna Asaf Ali, Dec. 18, 1946.

26 Aruna Asaf Ali: *A Life Sketch* (Lahore: New India Publications, 1947), p. 105.

27 Raghavan (ed.), *M. Asaf Ali's Memoirs*, p. 352. Undated.

28 Ibid. See also G. N. S. Raghavan, *Aruna Asaf Ali: A Compassionate Radical*, pp. 93–7.

29 IOR L/E/8/2602. Oct. 1945.

30 Compton Mackenzie, *All Over the Place*, p. 64.

31 NARA, Provost Marshal Activity Reports, Box 779. Report dated 4 Feb. 1946.

32 *Records of the Hajj: A Documentary History of the Pilgrimage to Mecca*, vol. 7 (1993), p. 411. From Foreign Office to India Office, 9 May 1940. In 1940 this proposal was rejected by the Government of India for fear of 'subversive influences' but was considered a possibility for consideration at the end of the war.

33 Penderel Moon, *The Future of India* (London: Pilot Press, 1945).

23 The Sepoy's Return

1 Ramesh Benegal, *Burma to Japan with Azad Hind*, p. 140.

2 Ibid., p. 142.

3 H. M. Close, *A Pathan Company*, p. 302.

4 Ashali Varma, *The Victoria Cross.*

5 Gian Singh, *Memories of Friends and Foes*, p. 18.

6 National Army Museum, J. H. Voice, draft of unpublished memoirs, Ref: 2009–06–11. Written in 1974.

7 National Army Museum, 'Memoirs of an old Koi Hai' (John Ffrench, unpublished manuscript, National Army Museum) 9507–79. Written in 1989.

8 Ibid.

9 National Army Museum, Ref: 1993–04–13, Capt R. A. Newman Papers. Letter from Kartar Singh in Waziristan to Newman Nov. 1946.

10 H. M. Close, *A Pathan Company*, p. 316.

11 IOR MSS Eur F152/70 Papers of Frank Lugard Brayne. Lectures to demobilising troops and pamphlets published by Punjab ministry, 1945.

12 Ibid.

13 CSAS, B. C. Dutt, interviewed by Arun Gandhi in 1970. There was also a feeling among some of their relatives that the men had been hardened by their experiences. Distances between families and men after long separations could not be easily breached. The novel *Aadha Gaon* gave voice to this common assumption about returning sepoys, evoking the sense of unknoweable experiences and their alienation from home: 'Tannu returned as Major Hasan. The softness natural to a Saiyid had disappeared from his face and he looked as stiff and hard as a shoe which had dried in the monsoon rain . . . Now he carried the pictures of several girls in his case. He had forgotten their names. He just remembered their bodies.' Rahi Masoom Reeza, *The Feuding Families of Village Gangauli: Aadha Gaon*, trans. Gillian Wright (Delhi: Penguin, 1994).

14 B. L. Joshi and Leo Rose, *Democratic Innovations in Nepal* (Berkeley: University of California Press, 1966), p. 59.

15 B. L. Raina, *Official History of the Indian Armed Forces in the Second World War (1939–45): Medical Services, Administration* (New Delhi: Combined Inter-Services Historical Section, 1990 [1953]), p. 495.

16 Ibid.

17 *The Times*, London, 16 Aug. 1947.

18 National Archives, Kew, KV 2/2510, Security Service files on Menon.

19 Transcript of interview conducted with Rajinder Singh Dhatt by Dr Kanwaljit in Hounslow, *c.* 2008. Also, author's communication with Rajinder Singh Dhatt, 2011.

20 Raina, *Official History*, p. 460. Indian restaurants in fact date back to at least 1809 in the UK, and there had long been a presence of Indian cooks in Britain although their popularity and presence of Indian restaurants spread after 1945. See Liz Buettner, 'Going for an Indian: South Asian Restaurants and the Limits of Multiculturalisation in Britain', *Journal of Modern History* 80: 4 (2008), pp. 865–901.

21 IOR L/WS/1/962. Proposed Memorial to soldiers of the Indian Army, Auchinleck to Secretary of State, 26 June 1949.

22 Ibid.

23 Commonwealth War Graves Commission Archives, A171 part 2, 20 Sept. 1955. Memorials for India and Pakistan.

24 Aruna Asaf Ali, 'Memories of 1942' (undated, *c.* 1960) in *Fragments From the Past: Selected Writings and Speeches of Aruna Asaf Ali* (New Delhi: Patriot Publishers, 1989), p. 148.

25 Compton Mackenzie, *All Over the Place* (London: Chatto & Windus, 1948), p. 19.

Bibliography

ARCHIVES AND UNPUBLISHED SOURCES

British Library, Oriental and African Studies, London
Cambridge Centre for South Asian Studies, Oral History Collection
Commonwealth War Graves Commission Archives, Maidenhead
Imperial War Museum, London
National Archives, Kew
National Archives and Records Administration, Washington DC
National Archives of India, New Delhi
National Army Museum, London
Nehru Memorial Museum and Library, New Delhi
School of Oriental and African Studies, London

PERSONAL RECOLLECTIONS AND PUBLISHED PRIMARY SOURCES

Abbas, Khwaja Ahmad, and N. G. Jog Shankar. *A Report to Gandhiji: A Survey of Indian and World Events During the 21 Months of Gandhiji's Incarceration.* Bombay: Hind Kitab, 1944.

Abse, D. Wilfred. *The Diagnosis of Hysteria, etc.* Bristol: John Wright & Sons, 1950.

Ahmad, J. (ed.), *Speeches and Writings of Mr Jinnah*, vol. 2. Lahore: Shaikh Muhammad Ashraf, 1964.

Allana, G. *Pakistan Movement: Historic Documents.* 4th edition. Lahore: Islamic Book Service, 1988.

Anand, M. R. *Across the Black Waters.* Delhi: Orient Paperbacks, 2000. Original edition 1939.

Anand, M. R. *Conversations in Bloomsbury.* New York: Oxford University Press, 1995.

Anand, M. R. *Coolie*. London: Bodley Head, 1972. Original edition 1936.

Anand, Roshan Lal. *Soldiers' Savings and How They Use Them*. Lahore: Civil and Military Gazette, 1940.

Anon. *Jai Hind: The Diary of a Rebel Daughter of India with the Rani of Jhansi Regiment*. Bombay: Janmabhoomi Prakashan Mandir, 1945.

Asaf Ali, Aruna. *A Life Sketch*. Lahore: New India Publications, 1947.

Asaf Ali, Aruna. *Fragments from the Past: Selected Writings and Speeches of Aruna Asaf Ali, with a Biographical Introduction*. New Delhi: Patriot Publishers, 1989.

Asaf Ali, Aruna. *The Resurgence of Indian Women*. New Delhi: Radiant Publishers, 1991.

Asaf Ali, Aruna, and G. N. S. Raghavan. *Private Face of a Public Person: A Study of Jawaharlal Nehru*. London: Sangam, 1989.

Association of Poles in India. *Poles in India 1942–1948*. London: Amolibros, 2013.

Azad, Maulana Abul Kalam. *India Wins Freedom*. New Delhi: Orient Longman, 1959; new edn, 1988.

Basu, Satyen. *A Doctor in the Army*. Calcutta: Sri Bajendranath Bose, 1960.

Benegal, Ramesh S. *Burma to Japan with Azad Hind: A War Memoir 1941–1945*. Olympia Fields, IL: Lancer, 2009.

Bhore Report, see *The Health Survey*

Bolton, Angela. *The Maturing Sun: An Army Nurse in India, 1942–45*. London: Imperial War Museum, 1986.

Bose, Jyoti. *The Man-made Famine*. Cambridge: B. Rajan & D. Sen, 1943.

Bose, Sisir K., and Sugata Bose (eds). *Azad Hind: Subhas Chandra Bose, Writing and Speeches 1941–1943*. 2nd edition. London: Anthem Press, 2004.

Boss, Joan. *Love and War in India: My War Years, 1942–1945*. (vol. 2) Boss Bros, 2005.

Branson, Clive. *British Soldier in India: The Letters of Clive Branson*. London: International Publishers, 1945.

Brett-James, A. *Ball of Fire: The Fifth Indian Division in the Second World War*. London: Gale & Polden, 1951.

Carter, Lionel (ed.). *Punjab Politics 1936– 1939: The Start of Provincial Autonomy: Governors' Fortnightly Reports and Other Key Documents*. Delhi: Manohar, 2004.

———. *Punjab Politics, 1940–1943: Strains of War: Governors' Fortnightly Reports and Other Key Documents*. New Delhi: Manohar, 2005.

Chopra, Pran Nath, and S. R. Bakshi (eds). *Quit India Movement: British Secret Documents*. New Delhi: Interprint, 1986.

Chowdhary, Savitri. *I Made My Home in England*. Laindon: Grant West, n.d.

Close, H. M. *A Pathan Company*. Islamabad: National Book Foundation, 1994.

Cochrane, Peter. *Charlie Company: In Service with C Company 2nd Queen's Own Cameron Highlanders, 1940–44*. Stroud: Spellmount, 2007.

Cole, B. L. *The Recruiting Handbook for the Rajputana Classes*. Simla: Government of India, 1922.

Craine, Eric R. *Burma Roadsters*. Tucson, Ariz.: Western Research Company, 1992.

Crasta, John Baptist, with intro. by Richard Crasta. *Eaten by the Japanese: The Memoir of an Unknown Indian Prisoner of War*. 3rd edition. New York: Invisible Man Press, 2013.

Darling, Malcolm. *At Freedom's Door*. London: Oxford University Press, 1949.

Dhillon, Gurbaksh Singh. *From My Bones: Memoirs of Col. Gurbaksh Singh Dhillon of the Indian National Army, Including 1945 Red Fort Trial*. New Delhi: Aryan Books International, 1998.

Durrani, Mahmood Khan. *The Sixth Column: The Heroic Personal Story of Lt.-Col. Mahmood Khan Durrani*. London: Cassell, 1955.

Evatt, J., *Garhwalis Handbook*. Calcutta: Government of India, 1924.

Famine Inquiry Commission. *Report on Bengal*. Delhi: Government of India, 1945.

Fessler, Diane Burke. *No Time for Fear: Voices of American Military Nurses in World War II*. East Lansing: Michigan State University Press, 1996.

Gandhi, Mahatma. *The Collected Works of Mahatma Gandhi*. Delhi: Publications Division, Ministry of Information and Broadcasting, Government of India, 1999.

Glendevon, John. *The Viceroy at Bay: Lord Linlithgow in India, 1936–1943*. London: Collins, 1971.

Gopal, S. (ed.) *Selected Works of Jawaharlal Nehru*. New Delhi: Orient Longman, 1972–1982.

Harrer, Heinrich. *Seven Years in Tibet*. London: Harper, 2005. Original edition 1953.

The Health Survey and Development Committee Report [Bhore Report]. New Delhi: Government of India, 1946.

The I N A Heroes: Autobiographies of Maj. Gen. Shahnawaz, Col. Prem K. Sahgal [and] Col. Gurbax Singh Dhillon of the Azad Hind Fauj. Lahore: Hero Publications, 1946.

India Office, Information Department. *India at War, Rising Flood of Vast Resources*. London: Ministry of Information, 1941.

India. Legislation and orders relating to the war. Delhi: Manager of Publications, 1942.

Kaul, T. N. (ed.). *Aruna Asaf Ali: A Profile.* Delhi: Lancer Press, 1990.

Khan, Gul Hassan. *Memoirs of Lt. Gen. Gul Hassan Khan.* Karachi: Oxford University Press, 1993.

Khan, Sayeed Hasan. *Across the Seas: Incorrigible Drift.* Karachi: Ushba, 2013.

Khanolkar, G. D. *Walchand Hirachand: Man, His Times and Achievements.* Bombay: Walchand & Co., 1969.

Kiernan, V. G. 'The Communist Party of India and the Second World War: Some Reminiscences', *South Asia*, 10, no. 2 (1987): 61–73.

Lele, P. R. *War and India's Freedom.* Bombay: Popular Book Depot, 1940.

Mackenzie, Compton. *All Over the Place.* London: Chatto & Windus, 1948.

Mackenzie, Compton. *Eastern Epic.* London: Chatto & Windus, 1951.

Mansergh, Nicholas, and E. W. R. Lumby (eds). *Constitutional Relations between Britain and India: the Transfer of Power, 1942–7.* London: HM Stationery Office, 1970–1983.

Mason, Philip. *A Matter of Honour: An Account of the Indian Army, Its Officers and Men.* London: Jonathan Cape, 1974.

Mehta, Chitra P. *I Fought for My Country's Freedom.* Bombay: Hamara Hindoostan Publications, 1946.

Moon, Penderel. *The Future of India.* London: Pilot Press, 1945.

Menon, Krishna. *India, Britain & Freedom.* London: The India League, 1942.
——. *Why Must India Fight?* London: The India League, c. 1940.

Mitra, Asok. 'Famine of 1943 in Vikrampur Dacca', *Economic and Political Weekly* 24, no. 5 (1989).

Mitra, Asok. *Towards Independence: Memoirs of an Indian Civil Servant, 1940–1947.* Bombay: Popular Prakashan, 1991.

Moraes, Frank. R. *Witness to an Era: India 1920 to the Present Day.* London: Weidenfeld & Nicolson, 1973.

Nehru, Jawaharlal. *The Discovery of India.* New Delhi: Penguin Books, 2004.

Orwell, George. *The Complete Works of George Orwell.* London: Secker & Warburg, 1998.

Orwell, George. *Orwell and Politics.* London: Penguin, 2001.

Orwell, George. *Orwell: the Observer Years.* London: Atlantic Books, 2003.

Pant, Govind Ballabh, and B. R. Nanda. *Selected Works of Govind Ballabh Pant.* Delhi and Oxford: Oxford University Press, 1997.

Philips, Cyril Henry, and M. Doreen Wainwright. *Partition of India: Policies and Perspectives, 1935–47*. London: Allen & Unwin, 1970.

Pignede, Bernard. *The Gurungs: A Himalayan Population of Nepal*. English edition edited by Sarah Harrison and Alan Macfarlane. Kathmandu: Ratna Pustak Bhandar, 1993.

Pilcher, A. H. *Navvies to the Fourteenth Army*. Calcutta, *c.* 1945.

Prebble, E. E. 'Venereal Disease in India', *Sexually Transmitted Infections* 22, no. 2 (June 1946): 55–62.

Quraishi, M. A. *Indian Administration, Pre & Post Independence: Memoirs of An ICS*. Delhi: BR Publishing, 1985.

Raghavan, G. N. S. *Aruna Asaf Ali: A Compassionate Radical*. New Delhi: National Book Trust, India, 1999.

———. *M. Asaf Ali's Memoirs: The Emergence of Modern India*. Delhi: Ajanta, 1994.

Raina, B. L. *Official History of the Indian Armed Forces in the Second World War (1939–45): Medical Services, Administration*. New Delhi: Combined Inter-Services Historical Section, first published 1953. (1990 edition cited.)

Raina, B. L. *World War II: Medical Services, India*. New Delhi: Commonwealth Publishers, 1990.

Ram, Janaki. *V. K. Krishna Menon: A Personal Memoir*. Delhi: Oxford University Press, 1997.

Rau, Santha Rama. *Home to India*. London: Victor Gollancz, 1946.

Reiss, Stephen (ed.). *From Burma with Love: Fifteen Months of Daily Letters between Irwin and Mary Reiss during World War II*. Bloomington, IN: Author House, 2011.

———. *Stilwell's Command Problems*. Washington, DC: Office of the Chief of Military History, 1956.

Romanus, Charles F., and Riley Sunderland. *Stilwell's Mission to China*. Washington DC: Office of the Chief of Military History, 1953.

———. *Time Runs Out in CBI*. Washington DC: Office of the Chief of Military History, 1959.

Sahgal, Lakshmi. *A Revolutionary Life: Memoirs of a Political Activist*. New Delhi: Kali for Women, 1997.

Sareen, T. R. (eds). *Select Documents on the Indian National Army*. Delhi: Agam Prakashan, n.d.

Saunders, Hilary Aidan St George. *Valiant Voyaging: A Short History of the British India Steam Navigation Company in the Second World War, 1939–1945*. London: Faber & Faber, 1948.

Saville, John. *Memoirs from the Left*. Talgarth: Merlin, 2003.

Sengupta, Syamalendu, Gautam Chatterjee and National Archives of India. *Secret Congress Broadcasts and Storming Railway Tracks during Quit India Movement*. New Delhi: Navrang, 1988.

Singh, Gian. *Memories of Friends and Foes*. Neath: Cwmnedd Press, 1995.

Singh, Navtej, and Avtar Singh Jouhl, (eds). *Emergence of the Image: Redact Documents of Udham Singh*. New Delhi: National Book Organisation, 2002.

Slim, William Joseph. *Defeat into Victory*. London: Pan, 2009.

Smith, E. D. *Even the Brave Falter*. London: Robert Hale, 1978.

The Statesman. Calcutta, 1940–1945

Symonds, Richard. *In the Margins of Independence: A Relief Worker in India and Pakistan, 1942–1949*. Karachi: Oxford University Press, 2001.

Tewari, Krishna Kumar. *A Soldier's Voyage of Self-discovery*. Auroville: Tewari, 1995.

The Tiger Strikes?: India's Fight in the Middle East. Calcutta: Government of India, 1943.

Thompson, Edward John. *Enlist India for Freedom!* London: Victor Coollancz, 1940.

Thorner, Daniel. 'Problems of Economic Development in India', *Annals of the American Academy of Political and Social Science* 268 (March 1950): 96–7.

Toschi, Elios. *Ninth Time Lucky*, trans. James Cleugh. London: William Kimber, 1955.

Tuker, Francis. *Gorkha: The Story of the Gurkhas of Nepal*. London: Constable, 1957.

Tyson, Geoffrey. *Forgotten Frontier*. Calcutta: W. H. Targett, 1945.

Varma, Ashali. *The Victoria Cross: A Love Story*. Delhi: Pearson, 2013.

Wavell: The Viceroy's Journal, ed. Penderel Moon. Oxford: Oxford University Press, 1973.

Yeats-Brown, Francis. *Martial India*. London: Eyre & Spottiswoode, 1945.

Young, Desmond. *Try Anything Twice*. London: Hamish Hamilton, 1963.

Zaidi, A. *The Way Out to Freedom: An Enquiry into the Quit India Movement Conducted by Participants*. New Delhi: Orientalia India, 1973.

SECONDARY SOURCES

Ahmed, Rafiuddin. *History of the Baloch Regiment 1939–1956*. Uckfield: Naval and Military Press, 2005.

Ahmed, Rehana, and Sumita Mukherjee (eds). *South Asian Resistances in Britain, 1858–1947*. London and New York: Continuum, 2012.

Ahmed, Talat. *Literature and Politics in the Age of Nationalism: The Progressive Episode in South Asia, 1932–56*. New Delhi: Routledge, 2009.

Ahuja, Ravi. 'Networks of Subordination – Networks of the Subordinated: The Ordered Spaces of South Asian Maritime Labour in an Age of Imperialism (*c.* 1890–1947)', in Ashwini Tambe and Harold Fischer-Tiné (eds). *The Limits of British Colonial Control in South Asia*. Abingdon, Oxon, and New York: Routledge, 2009.

Amin, Shahid. *Event, Metaphor, Memory: Chauri Chaura, 1922–1992*. Berkeley: University of California Press, 1995.

Amrith, S. 'Reconstructing the "Plural Society": Asian Migration Between Empire and Nation, 1940–1948', *Past and Present* 210, no. suppl. 6 (2011): 237–257.

Amrith, S. S. 'Food and Welfare in India, c. 1900–1950', *Comparative Studies in Society and History* 50, no. 4 (2008): 1010–35.

———. 'Tamil Diasporas Across the Bay of Bengal', *The American Historical Review* 114, no. 3 (2009): 547–72.

Amrith, Sunil S. *Crossing the Bay of Bengal: The Furies of Nature and the Fortunes of Migrants*. Cambridge, MA: Harvard University Press, 2013.

———. *Decolonizing International Health: India and Southeast Asia, 1930–65*. New York: Palgrave Macmillan, 2006.

———. *Migration and Diaspora in Modern Asia*. Cambridge and New York: Cambridge University Press, 2011.

Anders, Leslie. *The Ledo Road: General Joseph W. Stilwell's Highway to China*. Oklahoma: University of Oklahoma Press, 1965.

Anderson, Clare. *Subaltern Lives: Biographies of Colonialism in the Indian Ocean World, 1790–1920*. Cambridge: Cambridge University Press, 2012.

Anderson, Robert S. *Nucleus and Nation: Scientists, International Networks, and Power in India*. Chicago: Chicago University Press, 2010.

Ansari, Sarah F. D. *Sufi Saints and State Power: The Pirs of Sind, 1843–1947*. Cambridge and New York: Cambridge University Press, 1992.

Appadurai, Arjun. 'Review: How Moral Is South Asia's Economy? – A Review Article', *Journal of Asian Studies* 43, no. 3 (1 May 1984): 481–97.

Arnold, David. *Everyday Technology: Machines and the Making of India's Modernity*. Chicago: University of Chicago Press, 2013.

———. *Science, Technology and Medicine in Colonial India*. New York: Cambridge University Press, 2000.

Arnold, David, and Stuart Blackburn (eds). *Telling Lives in India: Biography,*

Autobiography, and Life History. Bloomington: Indiana University Press, 2004.

Ashplant, T. G., G. Dawson and M. Roper. *The Politics of War Memory and Commemoration*. London: Routledge, 2000.

Balachandran, Gopalan. *Globalizing Labour? Indian Seafarers and World Shipping, c. 1870–1945*. New Delhi: Oxford University Press, 2012.

Barkawi, Tarak. 'Culture and Combat in the Colonies: The Indian Army in the Second World War', *Journal of Contemporary History* 41, no. 2 (1 April 2006): 325–55.

———. *Globalization and War*. Washington DC: Rowman & Littlefield, 2005.

Bates, Crispin. *Subalterns and Raj: South Asia Since 1600*. New edition. Abingdon, Oxon, and New York: Routledge, 2007.

Bayly, C. A., and T. N. Harper. *Forgotten Armies: Britain's Asian Empire and the War with Japan*. London: Penguin, 2005.

———. *Forgotten Wars: The End of Britain's Asian Empire*. London: Allen Lane, 2007.

Bellamy, Chris. *The Gurkhas: Special Force*. London: John Murray, 2011.

Bhattacharjee, Anuradha, and Franek Herzog. *The Second Homeland: Polish Refugees in India*. Los Angeles: Sage, 2012.

Bhattacharya, Sanjoy. 'British Military Information Management Techniques and the South Asian Soldier: Eastern India During the Second World War', *Modern Asian Studies* 34, no. 2 (1 May 2000): 483–510.

———. *Propaganda and Information in Eastern India 1939–45: A Necessary Weapon of War*. Kolkata: Routledge, 2000.

Black, Jeremy. *Rethinking Military History*. London and New York: Routledge, 2004.

Blackburn, Kevin. 'Recalling War Trauma of the Pacific War and the Japanese Occupation in the Oral History of Malaysia and Singapore', *Oral History Review* 36, no 2 (2009): 231–52.

———. 'Reminiscence and War Trauma: Recalling the Japanese Occupation of Singapore, 1942–1945', *Oral History* 33, no. 2 (1 October 2005): 91–8.

Blackburn, Kevin, and Karl Hack (eds). *Forgotten Captives in Japanese Occupied Asia*. Abingdon, Oxon, and New York: Routledge, 2007.

Blunt, Alison. 'Imperial Geographies of Home: British Domesticity in India, 1886–1925', *Transactions of the Institute of British Geographers* 24, no. 4. New Series (1 January 1999): 421–40.

———. '"Land of Our Mothers:" Home, Identity, and Nationality for Anglo-Indians in British India, 1919–1947', *History Workshop Journal* no. 54 (1 October 2002): 49–72.

Bose, Sugata. *A Hundred Horizons: The Indian Ocean in the Age of Global Empire*. Cambridge, MA: Harvard University Press, 2006.

——. *His Majesty's Opponent: Subhas Chandra Bose and India's Struggle Against Empire*. Cambridge, MA: Harvard University Press, 2011.

Bose, Sugata, and Kris Manjapra (eds). *Cosmopolitan Thought Zones: South Asia and the Global Circulation of Ideas*. Basingstoke: Palgrave Macmillan, 2010.

Brown, Judith M. *Nehru: A Political Life*. New edition. New Haven, CT: Yale University Press, 2005.

Buchanan, Andrew N. 'The War Crisis and the Decolonization of India, December 1941–September 1942: A Political and Military Dilemma', *Global War Studies* 8, no. 2 (2011): 5–31.

Buettner, E. 'Cemeteries, Public Memory and Raj Nostalgia in Postcolonial Britain and India', *History and Memory* 18, no. 1 (2006): 5–42.

——. 'Problematic Spaces, Problematic Races: Defining "Europeans" in Late Colonial India', *Women's History Review* 9, no. 2 (2000): 277–98.

Buettner, Elizabeth. *Empire Families: Britons and Late Imperial India*. New edition. Oxford: Oxford University Press, 2005.

Burton, A. 'Who Needs the Nation? Interrogating "British" History', *Journal of Historical Sociology* 10, no. 3 (1997): 227–48.

Calder, Angus. *The People's War: Britain 1939–1945*. London: Pimlico, 1992.

Caplan, Lionel. *Warrior Gentlemen: 'Gurkhas' in the Western Imagination*. Providence: Berghahn Books, 1995.

Chakrabarty, B. 'Political Mobilization in the Localities: The 1942 Quit India Movement in Midnapur', *Modern Asian Studies* 26, no. 4 (1992): 791–814.

Chakrabarty, Bidyut. *Local Politics and Indian Nationalism: Midnapur, 1919–1944*. New Delhi: Manohar, 1997.

Chandavarkar, Rajnarayan. *Imperial Power and Popular Politics: Class, Resistance and the State in India c. 1850–1950*. Cambridge: Cambridge University Press, 1998.

Clymer, K. J. *Quest for Freedom: The United States and India's Independence*. New York: Columbia University Press, 1995.

Cockburn, Cynthia. *From Where We Stand: War, Women's Activism and Feminist Analysis*. London: Zed Books, 2007.

Cohn, Bernard S. *Colonialism and Its Forms of Knowledge: The British in India*. Princeton, NJ: Princeton University Press, 1996.

Collingham, Lizzie. *The Taste of War: World War Two and the Battle for Food*. London: Penguin, 2012.

Connerton, Paul. *How Societies Remember*. Cambridge: Cambridge University Press, 1989.

Copland, Ian. *The Princes of India in the Endgame of Empire, 1917–1947*. Cambridge: Cambridge University Press, 2002.

Cross, J. P., and Buddhiman Gurung. *Eyewitness Accounts from World War II to Iraq*. London: Greenhill Books, 2007.

Daechsel, Markus. *The Politics of Self-Expression: The Urdu Middle-Class Milieu in Mid-Twentieth-Century India and Pakistan*. Royal Asiatic Society Books. London: Routledge, 2006.

———. 'Scientism and Its Discontents: the Indo-Muslim Fascism of Inayatullah Khan al-Mashriqui', *Modern Intellectual History* 3, no. 3 (2006): 443–72.

Damodaran, Vinita. *Broken Promises: Popular Protest, Indian Nationalism and the Congress Party in Bihar, 1935–46*. Delhi and New York: Oxford University Press, 1993.

Das, Santanu (ed.). *Race, Empire and First World War Writing*. Cambridge: Cambridge University Press, 2011.

Dasgupta, Jayant. *Japanese in Andaman and Nicobar Islands: Red Sun over Black Water*. New Delhi: Manas, 2002.

Dear, Ian, and M. R. D. Foot (eds). *Oxford Companion to World War II*. New edition. Oxford: Oxford University Press, 2001.

Des Chene, Mary. *Relics of Empire: A Cultural History of the Gurkhas*. PhD thesis, Stanford University, 1991.

Des Chene, 'Traversing Social Space: Gurung Journeys', *Himalayan Research Bulletin*, vol. 12.1 (1992): 1–11.

Deshpande, A. 'Hopes and Disillusionment: Recruitment, Demobilisation and the Emergence of Discontent in the Indian Armed Forces After the Second World War', *Indian Economic and Social History Review* 33, no. 2 (1996): 175–207.

———. 'Sailors and the Crowd: Popular Protest in Karachi, 1946', *Indian Economic and Social History Review* 26, no. 1 (1989): 1–28.

Devji, Faisal. *The Impossible Indian: Gandhi and the Temptations of Violence*. London: Hurst, 2012.

Dewey, Clive. *Anglo-Indian Attitudes: The Mind of the Indian Civil Service*. London: Hambledon Press, 1993.

Douds, G. J. 'The Men Who Never Were: Indian POWs in the Second World War', *South Asia: Journal of South Asian Studies* 27, no. 2 (2004): 183–216.

Dutta, Krishna, and Andrew Robinson. *Rabindranath Tagore: The Myriad-minded Man*. London: Bloomsbury, 1995.

Egorova, Yulia. *Jews and India: Perceptions and Image*. Abingdon, Oxon: Routledge, 2006.

Enloe, Cynthia. *Bananas, Beaches and Bases: Making Feminist Sense of International Politics*. Berkeley: University of California Press, 2001.

————. *Maneuvers: The International Politics of Militarizing Women's Lives*. Berkeley: University of California Press, 2000.

Fay, Peter Ward. *The Forgotten Army: India's Armed Struggle for Independence, 1942–45*. Delhi: Rupa, 1997.

Fischer-Tiné, Harald. '"White Women Degrading Themselves to the Lowest Depths"': European Networks of Prostitution and Colonial Anxieties in British India and Ceylon ca. 1880–1914', *Indian Economic Social History Review* 40, no. 2 (2003): 163–90.

Gawankar, Rohini. *The Women's Regiment and Captain Lakshmi of INA: An Untold Episode of NRI Women's Contribution to India's Freedom Struggle*. New Delhi: Devika Publications, 2003.

George, Thayil Jacob Sony. *Krishna Menon: A Biography*. First edition. London: Jonathan Cape, 1965.

Ghosh, Amitav. *The Glass Palace*. London: HarperCollins, 2001.

Gilmartin, David. *Empire and Islam: Punjab and the Making of Pakistan*. Berkeley: University of California Press, 1988.

Gilroy, Paul. *Postcolonial Melancholia*. New York: Columbia University Press, 2006.

Glancey, Jonathan. *Nagaland*. London: Faber & Faber, 2007.

Go, J. *American Empire and the Politics of Meaning: Elite Political Cultures in the Philippines and Puerto Rico During US Colonialism*. Durham, NC: Duke University Press, 2008.

Gordon, Leonard A. *Brothers Against the Raj: A Biography of Indian Nationalist Leaders Sarat and Subhas Chandra Bose*. New York: Columbia University Press, 1990.

Gould, Tony. *Imperial Warriors: Britain and the Gurkhas*. London: Granta Books, 1999.

Gould, William. *Bureaucracy, Community and Influence in India*. London: Routledge, 2010.

————. *Hindu Nationalism and the Language of Politics in Late Colonial India*. Cambridge: Cambridge University Press, 2010.

Green, L. C. 'The Indian National Army Trials', *The Modern Law Review* 11, no. 1 (1 January 1948): 47–69.

Greenough, P. R. 'Political Mobilization and the Underground Literature of the Quit India Movement, 1942–44', *Modern Asian Studies* 17, no. 3 (1983): 353–86.

Greenough, Paul R. *Prosperity and Misery in Modern Bengal: The Famine of 1943–44*. Oxford: Oxford University Press, 1983.

Grover, Verinder, and Ranjana Arora (eds). *Great Women of Modern India, vol. 8: Aruna Asaf Ali*. Delhi: Deep and Deep, 1993.

Guite, Jangkhomang. 'Representing Local Participation in INA–Japanese Imphal Campaign: The Case of the Kukis in Manipur, 1943–45', *Indian Historical Review* 37, no. 2 (2011): 291–309.

Gupta, Partha Sarathi. *Radio and the Raj 1921–47*. Calcutta: K. P. Bagchi Centre for Studies in Social Sciences, 1995.

Gurkha Army Ex-Servicemen's Organization, and International Commission of Inquiry on Discrimination against British Gurkhas. *The Gurkhas: The Forgotten Veterans*. Kathmandu: Gurkha Army Ex-Servicemen's Organization, 2005.

Hall, Catherine. *Cultures of Empire: A Reader – Colonisers in Britain and the Empire of the Nineteenth and Twentieth Centuries*. Manchester: Manchester University Press, 2000.

Harrison, Mark. *Medicine and Victory: British Military Medicine in the Second World War*. Oxford and New York: Oxford University Press, 2004.

Hauner, Milan. 'One Man Against the Empire: The Faqir of Ipi and the British in Central Asia on the Eve of and During the Second World War', *Journal of Contemporary History* 16, no. 1 (1 January 1981): 183–212.

Hauser, Walter. 'From Peasant Soldiering to Peasant Activism: Reflections on the Transition of a Martial Tradition in the Flaming Fields of Bihar', *Journal of the Economic and Social History of the Orient* 47, no. 3 (1 January 2004): 401–34.

Hayes, Romain. *Subhas Chandra Bose in Nazi Germany: Politics, Intelligence and Propaganda, 1941–1943*. London: Hurst, 2011.

Horne, Gerald. *The End of Empires: African Americans and India*. Philadelphia, PA: Temple University Press, 2008.

Hutchins, Francis G. *India's Revolution: Gandhi and the Quit India Movement*. Cambridge, MA: Harvard University Press, 1973.

Jackson, A. '"Defend Lanka Your Home": War on the Home Front in Ceylon, 1939–1945', *War in History* 16, no. 2 (2009): 213–38.

Jackson, Ashley. *The British Empire and the Second World War*. London and New York: Hambledon Continuum, 2006.

Jalal, Ayesha. *Partisans of Allah: Jihad in South Asia*. Cambridge, MA: Harvard University Press, 2008.

Jeffreys, Alan, and Patrick Rose. *The Indian Army, 1939–47: Experience and Development*. Farnham, Surrey, and Burlington, VT: Ashgate, 2012.

Joshi, B. L., and Leo Rose. *Democratic Innovations in Nepal*. Berkeley: University of California Press, 1966.

Kamtekar, Indivar. 'The Shiver of 1942', *Studies in History* 18, no. 1 (2002).

————. 'A Different War Dance: State and Class in India 1939–1945', *Past and Present* no. 176 (2002): 187–221.

————. *What Caused the 'Quit India' Movement?* Calcutta: Indian Institute of Management, 1990.

Keane, Fergal. *Road of Bones: The Epic Siege of Kohima*. London: HarperPress, 2011.

Khan, Yasmin. *The Great Partition: The Making of India and Pakistan*. London: Yale University Press, 2007.

————. 'Sex in an Imperial War Zone: Transnational Encounters in Second World War India', *History Workshop Journal* 73, no. 1 (1 April 2012): 240–58.

Killingray, David. *Fighting for Britain: African Soldiers in the Second World War*. London: James Currey, 2012.

Killingray, David, and David E. Omissi (eds). *Guardians of Empire: The Armed Forces of the Colonial Powers c. 1700–1964*. Manchester: Manchester University Press, 1999.

Killingray, D., and R. Rathbone. *Africa and the Second World War*. Basingstoke: Macmillan, 1986.

Koerner, Brendan I. *Now the Hell Will Start: One Soldier's Flight from the Greatest Manhunt of World War II*. New York: Penguin Press, 2008.

————. *Piano Demon: The Globetrotting, Gin-soaked, Too-short Life of Teddy Weatherford, the Chicago Jazzman Who Conquered Asia*. New York: Penguin, 2008.

Kudaisya, Medha M. *The Life and Times of G. D. Birla*. Delhi: Oxford University Press, 2003.

Kuracina, William F. 'Sentiments and Patriotism: The Indian National Army, General Elections and the Congress's Appropriation of the INA Legacy', *Modern Asian Studies* 44, no. 4 (2010): 517–86.

Lall, B. B. *A Regime of Fears and Tears: History of the Japanese Occupation of the Andaman Islands*. Delhi: Farsight, 2000.

Legg, S. 'Governing Prostitution in Colonial Delhi: From Cantonment Regulations to International Hygiene (1864–1939)', *Social History* 34, no. 4 (2009): 447–67.

————. 'An Intimate and Imperial Feminism: Meliscent Shephard and the Regulation of Prostitution in Colonial India', *Environment and Planning D: Society and Space* 28, no. 1 (2010): 68–94.

Levine, Philippa. *Gender and Empire*. Oxford: Oxford University Press, 2007.

————. *Prostitution, Race and Politics: Policing Venereal Disease in the British Empire*. 1st edn. New York and London: Routledge, 2003.

————. 'Venereal Disease, Prostitution, and the Politics of Empire: The Case of British India', *Journal of the History of Sexuality* 4, no. 4 (1 April 1994): 579–602.

Levine, Philippa, and Susan R. Grayzel (eds). *Gender, Labour, War and Empire: Essays on Modern Britain*. Basingstoke: Palgrave Macmillan, 2008.

Liebau, Heike. *The World in World Wars: Experiences, Perceptions and Perspectives from Africa and Asia*. Leiden, The Netherlands, and Boston, MA: Brill, 2010.

Lokendra, N. *Manipur during World War II, 1941–45: Socio-economic Change and Local Responses*. Imphal: Manipur State Archives, Directorate of Arts & Culture, Govt of Manipur, 1993.

Louis, W. R. 'American Anti-colonialism and the Dissolution of the British Empire', *International Affairs (Royal Institute of International Affairs 1944– 61)*, no. 3 (1985): 395–420.

————. *Ends of British Imperialism: The Scramble for Empire, Suez and Decolonization: Collected Essays*. London: I. B. Tauris, 2006.

————. *In the Name of God, Go!: Leo Amery and the British Empire in the Age of Churchill*. New York: W. W. Norton, 1992.

MacKinnon, Stephen R., and Robert Capa. *Wuhan, 1938: War, Refugees, and the Making of Modern China*. Berkeley: University of California Press, 2008.

Majeed, Javed. *Autobiography, Travel and Postnational Identity: Narratives of Selfhood in Gandhi, Nehru and Iqbal*. Basingstoke, Hants: Palgrave Macmillan, 2007.

Manjapra, Kris. *M. N. Roy: Marxism and Colonial Cosmopolitanism*. Delhi: Routledge India, 2010.

Manjapra, Kris, and Sugata Bose (eds). *Cosmopolitan Thought Zones: South Asia and the Global Circulation of Ideas*. Basingstoke: Palgrave Macmillan, 2010.

Markovits, C. *The Global World of Indian Merchants, 1750–1947: Traders of Sind from Bukhara to Panama*. Cambridge: Cambridge University Press, 2000.

————. *Indian Business and Nationalist Politics 1931–39: The Indigenous Capitalist Class and the Rise of the Congress Party*. Cambridge: Cambridge University Press, 1985.

Marston, Daniel. *The Indian Army and the End of the Raj*. Cambridge: Cambridge University Press, 2014.

Marston, D. P. 'The Indian Army, Partition, and the Punjab Boundary Force, 1945–1947', *War in History* 16, no. 4 (2009): 469–505.

Marston, D., and C. S. Sundaram (eds). *A Military History of India and South Asia: From the East India Company to the Nuclear Era*. London: Praeger, 2006.

Masters, John. *The Road past Mandalay*. London: Cassell Military, 2002.

Mazarella, William. 'A Torn Performative Dispensation: The Affective Politics of British Second World War Propaganda in India and the Problem of Legitimation in an Age of Mass Publics', *South Asian History and Culture* 1, no. 1 (2010): 1–24.

Mazower, M. 'Violence and the State in the Twentieth Century', *American Historical Review* 107, no. 4 (2002): 1158–78.

Mazower, Mark. *Dark Continent: Europe's Twentieth Century*. New York: Vintage Books, 2000.

McBryde, Brenda. *Quiet Heroines: Nurses of the Second World War*. Saffron Walden: Cakebreads, 1989.

McLynn, Frank. *The Burma Campaign: Disaster into Triumph 1942–5*. London: Vintage, 2011.

Mitter, Rana. *China's War with Japan, 1937–1945: The Struggle for Survival*. London: Allen Lane, 2013.

Moon, Katharine H. S. *Sex Among Allies*. New York: Columbia University Press, 1997.

Moore, R. J. *Churchill, Cripps, and India, 1939–1945*. Oxford and New York: Oxford University Press, 1979.

Mukerjee, M. *Churchill's Secret War: The British Empire and the Ravaging of India During World War II*. New York: Basic Books, 2010.

Mukherjee, Janam. *Hungry Bengal: War, Famine and the End of Empire*. London: Hurst, 2015.

Mukherji, Santosh Kumar. *Indian Sex Life and Prostitution*. Burnpur, Burdwan: Anil Kumar Das Gupta, 1945.

Nair, Janaki. *Mysore Modern: Rethinking the Region under Princely Rule*. Minneapolis: University of Minnesota Press, 2011.

Ó Gráda, Cormac. *Famine: A Short History*. Princeton: Princeton University Press, 2009.

Omissi, D. 'Martial Races: Ethnicity and Security in Colonial India', *War and Society* 9, no. 1 (1991): 1–27.

———. *The Sepoy and the Raj: The Indian Army, 1860–1940*. Basingstoke: Macmillan, 1994.

Ondaatje, Michael. *The English Patient*. London: Bloomsbury, 2004.

Onta, Pratyoush. 'The Politics of Bravery. A History of Nepali Nationalism' (Unpubd PhD thesis, University of Pennsylvania, 1996).

Owen, N. J. *The British Left and India: Metropolitan Anti-imperialism, 1885–1947*. New York: Oxford University Press, 2007.

————. 'The Cripps Mission of 1942: A Reinterpretation', *Journal of Imperial and Commonwealth History*, 30 no. 1 (2002): 61–98.

Panayi, Panikos, and Pippa Virdee. *Refugees and the End of Empire: Imperial Collapse and Forced Migration in the Twentieth Century*. Basingstoke, Hants: Palgrave Macmillan, 2011.

Pandey, Gyanendra. *A History of Prejudice: Race, Caste, and Difference in India and the United States*. Cambridge and New York: Cambridge University Press, 2013.

————. *The Indian Nation in 1942*. Calcutta: Published for Centre for Studies in Social Sciences, Calcutta, (ed). K. P. Bagchi, 1988.

————. *Remembering Partition Violence, Nationalism, and History in India*. Cambridge and New York: Cambridge University Press, 2001.

————. *Routine Violence: Nations, Fragments, Histories*. Stanford, CA: Stanford University Press, 2006.

Parratt, John. *Wounded Land: Politics and Identity in Modern Manipur*. New Delhi: Mittal Publications, 2005.

Pau, Pum Khan. 'Situating Local Events in Geo-Political Struggles Between the British and Japanese Empires: The Politics of Zo Participation During the Second World War', *Journal of Imperial and Commonwealth History* 42, no. 4 (2014): 667–92.

————. 'Tedim Road – the Strategic Road on a Frontier: A Historical Analysis', *Strategic Analysis* 36, no. 5 (2012): 776–86.

Pocock, Tom. *Alan Moorehead*. London: Pimlico/Random House, 1991.

Potter, David C. *India's Political Administrators, 1919–1983*. Oxford: Clarendon, 1986.

Prabhu, H. R. A. 'Military Psychiatry in India', *Indian Journal of Psychiatry*, no. 52 (Jan. 2010).

Procida, Mary A. *Married to the Empire: Gender, Politics and Imperialism in India, 1883–1947*. Manchester: Manchester University Press, 2002.

Rahman, Tariq. 'The British Learning of Hindustani,' *Contemporary Perspectives*, 2.1 (2008): 46–73.

Ramusack, Barbara N. *The Indian Princes and Their States*. Cambridge and New York: Cambridge University Press, 2004.

Reinisch, Jessica. *The Disentanglement of Populations: Migration, Expulsion and Displacement in Post-war Europe, 1944–49*. Basingstoke, Hants: Palgrave Macmillan, 2011.

Reza, Rahi Masoom. *The Feuding Families of Village Gangauli: Aadha Gaon*. Trans. from Hindi by Gillian Wright. Delhi: Penguin, 1994.

Robbins, Jane. 'Freedom Under Britain or Freedom Under Japan: The Radio Battle for India, December 1941–September 1945', *Japan Forum* 7, no. 2 (1995): 217–24.

Rose, Sonya O. 'Girls and GIs: Race, Sex, and Diplomacy in Second World War Britain', *International History Review* 19, no. 1 (1 February 1997): 146–60.

———. 'Sex, Citizenship, and the Nation in World War II Britain', *American Historical Review* 103, no. 4 (1 October 1998): 1147–76.

———. 'The "Sex Question" in Anglo-American Relations in the Second World War', *International History Review* 20, no. 4 (1 December 1998): 884–903.

———. *Which People's War?: National Identity and Citizenship in Wartime Britain 1939–1945*. Oxford: Oxford University Press, 2004.

Roy, K. 'Axis Satellite Armies of World War II: A Case Study of the Azad Hind Fauj, 1942–45', *Indian Historical View* 35, no. 1 (2008): 144–72.

———. 'Discipline and Morale of the African, British and Indian Army Units in Burma and India During World War II: July 1943 to August 1945', *Modern Asian Studies* 44, no. 06 (April 2010): 1255–82.

———. 'Military Loyalty in the Colonial Context: A Case Study of the Indian Army During World War II', *Journal of Military History* 73, no. 2 (2009): 497–529.

———. (ed). *War and Society in Colonial India, 1807–1945*. New Delhi: Oxford University Press, 2010.

Sareen, T. R. *Japanese Prisoners of War in India, 1942–46: Bushido and Barbed Wire*. Folkestone, Kent: Global Oriental, 2006.

———. *Conspiracy of Silence: Japanese Prisoners of War in India, 1942–1946: Selected Source Materials*. New Delhi: Life Span Publishers & Distributors, 2010.

———. *Sharing the Blame: Subhash Chandra Bose and the Japanese Occupation of the Andamans, 1942–1945*. Delhi: S.S. Publishers, 2002.

Sarkar, S. 'The Communists and 1942', *Social Scientist* 12, no. 9 (1984): 45–53.

———. *Modern India, 1885–1947*. Basingstoke: Macmillan, 1989.

Schofield, Victoria. *Wavell: Soldier and Statesman*. London: John Murray, 2007.

Sen, Amartya Kumar. *Poverty and Famines: An Essay on Entitlement and Deprivation*. Oxford and New York: Oxford University Press, 1982.

Sen, Satadru. *Disciplining Punishment: Colonialism and Convict Society in the Andaman Islands*. New Delhi, Oxford and New York: Oxford University Press, 2000.

Shephard, Ben. *A War of Nerves: Soldiers and Psychiatrists, 1914–1994*. London: Pimlico, 2002.

Sherman, Taylor C. 'From "Grow More Food" to "Miss a Meal": Hunger, Development and the Limits of Post-Colonial Nationalism in India,

1947–1957', *South Asia: Journal of South Asian Studies* 36, no. 4 (2013): 571–88.

———. 'From Hell to Paradise? Voluntary Transfer of Convicts to the Andaman Islands, 1921–1940', *Modern Asian Studies* 43, no. 2 (2009): 367–88.

———. *State Violence and Punishment in India*. London: Routledge, 2012.

Singh, Gajendra. *The Testimonies of Indian Soldiers and the Two World Wars: Between Self and Sepoy*. London and New York: Bloomsbury Academic, 2014.

Sinha, Jagdish N. *Science, War and Imperialism: India in the Second World War*. Leiden: Brill, 2008.

Slate, Nico. *Colored Cosmopolitanism: The Shared Struggle for Freedom in the United States and India*. Cambridge, MA: Harvard University Press, 2012.

Somerville, Christopher. *Our War: How the British Commonwealth Fought the Second World War*. London: Phoenix, 2005.

Spurling, Hilary. *Paul Scott: A Life*. London: Pimlico, 1991.

Srivasthan, A. 'When 5 Lakh Fled the City in 2 Weeks', *The Hindu*, 3 October 2012.

Stanley, Peter. '"Great in Adversity": Indian Prisoners of War in New Guinea', *Journal of the Australian War Memorial* (November 2002), https://www.awm.gov.au, accessed 2013.

Talbot, Ian. 'The Role of the Crowd in the Muslim League Struggle for Pakistan', *Journal of Imperial and Commonwealth History* 21, no. 2 (1993): 307–33.

Tambe, Ashwini, and Harald Fischer-Tiné (eds). *The Limits of British Colonial Control in South Asia: Spaces of Disorder in the Indian Ocean Region*. London: Routledge, 2009.

Tinker, H. 'A Forgotten Long March: The Indian Exodus from Burma, 1942', *Journal of Southeast Asian Studies* 6, no. 1 (1975): 1–15.

Tomlinson, B. R. *The Economy of Modern India, 1860–1970*. Cambridge: Cambridge University Press, 1996.

Virk, Daljit Singh. *Indian Army Post Offices in the Second World War*. New Delhi: Army Postal Service Association, 1982.

Visram, R. *Ayahs, Lascars, and Princes: Indians in Britain, 1700–1947*. London: Pluto Press, 1986.

Voigt, Johannes H. *India in the Second World War*. New Delhi: Arnold-Heinemann, 1987.

Wald, E. 'Defining Prostitution and Redefining Women's Roles: The Colonial

State and Society in Early 19th Century India', *History Compass* 7, no. 6 (2009): 1470–83.

Webster, Wendy. *Englishness and Empire 1939–1965*. Oxford: Oxford University Press, 2007.

Willoughby, John. 'The Sexual Behavior of American GIs During the Early Years of the Occupation of Germany', *Journal of Military History* 62, no. 1 (1 January 1998): 155–74.

Wills, C. *That Neutral Island: a Cultural History of Ireland During the Second World War*. Cambridge, MA: Belknap Press, 2007.

Woods, Philip. '"Chapattis by Parachute": The Use of Newsreels in British Propaganda in India in the Second World War', *South Asia: Journal of South Asian Studies* 23, no. 2 (2000): 89–110.

Yong, T. T. 'Mobilisation, Militarisation and "Mal-contentment": Punjab and the Second World War', *South Asia: Journal of South Asian Studies* 25, no. 2 (2002): 137–51.

———. *The Garrison State: Military, Government and Society in Colonial Punjab, 1849–1947*. London: Sage Publications, 2005.

———. 'Maintaining the Military Districts: Civil–Military Integration and District Soldiers' Boards in the Punjab, 1919–1939', *Modern Asian Studies* 28, no. 4 (1994): 833–74.

Zachariah, Benjamin. *Developing India: An Intellectual and Social History, c. 1930–1950*. New Delhi: Oxford University Press, 2005.

———. *Nehru*. London: Routledge, 2004.

———. 'Rewriting Imperial Mythologies: The Strange Case of Penderel Moon', *South Asia: Journal of South Asian Studies* 24, no. 2 (2001): 53–72.

———. 'The Creativity of Destruction: Wartime Imaginings of Development and Social Policy, c. 1942–1946', in Heike Liebau, Katrin Bromber, Katharina Lange, Dyala Hamzah and Ravi Ahuja (eds). *The World in the World Wars*. Leiden: Brill, 2010, pp. 547–78.

Index